Date Due

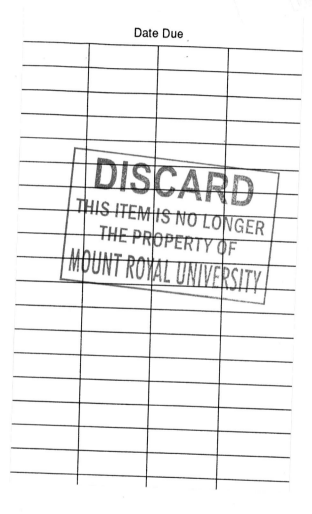

# Imagining the Impossible

## Magical, Scientific, and Religious Thinking in Children

*Edited by*

Karl S. Rosengren
*University of Illinois*

Carl N. Johnson
*University of Pittsburgh*

Paul L. Harris
*Oxford University*

CAMBRIDGE
UNIVERSITY PRESS

PUBLISHED BY THE PRESS SYNDICATE OF THE UNIVERSITY OF CAMBRIDGE
The Pitt Building, Trumpington Street, Cambridge, United Kingdom

CAMBRIDGE UNIVERSITY PRESS
The Edinburgh Building, Cambridge CB2 2RU, UK
http:\\www.cup.cam.ac.uk
40 West 20th Street, New York, NY 10011-4211, USA
http:\\www.cup.org
10 Stamford Road, Oakleigh, Melbourne 3166, Australia
Ruiz de Alarcón 13, 28014 Madrid, Spain

First published 2000

Printed in the United States of America

*Typeface* Palatino 10/13 pt.   *System* DeskTopPro$_{/UX}$ [BV]

*A catalog record for this book is available from the British Library.*

*Library of Congress Cataloging in Publication Data*
Imagining the impossible : magical, scientific, and religious thinking in children / edited by Karl S. Rosengren, Carl N. Johnson, Paul L. Harris.
    p. cm.
Includes bibliographical references and index.
ISBN 0-521-59322-0 (hb)
1. Cognition in children.   2. Magical thinking in children.   3. Children –
Religious life.   4. Reasoning in children.   I. Rosengren, Karl Sven.
II. Johnson, Carl N.   III. Harris, Paul L.

BF723.C5.I43 2000
153.4'083 – dc21
                                                                99-087643
ISBN 0 521 59322 0 hardback
ISBN 0 521 66587 6 paperback

*We dedicate this book to our children and their questions:*

*Emily & Julia*

*Eve & Jeremy*

*Simon, Rémi, & Louis*

# Contents

# Contributors

**Kristin Alexander,** 4250 W. Lake Sammamish Parkway N. E. #2048, Redmond, WA 98052

**Pascal Boyer,** Dynamique du Langage, 14 Avenue Berthelot, 69363 Lyon, France

**William F. Brewer,** Department of Psychology, University of Illinois, 603 E. Daniel Street, Champaign, IL 61820

**Stephanie M. Carlson,** Department of Psychology, University of Oregon, Eugene, OR 97403

**Clark A. Chinn,** Department of Educational Psychology, Graduate School of Education, Rutgers University, 10 Seminary Place, New Brunswick, NJ 08903

**E. Margaret Evans,** Department of Psychology, University of Toledo, Toledo, OH 43606-3390

**Paul L. Harris,** Department of Experimental Psychology, Oxford University, South Parks Road, Oxford, United Kingdom OX1 3UD

**Julie Hengst,** Department of Speech Communication, University of Illinois, 702 S. Wright Street, 244 Lincoln, Urbana, IL 61601

**Anne K. Hickling,** Department of Psychology, University of North Carolina at Greensboro, Greensboro, NC 27412

**Carl N. Johnson,** Child Development/Child Care, University of Pittsburgh, 1717 Cathedral of Learning, Pittsburgh, PA 15260

**Peggy J. Miller,** Department of Psychology, University of Illinois, 603 E. Daniel Street, Champaign, IL 61820

**Kristin Neff,** Educational Psychology Department, University of Texas, George Sanchez Building 504, Austin, TX 78722

**Carol Nemeroff,** Department of Psychology, Arizona State University, Tempe, AZ 85287-1104

**Karl S. Rosengren,** Department of Psychology, University of Illinois, 603 E. Daniel Street, Champaign, IL 61820

**Paul Rozin,** Department of Psychology, University of Pennsylvania, 3815 Walnut Street, Philadelphia, PA 19104

**David E. Schrader,** Department of Philosophy, Washington & Jefferson College, Washington, PA 15301

**Linda L. Sperry,** Education and School Psychology, Indiana State University, Terre Haute, IN 47809

**Eugene Subbotsky,** Psychology Department, Lancaster University, Lancaster, United Kingdom LA14YF

**Marjorie Taylor,** Department of Psychology, University of Oregon, Eugene, OR 97403

**Elliot Turiel,** School of Education, University of California, Berkeley, CA 94729

**Sheila Walker,** Department of Psychology, Scripps College, Claremont, CA 91711

**Jacqueline D. Woolley,** Department of Psychology, The University of Texas, Mezes 330, Austin, TX 78712

# Acknowledgments

We would like to thank all of our authors; we asked a lot of them, and we learned a great deal from them. We also thank Julia Hough, Kelly Hamilton, and Christine Hahn for their help and support throughout the editorial process.

# Preface

This volume is about the development of human thinking that stretches beyond the ordinary boundaries of reality. Various new research initiatives have emerged in the past decade exploring such matters as children's thinking about imaginary beings, magic, and the supernatural. The purpose of this volume is to capture something of the larger spirit of these efforts. Here we identify three recurrent themes: *going beyond the possible; beyond scientific rationality;* and *shaping the metaphysical.*

## Going Beyond the Possible

In many ways, this new work offers a counterpoint to research on the development of children's domain-specific knowledge about the ordinary nature of things. In acquiring an intuitive understanding of the physical, biological, or psychological domains, even young children recognize that there are constraints on what can happen. However, once such constraints are acknowledged, children are in a position to think about the violation of those very same constraints – to contemplate the impossible. In the words of William James (1902/1990), knowledge of the constraints of the "given world" brings into consideration the realm of "something more." Thus, many of the chapters consider the ways that children define and construct ideas about the supernatural, magical, or metaphysical against a background understanding of what is natural (see chapters by Boyer & Walker, Chinn & Brewer, Evans, Harris, Johnson, Rosengren & Hickling, Shrader, and Woolley). From this standpoint, thinking beyond the ordinary boundaries of understanding is considered to be a developmental achievement rather than a primitive form of confusion.

Consideration is also given to the existence of more unreflective forms of magical and phenomenalistic thinking (see chapters by Nemeroff & Rozin and Subbotsky), raising the question of how magical thinking eventually becomes articulated in terms of reflective ideas or ideologies about the magical or supernatural.

## Beyond Scientific Rationality

A standard view of development is that children increasingly cast aside any tendency to either think about supernatural possibilities or to engage in magical thinking. Instead, they gradually adopt a more disciplined, scientific, and rational conception of the world. The chapters in this volume consider alternatives to this standard, developmental account. One major alternative, adumbrated above, is that thoughts about magic – far from making an early appearance in development – depend on the establishment of various everyday principles and constraints. Moreover, to the extent that those everyday principles and constraints are themselves revised and elaborated, so too the metaphysical possibilities that the child contemplates will be revised and elaborated. A second view, also elaborated in a number of chapters, is that two different modes of thinking, the rational and magical, are present throughout development and remain in competition with one another.

What these two alternatives have in common is a dissatisfaction with the notion that cognitive development can be adequately understood in terms of the development of scientific rationality alone. Instead, the development of such rationality needs to be considered in relation to forms of knowing that go beyond empirical verification or the construction of scientific theories. These forms of knowing necessarily raise issues of faith, values, and ideology (see especially chapters by Chinn & Brewer; Evans; Harris; Johnson; Miller, Hengst, Alexander, & Sperry; Nemeroff & Rozin; Subbotsky; and Turiel & Neff).

In sum, the research in this volume goes beyond looking at children as "little scientists," constructing causal explanatory "theories" of the world, to consider their thinking as "little magicians" (see chapters by Chinn & Brewer, Nemeroff & Rozin, Rosengren & Hickling, and Subbotsky), "little metaphysicians" (see chapters by Harris and Johnson), "little theologians" (see chapters by Boyer & Walker, Chinn & Brewer, Evans, and Woolley), and "little story tellers" or "dramatists" (see chapters by Miller, Hengst, Alexander, & Sperry; and Taylor & Carlson) who are capable of imagining and analyzing other-worldly possibilities.

## Shaping the Metaphysical

When children or adults contemplate possibilities that go beyond reality it is evident that their thinking will be less constrained by empirical observation and causal regularity than when they contemplate mundane reality. This raises the question of what, if anything, shapes their thoughts about such metaphysical possibilities. One plausible expectation is that the family and the wider cultural milieu play an influential role. With this expectation in mind, the volume marks a step away from abstract, stagelike descriptions of either the decline of magical thinking or the development of religious ideas, toward more grounded descriptions of the development of particular kinds of ideas in particular social cultural contexts. For example, studying midwestern American parents and children, Rosengren and Hickling look at how parents gradually devalue the role of "magic" as an explanation just at the age where Woolley shows that parents begin to commonly support beliefs in the power of prayer. Johnson looks at the development of thinking about "miracles," "immanent justice," and "souls" among Roman Catholic and Unitarian adolescents. Evans examines the development of creationist ideas among children growing up in Christian fundamentalist versus nonfundamentalist communities. Taylor and Carlson look at parental attitudes toward fantasy and children's fantasy behaviors in a Mennonite community, offering comparisons with Christian fundamentalist and Hindu traditions. With regard to moral ideas and religious beliefs, Turiel and Neff also consider Christian fundamentalism and Hinduism, pointing out that a so-called collective society like India has fostered a view that religion is more a private and personal matter than a public and social matter. Finally, Miller, Hengst, Alexander, and Sperry look at variations across culture, subculture, and gender in the extent to which self-narratives should be tightly restricted to literal truth.

Notwithstanding the variation across cultures in institutionalized modes of thinking or received beliefs explored in these various chapters, it may still be that collective representations are themselves governed and constrained by universal features of human mentation. On this view, notwithstanding the apparent heterogeneity of belief, we can expect to find certain recurrent features to metaphysical ideas even in the context of different cultural and religious traditions (see chapter by Boyer & Walker). Moreover, no matter what view we take of the nature of such collective representations, there is the further question of how children assimilate or reject ideas that may not fit their preexisting intuitive notions (see chapter by Harris).

## A Synoptic Overview

The first two chapters tackle the issue of magical thinking. In Chapter 1, Nemeroff and Rozin offer a fundamental revision of the classical notion of sympathetic magic. With rich new evidence, they demonstrate that such thinking exists and persists as a peculiar kind of local nonrational thinking, being especially prevalent in some individuals. Nonetheless, while elaborately documenting the operation of this form of thinking, Nemeroff and Rozin dismiss the traditional view that development is marked by a linear evolution from magical thinking to religious thought and finally scientific understanding. Instead, sympathetic magic is considered as a form of thinking that selectively functions in certain conditions and in potentially valuable ways.

In a similar vein, Subbotsky reinterprets the classical idea that development proceeds from phenomenalistic to rational conceptions. Just as Nemeroff and Rozin point out that magical thinking persists as a form of thinking, Subbotsky argues that phenomenalistic thinking also persists in some contexts. Similarly, he challenges the traditional linear, "replacement" model of development characterized by increasing rationality with evidence that different ways of framing reality coexist and "fight for dominance." Phenomenalistic thinking, like magical thinking, is considered with regard to its local, pragmatic successes rather than solely in terms of its rational failures.

While these first two chapters focus on the characteristics of magical thinking, Rosengren and Hickling turn attention to the related but distinct issue of thinking about "magic." Magic is not simply a way of thinking; it is a potential object of thought. In any case, Rosengren and Hickling look at development in terms of dynamic processes, regarding the attraction and selection of different kinds of interpretations. Their research looks at the interplay between individual and social forces in the development of children's ideas about magic. In this account, "magic" makes only a brief appearance as a special category of explanation among American children, before it is largely reduced to matters of illusion and trickery.

Woolley's chapter effectively takes up this developmental story where Rosengren and Hickling leave off. Woolley reports that just as children's beliefs in magic decline, so too do their beliefs in the power of wishing. At the same time, however, in her sample of American children she finds an increasing belief in the real, albeit highly selective, power of prayer. In this regard, Woolley begins to chart the development of ideas and beliefs about mental-physical causality as special categories, separated from the ordinary conceptions of the limited power of minds.

The nature of religious ideas is more broadly considered by Boyer and Walker. Outlining the many different components and functions of religion, attention is focused on the cognitive characteristics of supernatural beings. Religions commonly postulate the real existence of apparently impossible things. These supernatural beings stand out as attractors against a background of intuitive, common sense. On this basis, Boyer and Walker offer a revision of traditional accounts of the development of religious ideas, challenging normative assessments with a more concrete, dynamic look at the way that people actually think about supernatural things.

The chapters by Harris and Johnson take a similarly broad look at the development of supernatural ideas, framed under the more general category of "metaphysics." Attention is focused on the development of children's questions and thoughts about phenomena that stretch beyond the boundaries of the actual, given world. Harris looks at how children try to make sense of strange or anomalous religious ideas. He points out that children appear remarkably open to such strange possibilities, in part because their thinking is not directed exclusively toward actual reality. Moreover, the realm of the nonactual cannot be directly explored or empirically verified, but rests heavily on verbal information, especially in the form of collective representations. On this basis, Harris looks concretely at the different conditions – empirical and metaphysical – under which children's questions actually arise and solutions are discussed. Failing to assimilate supernatural ideas into their ordinary categories of understanding, he argues that children construct boundaries, or "double entries," that keep conflicting beliefs apart.

Whereas Harris focuses primarily on the anomalies that children face in trying to integrate collective theological ideas with intuitive expectancies, Johnson focuses on the anomalies that are inherent in the structure of intuitive understanding itself. Contrary to recent claims that children's intuitive understanding argues against any susceptibility to magical ideas, Johnson argues that such understanding provides the input for magical ideas. The very way in which the world is intuitively conceived presents conundrums that tend to lead children's thinking toward mystical and religious ideas. Piaget's early work is reexamined insofar as it highlighted children's metaphysical speculation – as distinct from their intuitive understanding. The capacity of children to intuitively distinguish between thoughts and things is seen as being a prerequisite for magical ideas about how these different things "participate" together. In addition, the later development and crystallization of metaphysical ideas is considered.

While the above chapters focus on how children think or theorize about alternative realities, Miller, Hengst, Alexander, and Sperry look at how children talk about alternative realities, especially in the context of narrative. Miller et al. present an overview of current theories of speech genres that goes beyond formal description to look at the dynamic ways that function as "ways of seeing" in the context of social life. From this standpoint, children are viewed as not only acquiring rich and differentiated tools for framing reality; they are also learning how to make use of these tools, weaving them together in different ways depending on norms, practices, and purposes that vary with culture, family, and individual. Attention is also given to ways in which affective concerns and cultural practices foster the "interanimation" of written and personal stories, such that fictional literature becomes woven into a child's everyday life.

Consistent with this cultural perspective, Taylor and Carlson examine ways in which religious ideology frames children's fantasy practices. By looking at three religious traditions – Hindu, fundamentalist Christian, and Mennonite – they are able to offer a particularly rich insight into the way in which metaphysics is connected to values and practices in everyday life. For example, Mennonite parents discourage children's questions and see fantasy play as frivolous and a threat to social cohesion in public, yet they allow for such fantasy in private. Fundamentalist Christians, in contrast, equate fantasy with lying, viewing it as a serious threat to truth; whereas Hindus value fantasy insofar as it is seen to be a connection to a spiritual realm. Within these different frameworks, children develop more or less public and more or less articulate ideas about the nature and value of their fantasy lives.

Turiel and Neff bring another perspective on the interplay between culture, knowledge, and values. Overall, they demonstrate how universality and heterogeneity go together in the development of moral and religious thinking. Different types or domains of judgment appear to be universally distinguished, separating moral issues from matters of personal choice, social convention, or authority. They demonstrate that even children can distinguish moral values from religious convention or authority. Ironically, it is the universal, transcendental quality of moral principles that sets them apart from mere religious tradition. Morality judgments have to do with universal issues that arise from the ways people relate to one another, in relation to both individual rights and collective responsibilities. Nevertheless, the application of moral principles depends on informational assumptions, including metaphysical beliefs (such as the existence of souls, before birth or after death). Thus, instead of construing individuals and cultures as operating within a homogeneous moral framework, attention is directed to the diverse ways that people establish individual and collective values.

The interplay between ideology and cognitive development is also examined in the chapter by Evans, who looks in detail at how tendencies in children's thinking intertwine with cultural and educational influences to yield various ideas about creation and evolution. Evans frames her developmental studies within the broader context of historical and cultural resistance to the idea of evolution. She then looks at how ideology and cognition conspire to pose persistent difficulties to acceptance of the theory of evolution. The theory not only poses a threat to traditional values that give special status to human souls, it is also hard to assimilate, because it runs counter to certain intuitive tendencies. Importantly, Evans' detailed investigation demonstrates that fundamentalist, creationist parents are not anti-scientific in general. Rather, they retain a more traditional view of science and religion, seeking to protect their children from the evidence provided by fossils and more generally from the relativity of values expressed in the humanities.

The final two chapters give further attention to the institutional and historical roles of science and metaphysics. Chinn and Brewer look at the central issue of anomaly and knowledge change, comparing experts in science, religion, and the paranormal, with the thinking of nonexpert adults and children. While noting that the same set of strategies is used to deal with anomalies in all of these cases, they emphasize that, institutionally, science is unique in two respects. First, scientific data are comparatively unambiguous, allowing for more definitive, progressive resolutions of empirical questions. Second, science is guided by epistemological assumptions, characterized as "organized skepticism." In contrast, the domains of religion and the paranormal appear to be inherently limited by the absence of clear evidence with a consequent reliance on "faith" rather than rigorous proof. The critical point, however, is that for children and nonexperts the distinctive nature of science largely disappears. The data that children are exposed to in their science classes are often quite ambiguous, and belief rests largely on faith in authority.

The final chapter, by Shrader, is distinguished by its focus on the historical interplay between developments in science and metaphysics, quite apart from the thinking of children. The chapter serves as a wider caution against the idea that religion and science are inherently at odds with one another, with science coming to ultimately triumph over religion. Instead, Shrader shows how historical developments in the science of physics have been deeply intertwined with historical developments in metaphysics and theology. Importantly, this development is not only marked by shifts at the boundaries, but also by a more radical demise of the idea of fixed essences combined with a more dynamic view of the nature of reality and knowledge. Although it is true that religious institutions have sometimes functioned as a conservative force resisting advances in scientific knowledge (see chapters by Chinn & Brewer and Evans), this chapter points out that great thinkers have long been open to new ideas and evidence, pushing the boundaries of knowledge beyond the domains of science to contemplate the larger nature of reality.

## Reference

James, W. (1990). *The Varieties of Religious Experience*. New York: Random House. (Original work published in 1902)

# 1 The Makings of the Magical Mind

## The Nature and Function of Sympathetic Magical Thinking

CAROL NEMEROFF AND PAUL ROZIN

Although the word magic is common in both scholarly and lay discourse, the variety of things to which it refers is far-reaching, ranging from a social institution characteristic of traditional societies, to sleight-of-hand or parlor tricks, to belief in unconventional phenomena such as UFOs and ESP, to sloppy thinking or false beliefs, and even to a state of romance, wonder, or the mysterious. One must at least entertain the possibility that there is no true category here at all. Instead, the term "magic" in current usage has become a label for a residual category – a garbage bin filled with various odds and ends that we do not otherwise know what to do with.

Yet to relegate "magic" to this status seems to us to be throwing out the baby with the bath water. Certain meaningful consistencies can be gleaned from a careful review of the historical and current approaches to magic, including our own recent empirical studies of "magical thinking." We turn now to a review of these approaches, with an eye toward outlining a working definition of magic. This is followed by a review of our empirical studies to date and some speculations, based on current thinking in diverse fields, regarding the origins, functions, and implications of magical thinking.

Current conceptualizations of magic in Western society are heavily based on the writings of a long line of anthropologists, sociologists, and historians. These include works from the last century by scholars Tylor (1879/1974), Frazer (1890/1959), Mauss (1902/1972), Durkheim (1915/1965), Levy-Bruhl (1923), Malinowski (1955), and others, as well as more recent writings by, for example, Evans-Pritchard (1937/1976), Horton (1967), Tambiah (1990), and Thomas (1971). In our own work we have attempted to derive a framework that can usefully direct empirical explorations of magic.

1

## Classical Definitions and Distinctions

The classical scholarly view of magic centers on a tripartite division between magic, religion, and science, with magic defined as the most primitive of these institutions. Over time, as man's causal thinking has rid itself more and more of false and mystical elements, religion was born, and eventually science. Magic is seen as false or failed science, and its primary flaw is its assumption that the world of reality functions according to the same principles as our thoughts.

From the classical view we take two major components of our working definition of magic: (1) Magic does not make sense in terms of contemporary understandings of science, and (2) magic typically relies on subjective evidence and involves a conflation of internal and external worlds. We discard, however, the notion of an evolutionary sequence from magic-to-religion-to-science, based primarily on our own evidence of the abundant presence of all three simultaneously in modern Western societies and in the thinking of individuals within those societies (see Thomas, 1971). We also discard the notion of defining magic based on its real-world efficacy or lack thereof. Today's magic sometimes becomes tomorrow's science (as with germ theory), and today's science is sometimes tomorrow's magic (e.g., phlogiston).

The writings of Malinowski (e.g., 1955) provide another key element for our conceptual framework. In his view, magic is a misguided attempt to gain control over nature, applied primarily in cases where technology alone is insufficient to control uncontrollable forces. Although he also agreed with Frazer and Mauss that magic was *false* science – a notion that we have already rejected as a defining feature of magic – Malinowski contributes two critical new ideas to our thinking. The first is that people may comfortably employ multiple modes of thinking and action, blending "scientific" with "magical" approaches in a complementary fashion. The second is that magic is not simply the result of sloppy thinking, but instead may serve important functions, even when it "fails" from a scientific standpoint.

Tambiah's (1990) recent writings on magic provide us with an important clarification of this latter point. Tambiah asserts that many magical acts or components of them are not in fact aimed at accomplishing concrete efficacy, but aim instead for dramatic effect. Their success is most appropriately gauged in terms of whether they effectively serve to create a meaningful structure – whether in terms of social convention, solutions of existential problems, or intellectual puzzles. Thus magic serves important functions but operates on a different wavelength from science. We add our own speculation that magic may have evolutionarily adaptive value. In short, we consider magic as worthy of respect as an important and potentially beneficial human function.

## Sympathetic Magic

Within the general framework described above we have chosen to focus our own work on a subset of magic that is more or less proto-typical and unambiguous in its "magical" status, namely, sympathetic magic. Sympathetic magic is characterized by three basic principles: the *law of similarity* (homeopathic magic); the *law of opposites* (the "inverse" of similarity and generally considered a subcase of it), and the *law of contagion* (contagious magic) (see Frazer, 1890/1959; Mauss, 1902/1972; Taylor, 1879/1974). It is also characterized by the concept of "mana," which can be described as the driving force, or essence, that travels along the lines determined by sympathy. We see the sympathetic magical laws and mana as comprising the core of the "magic" category. Abstracted from magical rites and beliefs from cultures worldwide (Frazer, 1890/1959), they were considered to be basic and universal features of "primitive" human thought. We tentatively agree with this premise (Frazer, 1890/1959; Mauss, 1902/1972).

Similarity may be summarized as "like produces like" (Frazer, 1890/1959), "the image equals the object" (Mauss, 1902/1972), or, more generally, "appearance equals reality;" it rests on the premise that things that resemble one another at a superficial level also share deeper properties. A prototypical example of similarity is the voodoo practice of burning a representation of an enemy to cause the enemy harm. Action on the image is believed to result in effects on the object that it represents. The law of opposites has the same form and content as similarity but relates opposite and opposed to similar entities.

The law of contagion is more complex. We begin by identifying one object as a source and another object as a target or recipient. The law of contagion holds that *physical contact between the source and the target results in the transfer of some effect or quality (essence) from the source to the target*. Qualities may be physical, mental, or moral in nature, and negative or positive in valence. When qualities and their effects are negative in valence, the terms "contamination" or "pollution" apply, while positive effects are sometimes referred to as "transvaluation."

Effects may be symmetrical, in that the same object, in the same contact, may act as both a source and a target. Furthermore, the contact between the source and the target may be direct, or it may be mediated by a third object ("vehicle") that contacts both the source and the target, either simultaneously or successively.

Critical to the law of contagion are the ideas that the *transfer of essence establishes a continuing "sympathetic connection" between the target and the source* (hence the summary description "once in contact, always in contact;" Mauss, 1902/1972) and that *essence contains all of the important properties of the source* ("the part equals the whole;" Mauss, 1902/1972). Following contact the target is changed in the direction of being more like and/or more connected to the source. In the case of a negative source, the target is contaminated, debased, or otherwise harmed. In the case of a positive one, the target is purified, elevated, or otherwise benefited. The continuing connection allows for the possibility that action taken against a vehicle or even against the target will affect the source. Thus typical examples of contagion include the voodoo burning or defacing of a garment, lock of hair, or fingernail parings from an enemy to effect some negative influence on him or her. Obviously there are real-world, scientifically validated instances of contagion, most notably germ and illness transmission. However, "magical" contagion is far broader than its scientific counterpart in terms of what may be transmitted and how.

Magical contagion shares two key characteristics with magical similarity. First, both involve a conflation of the internal/subjective and external/objective worlds. In similarity, perceived resemblance is taken to reflect a deeper level identity between two objects (or between an object and its representation). In contagion, the most relevant feature of a source – in the mind of the perceiver or practitioner – is what is believed to be transmitted; furthermore, both properties and modes of transmission may be metaphorical. Second, both similarity and contagion depend on the notion of a shared essence ("mana"), between the object and the representation in similarity, and between the source and the target in contagion.

Mana, then, may be understood as pure efficacy or identity (hence "essence"). It is the driving force behind the effects, the stuff that travels along the routes laid out by similarity and contagion.

*A Working Definition of Magic*

To summarize, our delineation of magic is comprised of the following elements:

1. Magic is an intuitive, and possibly universal, aspect of human thinking. As corollaries, (a) magic is defined in terms of a belief or set of related beliefs, and (b) these beliefs may be held at different levels of explicitness, ranging from spontaneous, vague, "as if" feelings, all the way to explicit, culturally taught beliefs.
2. Magic generally does not make sense in terms of the contemporary understanding of science.
3. Magic typically relies on subjective evidence and involves the assumption – whether explicit or implicit – of correspondence or conflation between the subjective, internal world and the world of reality.
4. Magic may serve important functions (e.g., cognitive, emotional, social, or adaptive functions.)
5. Magic in its most prototypical form involves the sympathetic principles of similarity and contagion, and the notion of an imperceptible force (essence) that drives, carries, or provides the mechanism for effects.

These elements can be loosely summed up as: Magic is a cognitive intuition or belief in the existence of imperceptible forces or essences that transcend the usual boundary between the mental/symbolic and physical/material realities, in a way that (1) diverges from the received wisdom from the technocratic elite, (2) serves important functions, and (3) follows the principles of similarity and contagion.

## Sympathetic Magical Thinking

Our research on the laws of sympathetic magic was stimulated by the observation that the contamination properties of disgusting stimuli, for Americans, manifested themselves according to the laws of sympathetic magic: Replicas of disgusting objects are treated as disgusting (similarity), and brief contact between disgusting entities and acceptable foods renders those foods disgusting (contagion) (Rozin, Millman, & Nemeroff, 1986). In fact, Rozin and Fallon's (1987) definition of disgust included the contagion feature. Subsequent work has established that both laws of sympathetic magic operate in a salient and frequent way in the thinking of educated, Western adults. In the following sections we will provide evidence for this claim and analyze the properties, origins, and functions of the two laws.

## The Law of Similarity

In a first study Rozin, Millman, and Nemeroff (1986) demonstrated various reactions consistent with the law of similarity among American undergraduates. In the domain of disgust, most participants showed a preference for a normally shaped piece of fudge over fudge shaped like dog feces. Many were far less willing to hold fake "vomit" made of rubber in their mouths than a clean new rubber sink stopper. Examples of similarity in the interpersonal domain included poorer accuracy in throwing darts (aiming between the eyes) at photographs of good (e.g., John F. Kennedy) or imagined liked persons, relative to evil (e.g., Adolph Hitler) or imagined disliked persons.

Rozin, Millman, and Nemeroff (1986) and Rozin, Markwith, and Ross (1990) also explored the phenomenon of nominal realism, identified by Piaget (1983) as a feature of thinking in young children. Nominal realism involves the child's failure to appreciate the arbitrary relationship between a word and its referent. Rather, toddlers assume that the name of an entity carries its very nature within it (i.e., the name/image equals the referent/object). We demonstrated this in undergraduates, who saw two empty, clean bottles and watched while some sugar powder from a commercially labeled sugar box was poured into each. The participant was then given two labels, one with "sucrose" written on it and the other with "sodium cyanide, poison" written on it. Participants were instructed to attach one label to each bottle, as they preferred. After powder from each bottle was stirred into a separate glass of water, participants were asked to rate their willingness to take a sip from each glass, and then to do so. Many were reluctant to drink from the glass with the cyanide-labeled sugar in it, and there was a significant preference for the sugar-labeled bottle (Rozin, Millman, & Nemeroff, 1986; Rozin, Markwith, & Ross, 1990). Participants acknowledged that their negative feelings were unfounded, in that they knew only sugar was in both glasses. In a subsequent study it was shown that this similarity-based rejection occurred even if the "cyanide" bottle was labeled "not sodium cyanide, not poison" (Rozin, Markwith, & Ross, 1990), potentially supporting Freud's (1920/1966) claim that the unconscious does not process negatives.

These demonstrations raise a particularly important issue in the study of magical thinking, namely, that notions of magic may exist at different levels of awareness and explicitness, depending on the individual, situational, and cultural contexts. Thus magical responses can range from a spontaneous, ineffable, intuitive sense of connection between things, all the way to an explicit, rationalized, culturally supported belief in such a connection.

The similarity magic mode of thought seems "primitive," and indeed Flavell (1986) has shown that a confusion of appearance and reality characterizes the thinking of young children. Similarity magic is related to the principle of generalization. This is a property that, appropriately constrained, is fundamental to survival across species, because even the same thing rarely looks exactly the same from moment to moment, and different exemplars of a category usually differ to some extent. Thus treating appearance as reality, as young children have been shown to do (Flavell, 1986), or "like as like," is generally very useful. This strategy occasionally goes awry in nature (as in cases of mimicry), but goes awry more often in *Homo sapiens*, where three- and two-dimensional images of real objects are commonly produced, and where symbols are often utilized. The possibilities for magical similarity are abundant in humans largely because of the world of artifacts (words, symbols, images, etc.) that humans have produced.

## The Law of Contagion

In a sense, contagion is the opposite of similarity. Contagion holds that things are often not what they seem. Rather, their history, which is not necessarily manifested in their appearance, constitutes an essential part of them. Contagion has to do with what and whom we wish to merge with, versus separate from, in the world. Contact with a host of negative things, including unknown strangers, malicious others, their possessions or bodily residues, death, and physical "corruption" of any kind (e.g., rotting matter, most insects, and virtually any other disgusting item), is felt to be physically endangering and/or morally debasing to the self. Contact with a smaller set of positive things – loved ones or kin in a nontabooed relationship, personifications of goodness or holiness (e.g., Mother Theresa), or their possessions or residues, can be felt to enhance or elevate the self. Proscriptions, taboos, and various forms of physical and symbolic purifications are utilized cross-culturally to manage negative contagion, while mementos, tokens, and avoidance of purification are used to maximize positive effects. We will first review magical contagion, and then examine the characteristic conflation of moral and physical realms, the basic principles of contagion, and typical ways of managing and conceptualizing it.

Contagion operates very powerfully in the food domain, within both traditional and modern cultures. Rozin, Millman, and Nemeroff (1986) demonstrated this with young adults. In one manipulation, a dead, sterilized cockroach was placed in a glass of the participants' preferred flavor of juice, and then removed. A strong aversion to drinking juice of a preferred flavor after it had been "roached" in this fashion was demonstrated.

There are abundant examples of food contamination of this sort. The contaminants are typically disgusting (rotting things, contact with a disliked person) or dangerous (contact with something that is toxic at high levels). Thus, people are reluctant to consume juice that had sodium cyanide added, at a dose level 1/1000 of the lethal level, a level that will have no harmful effects (since cyanide is not a cumulative poison), and a level that is common in everyday foods.

If contagion is based in contact, ingestion is certainly the most intimate form of contact – namely, the complete incorporation of an item into one's body. In a very concrete sense, the mouth is the principal incorporative organ, where almost all of the material transaction between self and world occurs, and ingestion is a major activity and concern of humans (Rozin, 1996). The mouth serves a particularly important function for omnivores as the final checkpoint where toxins can be distinguished from foodstuffs and rejected. It is small wonder that disgust is such a powerful emotion, or that food taboos are so common and important cross-culturally – or that the magical maxim "you are what you eat" can be identified cross-culturally (Frazer, 1890/1959; Nemeroff & Rozin, 1989). This principle states, in brief, that one will take on the properties of the things one ingests. For example, Meigs (1984) cites the belief of the Hua of Papua New Guinea that young male initiates should eat fast-growing leafy green vegetables to help them grow fast.

Nemeroff and Rozin (1989) looked for evidence of belief in "you are what you eat" among American undergraduates, creating scenarios of two fictitious cultures within which was embedded information about the foods typically eaten by members of each culture. There were two versions of each scenario (the Asch impressions technique), which were identical *except* for the specific food staple identified as eaten by culture members. The Chandoran islanders were described as hunting both marine turtles and wild boars, but in version 1 the turtle was a favorite food and the boar hunted only for its tusks. In version 2 this was reversed, with the turtle hunted only for its shell. Participants read the description, and then rated the average Chandoran on an adjective checklist including items descriptive of boars and turtles (e.g., hairy, aggressive, good runners). Boar eaters were rated as more boarlike than turtle eaters. In a replication of this effect, the Hagi were either vegetarian but hunted elephants to sell their tusks, or consumed elephant meat but grew vegetables to sell. Elephant eaters were rated more animal-like in general, and elephantlike in particular, relative to vegetarians. Although the pattern of ratings was clear, the magnitude of individual effects was small and the belief seemed to operate at an implicit level. That is, few of our participants would have admitted to, or been aware of, holding such beliefs.

The idea that one takes on properties of the things one ingests is not preposterous. It is in accord with daily experience; generally, when two entities combine, the product shows characteristics of both entities. In a few cases, you are what you eat actually holds true: Ingestion of high levels of orange-colored (beta-carotene containing) foods may lead to an orange-pigmented skin; similarly, ingestion of high fat foods may lead to becoming fat.

Given the power of magical contagion to elevate or debase the self, and the potency of ingestion as a form of contact, it is hardly surprising that food and the act of eating are almost universally moralized. A familiar example is the quasi-moral attitude to obesity and "bad foods" in many segments of American culture. In an American version of "you are what you eat," Stein and Nemeroff (1995) asked undergraduates at a southwestern university to identify several "good" and "bad" foods and explain what made them so. Their answers were cast in terms of the healthiness and fatteningness of foods. New students then read one of two scenarios describing a fictitious undergraduate. The scenarios were identical except for the foods usually eaten, which were "good" in one case (e.g., fruit, salad, chicken) and "bad" in the other (e.g., steak, french fries, doughnuts). After reading one version of the description, the students rated the target person on an adjective checklist that included a series of moral traits. Good food eaters were seen as strikingly more moral than bad food eaters. Contagion beliefs, specifically, ideas about moral and/or physical pollution resulting from ingestion of the foods, accounted for much of the moral-food effect.

The contagious world view assumes a notion of "self" that is both shed continuously (therefore, contagious and potentially polluting) and permeable to outside influences (therefore, potentially vulnerable), particularly at the apertures of the body (mouth, nostrils, etc.) (Rozin, Nemeroff, Horowitz, Gordon, & Voet, 1995). Noting that eating disorders are characterized by identity deficits on the one hand, and a strong tendency to moralize food on the other, Schupak-Neuberg and Nemeroff (1993) speculated that contagious thinking might play an important role in bulimia nervosa. They hypothesized that (1) bulimics binge in part to obliterate their sense of self by flooding it with outside "stuff;" (2) purging helps to expel a sense of negativity or pollution from the body-self; and (3) bulimics should be hypersensitive to contagion scenarios in general, not just those pertaining to food. In a questionnaire study comparing bulimics with binge eaters and normal controls, all of these predictions were supported. A follow-up study comparing anorexics with restrained eaters (dieters) and controls (Nemeroff, Schupak-Neuberg, & Graci, 1996) is producing similar findings with regard to general avoidance of contagious contact.

Microbial contamination can be viewed as an empirically validated subcase of magical contagion, wherein an influence (i.e., illness) is transmitted from a contagious source to a recipient through contact that allows a contagious entity (in this case, microbes) to travel from one to the other. It is possible that the danger of microbe-borne physical illness, particularly via the mouth, is the original domain of contagion. Some of the basic properties of contagion (particularly contact and dose insensitivity, described below) make adaptive sense with respect to infection. Part of the contagion of decayed food may be attributed to an appropriate fear of illness, as can the contaminating value of many insects, other people and their residues, and contact with a dead body (e.g., Rozin, Markwith, & McCauley, 1994). Many illness sources have disgust properties, including food, body products, poor hygiene, body malformations, and death (Rozin et al., 1993). However, in the pure case of presence of microbes, the contagion fear seems directly linked to the threat of physical illness, rather than disgust.

A principal domain of both disgust and contagion is other people (Nemeroff & Rozin, 1994; Rozin et al., 1993; Rozin, Markwith, & McCauley, 1994). Generally, people other than those in one's immediate family and friendship group are treated as negative entities, at least with respect to the prospects of contact. For example, in the United States and Japan, there is a marked reluctance by many people to wear used clothing. Of course there is a special positive value – and positive contagion – about direct or indirect contact with highly admired persons; this is reflected in the monetary value of clothing worn by famous people, or their possessions.

Questionnaire studies of undergraduates confirm the high negative value of contagious contact with negative others (e.g., disliked or unsavory persons) and an apparently weaker and less universal positive value of contact with respected or loved others (Nemeroff & Rozin, 1994; Rozin, Nemeroff, Wane, & Sherrod, 1989). Undergraduates often show an aversion to wearing laundered clothing worn once for a brief time by an unknown healthy person (in comparison to new, otherwise identical items) (McCauley, Markwith & Rozin, 1997, Rozin, Markwith, & McCauley, 1994). While this negativity is not shown by everyone, a stronger negativity is shown by virtually all participants if negative information about the former wearer is communicated. For example, if a sweater was worn (for one hour, followed by laundering) by someone who experienced a misfortune (e.g., an amputated leg), had a disease (e.g., tuberculosis), or had a moral taint (e.g., a convicted murderer), there is usually a strong aversion to wearing the sweater. Similar results are reported for objects other than clothing (Rozin, Markwith, & McCauley, 1994).

It is worth noting, considering the centrality of germs and illness in contagion, that illness transfer in humans usually involves a human vector, and hence is interpersonal. Common vehicles are food, air, and shared objects and residues. Interpersonal contagion is manifested in the domain of food, because food is a highly social entity that is procured, handled, prepared, or eaten and shared with others. These multiple other contacts allow for widespread interpersonal contagion influences, no doubt enhanced by the particular intimacy of the act of ingestion. The "you are what you eat" principle, in the pure sense, would apply to other humans only for the rare cases of cannibalism. But when coupled with the principle of contagion, you are what you eat promises an enormous range for the passage of personal influence by food (Rozin, 1990).

Cross-culturally, one finds an extraordinary elaboration of interpersonal contagion. In Hindu India, for example, the caste system is maintained, in large part, by food transaction rules based on avoiding consumption of foods that bear contagious essences of lower castes (Appadurai, 1981; Marriott, 1968). Other forms of contact with lower castes are also shunned. There is a weaker, positive contagious experience that results from sharing food with close relatives or deities (via the donation of foods at a Temple).

The limits of the moral domain are fuzzy, at best. Consistent with our working definition of "magic," we regularly find what we call moral/physical conflation (Rozin & Nemeroff, 1990), that is, extensive spill-overs from the hypothetically separate moral and physical domains. There is a large literature suggesting that physical afflictions, such as illness, are interpreted in moral or quasi-moral terms by individuals in many cultures (reviewed in Brandt & Rozin, 1997). For example, the extent of an aversion to wearing a convicted murderer's sweater correlates substantially with the aversion to wearing the sweater of someone with an amputation, or tuberculosis (Rozin, McCauley, & Markwith, 1994). There seems to be a common, shared negative core to both moral and physical shortcomings.

This is not to say that moral contagion is indiscriminable from "physical" contagion. For example, for most people the moral contagious entity has somewhat different properties than the disease contagious entity; only the latter is effectively purified by washing or sterilization (Nemeroff & Rozin, 1994). However, in applying these models of contagious entities, about 15–30% of people ascribe a physical essence to negative moral sources (enemies or evil people) and/or think about illness (hepatitis, AIDS) in terms of a moral entity.

Failure to distinguish moral from physical causes can result in "immanent justice" beliefs. Immanent justice refers to the notion that one's behavior will inevitably lead to appropriate rewards or punishments – essentially, that God's judgment or "cosmic justice" will prevail. Such beliefs can make people feel more or less vulnerable to illness (illness representing "cosmic punishment") as a function of how personally guilty or innocent they feel. Nemeroff et al. (1994) explored the relative contributions of people's sense of guilt, their knowledge about how AIDS is transmitted, and their actual behavioral risk factors to determining how worried they felt about contracting AIDS. In this study, guilt actually accounted for more of the variance in the worry measure than did the participants' knowledge and behavioral risk factors combined.

Interestingly, the effect was reduced when the "worry" outcome measure was replaced by a "likelihood estimate" as an outcome measure (i.e., "how likely do you think you are to contract AIDS? . . ." rather than "how worried are you about contracting AIDS?"). Guilt predicted likelihood estimates far less than it predicted worry, and knowledge and behavioral risks proved to be the more powerful predictors for likelihood. We interpreted these discrepancies in terms of a "head" versus "heart" distinction. When one asks a question in emotion-laden terms – "How worried are you?" – one seems to be accessing an emotional or "gut-level" response system, which follows magical principles, and immanent justice is evoked. In contrast, when one asks a more cognitively/objectively worded question (as in a mathematical probability estimate) more "rational" processes come into play.

This same head versus heart distinction was found by Nemeroff (1995) in a study where the participants imagined themselves coming into brief contact with one of three people with the flu: a lover, an enemy, or a stranger. The participants rated the likelihood that they would get the flu from the contact, and then how sick they would get if they did contract it. They felt that they would get most severely sick from their enemy's germs and least severely sick from their lovers' germs (moral-germ conflation); but intriguingly, there were once again no significant differences in likelihood estimates.

Moral-germ conflation may provide an explanation for some of the high AIDS-risk behaviors engaged in by young adults who would otherwise appear to be fully aware of the dangers of unprotected sex. Young adults have been shown to draw a distinction between "regular" and "casual" partners in terms of their likelihood of using condoms with those partners. It has been unclear whether this is a reasonable strategy borne of AIDS-relevant differences between partner types (e.g., explicit agreements about monogamy, degree of knowledge of one's partner's sexual history, etc.) or the result of illusory feelings of physical safety based in a sense of emotional safety. Comer and Nemeroff (in press) demonstrated that, among undergraduates, perceived physical risk follows emotional safety rather than objective risk factors, apparently reflecting the belief that "my lovers' germs won't hurt me, though a stranger's might well."

The head versus heart distinction routinely comes up in laboratory studies on both contagion and similarity. Participants often acknowledge that their feelings (e.g., negativity toward a beverage touched by a dead, sterilized cockroach) are "irrational." But they still do not want to drink the juice, wear the Nazi garment, or hear that their enemy has their hairbrush.

## Principles of Contagion

We elaborate here on what we take to be the basic principles of contagion (Rozin & Nemeroff, 1990), based on evidence principally from our empirical work. We have typically included AIDS as a contagious entity in part because, in people's minds, AIDS involves a potent mix of infectious and moral factors.

In magical contagion, actual *physical contact* – whether direct or indirect – is critical in determining transmission. We have had participants rate, on a scale ranging from −100, the worst feeling you can imagine, to +100, the best feeling you can imagine, how they would feel about wearing a sweater worn (but not owned) for a day by someone with AIDS (and then washed), as opposed to a sweater owned, but never worn, by someone with AIDS (Rozin et al., 1992). The ratings are uniformly much lower for the worn sweater.

The effects of even minimal contact tend to be relatively *permanent*. We demonstrated this by having participants rate a sweater one day to one year after it had last been worn by someone with AIDS: 54% of the participants showed a flat function over time, and overall 92% of the one-day effect remains after one year. The results were similar with an eating utensil as the vehicle (Nemeroff et al., 1994; Rozin et al., 1992).

Magical contagion is isomorphic, in the metonymic sense of the part being equivalent to the whole. We have referred to this as the *holographic* property of essence, and noted that it results in relative *dose insensitivity* (i.e., even very brief contact is capable of transmitting substantial effects) and *route insensitivity* (i.e., any part of Hitler, from heart to fingernails, is equally evil and can transmit his evil). A sweater worn for only five minutes by a person with AIDS (and then washed) manifests a significant drop in desirability (Rozin et al., 1992). Participants rated their feelings about learning that a single live AIDS virus had entered their body as equal with 100, 10,000, or 1,000,000 viruses (one was as bad as one million). For route insensitivity, 43%

of the participants reported that there was no place at all on the body of a person with AIDS that they would feel comfortable touching, compared with the same places on the body of a healthy stranger (Nemeroff et al., 1994).

Ethnographic evidence, most strikingly from societies such as Hindu India (Appadurai, 1981) or the Hua of Papua New Guinea (Meigs, 1984) suggests that *negative contagion may be more prevalent and more powerful than positive contagion.* In India, while contact with a lower caste is polluting and diminishing, there is virtually no enhancement effect of contact with a higher caste (although various products of the cow – considered a lower order deity – including milk, urine, and dung, can be used as purifiers). American undergraduates on average show substantially stronger contagion effects for objects (sweaters, hairbrush, food) that have contacted negative interpersonal sources (an unsavory person or a disliked individual) than objects that have contacted positive sources (friends or lovers). Furthermore, while virtually all participants show negative contagion effects, only about one-third show positive contagion effects in these contexts (Nemeroff & Rozin, 1994; Rozin, Nemeroff, Wane, & Sherrod, 1989), even when they are allowed to select their own personalized, positive source person (e.g., Mother Theresa, Princess Diana) to ensure the best chance of identifying a potent one. This apparent *negative bias* may be based in adaptive considerations: Few things are as strongly positive as contagious illness or as negative as death.

Almost any type of property is considered transmissible in *magical contagion*, including physical attributes (color, growth rate), abilities (strength, coordination), and dispositions (personality characteristics, moral worth, and intentions). The basic principles of contagion seem to hold independent of the property.

In forward contagion, influence flows from a contagious source to a recipient in much the same way that germs are transmitted from an individual contagious with the flu to a new victim. *Contagion effects* can also occur in the opposite direction. Thus a target may cause harm to the source by burning a lock of the source's hair, or attract the source by placing it in a love potion. A questionnaire explored *backward contagion* beliefs among undergraduates by describing their own hairbrush (given away, and never to be seen again) or lock of hair coming into the possession of either an unsavory or disliked person, or a good friend or lover. Although the effects were small, there was clear evidence of feelings consistent with belief in backward contagion, with about 30% of the participants showing some discomfort at the idea of negative people possessing these objects and about 37% showing some pleasure at the thought of friends or lovers having them (Rozin et al., 1989). The widely publicized reluctance of many Americans to donate blood since AIDS may be caused by backward contagion beliefs.

## Mental Models of Contagion

We have noted that all sorts of properties, ranging from influenza to goodness or evil, are transmitted in magical contagion. While all of these properties follow the basic laws of contagion, we thought it possible that the "mana," that is, the contagious essence involved, might be different for different types of properties. This concern motivated an intensive interview exploration of the psychological nature of the contagious entity.

Nemeroff and Rozin (1994) had participants imagine various source people coming into contact with several objects including a sweater, and then rate how they would feel about wearing the sweater after it had been "purified" in different ways – based on the logic that one can deduce the nature of the contagious entity by seeing what is most and least effective at undoing it. Sources included both positive and negative interpersonal ones (e.g., lover, good person, enemy, evil person); physical illness (hepatitis, AIDS); and disgust (dog feces). Purifications were physical (e.g., sterilize the sweater), symbolic (e.g., unravel or gash it), or "spiritual" (e.g., have Mother Teresa wear Hitler's sweater, to basically cancel out his "vibes" or "soul-stuff" with her own). Individual and averaged response patterns were compared to five possible models of contagious essences: germ, residue, symbolic interaction, associative, or spiritual essence models. The first two are both physical models, and differ primarily in terms of whether a living entity is involved (germ), as opposed to trace residues of substances that are not alive, such as sweat. The latter three are nonphysical models, with symbolic interaction referring to the meaning inherent in, or implied by, the particular interaction with the sweater (e.g., wearing Hitler's sweater as a statement supporting his views); association referring to the elementary notion of things being "paired" in one's mind (i.e., the "reminding value" of the sweater); and spiritual essence referring to Frazer's notion of personalized "soul-stuff" residing in the sweater (perhaps analogous to new-age "vibes," as well as to the "causal essence" discussed by Gelman & Hirschfeld, 1999).

On average, the residue model was the best match for all physical sources (i.e., illness and disgust) while the three nonphysical models were better matches for all interpersonal sources (including all positives). Thus, there seem to be at least two broad models of contagious essence: One is material and is effectively moderated by washing; the other is nonphysical, is reduced much less by washing, is very difficult to erase, and is most effectively reduced by opposite valence contact.

*Individual Differences in Contagion*

The thirty-six participants in the above study on contagious essence (Nemeroff & Rozin, 1994) did not think uniformly about contagion. Only about two-thirds behaved as described on average, with a material type of essence for illness sources and a spiritual type of essence for interpersonal-moral sources. However, one-sixth of the participants seemed to employ a spiritual essence model for all types of contact, and another sixth employed material essence models for all types of sources. Besides such variations in the quality of the contagion, there are large individual variations in sensitivity to contagions. This was gauged initially by a twenty-one-item measure of contagion sensitivity (Rozin, Fallon, & Mandell, 1984). Interestingly, parents' scores correlate significantly with their children's scores. More recent results, based on a more sophisticated, reliable, and valid instrument (the D-scale; Haidt, McCauley, & Rozin, 1994; see also Rozin, Haidt, McCauley, Dunlop, & Ashmore, 1997) confirm wide variability in contagion sensitivity across a number of different American samples. In general, sensitivity is higher in females than males.

*Managing Contagion: Framing*

The world is filled with contagious entities, especially negative ones, such as traces of unknown, other human beings. Every piece of money or doorknob is a veritable storehouse of interpersonal contagion. An attentive, contagion-sensitive person could be literally crippled into inaction by the prospects. Yet, even in highly contagion-conscious cultures, like Hindu India or the Hua of Papua New Guinea, life goes on. Two fundamental mechanisms seem to be at work to contain contagion. One has to do with the establishment of ritual boundaries to limit low levels of contagion, and related ritual purifications to eliminate contagious effects. A particularly clear ritual boundary is the one-sixtieth rule of Kashrut, relating to the contamination of kosher foods by nonkosher entities (Nemeroff & Rozin, 1992). According to this rule, if contamination occurs by accident and the contaminant is less than 1/60th of the total volume of the contaminated entity, the food remains kosher. A second, more mundane way to cope with contagion threats is through framing and associated attentional effects. Thus, most Americans just do not think of the past interpersonal history of the doorknobs or the money that they encounter. Here, there are substantial within and between-culture differences. For example, the contamination produced by the bottoms of shoes bringing outside filth into the home is salient for most Japanese, and not attended to by most Americans. On the other hand, Japanese traditionally share their bath water with family members and guests, while Americans find that offensive.

## Development and Adaptive Value of Contagion

Contagion is a sophisticated idea, since it overrides appearances, and frequently invokes invisible entities. Since contagion involves the apparently rather complex notion of an imperceptible quality based in a history of contact, persisting in its effects over time, we do not find it surprising that very young children do not show contagion, per se. That is, although they may reject a disgusting source (e.g., a cockroach), and when just a bit older, reject an item that is currently in contact with that source, they will readily drink a beverage that has previously contacted a cockroach. Early work suggested that contagion in its full-blown sense becomes an active principle, at least in the domain of food and disgust for American children, at six to eight years of age (Fallon, Rozin, & Pliner, 1984; Rozin, Fallon, & Augustoni-Ziskind, 1985; 1986). More recent work on Australian preschoolers, using more sensitive measures, suggests that children as young as four years of age may show a degree of contagion sensitivity in the food domain (Siegal & Share, 1990), for example, rejecting moldy bread even if the mold is hidden by jam. No systematic research that we know of has been done to date investigating positive contagion in young children, but this may be a fruitful area for exploration, given the anecdotally common phenomenon of special objects of attachment such as soft blankets or stuffed toys. Also, little is known as yet regarding how socialization, specific experience, and so on might contribute to the development of contagion sensitivity. However, assuming that contagion follows a development course similar to essentialism, the available research does not appear to support a major role for the direct teaching of the concept (see Gelman & Hirschfeld, 1999).

Contagion has an adaptive value in at least three domains. In the food domain, it protects against microbial infection, and perhaps against potent toxins as well. In the interpersonal domain, it also protects against the transmission of infectious diseases and serves an important function in the defining and maintenance of social boundaries between groups. Finally, contagion thinking is salient as a representation of kin relations and love bonds. With the exceptions of tabooed relationships or states (e.g., menstruation), close kin are generally less contaminating and may give rise to positive contagion, hence cementing closeness and commitment among related individuals. Sharing food, for example, is a common behavior that centers on kin-related groups, and sexual intimacy involves highly contagious contact.

## Possible Origins of Magical Thinking

We believe that magical thinking is universal in adults; although the specific content is filled in by one's culture, the general forms are characteristic of the human mind. However, we have not yet addressed the question of the origins of such thinking. Historically, Tylor, Frazer, and Mauss saw magical similarity and contagion as based in the (psychological) laws of association of ideas, with the additional step of assuming that the external world followed the same pattern as one's thoughts. Freud (e.g., 1913/1950, 1920/1966) and Piaget (e.g., 1983) both discussed magic as a primitive level of confused thinking. Freud related it to the "primary process," which he described as unconstrained by the objective world, and antithetical to linear, logical, and adaptive "secondary process" thought. Piaget construed it as based in a childlike failure to fully differentiate self from world, resulting in the tendency to mistake ideational connections for real ones. Both described magical thinking as more or less operating uniformly across content domains.

Modern theorists appear to be converging on the idea that magical thinking is a very natural and intuitive way of thinking, arising as a natural by-product of the adaptive functioning of the mind. In the following section, we will review relevant ideas from theorists who have not explicitly related their work to magical thinking, as well as ideas from those working directly in this area.

## Information-Processing Accounts of Magic

Although the field of cognitive psychology has not explicitly discussed or explored magical thinking, we can fruitfully apply a cognitive approach to similarity and contagion based on inquiries into the limits of human cognitive capacities. The main thesis of such approach begins with the claim that there are normatively appropriate strategies that should guide inferences pertaining to correlation and causality. A good deal of evidence has demonstrated that people underutilize these strategies and overutilize more primitive, intuitive ones in making daily life judgments. Two views (not mutually incompatible) have been presented to explain why we make these "profound, systematic, and fundamental errors" in judgments and inferences (Nisbett & Ross, 1981). The first claims that they are labor-saving devices allowing a limited cognitive system to take short-cuts (Kahneman, Slovic, & Tversky, 1982) while the second construes them as cognitive illusions, comparable to visual illusions that are the inevitable result of the structure of the system. As Nisbett and Ross (1980) note, the visual system generally works extremely well to extract a constant, interpretable, and useful visual world from a shifting morass of stimulus energies. However, because of the built-in strategies used to accomplish this, the system will inevitably be fooled under certain circumstances. Analogously, the cognitive system can be construed as having a particular architecture that works well for everyday purposes but will inevitably fail on occasion. Central to both the successes and failures of the cognitive system is the operation of judgmental heuristics, or "rules of thumb."

The representativeness heuristic (Kahneman, Slovic, & Tversky, 1982) results in the assignment of a case or event to a category based on the similarity of its principle features to other members of that category. One version of representativeness is the tendency to expect a cause to resemble its effects. Thus, if AIDS is incurable and lethal, highly menacing and tenacious, we are likely to consider HIV to be the same, so that information about its fragility outside the human body (it does not survive on toilet seats) does not much change our thinking.

Shweder (1977) applied this approach to magical thinking. He asserted that magical thinking is an expression of a universal disinclination of normal adults to draw correlational lessons from their experiences, coupled with a universal inclination to seek symbolic and meaningful connections (likenesses) among objects and events ". . . an expression of a cognitive-processing limitation of the human mind" (p. 637). The law of similarity, for Shweder, is really a subset of the representativeness heuristic, which he claims is what generally replaces both correlation and contingency in everyday thinking. Thus the Zande believe that fowl excrement cures ringworm simply because, for them, fowl excrement and ringworm go together.

Shweder's definition of likeness/resemblance is so broad, encompassing all of the notion of "what goes with what" conceptually, that examples of part-whole relatedness and the law of contagion are included in his version of "similarity." While he collapses the two magical laws, we find it useful to retain the distinctions, and a more concrete level of focus, for our purposes. We agree that the law of similarity is obviously related to the representativeness heuristic, but suggest that the law of contagion can usefully be construed as an additional heuristic, along the lines of "contact causes influence," that substitutes for actual causal analysis.

A second source of error in the cognitive system, according to Nisbett and Ross (1980), comes from knowledge structures, which are preexisting systems of schematized and abstracted knowledge, such as beliefs, theories, and so on. These become problematic either inasmuch as they are inaccurate representations of the world, or inasmuch as we process an event through a knowledge structure that is inappropriate to that event. One can understand the moral-physical conflation characteristic of magical contagion in terms of easily available social schemata intruding inappropriately into the physical domain, and vice versa. This most likely happens in part because illness transmission occurs between people, and because possessions and ownership represent self and social and power relations. Inappropriate schemas are most likely to intrude when the appropriate schema for a given situation is weak – as seems to be the case for both random chance and contingency (see Kahneman, Slovic, & Tversky, 1982; Langer, 1975; Nisbett & Ross, 1980; Shweder, 1977).

*Domain-Specific Origins of Magical Thinking*

An alternative (though not incompatible) approach rests on the phenomenological experience of living in a human body, and the role of this "embodied experience" in our abstract reasoning and inferential patterns. Johnson (1987), Lakoff (1987), and Lakoff and Johnson (1980) have argued that our bodies provide us with preconceptual structures that shape our experiences and concepts. Both bodily movements and perceptual interactions with the world involve recurrent sensorimotor patterns, which give rise to "image schemata" (gestalt abstract structures by which we make sense of things). These image schemata are "metaphorically projected" to give structure to a wide variety of domains. Within this framework, the contagion principle would arise naturally from our physical interactions with the world as a result of the combination of basic schemata, such as a "container" schema (arising from the experience of body as container) plus a "trajectory" schema (whereby properties from one container are transmitted to another). A "force" or vector schema also seems implicit in the notion of mana or essence and, for cases of indirect transmission, a "link" schema as well (see Lakoff & Johnson, 1980, for descriptions of basic schemata). A strength of this approach is that it easily accounts for both the breadth of magical contagion and for moral-germ conflation: Given the body as a starting point, metaphorical extensions presumably can occur just as easily to one realm (e.g., social-moral) as to another (e.g., physical).

Along somewhat similar lines, Rozin has provided an analysis of the cultural evolution of disgust, suggesting that disgust originated in the food-selection system and later expanded into other domains, including the interpersonal and moral. That is, the expressive-behavioral-physiological disgust "program" that evolved as part of food rejection became applied over time to a wider and wider range of elicitors spanning multiple domains. Along with this process went an extension of meaning, from ridding the self of a food threat to ridding oneself of a threat to the self (Rozin et al., 1993, 1997). Since contagion is a feature of disgust, the expansion of the domains of disgust could have led directly to expansion of the domains of contagion as well.

Alternatively, it is plausible that similarity and contagion might be more directly "preprogrammed," in the sense of having been subject to natural selection pressures. Shweder (1977) distinguished between intuitive and nonintuitive concepts: The former are easily acquired, even under highly degraded learning conditions (few acquisition trials, little conscious effort expended, etc.), whereas nonintuitive concepts are not necessarily acquired even under optimal learning conditions. This notion is based on the ideas of predisposition, preparedness, and constraints in learning (see Garcia & Koelling, 1966; Rozin & Kalat, 1971; Seligman, 1970; Shettleworth, 1973). Based on the evolutionary history of a species (say these authors), certain relationships are learned more readily than others. These predispositions generally make adaptive sense, such as the tendency to associate nausea with something recently tasted or eaten rather than something seen or heard. Shweder suggests that concepts can be arranged along a continuum of intuitiveness, with some so intuitive that they will be attained "... regardless of variations in physical, social, or cultural environment," whereas others – such as contingency and correlation – are so difficult to learn that they are "absent from the thinking of most normal adults" (1977, p. 638). The laws of similarity and contagion and the mana concept may be examples of highly intuitive concepts in this sense. It is interesting to note that in humans, who, like rats, acquire taste aversions very easily, the persistence of an aversion is *not* affected by knowledge that the association between taste and nausea was spurious (i.e., that the substance ingested did not cause the nausea) (Pelchat & Rozin, 1982; Stunkard & Garb, 1974). Along similar lines we have noted that responses based in magical contagion seem robust, being resistant to attempts to override them by "rational" processes.

It is important to note that a "prepared" concept need not necessarily be present from birth. Preparedness simply implies that a particular relation or concept will be relatively easily learned. Some input – however indirect or minimal – is necessary, though, for it to be learned; nor does preparedness rule out the possibility of a maturational course. Current clinical theorizing about the nature and development of phobias, for example, draws heavily on the preparedness idea to explain the preponderance of phobias of animals and insects, and the relative lack of phobias of artifacts such as guns and knives. Yet there is also a clearly delineated normal childhood progression through a series of fears (animals, insects, the dark, etc.), most of which are outgrown over time.

Boyer (1993, 1994, 1995) presents a somewhat different spin on the idea of constraints on learning as they apply to magic. Boyer draws on the growing trend, particularly within developmental psychology, to think in terms of distinct cognitive domains and relatively domain-specific causal principles. According to this view, the causal principles learned regarding animate objects are distinct from those learned regarding inanimates, and those pertaining to natural kinds are different from those for artifacts (see Bullock, 1985; Gelman, 1990; and Keil, 1989), although there appear to be universal cognitive constraints on how domains are divided and what may be learned about objects and events within them. According to Boyer, domain-specific principles constitute the skeleton of intuitive or naive theories for a given domain, which are then completed by a process of "enrichment" that is, at least in part, the product of culture.

While anthropologists have often assumed that people engaged in magical or religious activities must suspend the constraints of their everyday concepts of causality, Boyer claims that in fact it is empirical expectations, rather than principles of causation, that are suspended. Since principles of causation are not general at all, but are instead based on specific expectancies with regard to the type of events or objects in question (i.e., domains), magical practitioners can determine which causal rules are relevant in a given situation by transforming the understanding of the nature of the objects involved. An example might be to treat an inanimate object as animate: In doing so, causal thinking per se is not suspended, but intuitive expectations normally applying to inanimates are suspended in favor of expectations normally governing animates. (This seems closely related to the cognitive psychology notion of causal schemata from one domain intruding into another, a major difference being that the magical or religious practitioner apparently creates and directs such intrusions intentionally.)

We find it eminently reasonable to presume that, if humans can be biologically predisposed to consider tastes as more likely to be connected with nausea than sights or sounds, then they can also be predisposed to see intentions as more likely causal candidates in the social domain and physical contact as a more likely causal candidate in the mechanistic physical domain. However, we are not in full agreement with Boyer's account, in which he describes religious and magical phenomena as "counterintuitive" attention-getters that are then subjected to more normal intuitive treatment. On the contrary, we presume that many magical principles and supernatural inventions were constructed to help make sense of a difficult-to-understand world, rather than to attract attention (see Gelman & Hirchfeld, 1995, for a similar account of the origins of essentialist thinking). Furthermore, we do not find these creations to be as counterintuitive or bizarre as Boyer implies. It is a common part of normal life to experience the action of invisible forces, such as gravity, infectious diseases, and most forms of electromagnetic radiation, and the entire social world functions based on "invisible" forces – emotions, beliefs, intentions, thoughts, and relationships. It seems more plausible to us that the general set of invisible, insensible forces that can cause illness, death, disaster, and social effects might constitute a cognitive domain with its own relevant set of rules and principles – such as contagion, which deals with situations where things are not as they seem, where there is more to the eye than the obvious, and where imperceptible, transmissible forces exert their influences.

### Why Is Magic so Attractive? Pragmatic Functions of Magical Thinking

Magical thinking is extremely common cross-culturally, spanning traditional and modern societies and all levels of education. This is so whether we mean magic in the sense of isolated beliefs and practices consistent with the laws of sympathetic magic and the mana concept, or in the sense of broadly magical world views. Magical thinking has stubbornly resisted the aggressive expansion of modern science (Humphrey, 1996) and, if anything, appears to be making a major resurgence in terms of explicit and culturally (or at least, subculturally) supported beliefs. We have seen that magic may be a particularly natural and intuitive mode of thought, which explains in part why it is so attractive and compelling. We turn now to consider the question: What functions – positive or negative – might magical thinking serve?

*Magical Thinking Provides an Experience of Connection, Participation, and Meaning*

As reflected in our working definition, magic involves a blurring of the usual, mundane boundary between internal/self and external/world; this blurring is the basis for magical "participations" between an object and one's will, and so on. The phenomenology of the loss of self-boundaries has been described in many contexts, generally in very positive terms. For example, Maslow (1970, 1971/1993) described "peak experiences," Csikzentmihalyi (1990) writes about "optimal experience" or "flow," and Tellegen and Atkinson (1974) write about "absorption." Virtually all religions, and particularly mystical sects, refer to the experience of a loss of a sense of self separate from the world; feelings of oneness with creation, the environment, and/or other people; alteration in the perception of time; and a sense of profound yet effortless involvement. Many religious rituals appear to be designed specifically to elicit this kind of participatory or flow state, via "ecstatic" music, dance, and simultaneous participation by a group of people in the same event in the same way, doing, thinking, and feeling the same thing. Indeed, Durkheim (1915/1965) referred to the participatory group experience as "mana-feeling" and believed it to be the very core of religious experience.

A different sense of connection or participation between self and world is alluded to by Tambiah (1990), who describes the primary value of magic as its ability to bring meaning by providing a way to situate oneself, one's traumas, or one's life in a broader context that simplifies, validates, and brings acceptance – in short, knowing where one stands in the cosmos.

Both senses of participation are acknowledged by Griffin (1988) in his discussion of the contrast between the magical-participatory, versus the scientific machine, metaphor of the universe. The magical universe is responsive to will, with entities blending, joining, and hence influencing each other based on sympathy. In contrast, in the scientific universe, separate, isolated parts act in a mechanistic fashion; nature is denied all subjectivity, experience, or feeling, and there is no place for values, purposes, freedom, or divinity. Modern science, says Griffin, is experienced as alienating people from their subjective experience while magic is closer to our experiential base, and hence more absorbing and richer emotionally.

Finally, magical thinking furthers feelings of connection in the context of contagious thinking about object history. Grandmother's ring was a part of her in a meaningful sense, so that wearing it constitutes a connection with her (see Csikzentmihalui & Rochberg-Halton, 1981, for a more in-depth analysis of the meanings of objects, history, and identity). The history of the object comprises an important part of its identity, which is no less real for being intangible.

*Magical Thinking Allows a Sense of Prediction and Control*

Another obviously attractive aspect of magic is that it can give rise to a sense of control over domains that otherwise feel unpredictable and uncontrollable (see Malinowski, 1995; Shweder, 1977). Gmelch (1971) observed that the extent to which players of different sports engage in personal rituals and superstitions is directly related to the extent to which luck, as opposed to skill, is responsible for outcomes in their particular sport. To borrow Malinowski's words, when mundane or scientific explanations fail or reach their limits, the remaining "uncharted territory" is frightening and frustrating; this is where magico-religious explanations are invoked, to fill the gap.

Langer (1975) observed that human beings do not appear to readily accept or even comprehend the notion of chance (see also Rosenberg, 1997). But illusions of control are not necessarily a bad thing. In an adaptive sense, it is surely more constructive to assume more control than one actually has, as opposed to assuming less control than one has and giving up prematurely (Matute, 1996). A large clinical literature shows that "learned helplessness" is linked to depression, stress, physical symptoms, and poorer overall performance in life while illusions of control may predict positive health outcomes (see Kamen & Seligman, 1987; Peterson, Seligman, & Vaillant, 1994; Seligman, Kamen, & Nolen-Hoeksma, 1988; Taylor & Brown, 1988).

### Real-World Magic

We have attempted thus far to explain why magical thinking feels good largely without regard to the issue of how such thinking relates to reality. But as we have noted throughout this chapter, so-called magical thinking is not necessarily false. We now briefly examine some ways and instances in which magic may be quite literally true.

The most obvious case is when a magical belief is borne out by factual evidence. Magical contagion has many real-world counterparts. In addition to microbial contamination, the entire social realm is replete with contagious effects. Emotions are contagious (see Hatfield, Cacioppo, & Rapson, 1994); behaviors, attitude, and even events may be as well (hence cautions against contact with "bad company," which can result in a variety of effects ranging from harm to one's reputation, to personal involvement in drive-by shootings). Contagion in the sense of residues containing essence is also borne out by scientific fact. Fingerprints are an excellent example, as is DNA analysis and, most recently, cloning. We do indeed leave trace bits of ourselves everywhere we go; our identity can be reconstituted from them, and they can be used against us.

Magical similarity is factually borne out in phenomena such as vaccinations, allergy shots, and administration of the stimulant Ritalin to hyperactive children. It is real as well in the sense that practice of a behavior in fantasy or ritual form frequently leads to the real thing – as both critics of TV violence and fans of Star Trek will attest.

Similarity, contagion, and mana can also act concretely through the effects of symbols, which have powerful influences, not only on thinking and behavior, but even on physiology. Mana has a close relative in the real world – money, which is literally both a symbol and a transmissible physical substance, and is undoubtedly one of the most powerful influences in the modern world. And a curse placed on a person can effectively kill him, either because his belief in it and the ensuing hopelessness leads him to stop eating and drinking, or through direct physiological effects (see Cannon, 1957; Frecska & Kulcsar, 1989)

Some, perhaps most, magical rituals act through multiple mechanisms, all of them quite real. The process of Haitian zombification (Davis, 1988) is an excellent case in point. Tetrodotoxin from the puffer fish provides the physiological mechanism, inducing an initial state nearly indistinguishable from biological death, with continued small doses maintaining near-catatonia. Family and community provide a social mechanism: The individual is treated as dead, their property is distributed among their heirs, and, even if they physically return to the community (as rarely happens), their social status is irrevocable. Psychologically, the zombie believes him- or herself to have died and been resurrected in incomplete fashion. Thus this "magical" phenomenon is effectively real across biological, social, and psychological realms.

Centuries ago, "action at a distance" was considered the hallmark of magic; the notion of gravity was initially rejected on that basis. Today, remote controls and sound and light sensors are commonplace. Until recently, "mind over matter," including the idea that the mind can affect the health of the body in any serious way, was considered "magical." Yet we now have a subdiscipline called psychoneuroimmunology, and acknowledge that placebo effects constitute a substantial part of the effects of drugs acting on body organs. We urge humility in the face of magical thinking, both because it is part of our nature and because it is the peak of hubris to assume that we, at the end of the twentieth century, happen to be at just that time in history when the findings and methodology of science have achieved a level of understanding that leaves no proper space for magical thinking. Time and again, magical thinking has played an important role in the history of science.

## Conclusions

Whether magic is the result of a primitive confusion, a developmental advance (in the case of contagion), the domain-general architecture of the human information-processing system, a natural outgrowth of embodied experience, or domain-specific preadapted or prepared modes of thought – clearly it is often useful. It seems to work more often than it does not. To say that magical thinking "works" can mean a number of things. Most literally, it implies that it actually maps the contingencies of the real world. "You are what you eat" is sometimes true, things that look like tigers usually are tigers, words are usually reliable indicators for what they stand for, and magical contagion maps many of the properties of the real world, including serving as a useful "proxy" for the germ model for millenia before the discovery of germs at the end of the nineteenth century. It still serves as a principal psychological vehicle for the internalization of those practices related to cleanliness and contact that help contain the effects of germs.

Magical thinking can also provide satisfying accounts, and put our mind at ease (as can religion). We can gain comfort by wearing the actual ring our grandmother wore. We can feel that we understand instances of what appear to be undeserved luck or misfortune. Our mind can then turn to more useful pursuits, and our stress level may be reduced at the same time. More generally, the history of the objects that we deal with, as we understand that history, is of great importance in human life. Magical thinking is part of the symbolic world that humans have created, and this world, in many ways, enriches the human experience.

We conclude that magical thinking is an important part of human life, yet it has been little studied and hence is poorly understood. Magical thinking is sometimes adaptive and sometimes problematic, but it is almost always a force to be reckoned with. In short, we see magic as fundamental to human nature and empirically addressable, and urge increased attention to it.

## References

Appadurai, A. (1981). Gastro-politics in Hindu South Asia. *American Ethnologist, 8*, 494–511.

Boyer, P. (1992). Causal thinking and its anthropological misrepresentation. *Philosophy of Social Science, 22*, 187–213.

Boyer, P. (1995). Causal understandings in cultural representations: cognitive constraints on inferences from cultural input. In: Dan Sperber, David Premack, and Ann James Premack (Eds.), *Causal Cognition: A Multidisciplinary Debate* (A Fyssen Foundation Symposium), (pp. 615–644). Oxford: Clarendon Press.

Brandt, A., & Rozin, P. (Eds.) (1997). *Morality and Health.* New York: Routledge.

Bullock, M., (1985). Animism in childhood thinking: a new look at an old question. *Developmental Psychology, 21*, 217–225.

Cannon, W. (1957). Voodoo death. *Psychosomatic Medicine, 19*, 182–190.

Comer, M., & Nemeroff, C. (in press). Conflations of emotional and physical safety in AIDS-risk perception among college students: the "casual-regular" partner distinction. *Journal of Applied Social Psychology.*

Csikszentmihalyi, M. (1990). *Flow: The Psychology of Optimal Experience.* New York: Harper Perennial.

Csikszentmihalyi, M.,& Rochberg-Halton, F. (1981). *The Meaning of Things.* Cambridge: Cambridge University Press.

Davis, W. (1988). *Passages of Darkness:. The Ethnobiology of the Haitian Zombie.* Chapel Hill, NC: University of North Carolina Press.

Durkheim, E. (1965). *The Elementary Forms of the Religious Life.* (J. W. Swain, Trans.) New York: MacMillan, The Free Press. (Original work published 1915)

Evans-Pritchard, E. E. (1976). *Witchcraft, Oracles, and Magic Among the Azande.* Oxford: Oxford University Press. (Original work published 1937)

Fallon, A. E., Rozin, P., & Pliner, P. (1984). The child's conception of food: The development of food rejections with special reference to disgust and contamination sensitivity. *Child Development, 55*, 566–575.

Flavell, J. (1986). The development of children's knowledge about the appearance-reality distinction. *American Psychologist, 41*, 418–425.

Frazer, J. G. (1959). *The Golden Bough: A Study in Magic and Religion.* New York: Macmillan. (Reprint of 1922 abridged edition, edited by T. H. Gaster; original work published 1890)

Frecska, E., & Kulcsar, Z. (1989). Social bonding in the modulation of the physiology of ritual trance. *Ethos, 17*, 70–87.

Freud, S. (1966). The Dream Work Lecture XI. In: J. Strachey (Ed. & Trans.), *Introductory Lectures on Psychoanalysis*, (pp. 170–183). New York: W. W. Norton & Co. (Original work published 1920)

Freud, S. (1950). *Totem and Taboo. Some Points of Agreement Between the Mental Lives of Savages and Neurotics.* (J. Strachey, Trans.). New York: W. W. Norton & Co. (Original work published 1913)

Garb, J., & Stunkard, A. J. (1974). Taste aversions in man. *American Journal of Psychiatry, 131,* 1204–1207.

Garcia, J., & Koelling, R. A. (1966). Relation of cue to consequence in avoidance learning. *Psychonomic Science, 4,* 123–124.

Gelman, R. (1990). First principles organize attention to and learning about relevant data: Number and the animate-inanimate distinction as examples. *Cognitive Science, 14,* 79–106.

Gelman, S. A., & Hirschfeld, L. A. (1999). How biological is essentialism? In: D. Medin and S. Atran (Eds.), *Folk Biology.* Cambridge, MA: MIT Press.

Gmelch, G. (1971). Baseball magic. *Society, 8,* 39–54.

Griffin, D. R. (Ed.) (1988). *The Reenchantment of Science. Postmodern Proposals.* Albany, NY: State University of New York Press.

Haidt, J., McCauley, C. R., & Rozin, P. (1994). A scale to measure disgust sensitivity. *Personality and Individual Differences, 16,* 701–713.

Hatfield, E., Cacioppo, J. T., & Rapson, R. L. (1994). *Emotional Contagion.* New York: Cambridge University Press.

Horton, R. (1967). African traditional thought and Western science. *Africa, 37* (1 & 2), 50–71, 155–187.

Humphrey, N. (1996). *Leaps of Faith.* New York: Basic Books.

Johnson, M. (1987). *The Body in the Mind. The Bodily Basis of Meaning, Imagination, and Reason.* Chicago: University of Chicago Press.

Kahneman, D., Slovic, P., & Tversky, A. (1982). *Judgment under Uncertainty: Heuristics and Biases.* Cambridge: Cambridge University Press.

Kamen, L. & Seligman, M. E. P. (1987). Explanatory style and health. *Current Psychology: Research and Reviews, 6* (3), 207–218.

Keil, F. (1989). *Concepts, Kinds and Conceptual Development.* Cambridge, MA: MIT Press.

Lakoff, G., & Johnson, M. (1980). *Metaphors We Live By.* Chicago: University of Chicago Press.

Lakoff, G., & Johnson, M. (1987). *Women, Fire, and Dangerous Things. What Categories Reveal About the Mind.* Chicago: University of Chicago Press.

Langer, E. J. (1975). The illusion of control. *Journal of Personality and Social Psychology, 32,* 311–328.

Levy-Bruhl, L. (1923). *Primitive Mentality.* The Herbert Spencer Lecture (L. Clare, Trans.) Oxford: Clarendon Press. (Original work published 1922)

Malinowski, B. (1955). *Magic, Science, and Religion.* New York: Doubleday.

Marriott, M. (1968). Caste ranking and food transactions: A matrix analysis. In: M. Singer and B. S. Cohn (Eds.), *Structure and Change in Indian Society,* (pp. 133–171). Chicago: Aldine.

Maslow, A. (1970). New introduction: Religions, values, and peak experiences. *Journal of Transpersonal Psychology, 2* (2), 23–90.

Maslow, A (1971). *The Farther Reaches of Human Nature.* New York: Arkana/ Penguin Books. (Reprinted in 1993)

Matute, H. (1996). Illusion of control: Detecting response-outcome independence in analytic but not in naturalistic conditions. *Psychological Science, 7,* 289–293.

Mauss, M. (1972). *A General Theory of Magic*. (R. Brain, Trans.) New York: W. W. Norton & Co. (Original work published 1902: Esquisse d'une theorie generale de la magie. L'Annee Sociologique, 1902–1903)

McCauley, C. R., Rozin, P., & Markwith, M. (1997). Aversion to interpersonal contact with strangers: A two component analysis. Unpublished manuscript.

Meigs, A. S. (1984). *Food, Sex, and Pollution. A New Guinea Religion*. New Brunswick, NJ: Rutgers University Press.

Murdock, G. P. (1980). *Theories of Illness: A World Survey*. Pittsburgh, PA: University of Pittsburgh Press.

Nemeroff, C. (1995). Magical thinking about illness virulence: Conceptions of germs from "safe" versus "dangerous" others. *Health Psychology, 14,* 147–151.

Nemeroff, C., & Rozin, P. (1989). "You are what you eat": Applying the demand-free "impressions" technique to an unacknowledged belief. *Ethos, 17,* 50–69.

Nemeroff, C., & Rozin, P. (1992). Sympathetic magical beliefs and kosher dietary practice: The interaction of rules and feelings. *Ethos, 20,* 96–115.

Nemeroff, C., & Rozin, P. (1994). The contagion concept in adult thinking in the United States: Transmission of germs and interpersonal influence. *Ethos, 22,* 158–186.

Nemeroff, C., Brinkman, A., & Woodward, C. (1994). Magical cognitions about AIDS in a college population. *AIDS Education and Prevention, 6,* 249–265.

Nemeroff, C. J., Schupak-Neuberg, E., & Graci, G. (1996). Je (ne) suis (que) mon corps: Pensee magique et troubles du comportement alimentaires. (My body, my self: Magico-metaphorical thinking in the eating disorders.) In: Claude Fischler (Ed.), *Pensee magique et alimentation aujourd'hui (Magical Thinking and Nutrition Today)*, (pp. 86–100). Cahiers de l'OCHA, Vol. 5.

Nisbett, R., & Ross, L. (1980). *Human Inference: Strategies and Shortcomings of Social Judgment*. Englewood Cliffs, NJ: Prentice-Hall.

Pelchat, M. L., & Rozin, P. (1982). The special role of nausea in the acquisition of food dislikes by humans. *Appetite, 3,* 341–351.

Peterson, C., Seligman, M. E. P., & Vaillant, G. E. (1994). Pessimistic explanatory style is a risk factor for physical illness: A thirty-five-year longitudinal study. In: A. Steptoe, J. Wardle: et al. (Eds.), *Psychosocial Processes and Health: A Reader*, (pp. 235–246). Cambridge, England: Cambridge University Press.

Piaget, J. (1983). *The Child's Conception of the World*. Totowa, NJ: Rowman & Allanheld (a division of Littlefield, Adams, & Co.). (Original work published 1929).

Rosen, A., & Rozin, P. (1993). Now you see it . . . Now you don't: The preschool child's conception of invisible particles in the context of dissolving. *Developmental Psychology, 29,* 300–311.

Rosenberg, C. (1997). Banishing risk: Continuity and change in the moral management of disease. In: A. Brandt, and P. Rozin (Eds.), *Morality and Health*, (pp. 35–51). New York: Routledge.

Rozin, P. (1990). Social and moral aspects of eating. In: I. Rock (Ed.), *The Legacy of Solomon Asch: Essays in Cognition and Social Psychology*, (pp. 97–110). Potomac, MD: Lawrence Erlbaum.

Rozin, P. (1996). Towards a psychology of food and eating: From motivation to model to meaning, morality and metaphor. *Current Directions in Psychological Science, 5*, 1–7.

Rozin, P., & Fallon, A. E. (1987). A perspective on disgust. *Psychological Review, 94*, 23–41.

Rozin, P., Fallon, A. E., & Augustoni-Ziskind, M. (1985). The child's conception of food: The development of contamination sensitivity to "disgusting" substances. *Developmental Psychology, 21*, 1075–1079.

Rozin, P., Fallon, A. E., & Augustoni-Ziskind, M. (1986). The child's conception of food: Development of categories of accepted and rejected substances. *Journal of Nutrition Education, 18*, 75–81.

Rozin, P., Fallon, A. E., & Mandell, R. (1984). Family resemblance in attitudes to food. *Developmental Psychology, 20*, 309–314.

Rozin, P., Haidt, J., & McCauley, C. R. (1993). Disgust. In: M. Lewis and J. Haviland (Eds.), *Handbook of Emotions*, (pp. 575–594). New York: Guilford.

Rozin, P., Haidt, J., McCauley, C. R., Dunlop, L., & Ashmore, M. (in press). An ecologically valid set of measures of disgust sensitivity and a validation of the D-Scale. *Journal of Research in Personality*.

Rozin, P., & Kalat, J. W. (1971). Specific hungers and poison avoidance as adaptive specializations of learning. *Psychological Review, 78*, 459–486.

Rozin, P., Markwith, M., & McCauley, C. R. (1994). The nature of aversion to indirect contact with another person: AIDS aversion as a composite of aversion to strangers, infection, moral taint and misfortune. *Journal of Abnormal Psychology, 103*, 495–504.

Rozin, P., Markwith, M., & Ross, B. (1990). The sympathetic magical law of similarity, nominal realism and the neglect of negatives in response to negative labels. *Psychological Science, 1*, 383–384.

Rozin, P., Millman, L., & Nemeroff, C. (1986). Operation of the laws of sympathetic magic in disgust and other domains. *Journal of Personality and Social Psychology, 50*, 703–712.

Rozin, P., & Nemeroff, C. J. (1990). The laws of sympathetic magic: A psychological analysis of similarity and contagion. In: J. Stigler, G. Herdt and R. A. Shweder (Eds.), *Cultural Psychology: Essays on Comparative Human Development*, (pp. 205–232). Cambridge, England: Cambridge University Press.

Rozin, P., Nemeroff, C., Horowitz, M., Gordon, B., & Voet, W. (1995). The borders of the self: Contamination sensitivity and potency of the mouth, other apertures and body parts. *Journal of Research in Personality, 29*, 318–340.

Rozin, P., Nemeroff, C., Wane, M., & Sherrod, A. (1989). Operation of the sympathetic magical law of contagion in interpersonal attitudes among Americans. *Bulletin of the Psychonomic Society, 27*, 367–370.

Schupak-Neuberg, E., & Nemeroff, C. (1993). Disturbances in identity and self-regulation in Bulimia Nervosa: Implications for a metaphorical perspective of "body as self." *International Journal of Eating Disorders, 13,* 335–347.

Seligman, M. E. P. (1970). On the generality of the laws of learning. *Psychological Review, 77,* 406–418.

Seligman, M. E. P., Kamen, L., Nolen-Hoeksema, S. (1988). Explanatory style across the life span: Achievement and health. In: E. M. Hetheringon, R. M. Lerner, et al. (Eds.), *Child Development in Life-Span Perspective,* (pp. 91–114). Hillsdale, NJ.: Lawrence Erlbaum Associates, Inc.

Shettleworth, S. J. (1973). Constraints on learning. In: D. S. Lehrman, R. A. Hinde, and E. Shaw (Eds.), *Advances in the Study of Behavior, Vol. 4.* New York: Academic Press.

Shweder, R. A. (1977). Likeness and likelihood in everyday thought: Magical thinking in judgments about personality. *Current Anthropology, 18,* 637–658.

Shweder, R. A., Much, N. C., Mahapatra, M., & Park, L. (1996). The "big three" of morality (autonomy, community, divinity), and the "big three" explanations of suffering. In: A., Brandt and P. Rozin, (Eds.), *Morality and Health,* (pp. 119–169). New York: Routledge.

Siegal, M., & Share, D. L. (1990). Contamination sensitivity in young children. *Developmental Psychology, 26,* 455–458.

Stein, R. I., & Nemeroff, C. (1995). Moral overtones of food: Judging others by what they eat. *Personality and Social Psychology Bulletin, 21,* 480–490.

Tambiah, S. J. (1990). *Magic, Science, Religion, and the Scope of Rationality.* Cambridge, England: Cambridge University Press.

Thomas, K. (1971). *Religion and the Decline of Magic.* New York: Charles Scribner's Sons.

Taylor, S. E., & Brown, J. D. (1988). Illusion and well-being: A social psychological perspective on mental health. *Psychological Bulletin, 103* (2), 193–210.

Tellegen, A., & Atkinson, G. (1974). Openness to absorbing and self-altering experiences ("Absorption"), a trait related to hypnotic susceptibility. *Journal of Abnormal Psychology, 83,* 268–277.

Tylor, E. B. (1974). *Primitive Culture: Researches into the Development of Mythology, Philosophy, Religion, Art, and Custom.* New York: Gordon Press. (Original work published 1871)

# 2 Phenomenalistic Perception and Rational Understanding in the Mind of an Individual

## A Fight for Dominance

EUGENE SUBBOTSKY

The distinction between phenomenalistic perception and rational understanding of the world is one of the classic distinctions in philosophy and psychology.[1] *Rational understanding* is usually viewed as being based on scientifically accepted theories, methods of analysis, measurement, and interpretation of experience. This type of understanding may differ substantially from the *phenomenalistic perception* of the same events and objects, that is, not mediated by scientific conceptions and theories. Attempts to reduce the distressing diversity of the phenomenal world to a limited number of mental constructions (e.g., "primary substances," numbers or atoms) can be traced back to antiquity (Sextus Empiricus, 1933), yet such attempts became particularly persistent in recent centuries. With the development of scientific knowledge and a rational means of analysis and explaining experience, rational interpretation began to be viewed as the "essential" and true interpretation, while phenomenalistic perception acquired the status of something that is not real but only apparent and illusory.

Descartes, referring to the relation between phenomenalistic and rationalistic descriptions of sound, wrote: "Most philosophers believe that sound is only a vibration of the air impinging on our ears; thus, if our sense of hearing conveyed to our thought a true image of its

---

[1] Insofar as "thinking," "perception," and "understanding" are psychologically related processes, these terms will sometimes be used interchangeably. However, as phenomenalistic assimilation is mainly unconscious and beyond voluntary control, and scientific understanding is conscious and voluntarily controlled, the term "perception" better fits the phenomenalistic view of the world, while the terms "thinking" and "understanding" better fit "scientific" and "rationalistic" assimilations of reality. In broader terms, phenomenalistic and rationalistic representations are different modes of assimilation of the world.

35

object, instead of giving us the ability to perceive sound, this would compel us to perceive the movements of the particles of air that at the time happen to be vibrating near our ears" (Descartes, 1957, p. 174). The distinction between phenomenalistic and rationalistic kinds of assimilation has important implications in psychology as well, relating to Vygotsky's distinction between everyday concepts and scientific concepts (Vygotsky, 1982).

The relations between phenomenalistic perception and scientific understanding of the same events can be quite complicated. On some occasions the advance of scientific understanding, which aims to reveal the illusory nature of certain phenomenalistic images, fails to destroy them; perceptual illusions are a good example of this. They are easy to "expose" by performing certain measurements, yet the illusion persists, constituting a kind of a special "layer" of phenomenal, perceptual experience (Gregory, 1980).

On other occasions scientific education does seem to "wipe out" the phenomenalistic perception. This is particularly evident in the case of the so-called Piagetian phenomena (e.g., conservation) that constitute a specific form of phenomenalistic perceptions of quantitative, spatio-temporal, and logical relations (Flavell, 1963; Piaget, 1930, 1969). These phenomenalistic perceptions, which are typical of children between four and six years, are gradually supplanted by rational, scientifically based interpretations in older children.

The term "phenomenalistic perception" should be distinguished from the classic idea of "phenomenological intuition" introduced by Husserl (1977). As noted by Piaget, phenomenalistic intuition is a complex idea that involves two components: a psychological and physical one and a logical and normative one (Piaget, 1971). Only the psychological component of phenomenalistic intuition is intended here by "phenomenalistic perception." In other words, phenomenalistic perception represents the world "as it seems," without the element of necessity that is part of the end product of Husserlian "phenomenalistic reduction."

Viewing phenomenalistic perception as a pure "impression" that we have about the world does not mean that this kind of perception lacks any structure whatsoever. That perception can, at some level, be mediated by knowledge is well-established in psychology (Brunner, 1974). In fact, even at the level of the most "raw" perceptual data (the level of phenomenalistic perception), perceptual processes can be internally structured. This idea was emphasized by theorists of "modularity" such as Fodor (1988), who referred to the Müeller-Layer illusion as an illustration of an irreducible "unit" built into the perceptual system, independent of knowledge and voluntary efforts (see also Leslie, 1986). However, encapsulated "modules" impenetrable to cognitive information are not the result of measurement or any kind of rational constructive activity. Thus, their presence does not undermine our definition of phenomenalistic perception as perception that is independent of rational and scientific thinking.

Another distinction can be drawn between phenomenalistic perception and intuitive knowledge. Some theorists distinguish between intuitive concepts (i.e., conservation) and nonintuitive ones (i.e., correlation) (Shweder, 1977). In our view, although some concepts (like conservation, class inclusion, etc.) can be acquired spontaneously and are culturally invariant, they are not phenomenalistic, because some or even considerable experience is needed for their acquisition (as is the case for many Piagetian concepts). Rather, intuitive and nonintuitive concepts belong to a level of functioning that is above the level of phenomenalistic perception, while the latter belongs to the level of preoperational intelligence.[2] In other words, the distinction between intuitive and nonintuitive concepts targets the area of rational understanding, demonstrating that even certain rational structures can be acquired spontaneously.

In sum, a distinction between phenomenalistic perception and a rational understanding of objects and events has often been made in psychology. These distinctions have typically been made with regard to children's and adults' verbal judgments about the world, and this has inevitably led to a peculiar kind of "linear perspective" in descriptions of cognitive development. In the beginning, mental development is viewed as dominated by phenomenalistic perception that is gradually replaced by rational forms of perception and thinking under the influence of instruction or an independent assimilation of experience (see Piaget, 1930). If projected on the development of causal reasoning, this perspective assumes that human psychology is fundamentally altered over development by the advance of technology. In other words, as a society becomes more technologically advanced, causal thinking of individuals should be dominated by scientific views. At the same time, these individuals should be less likely to believe in

---

[2] In fact, it is preoperational thinking that Piaget calls "intuitive," in contrast to Shweder.

magical or supernatural causal explanations. It is assumed that this "linear perspective" (or "replacement model") has only limited power and is not an adequate representation of the development of large areas of the mind. In fact, limitations of the linear, unidirectional model of cognitive development have been outlined by many theorists (Flavell, 1972; Van den Daele, 1966; Werner, 1948). We will show how these limitations operate with regard to one area of cognitive development: the relationship between phenomenalistic perception and rational understanding.

One limitation of the "replacement model" is that it only reflects cognitive development as manifested through individuals' verbal judgments. Indeed, in most studies of children's language development it appears that as soon as children acquire the correct rules of speaking or thinking about a certain area of reality (i.e., logical structures or scientific theories) the old ways of thinking are suspended and gradually disappear. However, even if we assume that the substitution of phenomenalistic thinking by scientific understanding does occur in children's verbal judgments, this does not necessarily mean that their nonverbal attitudes and actions are also based on that newly acquired understanding. In fact, it is often the case that individuals' deeds deviate from their words (Subbotsky, 1993; Wicker, 1971).

Although most of us are sure that we would not believe in the possibility of a magical or psychical transformation of a physical object, does this mean that under certain conditions we may not act as if we believed in the possibility of these kinds of causation? Indeed, as soon as nonscientific beliefs run up against the rational, scientific world view that dominates Western societies, we may be unwilling to overtly reveal our credulity to magic and parapsychology, or we may be unaware of the fact that we, in fact, hold such beliefs. However, if we are placed in a situation in which we are fully aware that if we ignore the possibility of magical transformations this can have some undesirable practical consequences for us (e.g., loss of a valuable object), we might reveal our hidden beliefs through actions.

If this were the case, then the fundamental assumption that human psychology in its development is altered by the advance of technology would collapse. In other words, if it is found that contemporary individuals are prepared to accept phenomenalistic, magical, and other nonscientifically based explanations, this would mean that the basic human mind is not altered by the technological advance of society. If it does change, the change is only superficial and can be easily reversed or eliminated if certain conditions are met. An alternative model of cognitive development predicts that phenomenalistic thinking and scientific understanding (when it appears) coexist in the mind throughout the life span. Reference to either phenomenalistic or scientific modes of thinking depend on varying circumstances. From this perspective, the relation between phenomenalistic perception and scientific understanding could be portrayed as a *permanent* "fight for dominance" over one's life, rather than as the steady replacement of phenomenalistic perception by scientific understanding.

Does the coexistence model add anything new to the widely accepted idea of multiple levels of processing? Piaget's stage theory has been thoroughly criticized in recent decades because cognitive development cannot be described in terms of rigidly ordered stages (Flavell, 1972). Various stages overlap and contrasting concepts and processes can function at one time in the mind of an individual. Developmental sequences cannot be reduced to the simple substitution of one type of cognitive functioning by another. Yet the stage concept does reflect a real feature of development. The question is, what aspects of cognitive development can be described in terms of linear progressive change, and what can be described in terms of "coexistence" and "fight for dominance"? The coexistence model is applied here with a more specific meaning than the simple assertion of "multiple levels of processing." On the one hand (as will be shown later), this model primarily targets the fundamental structures of the mind (alternative representations of causality, object, space, and time) and serves to create a new research methodology, rather than being merely a theoretical claim. On the other hand, the research methodology based on this model belongs to a more holistic and psychological level of functioning of the mind than the level of neuropsychological processes that has long been viewed in cognitive psychology in terms of multiple structures competing for attention. It is true that cognitive variability, rather than cognitive uniformity, is a major factor in cognitive development (Siegler, 1994). Yet cognitive variability is only a precondition for the coexistence of alternative structures in one mind. As some of the experiments reported here show, the variety of interpretations that children, and even one single child, give to one and the same phenomenon may or may not be a manifestation of coexistence. Cognitive variability can be viewed as coexistence only if the competing (ultimately, alternative) cognitive structures form a kind of "permanent partnership" in the mind of an individual, rather than being just a temporary "passing moment" in "cognitive progress." All of this makes the coexistence model irreducible to the previous views of multiple levels of processing and useful for making methodological and theoretical predictions about certain areas of functioning of the mind.

Two major predictions can be made on the basis of the coexistence model. First, under certain circumstances a discrepancy between participants' verbal judgments and their nonverbal practices can be expected to exist. In other words, in their verbal judgments participants will assimilate events on the basis of their rational (scientific) understanding, while in their practical actions participants will prefer to assimilate the events on the basis of their phenomenalistic perception of these events. Second, although certain rationalistic-based behaviors can be expected to exist in infants and young children,[3] under certain circumstances older children and adults can be expected to base their behaviors on their phenomenalistic perceptions and thinking rather than on acquired scientific understanding.

The studies presented here investigated these predictions. Although these studies dealt with a variety of objects and events, they all shared a common feature: The phenomenal perception of the objects and events differed substantially from their rational-scientific understanding. In one condition in these experiments, the participants were encouraged to assess and describe the events (objects) verbally. In another condition, they were asked to use these events (objects) to achieve some practical goal. If the participants based their judgments on their phenomenalistic perceptions of the events (objects), it was made clear that these perceptions were in fact illusory, and then the "correct," scientific-based versions of the events (objects) were presented to the participants. The purpose of this was to find out when acquired scientific explanations of events replace phenomenalistic perceptions, and in what circumstances they simply coexist with phenomenalistic perceptions without undermining the capacity of that mode of perception to affect the participants' actions.

---

[3] This has been shown in abundance in the recent studies of infants' cognition (Bower, 1974; Bremner, 1994).

## Phenomenalistic Perception and Scientific Understanding by Children

In the first group of studies children were tested for their phenomenalistic perception and rational understanding of quantitative and spatial relations between objects. As was already mentioned, phenomenalistic generalizations in the domain of quantitative relations were first studied by Piaget and referred to as intuitive thinking (Flavell, 1963; Piaget, 1969). The key feature of these phenomena is that children make judgments on the basis of perceptual properties of objects (such as length, height, etc.) and not on the basis of abstract, logical-quantitative relations. For example, if preschool children are shown two identical rows of black and white tokens arranged in a one-to-one correspondence and are asked which row contains more tokens or whether there is the same number in each, the children say that the rows contain equal numbers of tokens. But if the tokens in one of the rows are moved father apart from one another, many children say that there are more tokens in the longer row.

Of course, such an answer might not be viewed as incorrect, given children's abilities at this point. Specifically, because children have not yet developed the means of establishing quantitative equality, they are unable to distinguish between true (quantitative) and apparent (phenomenalistic) relations. However, today almost all children aged four and older can count up to ten. By making use of this ability, it is possible to "split" the perception of the array by contrasting the apparent relation (more tokens in the long row) with the true relation (same number of tokens). The next step was to find out whether the children actually used the acquired knowledge about quantitative equality, not only in their verbal judgments, but also in a practical situation where it was important which of the rows was chosen. The second goal of the experiment was to examine whether the acquired knowledge about the equality of objects in rows was retained after children mastered their choices in a practical situation.

During the experiment, which was a modified version of a traditional Piagetian test on number conservation, each child was individually presented with two rows each containing six identical pieces of chocolate (Subbotsky, 1990). One of the rows was twice as long as the other row. In the first condition of the experiment ("neutral" situation) the child was asked whether there was an identical number of pieces of chocolate in both rows or were there more pieces in one row. This was to determine whether the children were subject to phenomenalistic perceptions of the quantitative relations between the rows (i.e., whether most children judged that there were more pieces in the long row). If the children answered that there were more pieces of chocolate in the long row, they were asked to count the pieces in both rows and see for themselves that the rows contained the same number. In this way, a contrast between phenomenalistic perception (more objects in one of the rows) and rational understanding (equal numbers in both rows) was produced.

In the second condition of the experiment ("practical" situation) the child was distracted for a few minutes by a conversation about the imminent New Year holiday and presents, after which he or she was asked to choose one of the rows of chocolates as his or her New Year's present. It was assumed that if in this situation the children relied on their rational understanding of quantitative relations between the rows, the number of participants who chose each row would not differ. On the other hand, if the children were guided by their phenomenalistic perceptions, more children should choose the long row. In the third condition of the experiment children were asked how many pieces of chocolate were in each row. The purpose of this was to find out whether they retained a correct judgment of the equality of the rows.

The results of the experiment are shown in Table 2.1 Consistent with Piaget's data, most of the four-, five-, and six-year-old children said that there were more objects in the long row in the first condition. All children counted the objects easily and acknowledged that there was the same number in both rows. In the second condition, the number of children who chose the long row did not differ significantly

Table 2.1. *Results from Conservation of Number Task*

| Number of participants | Age | Responses | | |
|---|---|---|---|---|
| | | 1 More in long row | 2 Chose long row | 3 Same |
| 26 | 4–4.11 | 24* | 14 | 22 |
| 30 | 5–5.11 | 23† | 20 | 26 |
| 30 | 6–6.11 | 23† | 21 | 25 |

* $p < .01$.   † $p < .05$.

from chance. In the third condition, the vast majority of the children retained their knowledge of the equal number of pieces in the rows.

In sum, the results showed that the phenomenalistic perception of quantitative relations between the rows was quite unstable and collapsed under the pressure of rational understanding. These data support the "replacement" model and not the "coexistence" one. Considering that many of Piaget's nonconservation phenomena are quite fragile and vulnerable to a variety of contextual factors (Light, 1986), the "replacement" model seems the most suitable account for this kind of developmental phenomenon. The question to be answered is whether the same model also describes the fate of phenomena whose phenomenalistic perception is considerably more stable and powerful than that of nonconservation.

To examine this issue the Müeller-Layer illusion was used. Two rulers, each 40 cm long, were fastened parallel to one another on two pieces of plywood. The background consisted of right angles made from two similar 25-cm rulers nailed to the plywood. The long rulers were fastened so that each end was at the tip of a right angle. In one case the ends of the angles diverged upward and downward from the ruler (dovetail), and in the other they converged toward the center (arrow-tip).

In the first condition of the experiment, children were asked whether the rulers were identical in length, and if not, which one was longer. The purpose of this was to determine whether children indeed experienced the illusion that the dovetailed configuration seemed longer than the arrow-tip one. After their answer, the children were told that the rulers were the same lengths. The rulers were then removed from the background and placed side by side, so that the children could see that the rulers were of equal lengths. Then the rulers were again fastened to the background as the children watched. Thus, as in the preceding experiment, rational understanding of equality of length was contrasted with phenomenalistic perception (the Müeller-Layer illusion).

In the second condition of the experiment, immediately following the first, the child was told that the experimenter would like to test how skillful the child was. The experimenter then suggested that if the child could reach a pretty stamp with his or her hands without getting off the chair, then he or she could keep the stamp as a reward. The stamp was placed on the floor far enough away so that, even with the child's hand outstretched, there was still a gap roughly equal to the length of the ruler. After a number of unsuccessful attempts to get the object, the experimenter suggested, in a casual fashion, that the child could use one of the rulers used in the previous task. It was assumed that if the children were guided by their rational understanding of the lengths, they would choose either ruler with equal probability. But if they were guided by phenomenalistic perception, then more children would choose the dovetailed ruler than the arrow-tip one.

After a child had obtained the stamp with the aid of the ruler, the experimenter again asked whether the rulers were the same lengths or whether one of them was longer (a control condition). Then the child was asked to explain his or her choice in the practical situation.

As is evident from Table 2.2, all of the children in the first condition said that the dovetailed ruler was longer. However, after seeing the rulers together they all agreed that the rulers were equal in length. In the second condition the dovetailed ruler was chosen by significantly more of the children. A majority of the children retained their knowledge of length equality in the third condition. When asked why they chose the dovetailed ruler, the children had difficulty in offering an explanation: Some simply said, "I don't know," and others attempted to justify it in some way ("I liked it better," "It was easier to get to"). Ten of the children reverted to the previous interpretation (the dovetailed ruler was longer), and three said that the arrow-tipped ruler was longer.

In contrast to the previous experiment in which the data supported the "replacement model," in this experiment the results favor the

Table 2.2. *Results of Investigation Using Müeller-Layer Illusion*

| Number of participants | Age | Responses | | |
|---|---|---|---|---|
| | | 1 *Thought that dovetailed was longer* | 2 *Chose dovetailed rule* | 3 *Thought that rulers were the same lengths* |
| 26 | 4–4.11 | 26* | 23† | 22 |
| 30 | 5–5.11 | 30* | 28* | 27 |
| 30 | 6–6.11 | 30* | 24†† | 24 |

* $p < .001$.   † $p < .01$.   †† $p < .05$.

"coexistence model." Rational understanding alone failed to destroy the power of the illusion, which continued to exercise control over the children's behavior in the practical situation. Obviously, a key difference between the two experiments was in the strength of the phenomenalistic illusion. While the "nonconservation" illusion is a phenomenon that belongs exclusively to children younger than seven years of age, the Müeller-Layer illusion is more powerful and can be experienced by both children and adults. In this regard, the question arises whether the failure of rational understanding to take control of children's actions in the second experiment was a result of the relative immaturity of rationalistic thinking in preschool children in the face of a stronger illusion. If this were the case, then the development of thinking on a broader age scale could still be accounted for in terms of the "replacement model." It can be argued that the stronger the illusion the longer it takes for it to be replaced by mature, rationalistic understanding. With the growth of linguistic and cognitive abilities, children become able to coordinate alternative perspectives about the world, and rational understanding suppresses phenomenalistic perception. However, if the presence of the phenomenalistic perception is a permanent feature of the human mind, then this kind of perception should also be active in older children and adults, independent of cognitive and linguistic proficiency.

To investigate this possibility, a phenomenalistic illusion had to be chosen that could not be discounted as an illusion simply because of its artificial origin. At the same time, the impact of this illusion had to be equally strong for children and adults, implying that adults had to have little understanding of the illusion's psychological "mechanisms." The illusion described by Descartes (i.e., mistaking sensual qualities of physical objects for their real physical properties) met all of these conditions.

### Phenomenalistic Perception and Rational Understanding of Sensations and Physical Properties of Objects

The double character of reality is a fundamental idea that is deeply imbedded in Western thought. Indeed, the classic view of Descartes is still current. In fact, according to contemporary scientific theories, a physical object is viewed as a complex entity consisting of physical characteristics (Duncan, 1987; King 1962), whereas human sensations are interpreted as qualities produced by the human mind and sense organs whenever they are affected by the physical characteristics of objects (Geldard, 1972; Wyszecki & Stiles 1967).

Yet, even casual observation shows that children (and many adults) have poor awareness of the distinction between sensations produced by external objects in human sense organs and physical properties of objects "in their own right." The majority of people assume that it is not their sense organs and minds that produce sensations of "redness, warmth, and hardness," but rather it is the objects that are red, warm, and hard.[4]

This confusion, however important it is for establishing the feeling of the outer world's reality, nevertheless contradicts the scientific representation of objects as combinations of physical properties. In fact, one of the important objectives of scientific education is to create this distinction between subjective and objective ways of description. Thus, in physics textbooks (Duncan, 1987) light is described as rays entering eyes; color as a composition of light rays; sound as vibrations that travel through the air to our ears; weight as the force of gravity combined with the resistance of other objects; temperature as the average kinetic energy of the molecules, and so on.

Yet, in the case of rational understanding of object qualities, it seems that scientific education fails to achieve its main goal, that is, to create in students a special kind of "double vision" of reality. According to this vision, the same objects can be described in terms of sensations (redness) and in terms of physical characteristics (light rays) that trigger these sensations when they interact with sense organs and initiate cortical functions of the brain. If this is indeed the case, then it could be viewed as an empirical demonstration of the thesis of this chapter, namely, that the "coexistence" model is a better account of the development of certain aspects of thought than the "replacement" model. To examine this, five experiments were carried out (Subbotsky, 1997b).

The objectives of Experiment 1 were to examine whether six- and nine-year-old children and adults were able to appreciate that object sensations are produced by their minds and are not physical proper-

---

[4] Not to be confused with the "appearance-reality" illusion, where an object possessing certain qualities (i.e., an apple made of plastic) can be mistaken for another object that produces similar sensations but has different functions and chemical compounds (i.e., a real apple) (Brain & Shanks, 1965; Taylor & Flavell, 1984; Flavell, 1986).

ties of objects in their own right. In this experiment the participants were individually asked eight separate sets of questions. Each set consisted of a few preliminary questions and two key questions that targeted one of eight sensations.

For instance, with respect to color, a subject was shown a red pencil lying on a table and asked, "Can you see this pencil?" "What color is it?" Following these preliminary questions, the participants were asked the key questions, "And this redness of the pencil, where do you think it is: in the pencil or in your mind?" and "This redness of the pencil, where do you think it is: in the pencil or in your eyes?" (The order of target items and key questions was counterbalanced).

The questions were worded so that the mind and sense organs were not presented as alternatives (i.e., they were put as alternatives to the object but not to one another) and yet it was possible to assess the participants' preferences with regard to locating sensations mainly in the mind or in the sense organs. It was assumed that the spatial location employed in the questions (i.e., "in the mind" or "in the pencil") would stand for the distinction between the subjective and objective realities in a philosophically unsophisticated mind. It was further assumed that a child who allocated, for instance, warmth to the mind (or hands) rather than to the fire would mean that warmth is a subjective rather than an objective (physical) quality.[5]

Auditory (ringing of a bell), olfactory (odor of perfume), gustatory (sweetness of chocolate), thermal (warmth of fire), tactile (hardness vs. softness), weight (heaviness vs. lightness), and pain (caused by a needle) sensations were also examined. The specific questions were asked in the same way as color sensation.

No overall age effects were found in the participants' tendency to allocate sensations to the subject rather than to the object (see Figure 2.1). Thus, adults did not show a significant improvement in their understanding of the distinction between psychological and physical object descriptions compared to the six- and nine-year-olds.

---

[5] One possible objection to this can be that when participants claim that, for instance, redness is in the pencil and not in the mind (eyes), they actually mean the source of the redness (i.e., light rays of a certain wavelength) rather than the sensation of redness. Even if this was the case, it would show exactly what the question is supposed to test, that is, that the individual is unable to distinguish between the sensation and its source, identifying the sensation with its external source. Notice that the questions employed laymen equivalents for sensations (like "redness" or "heaviness") and not for the physical source of sensation ("red color" or "weight").

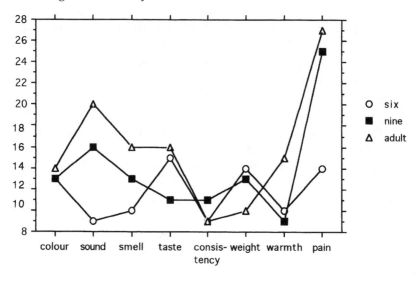

Figure 2.1. Numbers of answers (out of 32) in which sensations were localized in a subject and not in an object.

In spite of some indicators of age-related progress (e.g., a better appreciation of the subjective nature of pain by nine-year-olds and adults, as compared to six-year-olds), most participants considered sensations to be immanent properties of external objects. This finding obviously contradicts the image of the world given by modern science and reflected in educational programs and textbooks (Duncan, 1987). However, this contradiction is not stated explicitly in most textbooks for beginners but is explicated in more advanced texts. Thus, in a book for students who have good grounding in elementary college physics, definitions of temperature involving physiological sensations of hot-ness and coldness are qualified as "utterly unreliable" because "a piece of iron may *feel* colder than a block of wood though the two are at the same temperature as determined by any one thermometer" (King, 1962, p. 2). Instead, temperature is defined as "that property of a system which determines whether the system is in thermal equilib-rium with other systems" (King, 1962, p. 2). With respect to other senses (seeing, hearing, taste) similar distinctions between physical stimuli and sensations proper are made (Geldard, 1972; Wyszecki & Stiles 1967).

This way of representing modern scientific knowledge is expected to terminate the initial naive identification between sensations produced by objects and the objects described in physical terms, and induce the double picture of the world that consists of physical bodies and their subjective images. Our present knowledge does not allow us to assess to what extent the split between sensations and physical properties really occurs in individuals' minds as a result of scientific education.

To examine this, a series of intervention experiments were conducted to examine children's and adults' capacities to appreciate the difference between sensations and physical properties of objects. The intervention strategies included direct explanation, cognitive conflict treatment, and "personal views conflict treatment."

Experiment 2 used the same participants as Experiment 1. Three types of sensations (color, sound, and smell) were selected from those used in Experiment 1. The participants were tested individually. In the training session the participants were told a short story, accompanied by an illustration describing physical causes of subjective qualities. For example, for color sensation the participant was told: "You know, of course, that different objects have different colors, don't you? Now I'd like to explain to you how people can see colors, o.k.? Have you ever seen waves on the surface of water? You should know that each object produces a special sort of wave – the light waves. Look at this picture" (see Figure 2.2).

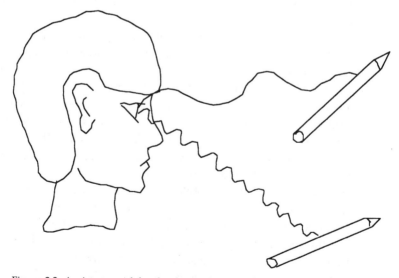

Figure 2.2. A picture used for the demonstration of the "light waves" – based theory of color perception.

"These waves – here they are. They are not colored themselves, but if they come into human eyes, people can see colors. Now look, some of the objects produce big and slow waves, the others produce small and quick waves. If big and slow waves come into our eyes, we can see a red color, and if small quick waves come into our eyes, we can see a green color."

After preliminary questions to establish that the story was understood, a set of key questions was asked as in Experiment 1. If the treatment affected the participant's tendency to identify sensations with the objects that produce them, then more participants should make this identification after the treatment than before the treatment.

The results showed that direct explanation was ineffective for children, and only moderately beneficial for adults. Adults made improved judgments after the treatment for sensation of smell, but not for color or auditory sensations. The partial success of direct explanation for adults (and not children) can be explained by the fact that adults were better prepared intellectually to benefit from the explanation than the children were. An alternative explanation is that adults simply benefited from their superior linguistic capacities. Although the children's answers to the preliminary questions showed that they understood the story, their capacity to benefit from this explanation may have been lower than that of adults. Whatever explanation is correct, it is obvious that the direct explanation was linguistically biased.

To assess this further, two experiments employing training strategies that were less language-dependent were conducted: a demonstration that one and the same object can change its color or relative weight if put in different conditions ("cognitive conflict"), and a demonstration that the same object can be perceived differently by different individuals ("individual views conflict"). These experiments yielded only partial success with adults. Taken together these studies suggest that adults have no better understanding of the subjective nature of sensations than do six- and nine-year-olds.

Why does the confusion between scientific and psychological descriptions of physical objects and events, typical for young children, remain largely intact despite scientific education? One possible answer is that children are not properly taught this subject (i.e., there is no program of psychological education in school curricula).

Another explanation of the poor progress in picking up this distinction may lie in the intrinsic nature of the distinction itself. Unlike other types of false beliefs (like nonconservation) that are relatively weak and situation biased (Light, 1986), the confusion between psychological and physical ways of describing objects is very stable, particularly for certain kinds of sensations. In everyday life individuals of all ages have very few incentives to overcome this confusion.

Obviously, in ordinary life some sensations can quite successfully represent their physical prototypes, making direct reference to these prototypes superfluous. For most practical situations, it is easier to view the world in terms of sensations "stuck" to objects than to keep permanently in mind a complicated distinction between sensations and the physical properties that elicit them. In other words, the confusion has a useful function for individuals, because it makes practical activity cognitively more simple and "economical." It belongs to a special class of "useful false beliefs" that (like the irreducible feeling that the Sun rotates around the Earth), although theoretically incorrect, can be helpful in certain areas of practical life (i.e., creating devices like a sundial).[6]

The results of this study, therefore, support the assumption that mistaking mental phenomena for physical properties of objects is not a situation-based illusion, but rather an indication of a fundamental feature of the mind – in which phenomenalistic thinking of certain objects coexists with a rationalistic understanding of the same objects throughout the life span. Of course, the ineffectiveness of rationalistic explanations, which was quite evident in this study, cannot be seen as a universal feature of education. Obviously, rationalistic understanding is powerless with regard to only a limited number of particularly strong phenomenalistic perceptions. There is no doubt that many of children's phenomenalistic perceptions are eventually replaced by rationalistic models in the course of scientific education. As the experiment with the Müeller-Layer illusion revealed, this replacement can be misleading in the sense that it only affects children's verbal judgments. Clearly, our understanding of certain events cannot be reduced to only what we *think* about the structure of the events, but also includes the way we *use* the events for practical purposes. It may be the case that rational understanding replaces phenomenalistic percep-

---

[6] With regard to the beliefs discussed, the term "false" is used in the context described earlier, that is, these beliefs were not unconditionally false; rather, they were attributed the status of false beliefs after "true" scientific rational models of the same objects and events had been created.

tion only in participants' judgments, whereas in their practical activity participants still rely on their phenomenalistic perceptions. This would suggest that the coexistence of alternative modes of representation of a certain event is not merely a mixture of alternative views in the participants' minds, but has a more complicated "multilevel" structure.

The idea that remnants of various stages of mental development coexist in the minds of adults has been frequently acknowledged (i.e., S. Freud, L. Levy-Brühl, Tul'viste,. L. Vygotsky, H. Werner, J. Wertsch, and others) (Cole & Subbotsky, 1993). Arguably, the heterogeneity of thinking was established even in ancient times (Shweder, 1984). The problem arises of how this heterogeneity should be understood.

The point to be clarified is the psychological nature of this coexistence, especially if it concerns the coexistence of alternative fundamental beliefs (such as beliefs in object permanence versus nonpermanence, magical causality versus physical causality). If such alternative structures coexisted on the same level of functioning of an individual's mind, for instance, on the level of verbal intelligence, it would make the individual very uncomfortable. Indeed, it is difficult to simultaneously believe in alternative versions of the same event and maintain peace of mind. The adherence of modern individuals to common logic and consistency of views would make a certain view of the world (i.e., scientific) become all-embracing and dominant. It is difficult to conceive how the "heterogeneity of mind" can be established when social and cultural settings consistently encourage homogeneity.

Yet, an individual's mind does not only consist of verbal beliefs; it also consists of nonverbal attitudes and actions. The problem of peaceful coexistence between alternative representations can be resolved by simply "divorcing" the alternative representations and assigning them to different levels of the mind's functioning. Indeed, an individual can believe in the universal nature of physical causality and yet act in certain circumstances as if magic were possible. After all, events that occur in our emotional life, dreams, or fantasies are often based on magic.

This peaceful noncompetitive coexistence of alternative structures of the mind involves two necessary conditions: a) the structures are at different levels of functioning (verbal/real), and b) they occur in different contexts (i.e., one structure dominates during scientific activity, and an alternative one is activated during art or religious practices). These conditions are essential for creating different realities of mind (Subbotsky, 1992).

If, however, the alternative beliefs are activated within one context (i.e., in everyday practices or scientific reasoning), they become competitive even if they exist at different levels of functioning. Thus, a person can believe in the universal nature of physical causality, yet in high risk situations may practice magic (crossing fingers, tapping on wood, etc.). At the end of the competition, one outcome favors phenomenalistic thinking and the other outcome favors rational understanding. The issue is, in what contexts and under what conditions are these possible outcomes realized?

To investigate this, a phenomenalistic belief was needed that had a direct "scientific alternative" and which was supposed to be replaced in the course of education. The question to be clarified was whether replacement, if it occurred in participants' verbal judgments, would automatically bring about appropriate changes in the participants' nonverbal practices. Alternatively, individuals might still employ the phenomenalistic version in their practical actions while "preaching" the scientific version in their verbal reasoning. Beliefs about causal relations met these requirements.

## Phenomenalistic Perception and Rational Understanding of Causal Relations

Among various causal relationships, psychological and natural-physical types of causality can be distinguished. In psychological causality, an individual's thoughts or wishes produce certain physical events either normally (as in the case of moving our bodies) or through magic. Natural-physical causality concerns causal relationships between two or more external physical events. This latter type of causality is typical of scientific explanations. There is, however, one more type of causal reasoning that is neither psychological nor natural-physical but is potentially open to both of these modes of interpretation. In this type of causal reasoning (referred to as phenomenalistic) events A and B are connected by certain associations (i.e., they happen at one time or have similar features or functions), but an individual is unable to offer any sensible explanation for this connection. While making this type of judgment the individual is subjectively biased and lacks understanding of the logical necessity of links between the events.

Unlike magical and physical causation that have provoked numerous studies (Berzonsky, 1971; Bullock, 1984, 1985; Bullock, Gelman & Baillargeon, 1982; Chandler & Lalonde, 1994; Johnson & Harris, 1994;

Phelps & Woolley, 1994; Rosengren & Hickling, 1994; Schultz, Altman & Asselin, 1986; Schultz, Fisher, Pratt & Rulf, 1986; Subbotsky, 1985), phenomenalistic causality has been studied only sporadically. In psychology the term "phenomenalism" was originally applied by Piaget (1986) to infants' "secondary circular reaction," a behavior that appears at around three to seven months of age. In this initial stage of causal behavior infants have a vague intuition of the connection between a certain action and effect. They will tend to reproduce the action, apparently hoping to evoke the effect, without paying any attention to the necessary connections between the event and the effect. At around eighteen months of age phenomenalistic causal behavior is replaced by behaviors based on the child's understanding of real mechanical causal links (which can be seen from the child's capacity to reconstruct the cause only on the basis of the effect). Phenomenalistic causality reappears later in children's verbal judgments about the causes of various events. Along with other types of "precausal reasoning" (artificialism, animism, etc.) the tendency to reason phenomenalistically lasts until the beginning of the concrete operational period (Piaget, 1930).

Clearly, Piaget's view on the development of causal thinking was strongly based on the replacement model, as were many subsequent studies (Huang, 1930; Raspe, 1924; Venger, 1958; Zaporojetz & Lukov, 1941). According to this view, phenomenalistic (and other "nonscientific") ways of causal thinking disappear from children's actions somewhere around age two, and after that age can only be detected in children's judgments. However, the "coexistence" model would predict a different picture of the development. According to this model, phenomenalistic causal thinking retains its power at the level of nonverbal attitudes and actions in older children and even adults.

To examine this issue a series of experiments was undertaken. In one of the experiments three small transparent beakers were placed before the child (Subbotsky, 1990). One contained a weak base solution (NaOH), the second contained a weak acid solution, and the third beaker contained phenolphthalein (an acid-base indicator). All of the solutions looked identical to water. Alongside the beakers were two small cardboard cylinders (red and white) that were equal in height to the beakers but somewhat greater in diameter.

In the first phase of the experiment, the children were shown the contents of all of the beakers and asked what color the water in them was. Hearing that the water was in each case "white," the experimenter asked what color the water would be if he poured water from one beaker (the one with phenolphthalein) into another (the base solution). While waiting for the child's answer, the red cylinder was placed around the beaker containing the base solution and the phenolphthalein was poured into it. The solution turned bright red before the child's eyes. After removing the cylinder, the experimenter asked what color the water became, and why.

After the child's answer, the experimenter asked what would happen if the "red water" was poured into the remaining beaker with the"white water" (the acid solution). On hearing the child's response, the experimenter placed the white cylinder around the beaker containing the acid and poured the red solution into it. This solution again became transparent. The experimenter then took the cylinder away and repeated his questions about what color the water became and why.

The purpose of this phase was to determine whether the children were prone to phenomenalistic perceptions of causal relations. It was assumed, as observed in Huang's (1930) experiment, that the children would view the cylinders as the cause of the color change because of the spatial proximity and similarity of the cylinders in color to the color of the solutions (even though it was clear that the cylinders never came in contact with the beakers).

The children who produced phenomenalistic answers were then given a rationalistic (somewhat "anthropomorphic") quasi-scientific explanation of the phenomenon. They were shown a picture (see Figure 2.3) and told a story that presented the color change in the beakers as a result of the "love-hate" relationships between small white invisible balls swimming around in the beakers.

Thus, as in the preceding experiment, each child was confronted with two contrasting representations of the same event (changing color in the solutions): a phenomenalistic interpretation (the change occurs because of the cylinders) and a rationalistic interpretation (the water changes its color because of the interaction of invisible little balls).

In the second phase of the experiment, using the same children, each child was given the original set of beakers and asked to "make the water in these beakers red and then white again." If they succeeded, the children were promised a nice stamp as a reward. In the third phase, the children were again asked to explain why, as a result of their actions, the water became red and then white.

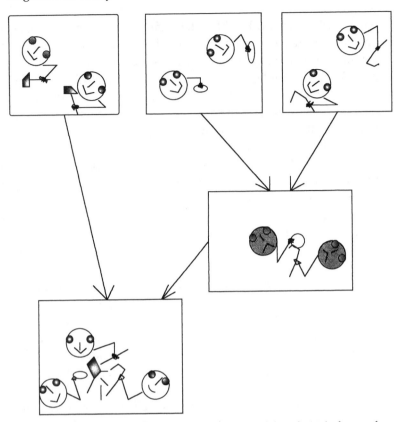

Figure 2.3. A rational explanation of the phenomenon of the solution's change of color.

In the first phase, almost all of the children (four-, five-, and six-year-olds) said that the cylinders were the cause of the color change. After hearing the experimenter's interpretation of the event, all of the children were able to repeat it and they agreed that the cardboard cylinders had no influence on the water color. Yet, in the second phase all of the participants (except four) used the cylinders to reproduce the phenomenon. The third phase showed that most of the four- and five-year-old children and some of the six-year-olds abandoned the rational representation given by the experimenter and said again that the cause of the color change was the cylinder.

However, in the third phase, the participants who did not use the cylinders in the second phase, as well as the thirteen children who did use them, retained the rationalistic version when asked to explain the causes of the color change. Significantly more six-year-olds than younger children retained the rationalistic view.

The results (shown in Table 2.3) highlight the role that verbal education may have in changing the existential status of various forms of causality. It is obvious that teaching is more than the communication of new knowledge about some piece of reality to a student. The new knowledge will inevitably struggle for dominance with older and spontaneously developed forms of perception and comprehension of the same piece of reality. As the experiments showed, not only did the phenomenalistic perception of causal relations resist attempts to be expelled from the children's minds, but it continued to exert an influence on their behaviors. Would this also be the case with adults?

Whereas phenomenalistic causal judgments about physical phenomena are viewed as a legitimate stage in the development of children's causal judgments, they are considered to be a regressive mode of thinking in adults (Piaget, 1986). Usually, phenomenalistic causal judgments in adults are produced in artificial conditions and the participants who make them are fully aware that they are talking about perceptual illusions rather than real events. For instance, it was found that if adults were shown a film in which one square approached another (immobile) one and the latter moved off, the participants reported the impression of a causal effect, even if they knew that there was no direct contact between the two squares (Michotte, 1962). In another group of studies (Rozin, Markwith, & Ross, 1986, Rozin, Millman, & Nemeroff, 1990) adults were shown to follow rules of contagion ("once in contact, always in contact") and similarity ("the image

Table 2.3. *Results of the Color Change Study*

| Number of participants | Age | Responses | | |
|---|---|---|---|---|
| | | 1 *Said cylinders caused color change* | 2 *Used cylinders to produce the color change* | *Said again that cylinders caused color change* |
| 20 | 4–4.11 | 20 | 19 | 18 |
| 20 | 5–5.11 | 20 | 19 | 17 |
| 20 | 6–6.11 | 16 | 18 | 8 |

equals the object") in some of their actions (see Nemeroff & Rozin, this volume). These studies show that even adults are not completely free from phenomenalistic perceptions of causal relations.

To determine the factors that lead the adults' to reason and behave phenomenalistically, a series of experiments were conducted (Subbotsky, 1997a). In these studies, a wooden box was used to create the impression of a sudden spontaneous transformation of a regular physical object (a postage stamp) into a different object. During the experiment, the participant was asked to examine the empty box, place a postage stamp into it and close the lid. Next, the experimenter did three manipulations: 1) He took a postage stamp lying next to him and put it in the empty envelope (object associated manipulation); 2) he drew a cross on a white paper square (Condition 1) or cut the paper square in half with scissors (Condition 2, action-associated manipulation); and 3) he transformed a plasticine ball into a sausage (irrelevant manipulation). The order of manipulations was randomized across participants.

On opening the box the participant found a changed object, which, in Condition 1 (low degree of oddity), was an identical postage stamp with a red cross drawn on it and in Condition 2 (high degree of oddity) was a stamp cut in half. After giving an explanation (or acknowledging that he or she had none) the participant was asked whether he or she thought that what the experimenter had done with the objects made the cross appear on the stamp (or had caused the stamp to be cut in half).

Six- and nine-year-old children and adults participated in this experiment. Children tended to accept that the experimenter's manipulations caused the unusual event, even though there was no spatial or other physical link between the manipulations and the objects. Thus, their belief in phenomenalistic causality was revealed. A stronger acceptance was found for the action-associated manipulation (cutting) than the object-associated manipulation (stamp) or irrelevant manipulation (plasticize ball transformation). In contrast to the children, almost all of the adults rejected the possibility of a phenomenalistic causal explanation. The oddity of the unusual phenomenon did not affect the participants' tendency to succumb to phenomenalistic causal reasoning.

Children's phenomenalistic judgments cannot be attributed to difficulty in understanding the questions because children as young as four have been shown to understand questions about causal relationships (such as "whether event A made event B happen or not"), provided that both events are clearly displayed (Bullock, 1984; Gelman & Kremer, 1991; Kun, 1978, 1985, Ruffman, Perner, Olson, & Doherty, 1993; Schultz, Altmann & Asselin, 1986; Schultz, Fisher, et al., 1986; Springer & Keil, 1991). Rather, many six- and nine-year-olds ignored that a necessary condition for physical causal links (i.e. physical contact, be it mechanical or by electromagnetic waves) was absent.

To check whether the children who gave phenomenalistic answers were prepared to acknowledge that what had happened in the box was in fact "magic," different six- and nine-year-olds were shown the phenomenon of the unusual object transformation (identical to that of Condition 2, Experiment 1). This time, however, the children were asked whether it was magic or not. Next they were shown a toy car moving by a remote control device and they were asked whether the car was being moved by magic. Then the question of whether cutting of the stamp had been done by magic was repeated.

When directly asked about magic, the children were inclined to interpret their phenomenalistic causal judgments as magical causations. Moreover, when shown an event that resembled the original phenomenon in its core feature (one physical object was affected by another physical object without any obvious physical contact) the children almost unanimously denied that this was magic; yet they continued to say that the original phenomenon was magic. This suggests that children's references to magic in their explanations of the original phenomenon is not an overextension of the term "magic" to include normal events with an unknown physical force involved. Rather, by acknowledging that cutting the postage stamp by means of cutting a square of paper was magic, children really meant the type of causation based on mental (psychological) influence on the physical object, that is, real magic.

Only a few children, however, in both experiments produced spontaneous "magical" explanations. This suggests that most children were not actually sure how (in magical or natural-physical terms) the connection between the two events should be viewed. Only after a direct question about magic was asked did most children opt for a magical explanation. It is possible that under other circumstances they might have chosen a natural-physical explanation for the same event. In fact, it has been shown that children often use the word "magic" simply to mark phenomena for which they lack immediate physical explanations (Chandler & Lalonde, 1994; Phelps & Woolley, 1994).

This confirms the claim that phenomenalistic causal judgment is not rooted in a particular scientific (or culturally imposed) tradition; rather, it is a simple empirical judgment about the causal connection between two events that is open to further consideration in either natural-physical or magical terms.

Taken together, the results of these experiments confirm that preschool children tend to make phenomenalistic judgments (Huang, 1930; Piaget, 1930; Raspe, 1924). The results also support the traditional "replacement model" of the development of the mind, according to which phenomenalistic causal judgments (along with other "exotic" kinds of causal reasoning, such as artificialistic, magical, and moralistic) belong exclusively to childhood and disappear in adults. This concordance should not come as a surprise, however, because the replacement model was originally devised to account for the development of verbal judgments rather then real actions.

A characteristic limitation of these experiments that is shared with previous studies is that only the participants' verbal judgments were taken as an indication of belief in phenomenalistic causality. It has been shown, however, that verbal judgments reflect only the participants' verbal attitudes and may be at odds with their nonverbal attitudes and behaviors (Eisenberg & Shell, 1986; La Pierre, 1934; McNemar, 1946; Subbotsky, 1985, 1992). There have been various attempts to account for these inconsistencies (Wicker, 1971). Among other factors that contribute to the discrepancy is the "cost," understood in the sense of the risk of some loss due to the commitment to certain principles and behaviors (Deutsch, 1949; Cook & Selltiz, 1964; Eisenberg & Shell, 1986). Basically, it is more "costly" to practice certain views and principles (i.e., moral standards) in behavior than to express them in verbal judgments.

The results of Experiment 1 raise the question of "cost" with respect to adults' causal behavior. Although the results clearly suggest that children are susceptible to phenomenalistic causal judgments and adults are not, certain doubts regarding adults' judgments still remain. It is possible to assume that phenomenalistic causal thinking, although denied by adults in their verbal judgments, can nevertheless affect adults' behavior if the cost of disregarding the possibility of phenomenalistic causal connections becomes relatively high. If this were the case, it would show that phenomenalistic causal thinking still exists in adults' minds in a "submerged" form. It is only the predominance of physicalistic and rationalistic ideology in modern Western cultures that prevents this kind of thinking to be openly displayed in adults' verbal judgments and behavior. If, however, the cost of physical causal beliefs becomes high, the hidden tendency to think in a phenomenalistic way could show itself indirectly through adults' actions.

To examine this possibility, adults were shown the phenomenon of the postage stamp cut in half, and then asked to put their driver's license into the box and close the lid. Next, the experimenter took the postage stamp out of the envelope, replaced the cut square of white paper with a new one, and transformed the plasticine sausage back into a ball. In the final instructions, the participants in the experimental group were assured that nothing would happen to their license if the experimenter did not repeat his actions with the objects. If, however, he did repeat the manipulations, he would not be able to guarantee that their licenses would remain intact. Thus, it was entirely the participants' responsibility whether to give the experimenter permission to do the manipulations again. The participants in the control group were given the same procedure apart from the wording of the final instruction. In this case, the participants were simply asked whether they would mind if the experimenter did the manipulations again.

In the experimental condition, a significant number of the participants asked the experimenter not to repeat certain actions, even though the actions had no obvious physical connections with the undesirable event (the destruction of the participants' licenses). In the control condition (where the cost of disregarding the possibility of phenomenalistic causal connection was lower than the experimental condition) all of the participants granted the experimenter permission to repeat the manipulations. The data confirmed that adults in their practical actions acknowledged the possibility of phenomenalistic causal connections when the cost of discounting this possibility was high.

In general, the data of Experiment 1 showed that most six-and nine-year-olds accept the possibility of phenomenalistic causal connections when they lack a plausible physical causal explanation of the observed phenomenon. The results are in concordance with earlier-reported data (Piaget, 1930; Huang, 1930; Subbotsky, 1990) in which preschool and primary school children were found to be susceptible to phenomenalistic causal thinking. There was, however, one major difference between Experiment 1 of this study and the previous studies. In the previous studies, the children were asked questions about either some natural phenomena (i.e., the causes of the wind) or about unknown physical phenomena (i.e., the unknown properties of chemical solutions), whereas in Experiment 1 of this study the children were confronted with a transformation of a simple physical object (a postage stamp) that occurred as a result of their own activity (putting the postage stamp into an empty box and closing the lid). This difference has an important implication with regard to the causes of phenomenalistic thinking in children. Traditionally, children's tendency to make phenomenalistic judgments has been explained by a lack of adequate domain specific knowledge about physical, chemical, biological, and so on, properties and laws, and a lack of personal experience experimenting with objects. This traditional explanation is unlikely for Experiment 1 of this study given that six-and nine-year-olds have had substantial experience handling pieces of paper and various boxes, and there was nothing in the event shown that would challenge their knowledge of various domains of science. Our data showed, however, that phenomenalistic causal reasoning can be reactivated in children as old as nine with respect to common objects, provided that the children have no immediate "normal" physical explanation of the phenomenon that occurred with the objects.

Subsequent experiments showed that children quickly transformed their phenomenalistic causal judgments into magical causal judgments (Experiment 2), and in doing so they meant genuine magic (i.e., acting on physical objects by means of psychological rather than an unknown physical power). They did not use the term "magic" in a broad sense to include ordinary tricks, but used it only when they were directly asked about the possibility of magic. This shows that the original phenomenalistic judgments can develop later into either magical or natural-physical explanations, depending on the circumstances. The results also confirm preschool children's remarkable proficiency in maintaining boundaries between magical and real phenomena (Rosengren & Hickling, this volume).

In contrast to the children, almost all of the adults did not accept the possibility of phenomenalistic causal connections in Experiment 1. Instead, they either produced a physical explanation ("invisible ink," "trick") or refused to give any causal judgment. It was not until the cost of sticking to physical causal beliefs was increased that a significant number of adults succumbed to phenomenalistic causal reasoning in their actions (but not in their verbal judgments).

In the reported study, phenomenalistic causal judgments were studied in abstract form (i.e., the events that accompanied the unusual phenomenon were not rooted in a certain general background – either scientific or nonscientific). The next step was to examine phenomenalistic causal judgments when the accompanying events become linked to a certain (scientific or nonscientific) ideology and lead to either physical-natural or magical interpretations. With this in mind, educated adults (university students) were shown an unusual event (an unexpected destruction of a plastic card in the box) framed in scientific or nonscientific contexts (Subbotsky, 1996). In the first condition of the experiment (scientific context), the transformation of the plastic card in a closed box happened after the unknown physical device (which produced light and sound effects) was switched on for some time. In the second condition (parapsychological context), the transformation occurred after the experimenter demonstrated "effort of will" with his trembling hands and strenuous facial expression. In the third condition, the transformation of the plastic card was preceded by the experimenter putting a "magic spell" on the box. In all of the conditions, the participant was first asked to give his or her spontaneous explanation of the event and then say whether he or she believed that the transformation had been caused by (1) the unknown device, (2) the experimenter's "psychic" capacity to destroy physical objects by his sheer "effort of will," or (3) the supernatural power of the "magic spell".

In Experiment 1 of this study (low risk), the participants were then asked to put their driver's license into the box and given a choice either to allow the experimenter to repeat the manipulation (in which case the experimenter refused to guarantee the safety of the license) or to ask the experimenter to abstain from the manipulation. The participants' reactions indicated whether their disbelief in this particular explanation (scientific or nonscientific) was strong enough to run the risk of losing a valuable object. In Experiment 2 (high risk) of this study, the cost of disregarding a particular explanation was further increased, with the participants putting into the box not their driver's license (which are easily replaceable) but their hands after seeing a piece of plastic being badly scratched in the box. To overcome an ethical problem that inevitably appears in experiments involving some (even if purely imaginary) risk, the participants were explicitly warned that they had full control over the situation and did not have to do anything that they did not want to do, even if asked by the experimenter. This made the participants feel that if they accepted a certain risk, then they did it voluntarily and not because they were forced to. At the same time, it was clear to the participants that they could avoid any risk at all if they asked the experimenter not to repeat his actions. In this case it would be clear that the participants believed that the experimenter's actions could causally affect their hands.

In their verbal judgments more participants thought that the plastic card had been affected by the physical device than acknowledged the possible effect of a magic spell. Yet, approximately equal (and small) numbers of participants in every condition asked the experimenter not to repeat his actions in order to keep their licenses safe. However, in Experiment 2, the number of participants who asked the experimenter not to repeat his magic spell (eight out of sixteen) was significantly higher than the number of participants who made the same request in Experiment 1 (two out of sixteen). This shows that technologically based (i.e., scientific) explanations of unusual phenomenon do indeed dominate over nonscientific explanations. Yet this dominance is only evident at the level of verbal judgments. At the level of nonverbal attitudes and actions, adults are prepared to consciously accept magical explanations to the same extent as scientific ones. Another interesting result was that the adults' credulity toward magic increased significantly as the cost of disregarding magical explanations increased.

These findings show that under certain conditions individuals living in a technologically advanced society are prepared to accept phenomenalistic and magical explanations. This means that the development of human thinking does not mirror the technological advance of society; rather, it follows its own unique path in which contrasting modes of coping with reality permanently coexist. The data also support the view that beliefs in mental-physical causality persist throughout the life span. In this regard adults are not fundamentally different believers from children (Woolley, 1996, and this volume).

If the findings reflect a "submerged" (and reactivated) susceptibility to phenomenalistic and magical thinking among adults, then these results can be viewed as further evidence in favor of the "coexistence model" of the development of fundamental structures of mind (Subbotsky, 1992). In this model none of the so-called primitive and childish modes of thinking totally disappear in adulthood.[7] Instead, mental

---

[7] Reference to magic as a so-called primitive mode of thinking is not to say that the concept of magic is indeed primitive. In fact, with the advance of rationality, even

development can be accounted for more accurately if it is viewed as a gradual change of spheres of influence for alternative beliefs and their fight for dominance at various levels of functioning, rather than a complete replacement of "primitive beliefs" by more advanced ones.

## Concluding Remarks

Several models have been proposed to account for the relations between varying cognitive "entities" in the course of development. Flavell (1972), basing his classification mainly on works by Piaget (1986), Werner (1948), and Van den Daele (1969), described five types of developmental sequences: addition, substitution, modification, inclusion, and mediation. In this chapter, these models (specifically addition, substitution, and inclusion) have been applied to the relationships between alternative structures of the mind (i.e., phenomenalistic, magical, rationalistic, scientific) (see Figure 2.4).

After being proven "false," an old representation (i.e., phenomenalistic) may vanish from the child's mind; it can be incorporated (as only partially true) into the new representation; or, finally, it can be conserved in its original form somewhere in the "depth" of the child's mind. If we consider the two most influential approaches to cognitive development – the Piagetian and Vygotskyan approaches – we can see that they differ in the way they tackle the problem of the relation between "old" and "new" knowledge. Whereas Piaget (1986) consistently argued that new mental structures replace old ones (i.e., conservation replaces nonconservation, logical reasoning replaces prelogical reasoning), Vygotsky (1982) instead viewed the relations in terms of "fusing" and "merging" between the new (scientific) and the "old" (spontaneous) mental structures. Piaget's vision of the problem predominantly conforms to Model 1 of the relation between alternative structures of the mind, while Vygotsky's approach is more consistent with Model 2. Although both versions accurately reflect the development of certain areas of knowledge and cognitive function, they cannot satisfactorily explain the development of fundamental beliefs about the world, such as beliefs in magical or physical causality, or in the permanence (or nonpermanence) of a physical object.

Indeed, beliefs as fundamental as these can neither replace one

magical beliefs become viewed in terms of science, as in the studies of telepathy, in which the "psi-mediated" communication is interpreted as a weak signal that is normally overwhelmed by internal and external sensory noises (Bem & Honorton, 1994).

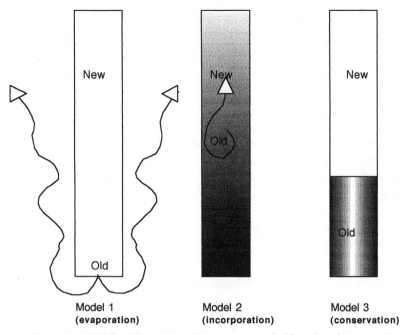

Figure 2.4. Models of the relations between new and old modes of representing reality in an individual's mind.

another (because they are interdependent) nor incorporate one another (because they are alternatives that have no common ground); they can only coexist. The problem of the relations between these kinds of beliefs in the course of individual development can be resolved only in accordance with Model 3. In fact, Model 3 also accounts for certain features of the development of "ordinary knowledge." It was shown that children's "false" representations about the world are often preserved in a certain form even after they have been "devaluated" in the face of "true" knowledge. However, even if they are preserved in the mind over development, their existential status may vary. They can be retained, for instance, as "stable illusions" that have only intangible and "ethereal" being. Numerous examples of this type of conservation of old knowledge can be found in studies of children's ability to distinguish between "appearance" and "reality." As they grow older, children acquire the capacity to distinguish between phenomenal images of objects and their rational constructions (Flavell, 1986). Although the "appearances" do not disappear, children come to treat them as "false" and "unreal." This type of preservation of old representations is easy to trace in children's verbal judgments.

If, however, nonverbal attitudes and behaviors are examined, another type of conservation of old structures may be found. The "retired" structure, even when it is considered "false," may still retain its own autonomous power and even compete with new structures. It seems likely that this is what happens to "archaic" forms of causal beliefs. Interestingly, in one of the experiments described above, the introduction of a rational interpretation and even the direct statement by an adult that the cylinders had nothing to do with the effect observed failed to destroy the influence of the phenomenalistic perception of causal relations on children's behavior, and the rational interpretation proved unstable. Even in adults, phenomenalistic perceptions of certain "appearances" cannot be destroyed by introducing rationalistic "true" models, if the pull of "appearances" is strong (as was the case with the phenomenalistic identification between sensations and objective properties of physical objects).

How can these results be interpreted? It can be assumed that the relation between phenomenalistic perception and rational understanding depends essentially on their relative "strength" in participants' minds. The strength of phenomenalistic perception depends, among other factors (like level functioning and context), on the emotional salience and "distinctness" of the impression produced. Hence, it is quite likely that if the "salience" and distinctness of the phenomenon is less marked, the phenomenon cannot compete with rational understanding and simply disappears from the children's minds, as was shown with regard to Piagetian phenomena (consistent with Model 1, Figure 2.4). In other cases (conforming to Model 2, Figure 2.4) rational knowledge can indeed "fuse" with old knowledge and give the old knowledge new shape and meaning. For instance, children's "naïve" theory of "heavy" objects sinking and light objects floating in water is made more precise by their incorporation of the concept of density (Zaporojetz & Lukov, 1941). A different result can be expected in the case where a phenomenal impact is especially strong, as in the reported study in which children and adults retained their phenomenalistic vision of sensations "sticking" to the physical bodies of objects despite a direct explanation in which the falsity of this illusion was revealed (Model 3, Figure 2.4).

As for rational understanding, its psychological strength may depend on the level of the participants' knowledge and their capacity to operate fluently with the knowledge. It may be assumed that the relations between the relative psychological strength of phenomenalistic perception and rational understanding determine the status of the "primary" mental structures. If the phenomenalistic perception of a certain event is weak, the newly acquired scientific version of the event destroys the phenomenalistic version and completely replaces it both at the level of verbal judgments and at the level of practical actions. The inverse relation of power may be expected to produce the opposite result.

Yet, in certain circumstances both the phenomenalistic and scientific versions may coexist. This means that a dynamic equilibrium between the psychological strength of phenomenalistic perception and that of rational understanding is achieved. As was shown in one of the experiments described, the rational (physical) version of causal links can govern at the level of verbal judgments in a "theoretical" situation, while phenomenalistic or magical causality continues to rule at the level of practical actions. The same dynamic equilibrium was observed with regard to the Müeller-Layer illusion.

The question, however, remains, in what psychological terms can the metaphor of the psychological strength be accounted for. Obviously, what was referred to as the "psychological strength" of a mental structure goes beyond the scope of "cognitive" or "intellectual" activity. Indeed, even if the structure has zero psychological strength, it does not cease to exist, but simply cannot be traced in participants' judgments or behavior. Yet, under certain circumstances, the structure can "emerge," as if "diving out" from some "depth" in the mind. But where?

If we accept the "coexistence" model of cognitive development, we must assume that a special "compartment" exists in an individual's mind in which all fundamental "false beliefs" are stored, even after their "falsity" is discovered in the course of rational understanding and scientific education. The structures that were once active and powerful acquire an "ethereal" existential status of sheer illusions and lose their control over the individual's behavior. Yet the "retired" structures are still there and can be "reactivated" at any moment. What are the conditions for "reactivation?" To examine this, we have to address a psychological concept that takes us beyond the area of cognitive processes – the concept of "motivation."

Let us examine the "magic box" study again. Even if rational causal understanding completely overwhelms phenomenalitic causal thinking, as was the case with the adults in this study, the results should be treated with caution. Indeed, some experiments of this study showed that the balance between alternative fundamental beliefs (like that between physical and phenomenalistic causality) is maintained by the "play" of participants' motivations, so that when the strength of the motive to employ phenomenalistic or magical beliefs was increased, the participants acted as if they believed in the phenomenalistic or magical versions of events. In light of this experiment, the term "psychological strength" of a mental structure can be further elaborated in terms of specific motivations that make participants favor this or another structure in guiding their behavior. The problem for experimental research with older children and adults shifts, therefore, from examining the mode of knowledge acquisition to identifying specific motives that make it profitable and safe (for a variety of reasons) for individuals to reactivate the retired modes for assimilating certain events.

The last question to be addressed concerns the function of the "retired" modes of thinking. It seems strange that, instead of disposing of the ballast of these fundamental "false beliefs," the human mind systematically stores and preserves them. Perhaps these structures have certain attractions for the human individual. But what attractions? Let us examine the phenomenalistic perception of causality.

As has long been known, rational understanding of the external world is promoted as a result of comparisons between objects and events using special measuring procedures (see Subbotsky, 1992). These procedures allow one to overcome a relative instability and diversity of the phenomenal world and reduce it to a stable world of rational constructions (or rationalistic models).[8] This tendency can be seen clearly, for instance, in the painting style of the Renaissance, when the "naïve" and two-dimensional painting styles of the ancient world were replaced by pictures of well-calculated proportions and sophisticated spatial perspectives. But the area that benefited most of all from the advance of rational thought was, of course, science.

Yet the old phenomenalistic ways of viewing the world remain important. First, they represent the "raw material" of the world as it directly contacts our sense organs prior to undergoing any rationalistically based transformations (let us call this function a "setting func-

---

[8] What is meant here is not that the phenomenal world is chaotic (in fact, it is structured or "modular") (Gibson, 1979), but that each individual has his or her own vision of any one object (i.e., the table), while a rational description of this object (the table's measured dimensions, weight, shape, etc.) will be the same for all.

tion"). Second, phenomenalistic perception is potentially more "rich" and flexible than any of the existing rationalistic models and can, therefore, be an inexhaustible source of new models and variations. Indeed, phenomenalistic causal thinking alerts our minds to potential causal links between events that, from a rational point of view, have to be ruled out from the outset. This function enables us to rethink and reconsider our causal judgments, sometimes resulting in "crazy" ideas that from time to time become new scientific theories (a "creative" function). Third, phenomenalistic perception makes the world more "human" and "proportional" to an individual human being, creating a sort of a "cushion" between our feelings and the cold indifference of rational constructions. Imagine, for instance, a person who would try to see the world in terms of "electromagnetic waves" instead of seeing it in colors and temperatures (a "humanizing" function).[9] Fourth, the phenomenalistic view of the world creates a specific kind of reality – the so-called "productive illusions" that we have about certain people (ourselves included) and objects. These illusions exist independently of (and alongside) our rational images of the same people and objects and help us to cope with certain problems that we encounter. Most obviously, this specific reality is manifested in human feelings (as contrasted to emotions) such as love. However deceptive and misleading the image of a person we love can be from a rational point of view, it helps us to maintain human relations and combat the ever changing and unstable nature of our emotions (a "stabilizing function"). These are but a few functions that phenomenalistic perception performs in our thinking and emotional life. The possession of positive functions in our lives is what makes the fundamental "false beliefs" competitive in the face of advancing rationality. The rediscovery of these functions is a special task of psychology that, we hope, will be paid due attention in future research.

### References

Bem, D. J., & Honorton, C. (1994). Does psi exist? Replicable evidence for an anomalous process of information transfer. *Psychological Bulletin, 115* (1), 4–18.
Berzonsky, M. D. (1971). The role of familiarity in children's explanations of physical causality. *Child Development, 42*, 705–15.

---

[9] Was it not this function of the phenomenalistic perception that inspired the famous "impressionistic" trend in arts?

Bower, T. G. R. (1974). *Development in Infancy.* San Francisco: Freeman.

Brain, M. D., & Shanks, B. L. (1965). The conservation of shape property and proposal about the origin of conservation. *Canadian Journal of Psychology, 19,* 197–207.

Bremner, G. (1994). *Infancy* (2nd ed.). Cambridge, MA: Blackwell.

Bruner, J. S. (1974). *Beyond the Information Given: Studies in the Psychology of Knowing.* London: Allen and Unvin.

Bullock, M. (1984). Preschool children's understanding of causal connections. *British Journal of Developmental Psychology, 2,* 139–48.

Bullock, M. (1985). Causal reasoning and developmental change over the preschool years. *Human Development, 28,* 169–91.

Bullock, M., Gelman, R., & Baillargeon, R. (1982). The development of causal reasoning. In: W. E. Friedman (Ed.), *The Developmental Psychology of Time,* (pp. 209–54). New York: Academic Press.

Chandler, M. J., & Lalonde, C. E. (1994). Surprising, magical, and miraculous turns of events: Children's reactions to violations of their early theories of mind and matter. *British Journal of Developmental Psychology, 12,* 83–96.

Cole, M., & Subbotsky, E. (1993). The fate of stages past: Reflections on the heterogeneity of thinking from the perspective of cultural-historical psychology. *Schweizerische Zeitschrift für Psychologie, 52,* 103–13.

Cook, S., & Selltiz, C. (1964). A multiple-indicator approach to attitude measurement. *Psychological Bulletin, 62,* 36–55.

Descartes, R. (1957). *Selected Works.* Moscow: Politisdat.

Deutsch, M. (1949). The directions of behavior: A field-theoretical approach to the understanding of inconsistencies. *Journal of Social Issues, 5,* 43–49.

Duncan, T. (1987). *GCSE Physics* (2nd ed.) London: John Murray.

Eisenberg, N., & Shell, R. (1986). Prosocial moral judgment and behavior in children: The mediating role of cost. *Personality and Social Psychology Bulletin, 12* (4), 426–433.

Flavell, J. H. (1963). *The Developmental Psychology of Jean Piaget.* New York: Van Nostrand.

Flavell, J. H. (1972). An analysis of cognitive developmental sequences. *Genetic Psychology Monographs, 86,* 279–350.

Flavell, J. H. (1977). *Cognitive Development.* Englewood Cliffs, NJ: Prentice Hall.

Flavell, J. H. (1986). The development of children's knowledge about the appearance-reality distinction. *American Psychologist, 41* (4), 418–425.

Fodor, J. A. (1988). Precis of the modularity of mind. In N: Collins, and E. E. Smith (Eds.), *Readings in Cognitive Science. A Perspective from Psychology and Artificial Intelligence,* (pp. 73–78). San Mateo, CA: Morgan Kaufmann

Geldard, A. F. (1972). *The Human Senses* (2nd ed.). New York: John Wiley & Sons.

Gelman, S. A., & Kremer, K. E. (1991). Understanding natural cause: Children's explanations of how objects and their properties originate. *Child Development, 62* (2) 396–414.

Gibson, J. J. (1979). *The Ecological Approach to Visual Perception.* Boston: Houghton-Mifflin.

Gregory, R. L. (1980). *The Intelligent Eye.* London: Weidenfeld & Nicolson.

Huang, I. (1930). Children's explanations of strange phenomena. *Psychologische Forchung, 14,* 63–183.

Husserl, E. (1977). *Cartesian Meditations. An Introduction to Phenomenology.* The Hague: Martinus Nijoff.

Johnson, C., & Harris, P. L. (1994). Magic: Special but not excluded. *British Journal of Developmental Psychology, 12,* 35–52.

King, A. L. (1962). *Thermophysics.* London: Freeman & Co.

Kun, A. (1978). Evidence for preschoolers' understanding of causal direction in extended causal sequence. *Child Development, 49,* 218–22.

La Pierre, R. T. (1934). Attitudes versus actions. *Social Forces, 13,* 230–37.

Leslie, A. (1986). Getting development off the ground. Modularity and infant's perception of causality. In: P. L. C. van Geert (Ed.), *Theory Building in Developmental Psychology,* (pp. 405–37). Amsterdam: Elsevier Science Publishers (North Holland).

Levin, I., Siegler, R. S., Druyan, S., & Gardosh, R. (1990). Everyday and curriculum-based physics concepts: When does short term training bring change where years of schooling have failed to do so? *British Journal of Developmental Psychology, 8,* 269–79.

Light, P. (1986). Context, conservation and conversation. In: M. P. M. Richards, and P. Light (Eds.), *Children of Social Worlds: Development in Social Context,* (pp. 170–190). Cambridge: Polity Press.

McNemar, Q. (1946). Opinion-attitude methodology. *Psychological Bulletin, 43,* 289–374.

Michotte, A. (1962). *Causalité, permanence et réalité phenomenales.* Paris: Publications Universitaires de Louvan, Editions Beatrice-Nauwelaerts.

Phelps, K. E., & Woolley, J. D. (1994). The form and function of young children's magical beliefs. *Developmental Psychology, 30,* 385–94.

Piaget, J. (1930). *The Child's Conception of Physical Causality.* London: Keegan Paul.

Piaget, J. (1969). *Selected Psychological Works.* Moscow: Progress.

Piaget, J. (1971). *Insights and Illusions of Philosophy.* London: Routledge & Keegan Paul.

Piaget, J. (1986). *The Construction of Reality in the Child.* New York: Ballantine Books.

Raspe, C. (1924). Kindliche Selbstbeobachtung and Theorienbildung. *Zeitschrift für Angewandte Psychologie, 23,* 302–28.

Rosengren, K. S., & Hickling, A. K. (1994). Seeing is believing: Children's explanations of commonplace, magical, and extraordinary transformations. *Child Development, 65,* 1605–26.

Rozin, P., Markwith, M., & Ross, B. (1990). The sympathetic magical law of similarity, nominal realism, and neglect of negatives in response to negative labels. *Psychological Science, 1,* 6, 383–384.

Rozin, P., Millman, L., & Nemeroff, C. (1986). Operation of laws of sympathetic magic in disgust and other domains. *Journal of Personality and Social Psychology, 50,* 4, 703–712.

Ruffman, T., Perner, J., Olson, D. R., & Doherty, M. (1993). Reflecting on scientific thinking: Children's understanding of the hypothesis-evidence relation. *Child Development, 64* (6), 1617–36.

Schultz, T. R., Altmann, E., & Asselin, J. (1986). Judging causal priority. *British Journal of Developmental Psychology, 4,* 67–74.

Schultz, T. R., Fisher, G. W., Pratt, C. C., & Rulf, S. (1986). Selection of causal rules. *Child Development, 57,* 143–52.

Sextus Empiricus (1933). *Works,* (in 4 volumes), vol. 1. Cambridge, MA: Harvard University Press.

Shweder, R. A. (1977). Likeness and likelihood in everyday thought: Magical thinking in judgments about personality. *Current Anthropology, 18* (4), 637–58.

Shweder, R. A. (1984). Anthropology's romantic rebellion against the enlightenment, or there's more to thinking than reason and evidence. In: R. A. Shweder, and R. A. LeVine, (Eds.), *Culture theory. Essays on Mind, Self, and Emotion,* (pp. 27–66). Cambridge: Cambridge University Press.

Siegler, R. (1994). Cognitive variability: A key to understanding cognitive development. *Current Directions in Psychological Science, 3,* (1), 1–5.

Springer, K., & Keil, E. C. (1991). Early differentiation of causal mechanisms appropriate to biological and nonbiological kinds. *Child Development, 62* (4), 767–81.

Subbotsky, E. V. (1985). Preschool children's perception of unusual phenomena. *Soviet Psychology, 23* (3), 91–114.

Subbotsky, E. V. (1990). Phenomenal and rational perception of some object relations by preschoolers. *Soviet Psychology, 28* (5), 5–24.

Subbotsky, E. V. (1992). *Foundations of the Mind: Children's Understanding of Reality.* London–New York: Harvester Wheatsheaf.

Subbotsky, E. V. (1993). *The Birth of Personality: The Development of Independent and Moral Behavior in Preschool Children.* London: Harvester Wheatsheaf.

Subbotsky, E. V. (1996). Scientifically and nonscientifically based causal explanations and behaviors in children and adults in a technologically advanced society: Are we still prepared to believe in magic? Unpublished manuscript.

Subbotsky, E. V. (1997a). Explanations of unusual events: Phenomenalistic causal judgments in children and adults. *British Journal of Developmental Psychology, 15,* 13–36.

Subbotsky, E. V. (1997b). Understanding the distinction between sensations and physical properties of objects by children and adults. *International Journal of Behavioral Development, 20* (2), 321–347.

Taylor, M., & Flavell, J. H. (1984). Seeing and believing: Children's understanding of the distinction between appearance and reality. *Child Development, 55,* 1710–20.

Van den Daele, L. D. (1969). Qualitative models in developmental analysis. *Developmental Psychology, 1,* 303–310.

Venger, A. A. (1958). Razvitije ponimanija prichinnosti u detej doshkol'nogo vozrasta (The development of the understanding of causality in preschool-age children). *Voprosy Psikhologii, 2,* 87–99.

Vygotsky, L. S. (1982). *Myshleniye i retch (Thought and Language)*. Moscow: Pedagogica.

Werner, H. (1948). *Comparative Psychology of Mental Development*. New York: Follett.

Wicker, A. W. (1971). Attitudes versus actions: the relationships of verbal and overt behavioral responses to attitude objects. In: K. Thomas (Ed.), *Attitudes and Behavior*. Baltimore: Penguin Books.

Wyszecki, G., & Stiles, W. S. (1967). *Color Science. Concepts and Methods, Quantitative Data and Formulas*. New York: John Wiley & Sons, Inc.

Woolley, J. D. (1997). Thinking about fantasy: Are children fundamentally different thinkers and believers from adults? Unpublished manuscript.

Zaporojetz, A. V., & Lukov, F. L. (1941). Pro rozvitok mirkuvannija u ditiny molodshego viku (On the development of thinking in a young child). *Scientific Reports of Charkov's Pedagogical Institute, 5*, 139–150.

# 3 Metamorphosis and Magic

## The Development of Children's Thinking About Possible Events and Plausible Mechanisms

KARL S. ROSENGREN AND ANNE K. HICKLING

The world is filled with wonderful, fantastic, and even miraculous events. Animals change color, providing natural camouflage as part of seasonal variations. Tadpoles and caterpillars metamorphose into frogs and butterflies as part of their natural growth and development. Amazing events are not limited to living things. From the startling beauty of the motion of waves, rainbows, or sunsets to the tremendous destructive powers of volcanoes and hurricanes, nature is filled with awesome events and surprising phenomena. Changes in technology have also made wonderful events commonplace in our homes and offices. At the touch of a button or remote control, lights, televisions, computers, and all sorts of machines come to life. Adults in many cultures generally accept all of these events without question. We view these events as possible and governed by natural causes or ordinary human agencies.

At the same time, we do not always agree about the possibility of events or causal mechanisms that stretch or violate scientific principles. If asked about the possibility of life on Mars, time travel, fish that change from male to female, carnivorous mushrooms that devour worms, the existence of ghosts or angels, the efficacy of prayer, or the likelihood that certain individuals have telepathic powers, many adults are not quite sure what to think.[1] Most adults routinely place

---

[1] As an aside, some of these events are actually possible. For example, a number of species of fish change sex as a function of environmental pressures (Crews, 1994) and some mushrooms trap and eat worms (Thom & Barron, 1984). Even scientists disagree about the possibility of some events. Although the scientific community does not widely hold these beliefs, some physicists do question the impossiblity of time travel (Deutsch & Lockwood, 1994) and other scientists cite recent meteor findings as suggestive of Martian life.

still other events in the realm of pure fantasy (e.g., visits by the Tooth Fairy, wishes granted by genies). This boundary between fantasy and reality or possible and impossible is not impermeable or unchanging. It varies according to age, knowledge level, context, and culture.

Given the prevalence of amazing events in everyday life, observations of relatively routine phenomena such as rainbows and sunsets could plausibly lead to the expectation that anything is possible. Indeed, if caterpillars can turn into butterflies, why can't butterflies turn into birds and frogs into princes? Although traditional views of early childhood have implied just that, characterizing young children as engaged in a magical, fantasy world (e.g., Piaget, 1930), current research in developmental psychology suggests that even very young children competently draw boundaries between reality and its alternatives. Although we accept this view for the most part, we suggest that children differ importantly from adults in how they view the possibility of events and the plausibility of various mechanisms.

In this chapter we examine the origins and development of thinking about possible and impossible events. We address how children come to construct boundaries between what is possible in the world by ordinary means and what is impossible.[2] We also focus on how children's preferred explanations shift with context and development. We emphasize throughout that children's causal judgments and explanations, although sometimes different from adults', are quite sensible in light of information provided by direct experience, parents, and culture. Although young children do seem quite skilled at maintaining boundaries between reality and fantasy or magical and real, they also may rely on explanations that adults would reserve for different classes of events. Specifically, in this chapter we examine children's use of magic, an explanation that children come to use to describe certain

[2] We focus on issues of possibility in part because our initial investigations have explored this issue. At the same time, we realize that our findings should be considered with respect to children's views of probability rather than possibility. Our focus on possibility may create a somewhat artificial dichotomy of possible/impossible events when, in fact, children and adults may make judgments based on probability. At present very little is known about children's understanding of chance and probability. Interestingly, Lesser and Paisner (1985) suggested that concepts of chance and probability are central to adults' views of reality. Although Piaget (1930) did investigate children's understanding of chance to some extent, this is an area where more research is sorely needed.

real-world phenomena but that adults routinely reserve for the world of fantasy, imagination, or pretense.

## Defining Magic

Establishing the place and function of magic in the everyday thought of young children first requires sorting out definitions emerging from diverse social science traditions. We contrast two distinct senses of magic pertinent to children's thinking. One concerns magical thinking, the focus of many anthropological and psychological accounts characterizing thoughts of exotic populations (young children or adults in preindustrial cultures) as illogical or irrational. The other encompasses magical explanations and beliefs, a topic of growing interest within recent psychological models of the causal reasoning systems that children recruit to make sense of ordinary experiences. Although both senses of magic describe aspects of cognitive functioning, magical explanations more directly reveal the nature of magic from the child's point of view.

Magical thinking encompasses errors in everyday causal attribution. For example, Piaget (1929, 1930) observed several apparent confusions in children's understanding of cause-effect relations and characterized these as "magical." Following this tradition, phenomena such as realism, inappropriate causal inferences between the mind and the world (e.g., explaining illness in terms of immoral thoughts), or participation, unwarranted causal inferences linking merely coincidental events, contribute to a picture of childhood thought as pervasively immature and rigid.

In contrast, magical explanations, that is, "thinking about magic" (Chandler & Lalonde, 1994), reveal children's flexibility in selecting among several candidate belief systems to make sense of real-world events. We argue that children's use of the term "magic" appeals to a legitimate and relatively coherent system of causal beliefs. Far from reflecting a fragile understanding of cause-effect relations, "magic" may provide considerable explanatory power.

We view magic as one of several alternative causal models. We use the term "alternative" to set these causal beliefs apart from foundational (Wellman & Gelman, 1997) or primary theories (Horton, 1993). Throughout our discussion we will refer to causal belief systems or models rather than to theories. This terminology highlights less well-developed forms of reasoning and avoids some of the intellectual baggage that comes with the use of the term "theory" to describe everyday thinking.[3]

Like more foundational domains of thought (see Wellman & Gelman, 1997), magic provides a causal-explanatory system specifying a unique set of relevant mechanisms and agents. We argue that a belief in extraordinary, perhaps even supernatural, forces defines the causal core of this domain. In this way, magic contrasts with ordinary physical, biological, and psychological reasoning. We believe that it is also important to distinguish magic from other types of alternative causal models that children and adults treat as distinct and that may have independent developmental trajectories. For example, we view religion as a distinct reasoning system involving a unique set of causal principles, not as an extension of magic. Beliefs in magic, religion, and extrasensory perception may each form distinct causal models. Because research directly supporting this view has not yet been conducted, we present suggestive data from our own research and point out where more research is needed.

## The Origins of Magical Beliefs

A central issue in characterizing the role of magical explanations in children's developing an understanding of everyday events concerns when and how magical beliefs originate: Do magical beliefs inform thinking from the very beginning, and then gradually decline in explanatory power across early childhood with the construction of causal-explanatory beliefs in more "scientific" domains (i.e., naive physics, biology, and psychology), or do they emerge somewhat later, as afforded by the consolidation of core conceptual domains? We argue that the ability to make sense of ordinary events through core "theories" actually sets the stage for the consideration of extraordinary events through alternative causal models like magical beliefs. In this way, the emergence of magical explanations reflects a degree of cognitive sophistication, with the underlying magical beliefs arising

---

[3] The use of the term "theory" to capture the manner in which children represent the world, although fairly widespread in developmental psychology, meets with considerable resistance by scientists who interpret "theory" as synonymous with coherent, explicit, formal thought.

out of the interaction between knowledge acquisition and cultural support.

Although especially congenial with contemporary views of cognitive development as a process of constructing conceptual understanding in collaboration with more knowledgeable members of one's culture (Rogoff, 1990; Vygotsky, 1978; 1986), the notion of magical beliefs arising through interaction between the individual and the social context finds roots even in earlier accounts. Classic developmental theories primarily focused on "magical causality" (Piaget, 1930), young children's belief in their own ability to control events in the world through the power of thought alone. Within this framework, young children's belief in the principle of efficacy at a distance leads to faulty reasoning about the causal links between thought or desire and action. Accordingly, toddlers and preschoolers might view wishing as a productive way to obtain an attractive new toy, whereas only older children would know to rely on more direct means (see Woolley, this volume).

In spite of this emphasis on magical thinking as a developmental precursor to scientific and systematic causal reasoning, Piaget (1929) also recognized a class of "social magical beliefs" of a more enduring and stable nature than causal understandings that children construct purely on their own. These social magical beliefs resemble many commonsense cultural views of magic, in which certain individuals, such as fantastic beings (e.g., fairies, wizards, Santa Claus), are endowed with extraordinary powers or capabilities (Rosengren, Kalish, Hickling, & Gelman, 1994). However, Piaget addressed neither the origins of magical beliefs nor their relationship to developments in causal reasoning skills. These unresolved issues gain renewed interest in the context of recent theories of knowledge development as instantiated within distinct domains of thought (for reviews, see Wellman & Gelman, 1992, 1998). This attention to multiple belief systems informing early causal-explanatory reasoning provides an arena for fresh consideration of the origins and developmental trajectory of magical beliefs and their place in children's everyday world views.

Despite widespread agreement about the active role that young children play in creating their own everyday knowledge systems, the role of knowledge acquisition in the construction of magical beliefs in particular remains controversial. Whereas classic constructivist accounts support an early, perhaps innate set of quasi-magical beliefs that are reflected in a global "magical" orientation in young children, ample evidence points to an alternative developmental story. We argue that young children's growing understanding of causal mechanisms and principles, supported by socio-cultural input, provides the foundation and motivation for the development of magical beliefs and explanations (see also Chandler & Lalonde, 1994; Harris, 1994; Johnson & Harris, 1994). In other words, the very processes of knowledge acquisition long thought to replace a "magical" world view actually encourages its development. With respect to the origins and developmental role of magical explanation, Chandler and Lalonde (1994) propose that ". . . children's thoughts about magic are sometimes meant to help preserve rather than undermine their commitment to systems of natural law" (p. 84). Thus, magical beliefs emerge as young children come to recognize shortcomings in their more conventional belief systems.

Several phenomena central to the emergence of everyday concepts eventually lead children to actively, even consciously, entertain notions of magic. Broadly speaking, magical beliefs may originate from children's developing abilities to consider both possible events and plausible mechanisms. How do these competencies arise? One important foundation for this development may lie in an innate (or very early learned) disposition to expect causal regularity. During the first months and years of life, children show an impressive ability to interpret events in terms of diverse, domain-specific causal mechanisms (Hickling, 1996; Wellman & Gelman, 1998). The speed and apparent ease with which these early causal understandings emerge have led to speculation that causality comprises a developmental primitive (Wellman & Gelman, 1998). Causal determinism, a presumption that knowable (even if unknown) mechanisms underlie events, may guide the search for explanation and understanding (Gelman & Kalish, 1993). Evidence for this strong propensity to view events as caused comes from research suggesting that preschoolers sometimes refuse to accept the possibility of random (i.e., acausal) events and draw causal inferences between unrelated states of affairs (Piaget, 1930). Still more compellingly, preverbal infants show a similar drive to explain by using spatio-temporal cues to resolve physical anomalies (i.e., seemingly impossible displays) intended to violate their expectations (Baillargeon, 1994). Therefore, a causal presumption may operate from the beginning of life in a framework fashion, directing attention to and thinking about events even before learning about relevant domain-specific causes takes place (Wellman & Gelman, 1998). This bias may so powerfully compel young children to search for causes that they eventually must recruit a broad repertoire of specific causal factors to make sense of the diverse and increasingly complex events they observe and experience. Preschoolers may begin to recruit alternative causal models, especially magical beliefs, for those circumstances that violate their now rich causal-explanatory beliefs provided by more ordinary domains of thought.

In light of their overwhelming orientation to seek out causes of everyday events, what guides children to begin appealing to magical explanations in particular? Another early conceptual achievement, the ability to categorize events as impossible, sets the stage for the consideration of unconventional causal factors. Distinguishing impossible events from possible ones allows children to recognize a special class of magical occurrences (Harris, 1994). The possible-impossible distinction, which is evident from the first months of life (Baillargeon & DeVos, 1991), suggests an appreciation that causal principles constrain what can take place rather than just what usually or typically happens (Harris, 1994; Rosengren & Hickling, 1994). Thus, events that defy expectations do so because they contradict well-established causal beliefs, not merely because they involve rare or unfamiliar outcomes. This growing understanding of what is ordinarily impossible in the physical, biological, or psychological domains helps young children define boundaries between the magical and the commonplace. Preschoolers' emerging ability to think about fictional events in the contexts of fantasy, imagination, pretense, and dreams (see Taylor & Carlson, this volume; Woolley & Phelps, 1994) enriches and expands how they conceptualize possibility and, therefore, impossibility. Early in the preschool period, children come to view fictional contexts as free-wheeling and unconstrained. For example, children as young as three years appreciate the possibility of imagining an entity (e.g., a purple cow) having no real-world referent (Woolley & Wellman, 1993) and of pretending a state of affairs in direct conflict with the pretense of one's playmate (e.g., same glass simultaneously holds both pretend "orange juice" and "coke") (Hickling, Wellman, & Gottfried, 1997). This growing experience with thinking about both real and fictional possibilities makes impossible events increasingly more salient and, therefore, especially demanding of explanation.

Once the normal processes of cognitive development enable young children to notice this class of special, seemingly impossible events, how do they come to see magic as a plausible mechanism? In short, culture invites young children to embrace magical beliefs. Cultural or social support of magical beliefs takes several forms. Most generally, a wealth of cultural practices and materials introduce young children to extraordinary or supernatural entities and mechanisms. Books and movies designed for preschoolers expose them to both (seemingly ordinary) human and (obviously) fantastic beings capable of bringing about events deemed impossible in the real world. As portrayed in many classic fairy tales, as well as in their animated adaptations, a variety of trappings accompany magical feats. Common types of cues signaling magical events include special clothing, objects with unusual properties, or incantations and spells. Furthermore, ritual practices such as hanging stockings or donning Halloween disguises help children find a place for magic in the real world, at least on special occasions. All of these activities, along with imaginary and pretend play, give young children experience integrating the magical into everyday life.

Nonetheless, interactions within children's close relationships exert more immediate influence than broader forms of cultural support. Parental input may play an especially powerful role in the development and maintenance of young children's magical beliefs. What form might such encouragement take? One crucial source may come from parent-child conversations regarding magical events. Instances in which an adult labels an event as "magic" provide a direct source of input. Although many parents surveyed about their responses to preschoolers' causal questions reported a preference for "scientific" (i.e., mechanical or technical) explanations, some admitted to resorting to magical explanations when asked about especially unusual events (Rosengren & Hickling, 1994). These magical markers may well occur more commonly than parents report. Informal observations in preschool classrooms reveal that teachers and other adults often describe events as "magic" (Rosengren & Hickling, 1994). Similarly, parents' use of magical explanations to highlight interesting events (e.g., "It's the magic of the season.") or to explain an anomalous event of interest to the child could spark the construction or elaboration of magical beliefs. The impact of parental input may prove substantial until children eventually orient more to the wider culture of peer group and school.

To summarize, we suggest that magical reasoning stems from an interaction of knowledge acquisition (learning the limits of possibility), the emergence of pretense and imagination (opening up the realm of possibility), a search for causality (and a desire to categorize entities or events by domain), and cultural support for the existence of magical phenomena and mechanisms. These factors set the stage for a special developmental window within which magical explanation rises and falls.

## Age-Related Changes in Magical Beliefs

When do children's magical beliefs first emerge? Figure 3.1 shows one possible developmental trajectory. Based on Piaget's account of magical thinking, this depiction shows a stagelike increase in logical thought, accompanied by a complementary age-related decrease in illogical or magical thinking. Figure 3.2 shows a contrasting developmental story (for a third perspective, see Subbotsky, 1993; this volume). Based on our experimental work, we argue that children's magical beliefs emerge some time around the beginning of the fourth year of life, peak during the preschool years, and then decline as children enter school.

Several research findings support our claim that magical beliefs emerge during but not prior to the preschool period. First, toddlers and young preschoolers show little if any familiarity with magic. In a pilot study of preschoolers' magical explanations for physical events,

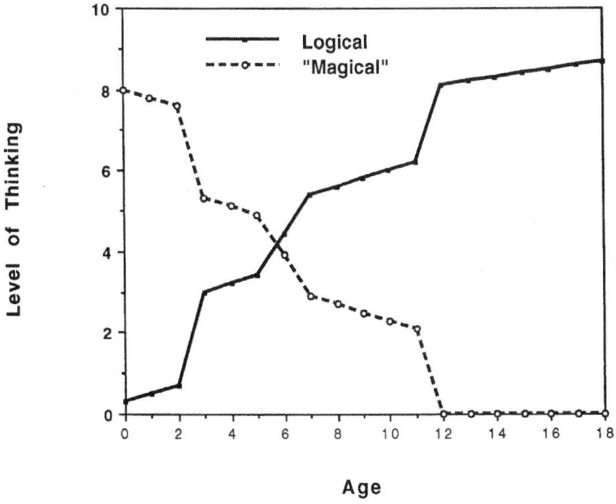

Figure 3.1. The traditional view of the development of logical and magical thinking.

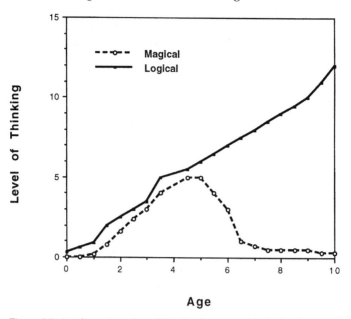

Figure 3.2. An alternative view of the development of logical and magical reasoning.

we found that children younger than age four did not know or use the term "magic." A longitudinal analysis of children's natural language supports this finding (Hickling, 1996). Children's first use of magical explanation in everyday conversation occurred on average at forty-two months, six to twelve months later than initial uses of physical, biological, psychological, or social explanations. Thus, magical reasoning emerges later than the more foundational forms of causal explanation.

Even if children do not commonly use magical words or explanations, they may still treat magical entities as belonging to a distinct category (or domain) from an early age. Determining whether children have a distinct magical domain of thought prior to the development of relevant language skills and vocabulary requires a method of tapping children's implicit magical knowledge. As a starting point, we investigated whether toddlers constrain the types of events they will attribute to different causal agents. Do toddlers associate magical events with specific sorts of causal agents (e.g., magicians), or do they think that anyone can perform magical events? In an exploratory study, we presented 2½-year-olds ($N = 11$) with a series of events (commonplace and magical ones) and then asked whether their teachers and parents could perform each one.[4] Ten of the eleven children judged that both the teacher and their parents could perform the commonplace events (blowing up a balloon, drawing a happy face, and cutting a triangle out of a paper circle). Six of the eleven children responded that they themselves would be unable to perform these commonplace events. This is not too surprising, because most of the commonplace events were beyond the motor skills of most children of this age.

More centrally, how did the children respond to the magical events? Seven of the eleven children judged that both the teacher and their parents could perform these events – and also responded that they themselves could not perform the events. Although preliminary, this finding suggests that toddlers may not restrict the causal agency of magical events. Some of these younger children appear to view all adults as equally capable of performing both commonplace and magical events. In contrast, we have found that somewhat older children are highly restrictive in who they believe capable of performing magic (Rosengren & Hickling, 1994). If this result holds up under more detailed exploration, it will provide greater evidence that young children do not start with a distinctly magical category.

When do children begin to embrace magic as a real, possible, explanation? We have found that preschoolers use magical explanations to explain impossible physical events. For example, in one study we presented four- and five-year-olds with a set of hypothetical object transformations (Rosengren & Hickling, 1994). These events included similar commonplace and magical events as in the study described earlier. In this study, however, we first showed specific objects (e.g., a piece of string, a coloring book with black and white line drawings) and then suggested hypothetical mechanisms for changing the object's appearance (i.e., making the string two pieces by cutting it with scissors, coloring the pages simply by flipping them). If the children said that the action we described could not cause the event to occur, we

---

[4] It is important with children of this age to spend a significant amount of time building rapport and to include questions to control for yes or no response biases. In this study, the head preschool teacher aided with both rapport and interpreting the children's responses. This was necessary because such young children often have idiosyncratic pronounciations that are understood only by familiar adults.

asked them to describe an action that would be successful. If the children accepted our action, we asked them for additional means for bringing about the event.

Children of both ages overwhelmingly judged the commonplace events to be possible and the magical ones to be impossible given the mechanisms we described. After actually viewing the events, most of the four-year-olds responded that the experimenter had performed magic. Children reserved magical explanations for only the events that they had previously described as impossible. The children did not generalize magical explanations to all of the events performed by the experimenter. In follow-up questions, the children of this age responded that the experimenter was in fact a magician, that magic can only be performed by certain individuals (i.e., magicians, and not teachers or parents), and that magic involves special powers.

These data also revealed striking age differences in the children's explanations. Most five-year-olds explained "impossible" events in terms of tricks (in contrast to real magic) and described magic as something that anyone may learn from experts or books. Although most four-year-olds embraced magic as a legitimate form of causal explanation and held a coherent set of magical beliefs, five-year-olds incorporated magical occurrences into their natural models of the world. Phelps and Woolley (1994) suggested a slightly older age for this decline in magical explanation ($\sim$ age 6). We suggest that timing will vary from one group to another depending on the level of support for magical beliefs in a given community. It is likely that this decline in magical beliefs coincides with the onset of formal schooling and a wider exposure to peer culture.

As mentioned earlier, we believe that changes in support provided by parents and the larger community in part account for age differences in magical explanations and beliefs. For the past few years we have collected a number of examples where parents or teachers use the term "magic." Although fairly rare in everyday speech, these instances seem to be associated with particular kinds of entities or events. For example, we have heard teachers of preschool and kindergarten children refer to magnets as "magic wands," chemical indicators as "magic potions," and color-changing paper as "magic." We have also found preschoolers' chemistry sets labeled as "mysterious or magical," science kits labeled as "Science Magic Tricks," or books that combine leaning science with magic (see, for example, Ladizinsky, 1994). Although these examples are compelling, anecdotal evidence alone cannot reveal how widespread this phenomenon might be. Thus, to explore this issue more systematically, we conducted a number of questionnaire studies and experimental manipulations.

The survey responses suggest age-related changes in parental perceptions and encouragement of preschoolers' magical beliefs. In one study (Rosengren et al., 1994), the parents of four-to six-year-olds (N = 70) reported relatively low levels of support for beliefs in various "magical" characters (e.g., magicians, witches) other than event-related figures such as Santa, the Easter Bunny, and the Tooth Fairy. Parents' reports of their children's beliefs significantly correlated with parental encouragement, especially for the event-related characters. A survey of parents whose children (ages four and five) participated in experimental research on preschoolers' magical explanations (Rosengren & Hickling, 1994) revealed similar results. These parents, however, received an additional set of questions that asked how they would respond if their children asked them about the reality status of certain figures (i.e., "is Santa real?"). Most parents responded that they would describe ghosts and magicians as not real, but would describe Santa, the Easter Bunny, and the Tooth Fairy as real. Most importantly, the parents also responded that their answers would change as their children grew older. The parents said that they would provide increasingly evasive answers (i.e., "what do you think?"), alternative responses (i.e., "Santa is real in the spirit"), or definite denials of reality status (i.e., "there really is no Santa").

Although anecdotal evidence and parents' own reports provide a starting place for examining parental encouragement of magical beliefs, we have also examined this issue in experimental work (Rosengren, Hickling, Jurist, & Burger, in preparation). In one study, parents and their four- or seven-year-old children (ten families per age group) watched a live magic show. The magician performed a series of magic tricks (e.g., making a rabbit appear in an empty box) as well as some commonplace events (e.g., blowing up a balloon, removing a ketchup bottle from a bag). For a week following the show, the parents kept a diary of their responses to the children's questions about the events performed by the magician. We coded the contents of the parents' explanations according to reasoning system (physical/natural, magic, or trick) and degree of encouragement in magic (affirm, evade, disconfirm). The parents of preschoolers generally provided magical explanations (of tricks) and affirmed the existence of magic.

When asked, "How did the man fold the money? Was it magic?" the parent of a preschooler responded, "Yes, it was!" The parents of the older children more often responded to the children's questions about the magic tricks by explicitly describing the event as a "trick" or by providing a physical/natural explanation. For example, when asked, "How did the magician make the bird come out of the balloon?" the parent of an elementary school age child replied, "I'm not sure. Sometimes magicians keep things up their sleeves and slip them down when you're not looking, but this takes a lot of practice." The parents of the older children generally disconfirmed the existence of magic.

How do parents explain magical events at the time they first observe them? In a second study, we examined the conversations between three- and five-year-old children and their parents watching a televised "magic show." A magician performed magical (i.e., our magic coloring book), commonplace (i.e., blowing up a balloon), and other extraordinary transformations (i.e., possible but dramatic events like mixing two colorless liquids to get a dark liquid). We recorded the parents' and children's spontaneous comments while watching the magic show. Here again we looked at the types of causal explanations given by the parents with a particular focus on whether the parents differentiated between the three types of events in their causal comments. The parents generally provided physical or natural explanations for the commonplace events, saying things like, "Hey that wasn't magic!" or "He's not a very good magician." The parents of the younger children (three-year-olds) often provided magical explanations for the magical events. For example, the following dialogue presents a conversation about a trick in which a brightly colored scarf vanished:

> CHILD: "It disappeared!"
> MOTHER: "It disappeared! That was pretty neat! He made the scarf disappear."
> CHILD: "How'd he do that?"
> MOTHER: "I don't know, it must be magic."
> CHILD: "Yeah!"

A number of parents engaged their children in explicit discussions regarding the nature of magic. For example, one mother walked her child through a number of events and evaluated whether each counted as magic.

MOTHER: "You know I think he's doing different things, where some things look like magic and some don't. Like blowing up a balloon, is that magic?"

CHILD: "No."

MOTHER: "I don't think so."

CHILD: "Blowing up a balloon is not magic."

MOTHER: "Yeah. . . . when he drew the happy face was that magic?"

CHILD: "NOOOOOO!!!!"

MOTHER: "Then he made the scarves change colors, was that magic?"

CHILD: "Yeah, that was magic!"

The parents of the older children in this study (five-year-olds) usually provided physical or natural mechanisms to explain magic tricks ("He put it [the scarf] in his pocket") or explicitly described the event in terms of trickery or deception.

Although the parents' comments clearly distinguished between the commonplace and magical events, we were particularly interested in how they talked about extraordinary events. Based on our anecdotal evidence we expected that the parents would describe these events as magic, especially in the context of a "magic show." Instead, we found that the parents talked about these events primarily by describing the event or using physical or scientific explanations. For example, the following dialogue presents a conversation about an event that involved mixing two colorless liquids together resulting in a dark liquid:

(*Magician holds two glasses containing colorless liquid*).

MOTHER: "What's he have in his hands?"

CHILD "Water."

(*Magician mixes liquids*)

MOTHER "Oh, cool, it turned black! Is it bubbling?"

CHILD "Yeah."

MOTHER "That's strange."

CHILD "Ooh, right?"

MOTHER "Yes, I think so."

MOTHER: "It's kind of mysterious. . . . That's chemistry you know, when you combine liquids, different liquids."

The parents rarely explained extraordinary events as magic or tricks (an average of less 0.3 utterances per parent). The parents of the older children provided significantly more physical or scientific explanations than the parents of the younger children.

Taken together, these studies suggest that parents clearly distinguish between magical and nonmagical events in both their spontaneous comments and responses to causal questions. In addition, parents of younger children (three- and four-year-olds) tend to provide encouragement of magical beliefs, whereas parents of older children (five- and seven-year-olds) tend to treat magic merely as clever trickery. This research suggests that parents support magical beliefs selectively. They and, most likely, the culture at large reserve magical explanations for particular situations, contexts, and events. This targeting of certain events as special or magical provides children with a structure to construct a unique causal belief model that applies to a constrained set of entities and events. Interestingly, soon after children construct this system of beliefs, parents begin to withdraw their support, providing less explicit encouragement and more evasive statements about the existence of magic. This raises an intriguing question. That is, if parents' ultimate goal is for children to have a clear understanding of the difference between magic or, more generally, fantasy and reality, why do they invest any energy in encouraging magical and fantasy beliefs? Several hypotheses for further consideration include that parents encourage such beliefs for fun, to support cultural rituals, or to recapture their own childhood.

## Contextual Issues

We do not view the developmental progression that we have just articulated as completely uniform or universal. We view this process as strongly influenced by the characteristics of the child, significant older individuals (specifically parents, teachers, and most likely older siblings), and the wider culture. Thus, we expect wide individual variation in the adherence to magical beliefs (see Johnson, this volume). We also suggest that young children do not show a generally magical orientation to events they confront in everyday life. Magical beliefs and explanations appear to arise in particular situations. In this section we explore the contexts that may elicit magical explanations.

In a series of studies of children's reasoning about the possibility of various biological and physical events (Rosengren et al., 1991, 1993, 1994; Rosengren & Hickling, 1994) we have found that: (1) young children are generally less accepting than older children and adults of events leading to dramatic changes in the appearance of an animal (i.e., metamorphosis) or object (i.e., changing from wood to metal); and (2) young children rarely provide spontaneous statements referring to magical means or entities. For example, of some 300 preschool children that we have interviewed in a variety of studies, only 3 have spontaneously provided any form of magical reasoning (DeHart, Rosengren, & Protska, under review; Rosengren, et al., 1991, 1994). Therefore, children ordinarily do not rely on magic as a default explanation. However, a number of situations may elicit children's magical beliefs. These include, but may not be restricted to: (1) situations violating children's causal expectations; and (2) special events explicitly labeled by parents and the culture as magical (i.e., magic shows).

It is important to point out that a violation of expectations alone is probably not sufficient for children to draw on magical beliefs. Two conditions must prevail as well. First, children must have experienced similar violations in the past where the event (or one highly similar to it) was explicitly labeled as magic. We expect that a few salient examples of parents or other adults labeling a dramatic event as magical may be enough to create this "magical category." Second, other alternative explanations cannot be readily available. Indeed, one reason that magicians perform each trick once per magic show and quickly move from one trick to the next is that these techniques do not enable the observer to spend any time pondering how any particular event was performed. Chandler and Lalonde (1994) showed that if children are allowed to repeatedly view an event, they rapidly give up their magical explanation in favor of a more mundane mechanism. Likewise, we have found that if children are provided with an alternative mechanism, even one that adults find highly implausible, they are less likely to resort to magical explanations. For example, in one study we presented children with a scenario where a machine would shrink and enlarge a room (DeLoache, Miller, & Rosengren, 1997). Although originally designed to examine children's symbolic understanding, this study also sheds light on situations that may violate children's expectations but not elicit magical explanations. In this study, the children were first introduced to "Terry the Troll," who was then shrunk by a "special machine." After successfully shrinking Terry, we enlarged him to his initial size and then hid him in a particular place in a larger room. We then turned the machine toward the room, activated it, and rendered the room approximately one-tenth of its previous size. The children were then asked to find Terry. During the actual shrinking or enlarging the children were in an adjoining room (for "safety") and the machine generated noises indicating the shrinking or enlarging of Terry or the room. Two-and-a-half-year-old children, who typically fail to find an object hidden in one space when it is hidden in an analogous space (such as a scale model), successfully find it in the shrinking room condition. This result suggests that toddlers accepted our transformation and viewed the room as the same room after it had been shrunk.[5] We have found that children under the age of five are quite accepting of our transformation – with many four-year-olds even refusing to accept our debriefing about the machine. The children would often ask us to "shrink" something else and would describe the machine to the parent who had not come into the laboratory as a "machine that can really shrink things." In only one case (out of approximately forty children) did we have a child describe the shrinking machine using magical terms. The few older participants (six-seven-year-olds) who completed this task began immediately looking for an alternative explanation and rapidly uncovered the real mechanism behind the transformation.

Overall, we interpret these findings as suggesting that young children are quite accepting that a machine can bring about an amazing transformation, one that they would normally view as impossible (see Rosengren et al., 1991, 1993). Given the prevalence of amazing machines such as televisions, CD players, and remote controls that have permeated most homes, it is not altogether surprising that children might believe that a shrinking machine was in the realm of possibility. This study also provides further evidence that children are not uniformly magical in their orientation to real-world events.

## Magical Beliefs and Other Forms of Causal Reasoning

How do magical beliefs and explanations relate to other forms of causal reasoning? Specifically, we return to the issue of whether magical reasoning should be considered as a distinct causal model.

We suggest that it might be useful to consider how different forms

---

[5] Success in the shrinking room condition appears to be due to the fact that, to perform successfully, children must treat the shrinking scenario in terms of an identity relation. Thinking about the large and small space in terms of identity is cognitively not as difficult as treating one space as a representation of other, even when the model and space are highly similar in appearance. See DeLoache et al. (1997) for greater detail.

of causal reasoning are related by thinking of different causal models as separate attractor states. In this view, the state of the system (here the possible causal reasoning systems that children may use) is modeled as a surface representing all possible states of the system (an attractor landscape). Depressions in the surface represent attractor states or regions where the system is likely to move under different conditions. The current state of the system can be represented in terms of a ball that rolls around on this surface. If the ball lands in one of the depressions in the surface, it will tend to remain in that location as long as the attractor well is sufficiently deep or the walls of the attractor region are sufficiently steep (symbolizing a strong attractor) and the conditions of the system remain relatively stable. However, if greater energy enters into the system, the ball will become more active and the likelihood that the system will move to a different attractor state will increase according to the overall characteristics of the attractor landscape.

Neither the attractor landscape nor the ball (the current state of the system) should be viewed as static. Rather, because biological systems are in constant flux, the ball should be viewed as constantly moving (similar in some regards to Piaget's view of dynamic equilibrium). These movements can be relatively small fluctuations or vibrations or be more vigorous in nature, depending on the level of energy or excitement in the system. Likewise with development, greater experience, or changes in context, new attractor states (new forms of causal reasoning) may emerge, while others deepen or become more shallow and still others may disappear completely.

Why adopt this metaphor for children's causal reasoning? One advantage of this type of description of cognitive development is that it provides a way of thinking about how different causal reasoning systems might relate and how children might shift from one form to another given different situations. This issue has been ignored for the most part as researchers have scrambled to describe domain-specific aspects of cognition and its early development (for a variety of views, see Hirschfeld & Gelman, 1994). This trend has been driven in part from the failure to find coherence in reasoning across domains and a general dissatisfaction with global descriptions of cognition (such as that proposed by Piaget). This approach enables us to think constructively about the variability in children's reasoning, an issue that has most recently been emphasized by dynamic systems theorists (see Thelen & Smith, 1994). However, other researchers in cognitive development have begun to examine more fully the nature of variability in children's thinking within particular domains (see Siegler, 1996: Rosengren, Taylor & DeHart, 1997). Few researchers or theorists have examined how domains might relate (but, see Hirschfeld, 1994; Taylor, Gerow, & Carlson, 1993).

From this perspective, each depression in the surface of the landscape, or attractor well, could represent one of the three foundational reasoning systems: physics, biology, and psychology. The exact shape and orientation of these domains (attractors) are yet to be determined (and in fact are most likely indeterminate). We view these wells as varying in depth to indicate that certain forms of causal reasoning may be more attractive than others. For example, the attractor state for physical reasoning would be relatively deep, indicating an "entrenched" causal model. In our view, an attractor landscape with three separate attractor wells representing naive physics, biology, and psychology would capture young children's default causal reasoning systems. That is, children primarily rely on one of these three causal models. If the event involves mechanical force, the attractor state for physical reasoning would deepen, and that form of explanation would become increasingly likely. Likewise, if the event involves mental states, the well corresponding to psychology would deepen, and the likelihood that children would reason about the event in psychological terms would increase.

At the boundary regions between attractor states the system may change in one direction or another, depending on the steepness or attractiveness of the different causal reasoning systems. Other attractor states may emerge in these boundary regions when more entrenched causal belief models fail to provide explanatory power (or when cultural support for a particular form of reasoning changes). For example, Hirschfeld (1995) suggested that reasoning about social phenomena (labeled as a Theory of Society) should be viewed as a distinct causal model (see also Hickling, 1996). This causal model may develop at the boundary between naive biology and naive psychology. Likewise, we suggest a causal model for magic emerging at the boundaries of physics and psychology. This attractor state deepens during the preschool period and then shrinks as children enter school. We view this causal reasoning system as distinct (and deserving of a separate attractor state) based on criteria articulated by Wellman and Gelman (1997). Specifically, magical reasoning involves a unique mode of causality (i.e., magic), nonobvious constructs (i.e., magical powers cannot be seen), and a relatively coherent set of interrelated concepts (i.e., magicians, magic wands, potions, special hats, etc.).

As magical explanation emerges and then declines, a religious causal reasoning system may form (see Wooley, this volume). Given developmental accounts of religious thinking, this attractor state may continue to deepen as children age (see Boyer & Walker, this volume). We suggest that these alternative causal models (i.e., magic or religion) will for the most part never become more attractive than the foundational domains for most individuals. The foundational reasoning systems will predominate in part because of greater experiential and cultural support. Cultural support for magical or religious reasoning (except in the case of isolated religious groups) may never be uniform enough, so that these causal models may become as entrenched or coherent as those for the foundational domains. Likewise, differing inclinations toward or support for magic or religion may influence whether either of these causal models emerge in the first place.

What causes a shift from one mode to another? Shifts in causal reasoning may occur due to changes in the entities involved in an event (i.e., objects, animals, or people), changes in context (i.e., home, school, farm or zoo, church or religious ceremony), heightened interest or curiosity about some type of phenomena (i.e., a child's fascination about magic leading to learning about the actual tricks), acquisition of new knowledge (i.e., learning why the sun appears to move), and changes in mood or emotional factors (i.e., hopelessness in one's current situation leading to the individual to turn toward religion). The nature of the attractor landscape is likely to vary across children as well. Children certainly vary with respect to their fantasy proneness (Taylor, Cartwright, & Carlson, 1993). Individuals also vary with respect to their beliefs in religion. Thus, the depth of particular attractor states, their location with respect to other causal reasoning systems, and the developmental course of attractors is likely to vary greatly across individuals.

## Conclusion

In this chapter we have outlined the development of children's beliefs and explanations about magic. Our view of the development of magical reasoning differs in two important ways from other accounts. First, we treat magical reasoning as carving out a distinct domain. In this view, magical reasoning represents an alternative form of causal reasoning that is distinct from both foundational forms of reasoning (i.e., physics, biology, and psychology) and other alternative forms of reasoning, such as religion. Traditionally, magic has primarily been viewed as an error in children's (or adult's) reasoning, and used to label any explanation that varied from the accepted logic. While we agree that children may sometimes make errors of logic and reasoning, we suggest that it is more fruitful to label these as just that, causal errors, and reserve the term magic for situations where individuals apply a specific type of causal reasoning, one that involves reference to specific supernatural powers.

We also differ from other researchers and theorists in that we view magical reasoning as emerging during the preschool years, rather than being present from the start. We have provided evidence that magical reasoning emerges in the fourth year of life, peaks sometime within in the next year or two, and then shows a relatively rapid decline as children enter formal schooling. This developmental trajectory is driven by a search for causal understanding, the acquisition of new knowledge, and changing cultural support. Like other contributors to this volume (most notably Woolley) we argue that it is important to consider how parents and culture provide support and encouragement for children's cognitive development.

Although we have argued that children's reasoning about magic should be viewed as distinct from other forms of causal reasoning, few researchers have explicitly addressed the relation between different causal modes of reasoning. Future research should examine more closely how magical reasoning relates to other types of reasoning, whether it truly represents a distinct form of reasoning, and the factors that cause children to switch from one mode of explanation to another.

## References

Baillargeon, R. (1994). Physical reasoning in young infants: Seeking explanations for impossible events. *British Journal of Developmental Psychology, 12*, 9–33.

Baillargeon, R., & DeVos, J. (1991). Object permanence in young infants: Further evidence. *Child Development, 62*, 1227–46.

Chandler, M. J., & Lalonde, C. E. (1994). Surprising, magical, and miraculous turns of events: Children's reactions to violations of their early theories of mind and matter. *British Journal of Developmental Psychology, 12*, 83–95.

Chiao, R. Y., Kiwiat, P. G., & Sternberg, A. M. (1993). Faster than light? *Scientific American, 269*, 52–60.

Crews, D. (1994). Animal sexuality.*Scientific American, 270,* 108–14.

DeLoache, J. S., Miller, K. F., & Rosengren, K. S. (1997). The credible shrinking room: Very young children's performance with symbolic and nonsymbolic relations. *Psychological Science, 8,* 308–313.

Deutsch, D., & Lockwood, M. (1994). The quantum physics of time travel. *Scientific American, 270,* 68–74.

Gelman, S. A., & Kalish, C. W. (1993). Categories and causality. In: R. Pasnak and M. L. Howe (Eds.), *Emerging Themes in Cognitive Development, Vol 2,* (pp. 3–32). New York: Springer-Verlag.

Harris, P. L. (1994). Unexpected, impossible and magical events: Children's reactions to causal violations. *British Journal of Developmental Psychology, 12,* 1–7.

Hickling, A. K. (1996). *The Emergence of Causal Explanation in Everyday Thought: Evidence from Ordinary Conversation.* Unpublished doctoral dissertation. University of Michigan. Ann Arbor, MI.

Hickling, A. K., Wellman, H. M., & Gottfried, G. M. (1997). Preschoolers' understanding of others' mental attitudes toward pretend happenings. *British Journal of Developmental Psychology, 15,* 339–354.

Hirschfeld, L. A. (1995). Anthropology, psychology, and meanings of social causality. In: D. Sperber, D. Premack, and A. James Premack (Eds.), *Causal Cognition: A Multidisciplinary Debate,* (pp. 313–50). Oxford: Oxford University Press.

Horton, R. (1993). *Patterns of Thought in Africa and the West: Essays on Magic, Religion, and Science.* New York: Cambridge University Press.

Johnson, C., & Harris, P. L. (1994). Magic: Special but not excluded. *British Journal of Developmental Psychology, 12,* 35–51.

Ladizinsky, E. (1994). *More Magical Science: Magic Tricks for Young Scientists.* Chicago: Contemporary Books.

Lesser, R., & Paisner, L. (1985). Magical thinking in formal operational adults. *Human Development, 28,* 57–70.

Kuzmak, S. D., & Gelman, R. (1986). Young children's understanding of random phenomena. *Child Development, 57(3),* 559–66.

Neusner, J. (1989). *Religion, Science, and Magic: In Concert and in Conflict,* New York: Oxford University Press.

Phelps, K. E., & Woolley, J. D. (1994). The form and function of young children's magical beliefs. *Developmental Psychology, 30,* 385–394.

Piaget, J. (1929). *The Child's Conception of the World,* London: Kegan Paul.

Piaget, J. (1930). *The Child's Conception of Physical Causality.* London: Kegan Paul.

Rogoff, B. (1990). *Apprenticeship in Thinking: Cognitive Development in Social Context.* Oxford: Oxford University Press.

Rosengren, K. S., Gelman, S. A., Kalish, C. W., & McCormick, M. (1991). As time goes by: Children's early understanding of growth in animals. *Child Development, 62,* 1302–20.

Rosengren, K. S., Kalish, C. W., Gelman, S. A., & Fealk, E. (1993). *No way? Children's Understanding of Possible and Impossible Transformations of Animals and Artifacts.* Unpublished manuscript.

Rosengren, K. S., & Hickling, A. K. (1994). Seeing is believing: Children's explanations of commonplace, magical, and extraordinary transformations. *Child Development, 65,* 1605–26.

Rosengren, K. S., Hickling, A. K., Jurist, M., & Burger, D. (in preparation). *Parent-Child Conversations about Magical, Extraordinary and Commonplace Events.*

Rosengren, K. S., Kalish, C. W., Hickling, A. K., & Gelman, S. A. (1994). Exploring the relation between preschool children's magical beliefs and causal thinking. *British Journal of Developmental Psychology, 12,* 69–82.

Rosengren, K. S. Taylor, M., & DeHart, G. (1997). Variability in children's biological reasoning, Symposium paper presented at the Biennial meetings of the Society for Research in Child Development, Washington, DC.

Siegler, R. S. (1996). *Emerging Minds: The Process of Change in Children's Thinking.* New York: Oxford University Press.

Subbotsky. E. V. (1992). *Foundations of the Mind: Children's Understanding of Reality.* Cambridge, MA: Harvard University Press

Taylor, M., Cartwright, B. S., & Carlson, S. M. (1993). A developmental investigation of children's imaginary companions. *Developmental Psychology, 29,* 276–285.

Taylor, M., Gerow, L. E., & Carlson, S. (1993). The relation between individual differences in fantasy and theory of mind. Symposium paper presented at the biennial meeting of the Society for Research in Child Development, New Orleans.

Thelen, E., & Smith, L. B. (1994). *A Dynamic Systems Approach to the Development of Cognition and Action.* Cambridge, MA: MIT Press.

Thom, R. G., & Barron, G. L. (1984). Carnivorous mushrooms, *Science, 224,* 76–78.

Wellman, H. M., & Gelman, S. A. (1992). Cognitive development: Foundational theories of core domains. *Annual Review of Psychology, 43,* 337–75.

Wellman, H. M., & Gelman, S. A. (1998). Knowledge acquisition in foundational domains. In: D. Kuhn and R. Siegler (Eds.), *Cognition, Perception, and Language.* Volume 2 of *Handbook of Child Psychology* (5th ed.) (W. Damon, Ed.-in Chief). New York: Wiley.

Woolley, J. D., & Phelps, K. E. (1994). Young children's practical reasoning about imagination. *British Journal of Developmental Psychology, 12,* 53–67.

Woolley, J., & Wellman, H. M. (1993). Origin and truth: Young children's understanding of imaginary mental representations. *Child Development, 64,* 1–17.

Vygotsky, L. S. (1978). *Mind in Society: The Development of Higher Psychological Process.* Cambridge, MA: Harvard University Press.

Vygotsky, L. S. (1986). *Thought and language.* Cambridge, MA: MIT Press.

# 4 The Development of Beliefs About Direct Mental-Physical Causality in Imagination, Magic, and Religion

JACQUELINE D. WOOLLEY

A fundamental ontological distinction that governs much of human behavior is that between the realms of the mental and the physical. An awareness of this distinction informs most, if not all, of adults' predictions for and explanations of events in the world. Thus, an important developmental question arises: When do children become aware of this distinction? Recent research has documented that, in their early years, children in Western cultures are acquiring considerable knowledge about how the mind and reality are both distinct and related. For example, children know that mental entities have very different properties from physical things (Estes, Wellman, & Woolley, 1989; Wellman & Estes, 1986). They also understand that mental states are related to the world in important ways, in particular in the form of beliefs and knowledge (Astington, 1993; Bartsch & Wellman, 1995; Perner, 1991; Astington, 1993). These pieces of knowledge are part of what many have called a "theory of mind" and arguably represent one of children's earliest bodies of knowledge to be used in understanding the world (Wellman, 1990).[1]

Yet a consideration of certain cultural practices in Western society

---

[1] As there is very little data on the development of a "theory of mind" in other cultures, the universality of early beliefs about the mind is as yet unknown. Although a "theory of mind" could be considered a cultural construct, I have chosen to speak of it here more as a body of knowledge that children acquire somewhat spontaneously, and to contrast it with particular constructs that are passed down more explicitly from generation to generation. I view the very early understandings and distinctions that children acquire about the mind as primarily untutored and implicit, and, as such, I think of their development as proceeding more similarly to development of knowledge about the natural world than to the acquisition of cultural constructs, such as magic and religion, which I expect to vary more between cultures. Of course this is still an open question (see, e.g., Lillard, 1997).

highlights a potential developmental oddity. At about the same age at which children begin to demonstrate that they have the basic components of a theory of mind, they are introduced by our culture to concepts that seem to contradict the knowledge that they are in the process of mastering. For example, around the time that children begin to demonstrate consistent knowledge of important causal relations between the mind and the world (see, e.g., Pillow, 1989; Pratt & Bryant, 1990), they are introduced to the concept of wishing. Shortly thereafter they are introduced to religious concepts such as God and prayer. Each of these cultural constructs involves processes (e.g., direct mental-physical causality in the case of wishing and possibly praying) or properties (e.g., immaterial beings with powers to affect the material) that appear to run counter to guiding principles in children's developing knowledge of mind-world relations. As Boyer (1995) puts it, "... religious assumptions in general seem to imply particularly strange notions as concerns the causal properties of particular objects or entities." This chapter explores the nature of the interplay between children's beliefs about natural mental-physical causal relations and their participation in the practices of imagination, magic, and religion.

### Causal Relations Between Mental and Physical

Before discussing relevant empirical findings, a discussion of causal relations must be undertaken. There is some debate as to whether humans operate with general causal principles or whether our causal reasoning is specific to particular domains (Spelke, Phillips, & Woodward, 1995). Subbotsky (this volume), for example, distinguishes two types of causality – psychological and natural-physical. The former involves a subject's wish or thought producing physical events either in a normal way (e.g., moving one's body) or via magic, and the latter involves interactions between physical events. He then adds a third type of causality – phenomenalistic causality – on which he focuses in his chapter.

For the purposes of the present chapter we can divide the world into two classes of processes – mental and physical – and two types of causal effects or changes – mental and physical. In doing so we can conceive of a number of different sorts of causal interactions, involving purely physical objects as well as intentional (or, for our purposes, human) beings. In fact, as illustrated in Table 4.1, these types of causal effects can be further subdivided into interindividual and intraindivi-

Table 4.1. *Instances of Direct Causal Processes and their Effects*

| | Nature of process | |
| --- | --- | --- |
| *Nature of change* | *Physical* | *Mental* |
| Physical | | |
| Interindividual | Launching event Push someone down | IMPOSSIBLE |
| Intraindividual | t.v. circuits | Decide to cross leg → crossing leg Chewing food → saliva |
| Mental | | |
| Interindividual | Hug someone → feel happy | IMPOSSIBLE |
| Intraindividual | Run for bus → memory of days as athlete | Think of event → feel sad |

dual. Much empirical work has documented that even infants are aware of the sorts of direct causal relations that exist between one physical object and another physical object (Leslie & Keeble, 1987; Oakes & Cohen, 1990; Spelke, Spelke, Phillips, & Woodward, 1995; see also upper left cell of Table 4.1). This work is important to consider because it challenges the traditional Piagetian view that infants' thinking is dominated by "magical" causality. Certain interactions between humans can also be placed in this cell, including events in which a physical action (e.g., pushing) has a direct physical effect (e.g., someone falling down). It is not yet clear what infants understand about these sorts of interactions, although Spelke et al. (1995) are also beginning to address this question in their research. We can also consider what sorts of interactions are possible not just between physical objects, but within them (i.e., intraindividually). For example, physical objects such as televisions and computers have electrical circuits that involve causal relations between various physical locations. Similarly, concerning humans, physical actions (e.g., chewing food) can directly cause certain physical reactions (e.g., production of saliva) within our own body.

Physical processes can also directly cause mental changes (lower left cell). Interindividually, a physical act, such as hugging, can cause someone to have a change in emotion (e.g., from sadness to happiness). Within an individual, a physical action, such as running to catch a bus, might produce a mental state of memory – in this case, one's days as a college athlete.

The cells of most interest for the purposes of this chapter are the two on the right, in which we consider the nature of direct causal relations involving mental processes. Intraindividual processes in the upper right cell represent psychophysical causality – even mental processes can directly result in physical changes within an individual. For example, one's decision or intention to cross one's leg (a mental event) will, in most cases, directly result in one's legs being crossed (a physical change). Research by Inagaki and Hatano (1996) reveals a sharp transition between the ages of three and four in children's understanding of the ways in which the mind can and cannot control bodily processes, with younger children seeming to overextend the limits of such controllability. Thoughts can also directly cause other mental events intraindividually; for example, if one thinks about a troubling event (a mental process), one may feel sad (a change in emotion; lower right cell). Importantly, however, the theory of mind of most Western adults does not allow for the extension of these processes interindividually. That is, most adults in our culture do not believe that their own thoughts alone may directly cause another individual to feel a certain way or to behave a certain way; one does not expect to make someone feel happy just by mentally "sending" them good thoughts (although it is surprising how often we engage in these kinds of casual interchanges with others, e.g., "I'll send some good vibes your way . . . ," etc.). Similarly, mental processes are not expected to have direct physical effects; that is, one does not expect to achieve changes in physical objects (e.g., opening a door) through mental activity alone (e.g., willing it to open). These two subcells are labeled "IMPOSSIBLE" in Table 4.1.

As discussed, direct mental-physical causality in the intraindividual sense is probably a fairly common experience, at least for adults. Thus it is possible that children's first experiences of mental-physical causality are of this sort. That is, young children may hold some awareness that they can, for instance, think about moving a part of their body, and that this thought alone can cause the movement. Even if this process is not available for conscious consideration, simply experiencing it may aid in children's expectations about causal processes. Because children experience this sort of causality within themselves, they may expect it to be a normal process that operates in other causal relations as well, such as between themselves and other people or between themselves and physical objects. It is also possible that children do not reflect at all on this process. For example, results from Johnson and Wellman (1982) suggest that these sorts of "brain activity causing physical action" processes are not available for conscious consideration until at least age nine, and maybe later. Finally, children may, at a very young age, have an awareness of this sort of causality but understand that it is not effective outside of the individual.

### Early Beliefs About Mental-Physical Causality

According to Piaget (1929), young children's confusion between thoughts and things results in a variety of mistaken beliefs about the causal relations between the mind and the physical world. These include beliefs that reality can be modified by a thought ("magic by participation between thoughts and things"), that an action or mental operation, such as counting to ten, can exert an influence on a desired event ("magic by participation between actions and things"), and that an object can be used to influence another object ("magic by participation between objects"). Piaget's interviews with children suggested to him that such beliefs are present through the concrete operations period, that is, until age eleven or twelve. Importantly, for Piaget, these sorts of "magical" beliefs are a direct outgrowth of children's confusion about the distinction between the mind and the world. Thus, it follows that once children have achieved a full understanding of the distinction between mental and physical, these types of magical thinking should cease or, at most, appear very infrequently and without much conviction.[2]

Although the bulk of research on children's theories of mind indicates that young children have impressive levels of understanding of the relations between thoughts and things, some research indicates that young children do entertain seemingly magical beliefs in mental-physical causality. Henry Wellman and I (Woolley & Wellman, 1993)

---

[2] Piaget (1929) distinguishes between "individual child magic" and "collective" or social magic. The sorts of beliefs discussed here refer to what Piaget termed "individual child magic." Piaget did believe that "collective" or social magical beliefs would increase with age as a function of exposure to adult cultural beliefs and practices, although he does not discuss this at any length.

investigated young children's beliefs about mental-physical causal relations in the domain of imagination. In one study, we told three- and four-year-old children stories about characters who were imagining the contents of a container. For example, a girl found a bag in her living room and imagined that there were some flowers in it. Children had to judge first whether these characters really believed that the object they had imagined was in the container, and, second, whether the characters would be likely to actually find the imagined objects when they looked in the containers. Although most children by the age of four judged imagination to be a poor guide to the nature of reality, a number of three-year-olds (43%) seemed to believe that imagination accurately reflected or possibly even created reality. These children claimed that the story characters, having imagined various objects in the containers, would actually find the objects when they looked inside. In a second study, the children themselves imagined objects inside empty boxes and then judged whether the objects really were inside. With this procedure, most older three-year-olds (83%) demonstrated an understanding that imagination does not reflect or create reality. Many younger three-year-olds (57%), on the other hand, exhibited what we termed the "true fiction" error, erroneously claiming that the objects they had imagined really existed inside the boxes.

A series of studies by Harris, Brown, Marriot, Whittall, and Harmer (1991) yielded similar findings, with a somewhat different developmental trajectory. Four- and six-year-old children were instructed to imagine that a monster was inside one empty box and that a puppy was inside another. Then the experimenter left the room and videotaped the children's behavior. These researchers found that even some six-year-old children acted as if the creatures were really inside the boxes, as reflected in their willingness to approach the "puppy" box and put their finger inside, and their avoidance and fear of the "monster" box. The authors suggest that children of this age may not know enough about the causal links between mind and reality to be sure that an imagined creature cannot become real.

Providing support for the claim that the aforementioned findings are not specific to supernatural creatures, Johnson and Harris (1994) used a similar procedure to Harris et al., but, instead of having the children imagine supernatural creatures, they had them imagine an everyday object, such as ice cream. They then assessed the children's behavior toward the box in which they had imagined the ice cream, and compared that to their behavior toward a box in which they had not imagined anything. They found similar results as in Harris et al., with three-to seven-year-old children acting as if they believed imagination to reflect reality. They suggest that, "when some children imagine an outcome, it leads them to wonder whether such an outcome has actually occurred, even if its occurrence would be magical" (Johnson & Harris, 1994, p. 21). However, Johnson and Harris argue that this does not imply that children are confused about mental-physical causal relations. Rather, drawing on Tversky and Kahneman's (1973) availability heuristic, they suggest that when children imagine an entity inside a box, the possibility that it might be there is judged as being more likely than it might otherwise be. This availability, in combination with latent magical beliefs that some children may possess, causes children to entertain seriously the possibility of the imagined object's existence.

Katrina Phelps and I (Woolley & Phelps, 1994) added a new dimension to this issue. In two studies, we assessed three-and four-year-old children's understanding of causal relations between imagination and reality. Our approach differed from that of Harris, et al. (1991) and Johnson and Harris (1994) in that the children were placed in what we considered a practical situation. Rather than simply making verbal judgments about the existence of the objects, as in my own earlier work, or behavioral decisions without clear consequences, as in Harris et al. and in Johnson and Harris, we required the children to make a behavioral response that had specific practical consequences for another person. We first asked the children to imagine an object in a box. After the children had imagined an object inside a box, an unfamiliar person entered the room and requested the very same type of object that the children had imagined. The children had to decide whether to give this person the box in which they had imagined the object. The results showed that children under these conditions rarely gave the person the box in which they had imagined the object. In other words, they rarely behaved as if they believed imagination to create reality. We concluded that, although young children at times may indulge in the possibility that imagination can directly alter physical reality, when there are real-world costs or consequences of their actions, they do not.

The results of this set of studies suggest that the practice of engaging in fantastical thinking regarding mental-physical causality may first involve a simple cost-benefit analysis. Children, and possibly also adults, before engaging in such thinking, may first assess both what the potential benefits are of doing so, and what the risks or costs might be. In our experimental situation (Woolley & Phelps, 1994) the children may have realized that acting as if the box did have the desired object inside would have a negative effect on another person or bring negative repercussions. As there was no clear advantage for them to engage in a fantastical response, the potential cost of doing so weighed more heavily than the benefit, leading them to produce a practical response. In other studies, for example, those of Harris and colleagues, there was no cost to children in their entertaining the possibility that their imagination had created the creatures, and there was a potential benefit. There is a clear benefit to entertaining the idea of a cute puppy appearing in a box, and there may even be some benefit of seriously considering the possibility that a monster is in a box (e.g., if you are being asked to put a finger into the box, as the children in these studies were, it may pay to err on the safe side).

Alternatively, it is also possible that different sorts of processes operate when children imagine negative versus positive things. Regarding positive things, the child's desire for the object may override his/her tendency to focus on the reality status of the item, leading to increased claims of its existence. Concerning negative items, simply imagining something scary may produce a feeling of fear in the child. In trying to interpret the source of the physiological symptoms they are experiencing, children may make something like the following assumption: Because the fear I feel is real, something real must have caused it. In other words, children may not be entirely aware that thoughts alone may be the direct cause of fear. This clearly is an empirical question.

However, despite children's apparent sophistication in the practical situation used by Woolley and Phelps (1994), beliefs in mental-physical causality do seem to be evident in young children in certain situations. What is the developmental future of these early beliefs in mental-physical causality? My own research on imagination (Woolley & Phelps, 1994; Woolley & Wellman, 1993) indicates that, in certain situations, children can demonstrate very mature beliefs about mental-physical causal relations, thus strongly suggesting that their thinking is not dominated by "magical causality." But do beliefs in mental-physical causality disappear entirely by the age of four? If this were true, this would be a very short chapter. In fact, focusing only on topics that fall squarely within children's "theories of mind," such as pretense and imagination, might lead to such a conclusion. But I will suggest that these beliefs do not disappear, but are reintroduced to children by our culture in a new form. That is, at about the age of three or four, children are introduced to various practices that promote the belief that one can bring about physical changes by engaging in mental activities. These include the activity of wishing.

*Beliefs in Wishing*

LISA:  Do plants wish for baby plants?

DEANA:  I think only people can make wishes. But God could put a wish inside a plant.

TEACHER:  What would the wish be?

DEANA:  What if it's a pretty flower? Then God puts an idea inside to make this plant into a pretty red flower – if it's supposed to be red.

TEACHER:  I always think of people as having ideas.

DEANA:  It's just the same. God puts a little idea in the plant to tell it what to be.

LISA:  My mother wished for me and I came when it was my birthday.[3]

As stated earlier, Piaget's (1929) position was that beliefs in magical processes such as wishing are a direct result of a lack of differentiation between the mental and physical. According to Piaget, mastering this distinction should lead to the end of this sort of magical thinking. The research reviewed in the previous section, along with much additional research on children's theories of mind, indicates that children have a solid grasp of the distinction between mental and physical by the age of three. Yet the sorts of ideas expressed in the conversation above are common among young children, or at least most of us believe that they are. Along with considerable anecdotal evidence, the folklore of childhood generally suggests that young children maintain beliefs in the magical process of wishing. These beliefs appear to linger long after children have achieved a sophisticated knowledge of mind-world relations.

How could this be? Resolution of this paradox could potentially be achieved in one of two ways: (1) It may be that anecdotal reports are

---

[3] Paley, V. G. (1981). *Wally's Stories*, pp. 79–80. Cambridge, MA: Harvard University Press.

misleading – empirical investigations may find that children really do not believe in wishing; or (2) empirical investigations may reveal that, despite considerable knowledge about the nature of mind-world relations, children still do believe in wishing. This latter conclusion would indicate that Piaget's proposed relation between children's mental-physical understanding and their magical thinking was wrong. The research discussed next is aimed at determining which of these proposals best resolves the paradox.

Beyond Piaget's writings, there has been almost no empirical work on children's beliefs about wishing. One published empirical study investigates children's beliefs about mental processes having mental effects, in other words, children's beliefs about their own and others' abilities to control other peoples' thoughts by thinking alone. Vikan and Clausen (1993) showed four- and six-year-old participants drawings of children in various scenes, for example, a picture of a child at school. The participants were told that the child in the drawing was making a wish in an attempt to influence a person depicted in another scene, for example, the child's mother, who was depicted as being at home. The children were then asked to indicate the effectiveness of the wish. The results showed that young children believe that they can influence others by wishing; 94% of the four- to six-year-old children tested professed a belief in what Vikan and Clausen term "control by thinking" at one or more points in the testing session. Vikan and Clausen (1993) interpreted their results as indicating that, "despite all modern evidence that suggests children are precocious rationalists, it would appear that the 'childish' young child is still with us" (p. 310).

Although this study is important in empirically demonstrating beliefs in wishing, it is limited in certain respects. First, Vikan and Clausen focused entirely on the children's beliefs about the efficacy of wishing; they did not assess the children's conceptions of the nature of wishing. Thus we do not know, for example, the extent to which children see wishing as more than just wanting something, nor what mental and/or magical processes children believe to be involved in wishing. Second, their questions regarding efficacy were arguably somewhat leading. The children were asked, "What do you think (the influencee) will (do, feel, think) when (the influencer) wishes that (the influencee) should (do, feel, think) a certain way?" It may have been difficult for the children to think of a response to this question other than the one suggested by the question, which may have led to an overestimation of the children's beliefs in efficacy. Finally, all of the stories dealt with influencing someone's mental processes through wishing; children's beliefs about affecting a physical object through wishing may differ.

Our first investigation into children's concepts of wishing involved fifty preschool-age children divided for purposes of analysis into older (five to six years old) and younger (three to four years old) groups (Woolley, Phelps, Davis, & Mandell, 1999). The children we tested were middle- to upper middle-class children, and were predominantly Caucasian. Approximately half attended a Montessori preschool, and the other half were recruited from birth announcements in the local paper. We began our investigation with a structured interview that assessed two issues: (1) children's wish concepts, and (2) children's beliefs in the efficacy of wishing (i.e., whether it "works"). Regarding children's conceptions of wishing, the interview included a number of questions as well as two embedded tasks. We began by asking the children questions about their familiarity with the general concept: The children were asked if they knew what it meant to make a wish, and whether they had ever made a wish. We also gave the children two structured tasks designed to assess what they thought were necessary components of wishing. The first task (the Entity Task) involved presenting the children with a number of entities (adults, children, babies, cats and dogs, flowers, and tables) and asking them to indicate which of these entities possessed the ability to make wishes. The second task (the Teaching Task) asked the children to instruct a naive puppet in the art of wishing. The puppet was presented as being ignorant of how to wish but wanting to learn, and the children were asked to teach him how.

To assess beliefs about efficacy, in the interview the children were asked whether their own past wishes had come true, and whether wishes in general come true. To further assess the children's beliefs about efficacy, we also gave the children a Prediction Task. In this task, the children made a wish for an object in a box and were asked to evaluate whether the object had materialized upon wishing for it. Finally, we concluded each session with a Judgment Task, aimed to provide information about the children's beliefs about the role of thinking in wishing. The children were shown line drawings of children who were described as being engaged in various activities, some

Table 4.2. *First Wishing Study: Percent Affirmative Responses to Interview Questions*

|  |  | Younger children (3–4) | Older children (5–6) |
|---|---|---|---|
| Interview questions |  |  |  |
| Do you know what it means to make a wish? |  | 65 | 93 |
| Have you ever made a wish? |  | 53 | 76 |
| Do wishes come true? | Always: | 22 | 0 |
|  | Sometimes: | 74 | 95 |
| Did your own wishes come true? |  | 56 | 38 |
| Prediction Task |  |  |  |
| Will the (object) be in the box? |  | 71 | 31 |

of which explicitly involved thinking, and others that did not. After hearing each story, the children were asked to indicate whether the child in the story was wishing.

The interview questions revealed considerable familiarity with wishing in both age groups, but significantly greater familiarity in the older group. As can be seen in Table 4.2, although a majority of the younger children knew about wishing, more older than younger children claimed to have such knowledge. More older than younger children also claimed to have made a wish themselves. Regarding beliefs about efficacy, the children tended to become more skeptical with age. For example, when asked whether wishing in general comes true, more older than younger children endorsed a response of "sometimes"; the younger children were more likely to endorse a response of "always" than were the older children. On the prediction task, in which the children had the opportunity to wish for an object of their choosing, the results revealed much stronger beliefs in the efficacy of wishing in the younger group. These results indicate that, as in Vikan and Clausen's (1993) study, preschool-age children do maintain beliefs in wishing, but beliefs in efficacy appear to decrease during these years.

One goal of our first study was to go beyond Vikan and Clausen in trying to determine what children believe to be the processes behind a wish. One way we did this was to ask the children to identify what sorts of entities have the ability to wish. We asked the children about adults, children, babies, cats and dogs, flowers, and tables. As is apparent in Table 4.3, almost all of the children acknowledged that

Table 4.3. *Entity Task: Results from First Wish Study and Prayer Study*

|  | 3- to 4-year olds | | 5- to 6-year-olds | | 7- to 8-year-olds |
|  | *Wish* | *Pray* | *Wish* | *Pray* | *Pray* |
|---|---|---|---|---|---|
| Adults | 96 | 94 | 91 | 100 | 100 |
| Children | 92 | 90 | 96 | 100 | 100 |
| Babies | 28 | 50 | 65 | 67 | 60 |
| Cats and dogs | 42 | 26 | 33 | 43 | 45 |
| Flowers | 27 | 15 | 10 | 36 | 10 |
| Tables | 15 | 22 | 9 | 27 | 7 |

children and adults can wish. The children also agreed that tables cannot wish. But the older children were significantly more likely than the younger children to say that babies can wish. Interestingly, the younger children more often responded that cats and dogs can wish than that babies can wish, whereas the reverse was true for the older children.

Information from both the Teaching Task and the Judgment Task provided further evidence about what children consider important components of wishing. When asked to teach the puppet how to wish, the majority of the children in both age groups told him that he needed to think of something. The children in the older age group instructed him that he needed to say something; the younger children were much less likely to do this. Many of the children also told the puppet that his eyes needed to be closed. When presented with a number of characters engaged in various activities, some of which were thinking and some not, the children were significantly more likely to claim that the characters who were thinking about something were wishing than to claim this for the characters who were described as: just wanting, having their eyes closed, rubbing an ordinary stone, and looking for something. Thus, children clearly see thinking as an important component of wishing.

The children's responses to the questions in this study revealed a growing awareness of the concept of wishing during the preschool years. Many children in both the younger and older age groups were familiar with the concept of wishing, although the results did reveal significantly greater familiarity and experience with wishing in the older group. Younger children tended to report less knowledge about wishing and claimed to have had fewer personal experiences with wishing. Interestingly, even though the older children appeared to be more familiar with the concept of wishing, they were also somewhat more skeptical about its efficacy. This sort of transition could result from a number of different processes. Older children may simply be becoming more critical or more skeptical in general. Alternatively, their skepticism may be empirically based and specific to wishing; they may have tried numerous times to wish for things without success and simply deduced that it does not work. It may also be that the sorts of things that younger children wish for are simpler and more likely to be obtained anyway, giving younger children the illusion that their wishing is working; whereas older children's wishes, being more complex, are less likely to be realized through other means. A systematic investigation of children's explanations for why wishes do not "work" might illuminate this issue further. In general, it seems that the span during which children are true believers in this means of direct mental-physical causality may be fairly short-lived: A beginning sense of the concept is present in young preschoolers, but doubts have already begun to appear by the late preschool years.

Results also indicated that, as children get older, they may perceive wishing to be more of a uniquely human activity. Although both the older and younger children claimed that adults and children can wish, the older children were more likely to claim that (human) babies can wish. Specifically, the older children were more likely to claim that babies can wish than that animals can wish, whereas the younger children said the reverse. However, even the youngest children acknowledged that wishing was the providence of animate or live beings only, as very few contended that tables have this ability. The younger children's claims that cats and dogs but not babies are capable of wishing may reflect a conception of wishing as an ability that one has to acquire with time, whether as a result of experience, teaching, or simply development.

In the Teaching Task, the children in both age groups consistently told the puppet that he needed to think of something. In the Judgment Tasks, the children of both age groups claimed that characters who were described as thinking about something were wishing. These results suggest that thinking is, for both age groups, a necessary component of wishing, which is consistent with the idea that beliefs about wishing involve beliefs about mental-physical causality. This finding may indicate that older children's greater tendency to say that babies can wish is due to a greater understanding that babies think. Oddly, the older children also seemed to believe that talking was necessary for wishing, which seems to contradict their claims that babies are able to make wishes. Solicitation of explanations would clarify some of these issues. We did this in a second study.

In this study we tested ninety-two children between the ages of three and six – forty-two younger preschool-age children and fifty older preschool-age children. These children were of similar race and social class as the children in Study 1, the only difference being that approximately half of the children attended a day-care center affiliated with a local Presbyterian Church. The goal of this study was to probe further how concepts of wishing are situated with regard to children's theories of mind and their beliefs about magic.

We used two tasks to address beliefs about the magical nature of wishing. The first task was designed to assess the children's beliefs about whether wishing is a magical process. The children were told, "Now we're going to talk about some different things that happen. Some of them are magic and some of them are not magic. This puppet doesn't know very much about all these things, and he wants you to help him figure out which things are magic and which things are not magic. I'll say the things, and you tell Sweet Pea whether they're magic or not magic. O.K.?" There were two prototypically magical events – a frog turning into a princess and a genie emerging from a lamp – and two natural events – water coming out of a faucet and a light being turned on. The children were asked, for example, for the faucet item, "When you turn on the faucet and water comes out . . . is that magic or not magic?" The purpose of presenting these items before the focal wishing item was twofold. First, we wanted the children to be aware that both affirmative and negative responses were valued. Second, we wanted to obtain a baseline rate of responding for both natural and magical events with which to compare the children's responses to the focal wish question. The events were presented in the following order: faucet, frog, genie, light. After responding to these four events, the children were asked whether a wish coming true is magical or not magical.

Second, the children were asked to make a wish of their own, predict whether it would come true, and explain the outcome of the wish. The purpose of this task was to determine whether the children explain successful acts of wishing by evoking magic. The experimenter showed the children a trick box that appeared to be empty. After agreeing that the box was empty, the children were encouraged to make a wish for a penny. Before the experimenter reopened the box, the children were asked if they thought that the penny would be there or not ("Tell me, what's in the box now – is there a penny in there, or is it empty?"). After it was revealed that there was a penny inside the box, the children were asked how it got there and if they thought that their wish made it happen. If the children claimed that they thought that their wish made the penny appear, they were asked if the event was magic or not magic. If the children responded that the event was magic, they were asked whether they considered it to be real magic or a trick.

To address relations between wishing and other mental activities in children's theories of mind we presented the children with a task concerning what types of entities can want, think, and make wishes. We asked about adults, babies, cats and dogs, and flowers. For wishing children were asked, "First I'm going to ask you about who can make wishes. Can_____wish for something?"; for thinking, "Now I'm going to ask you about who can think. Can_____think about something?"; and for wanting, "Now I want to ask you about who can want something. Can_____want something?" The purpose of asking about these different mental activities was to assess the children's beliefs about the roles of wanting and thinking in wishing. In other words, if a child judged an entity as being able to want or think something, would s/he also judge that the entity could wish? Similarly, if a child denied an entity the ability to wish, was it because this entity lacked the ability to want, or the ability to think? For the wishing questions, the children were asked to explain why each entity could or could not wish.

Finally, we also gave the children a magic trick task to assess their general magical orientation. This task involved a coin bank that had one transparent side and appeared to have a box suspended in the middle of it. The experimenter asked the children whether, if a coin was dropped into a slot at the top of the bank, it would hit the inner box. The experimenter then dropped the coin into the bank while the children looked through the transparent window. The coin seemed to disappear. The children were asked what happened to the coin and whether they thought it was magic. If they answered that they thought it was magic, they were asked if it was real magic or a trick. This task was selected from the tasks used in Phelps and Woolley (1994) as a task that yielded information that was representative of children's general magical orientation.

The results indicated that, for the most part, children believe wishing to be a magical and not an ordinary process. When asked to classify events as to their magical nature, the majority of the children (57% of the younger children and 74% of the older children) claimed that wishing involved magic. The older children were very clear in their classification of magical and nonmagical events. Whereas only 16% of the older children claimed that turning on a faucet and getting water was magical and only 18% claimed that turning on a light was magical, 78% claimed that a frog turning into a princess was magical.[4] Thus, with 74% claiming that wishing was magical, the older children were clearly grouping wishing with other magical events. The younger children's classifications were somewhat more ambiguous. Like the older children, many (67%) claimed that a frog turning into a princess was magical. At the same time, however, the same number (67%) claimed that turning on a light was also a magical event. However, as only a minority of the younger children (36%) claimed that turning on a faucet and getting water was magical, it was not the case that the younger children simply claimed that all of the presented events were magical. It seems that those young children who do view wishing as magical may cast a wider net over the things in their life that they see as involving magic.

Regarding those children who claimed, on seeing a wished-for penny appear in a previously empty box, that their wish had made the penny appear, almost all of these children claimed that this event was of a magical nature. Further, most (73%) claimed that it was real magic, and not a trick. A closer look at the data revealed that whereas most five-years-olds claimed that the magic involved in wishing was real, few six-year-olds made this claim. This indicated that, even though six-year-olds still claimed that wishing involved magic, the nature of the magic was for them in the form of a trick, and not of a direct mental-physical causal nature. This finding, that older children come to view magic in this way, is consistent with similar findings by Rosengren and Hickling (1994) and Phelps and Woolley (1994). Finally, the children who scored high in general magical orientation were more likely to say that wishing had caused the penny to appear in the box than were the children who scored low in magical orientation. These data indicate that children think of wishing as a magical

---

[4] Due to a lack of clarity in the phrasing of the question the genie question was dropped from the analyses.

rather than an ordinary process, and that children may situate their concepts of wishing more within their "theories" of magic than within their theories of mind.[5]

Regarding the sorts of mental processes that children implicate in wishing, we found that children of both younger and older age groups claimed that adults were able to wish, want, and think (see Table 4.4). Children of both age groups claimed that adults could do everything – wish, want, and think. Children of both age groups also claimed that babies could want, fewer claimed that babies could think, and even fewer claimed that babies could wish. This pattern suggests that neither wanting nor thinking is viewed as entirely sufficient for wishing. Responses for cats and dogs were nearly identical to the responses for babies. Lastly, 60% of the children claimed that flowers could want. Although 49% of the younger children claimed that flowers could think, only 17% of the older children made this claim. Very few children in either age group claimed that flowers could wish. This again suggests that wanting alone is not seen as sufficient for wishing and further supports the claim that, although thinking may be necessary, it also is not sufficient. Finally, inspection of the third column in Table 4.4, containing the percentage of children claiming that each entity could both want and think, reveals that wanting and thinking together still fall short of wishing; there is clearly something more involved in wishing.

To shed further light on this issue, children's explanations for why various entities could or could not wish were examined. These explanations typically fell into one of six categories: (1) appeals to mental states or processes (e.g., "they can use their imagination," "they don't know anything"); (2) appeals to verbal ability (e.g., "they can't talk"); (3) appeals to physical features (e.g., "because it has eyes," "it doesn't have a mouth"); (4) reference to the content of a wish (e.g., "they wish for water"); (5) appeals to the nature of the entity (e.g., "because they're just plants"); and (6) "don't know" or incomprehensible (e.g., "because"). Children in the younger age group most often appealed to physical properties (42%), but also often appealed to verbal abilities

---

[5] My use of the term *theory* here is not meant to imply any strong claims that children's early magical beliefs are theory-like, at least not to the degree that their beliefs about the mind are theory-like. Rather, I suspect that children's early magical beliefs form something more like what Rosengren and Hickling (this volume) term an "alternative causal model."

Table 4.4. *Second Wishing Study: Children's Responses to Who Can Wish, Think, and Want*

|  | Think | | Want | | Think and Want | | Wish | |
|---|---|---|---|---|---|---|---|---|
|  | Younger | Older | Younger | Older | Younger | Older | Younger | Older |
| Adults | 91 | 100 | 96 | 100 | 90 | 100 | 91 | 96 |
| Babies | 78 | 89 | 93 | 94 | 76 | 81 | 58 | 65 |
| Cats and dogs | 73 | 85 | 93 | 91 | 69 | 81 | 57 | 55 |
| Flowers | 49 | 17 | 58 | 62 | 40 | 17 | 20 | 13 |

*Note:* Responses reported are percentages.

(15%), mental states (10%), and the nature of the entity (19%). The modal explanation type of the older children was an appeal to mental states and processes when explaining why an entity could wish (32%) and to both mental states and talking (29% each) when explaining why an entity could not wish. To illustrate the types of mental explanations we received, in explaining adults' abilities to wish, children said things like "because they have brains" and "by using their mind." Children noted that babies can wish because they "say something in their mind" and "they use their heads – tiny wishes." In reference to cats and dogs, in explaining their inability, children said, "they don't know anything," and in explaining their ability, "they can think what they want to wish for."

Results of this second study confirm the pattern found in our first study, that children's beliefs in the efficacy of wishing begin to build in the early preschool years and appear to diminish by the end of the preschool years. Asking children about who can think and want, in tandem with asking them who can wish, yielded more precise information about what abilities children believe to be necessary for wishing to occur. Children's explanations indicate that linguistic and mental abilities are critical in being able to wish. Yet although children do consider wishing to involve both thinking and wanting, our tasks revealed that neither the ability to want nor the ability to think is sufficient for being able to wish. So wishing for something and simply thinking about something are not the same thing. Clearly there is something more and something special about wishing.

We hypothesized that this "something" may have to do with children's beliefs about magic. That is, we suspected that, although children implicate mental processes in wishing, they may subject the process of wishing not to their theories of mind but to their "theories" of magic. Our various tasks revealed that most of the children we tested viewed wishing as a magical process, not an ordinary one, although older children were slightly more likely than younger ones to espouse this belief. Children's beliefs about wishing also appeared to be related to their general magical orientation. Children with low beliefs in magic were unlikely to explain the "magical" appearance of an object in a box as being the result of wishing, whereas children with high magical beliefs did explain the event in terms of wishing.

The results of these two studies on children's beliefs about wishing indicate that many preschool-age children have a rich set of beliefs about wishing, and that they view it as a magical instance of mental-physical causality. Yet by the age of six, few children believe in the efficacy of wishing. However, I argue again, beliefs in mental-physical causality do not disappear entirely but are reaffirmed by our culture, this time via religion. The final area of research I discuss deals with children's beliefs about the nature of prayer.

## Beliefs about Prayer

Historically, one can find clear connections between magic and religion. According to Goode (1951), for example, magic and religion show the following similarities: Both are concerned with the nonempirical, both stand in opposition to science, both rely heavily on symbolism and rituals, and both deal with nonhuman forces and contain entities with human characteristics (see also Zusne & Jones, 1989, for discussions of similarities between magic and religion). Clearly there are also important differences between magic and religion, but the presence of these conceptual similarities urges consideration of possible relations between children's magical and religious beliefs. Specifically, for the purpose of this chapter, I will consider the nature of children's beliefs about prayer. Praying and wishing share a number of conceptual similarities, most notably that both involve internal mental processes aimed at bringing about external, often physical changes in the absence of intervening physical action on the part of the person wishing or praying. What do we know about young children's conceptions of prayers and praying?

Surprisingly, children's early understanding of prayer is an infrequently studied topic, even within the study of Western children's religious understanding. Goldman (1964), primarily interested in the effectiveness of religious education, carried out a study on the religious concepts of children aged six to sixteen. One of his foci was children's beliefs about the efficacy of prayer. He showed children a picture of a child praying, and found that almost all of the children he tested responded to the question, "Does what the child asks for in prayer ever come true?" in the affirmative. In soliciting children's explanations for how the child might know that the prayer came true, he suggests four stages in children's thinking. The first stage reflects what he calls "magical concepts," the second is "semi-magical," the third is nonmagical and incorporates more "rational" concepts, and the last is a more faith-based stage. The "magical stage" was found to characterize children's thinking up to the age of nine.

There are some studies of adolescents' understanding of prayer (e.g., Scarlett & Perriello, 1991), but there is only one comprehensive study of understanding of prayer that includes young children. I will describe this study in detail to provide the reader with some background and a sense of the extant state of our knowledge of this issue. Long, Elkind, and Spilka (1967) assessed elementary-school children's understanding of the nature, content, and affect of prayer. Framed within a Piagetian tradition, children's understanding of the nature of prayer was assessed by asking them to answer the question, "What is prayer?" The children's responses to this question were interpreted by the authors to indicate a stagelike progression in their understanding. At the age of five to seven years, children were found to have a "vague and indistinct notion of prayer," and a "dim awareness" that prayers were somehow linked with the term "God." Children of this age were also inconsistent and unclear regarding the capacity of animals (cats and dogs) for praying. There certainly was no evidence of an understanding that prayer involved anything like thinking, which casts doubt on the idea that young children might see it as a form of mental-physical causality.

Between the ages of seven and nine, children were reported to conceive of prayer "in terms of particular and appropriate activities." Children at this stage were said to conceive of prayer in terms of its associated behaviors, and still were not cognizant of its mental or affective aspects. Essentially, to children at this age prayer was synonymous with "verbal request." As a consequence children of this age judged that animals cannot pray simply because they cannot talk. Only by age nine or ten were children found to think of prayer "as a type of private conversation with God." At this age, according to the authors, children make a distinction between what one thinks and what one says; in other words, they recognize that prayer involves thought and belief. Children at this stage still claimed that animals cannot pray, but claimed that this was due to a lack of knowledge or intelligence rather than verbal skills. Around this age children also began to associate praying with believing in God. Interestingly, the authors also state that there was an increased recognition in these older children that "God[was] a helper and not a magic genie who simply[made]one's wishes come true," implying that this latter form was the way in which the younger children conceived of God. If this were true, it would suggest interesting and potentially important continuities between children's wish concepts and their early religious beliefs.

Finally, two of Long, et al.'s (1967) questions, "Where do prayers come from?" and "Where do prayers go to?" revealed some interesting ideas about causality. The youngest children seemed to view prayers as self-propelled, in that they often claimed that prayers "float," "fly," or "jump" to Heaven. Others at this age stated that God brought prayers to Heaven by magical means, again suggesting continuity between magical and early religious beliefs. The intermediate age group most often claimed that prayers were carried to God by messengers or intermediaries. Some children at this stage claimed that God actually came to pick up the prayers. These responses are interesting because they suggest other processes by which praying might operate than mental-physical causality. Finally, the oldest children claimed that prayers are heard by God directly, that praying is a form of direct communication.

Our research on children's understanding of prayer encompassed a variety of issues. Anecdotal evidence, as well as various findings from the Long et al. research, suggested resemblances of children's early prayer concepts to their concepts of wishing. To enable us to probe possible similarities and continuities, many of our interview questions paralleled those that we asked in the wish research. Thus, we asked the children if they knew what it meant to pray and whether they had ever prayed, as well as whether their own prayers had been granted and whether prayers in general are granted. We also addressed other issues specific to the nature of praying, such as the role of knowledge about God, and whether, when praying, one must say the prayer aloud or whether one can say it "in your head."

As in the wish studies, we employed a task in which the children were required to judge whether a variety of entities (adults, children, babies, cats and dogs, flowers, and tables) had the ability to pray. The children were also given a task in which they were asked to teach a puppet how to pray. They were told that the puppet's dog was sick and that he wanted to say a prayer for his dog but did not know how. The children were simply asked to tell him how.

Participants in this study were ninety-nine three to eight-year-olds. Approximately two-thirds were from day-care centers, one affiliated with a Methodist church and one with an Episcopal church, and the remaining third was recruited from birth announcements in local papers. The parents of all but three children described their religious affiliation as Christian, and most considered themselves moderately active in their religion. The parents reported an average of two different types of religious activities in which they regularly engaged at their home, and an average of two different activities in which they regularly engaged at their place of worship. These activities included praying, singing, Sunday school, and reading Bible stories. Sixty-seven percent of the parents reported that they prayed at home, and 67% reported that they attended church regularly.[6] Ninety-four percent reported that they talked regularly with their child about religion. Most parents reported moderate encouragement of their child's involvement in religious activities, which primarily involved prayer at home (68%) and attendance at church or Sunday school (68%).[7]

Results of this study indicated that, as with wishing, children become familiar with praying during the preschool years. There were sharp increases from age four to age five in children's claims that they knew what it meant to pray and that they had themselves prayed. What does prayer involve for these young children? As the topic of this chapter is children's beliefs about mental-physical causality, I will focus on children's responses regarding the role of thinking in prayer. We found a significant increase in the number of children who claimed that praying involves saying something "in your head" between the ages of four and five. Similarly, whereas only a minority of three and four-year-olds told the puppet he needed to think to pray, the majority of children five years and older instructed the puppet

[6] This is most likely a conservative estimate, as the majority of the remaining parents left this question blank. Because there was no "none" option for parents to check, it is not clear whether these parents truly did not engage in these activities or simply skipped this item for some reason.

[7] See note 5.

this way. In contrast, the majority of children in all age groups in the wish study told the puppet that to wish he needed to think of something. Thus it appears that, whereas wishing may involve thinking from the start, children may not conceive of prayer as involving mental activity until age five. This suggests that children do not immediately map prayer concepts onto their existing wish concepts; prayers are not automatically given all of the characteristics of wishes. Of course, this is not to imply that all children younger than five have a distinctly nonmentalistic view of prayer. It seems more likely that most three-year-olds and some four-year-olds do not have a clear sense of what prayer is. As the following results from the Entity Task suggest, however, a nonmentalistic conception of prayer probably does precede a mentalistic one. This is most evident in children's explanations for their denials that certain entities (e.g., babies and animals) can pray (discussed later in this section).

The present studies revealed a significantly earlier mentalistic understanding of prayer than what we would have expected based on the literature on prayer. Long et al.'s (1967) results indicated that children do not conceive of the mental nature of prayer until age nine or ten. One possible reason for this difference between their findings and ours is due to the nature of our samples. Our sample could be considered a fairly religious sample, as it was primarily drawn from schools with religious affiliations, whereas their participants were primarily drawn from private schools (Long et al. did not note any religious affiliation of these schools). Despite this, we suspect that it is more likely that the nature of our procedures was the critical factor. Long et al.'s procedures were open-ended, Piagetian-style interviews, that often tend to underestimate the level of children's knowledge, whereas our procedures involved, not only open-ended questions, but also forced choice response options and a variety of tasks, most of which placed very minimal verbal demands on the young children we tested.

As noted earlier, we also used the Entity Task to get at the question of the necessary components of prayer. As shown in Table 4.3, almost all of the children claimed that adults and children can pray, as they did when questioned about whether adults and children can wish. Approximately half of the children in each age group believed that babies can pray. The children's explanations suggest parallel patterns in the cases of wish and prayer. Early denials that babies can wish or pray appeared to be based on a belief that babies lack the required verbal abilities, whereas later denials were based on the idea that babies lack the required mental abilities. This is the same type of progression found by Long et al. regarding animals' abilities, however in their data the shift occurred slightly later. Regarding the abilities of cats and dogs, the younger children in our study (three- to five-year-olds) seemed to believe wishing to be something that these animals are more likely to be able to do than praying. This may be because of the importance of knowing about God for praying (to be addressed following). Although the children were even less likely to grant flowers and tables the ability to pray, a considerable number of five--to six-year-olds did claim this.

The judgment task yielded more information about children's beliefs in the mental concomitants of prayer. These patterns reinforce the above findings that prayer becomes mental for most children at around the age of five. There was a significant increase between four and five years of age in the number of children who claimed that a character who was thinking about something was praying. Relatedly, there was a significant decrease in claims that a character who was not thinking was praying. Interestingly, another mental aspect of prayer, knowledge about God, appears to begin to be understood slightly earlier than the mental activity aspect (i.e., thinking). Four-year-olds began to show some level of belief that to pray one must know about God; characters who were described as knowing about God were judged significantly more often to be praying than characters who were described as not knowing about God. But by age five, children were judging virtually all of the time that characters who knew about God were praying. Again, this association between praying and belief in God appeared earlier in our study (age five) than it did in Long et al.'s work (age nine to ten). As with our other findings, we suspect that our methods made it easier for the younger children to reveal their knowledge than did the methods used by these other researchers.

In general, there were age differences in children's beliefs about efficacy. Regarding the history of their own prayers, more older than younger children reported that their prayers had been granted. Interestingly, this is the opposite trend that was found in the wish data, where beliefs regarding the efficacy of children's past wishes decreased with age. It is not clear why this was the case. One interpretation is that the basis for assessing efficacy shifts from an early reliance on empirical observations (e.g., noticing how many times one actually got what one wished for) to a more faith-based method, in which "failed" attempts are reinterpreted or explained away. Another interpretation is that the content of children's prayers may be more realistic than the content of their wishes. For example, whereas children may often wish for extravagant material objects, they may be more likely to pray for things like "good health" or happiness. This sort of trend could also explain the claims of decreasing efficacy between younger and older children in the wish study. It is also possible that these differences are due to the differing levels of cultural support for religious versus fantastical beliefs.

In the aim of differentiating these hypotheses it would be interesting to know why children believe that prayers are sometimes unsuccessful. Children's reasons for unsuccessful acts of wishing included not trying hard enough, needing more magic, and simple skepticism. One might imagine that children might also refer to some of these reasons in explaining unsuccessful prayers, but might also marshal a number of additional reasons, such as it being God's will not to grant a certain prayer, or references to God's "availability" or "resources" at the time that the prayer was made. In Goldman's (1964) study, children were asked to explain unanswered prayers, and the six- to sixteen-year-old children he studied fell into three distinct stages. In the first stage, characterizing children up to age nine, failure of prayers was often due to moral issues, such as the child's being bad, but also concerned failing to pray correctly, as in not praying hard enough, politely enough, or loud enough. In the second stage (ages nine to twelve) children often referred more to the content of the prayers, for example, claiming that selfish or greedy prayers would not be answered. Finally, in the third stage, children cited more spiritual reasons, such as inconsistency with God's will. Children's reasons for the granting (and denial) of prayers should be explored further in future research.

This brings up the issue of children's efficacy beliefs concerning prayers of varying contents. There were clear age differences regarding the efficacy of prayers that might be considered of a questionable nature. Although few children at any age agreed that it was acceptable to pray for someone to get hurt, all of the three- and four-year-olds who said that this kind of prayer was acceptable also believed that it would be effective. Only about half of the five-year-olds felt this way, and almost none of the older children (six-to eight-year-olds) did. This age-related trend is consistent with Goldman's (1964) finding in children age nine and older that negative content of prayers is unacceptable and will result in denial of the prayer (e.g., "Stupid prayers don't get answered, like asking for money or a bicycle," p. 189).

In summary, it appears to be the case that right around the time at which children stop believing in mental-physical causality with respect to wishing, they begin to see prayer as an effective form of mental-physical causality. However, children's early prayer concepts do not appear equivalent to their concepts of wishing. First, early prayer concepts (prior to age five) do not appear to be mental. Second, prayer is clearly a more complicated process, as it involves an intermediary. At around the age of five, children begin to understand that God plays an important role in prayer. But importantly, by the age of five, children believe that thinking is involved, and it is the interaction between God and thoughts, not the usual physical activity associated with an event, that results in the efficacy of a prayer.

This research on children's understanding of prayer is only a first step in determining relations between children's religious beliefs and their knowledge about the mental world. These data indicate that mental-physical causality plays a large role in prayer for children five years of age and older. Not only do children believe thinking to be involved in praying but their beliefs in the efficacy of this form of mental-physical causality increase with age rather than decrease, as in the case of wishing. But praying is clearly a more complex process than is wishing. We need more work to determine exactly how children conceive of the process of praying, in particular, how it fits with their developing knowledge about both the physical and mental worlds. For example, one of the major developments in children's theories of mind at this age involves learning about communication. How do children conceive of the communication with God that is involved in praying as fitting with their developing knowledge about ordinary communicative processes? In a similar vein, Boyer (this volume) also argues that we need to view children's developing religious concepts in the context of their knowledge of the mind. More generally, he states that "children's religious statements cannot be properly explained (nor can development be adequately described) if we ignore the broader ontological background against which they are formulated." These are important directions that research on developing concepts of prayer and other religious concepts could take.

## Conclusions

In this chapter I have documented the presence of and changes in beliefs in mental-physical causality in young children. Children's beliefs in mental-physical causality are not for the most part a result of confusion about the distinction between mental and physical. Whereas very early beliefs may represent some blurring of this boundary, beliefs about wishing and prayer do not. Yet at the same time there is an important puzzle to be solved. Children appear to accept culturally sanctioned constructs, such as wishing and prayer, that endorse processes that run counter to the natural causal relations they are mastering. In beginning to solve this puzzle, I suggest that children in a sense may quarantine wishing from their developing theories of mind by labeling it a "magical" process.[8] Likewise they may do the same regarding prayer, holding it to religious rather than naive psychological constraints, although the data presented in this chapter are not yet enough to say this with certainty. Importantly, by making these processes subject to different laws children are spared the confusion they might otherwise face.

Clearly the role I have discussed for culture is somewhat different than the traditional view of the role of culture in the development of these concepts. According to Piaget, children's early misconceptions about causality were due to the immature nature of the child's mind. The influence of culture, then, was to correct these beliefs or supplant them with more "mature" ones. As paraphrased by Subbotsky (1993), according to Piaget, "This 'primitive' mind, however comes under the steady influence of culture, and children, through their numerous activities and communications with objects and people, eventually acquire the concepts of physical causality and permanence of objects..." (p. 82). Subbotsky's (1993; and this volume) position, and mine as well, is that children's minds are not inherently one way or

---

[8] The process I suggest here may be mistakenly construed as being more conscious and intentional than I intend. Rather than children making some conscious decision regarding the domain with which their beliefs fit, I envision the mechanism to be more implicit and not necessarily accessible to conscious awareness. Without proposing anything specific about how it would operate, I see it as potentially similar in this sense to the decoupling mechanism that Leslie (1987) has proposed to account for the fact that young children do not become confused by their pretend stipulations, or to the "slots" Boyer (this volume) proposes that children create for real, counterintuitive occurrences.

another – not inherently magical nor inherently rational. Culture does not "correct" initial misrepresentations about causality; rather, in this case, culture is responsible for introducing these "magical" ideas. It is quite possible that belief in mental-physical causality fulfills a useful function for both children and adults in our culture. Certainly for children, beliefs in magic and wishing allow participation in the cultural practice of fiction and enchantment, and thus can provide much joy. More generally, later beliefs in religion, in mental control over illness, and even in certain superstitious practices provide the role of "mediating and dominating the area of mental reality that is beyond the control of rational scientific methods" (Subbotsky, 1993, footnote p. 85), and thus can provide individuals with a comforting sense of control over events in their lives.

Until now, children's theorizing about mind-world relations has primarily been studied independently of the culture in which the child-theorizer is embedded. Because of this, it often appears that most of the interesting developments in children's theories of mind with respect to these relations have already taken place by the age of four, when, according to most, children have achieved a "representational understanding of mind" (Perner, 1991). What I hope to have made compelling in this chapter is the idea that many exciting new issues emerge when we consider potential interactions between developing knowledge of the mind and various cultural contexts, in this case, those of magic and religion. It is hoped that researchers studying the development of children's theories of mind, magic, and religion will continue to recognize the importance of the interaction between culture and cognition in the beliefs, theories, and behavior of young children.

## References

Astington, J. W. (1993). *The Child's Discovery of the Mind*. Cambridge, MA: Harvard University Press.

Bartsch, K., & Wellman, H. M. (1995). *Children Talk About the Mind*. Oxford: Oxford University Press.

Boyer, P. (1995). Causal understandings in cultural representations: Cognitive constraints on inferences from cultural input. In: D. Sperber, D. Premack, and A. J. Premack (Eds.), *Causal Cognition: A Multidisciplinary Debate*, (pp. 44–78). New York: Clarendon Press.

Estes, D., Wellman, H. M. & Woolley, J. (1989). Children's understanding of mental phenomena. In: H. Reese (Ed.), *Advances in Child Development and Behavior*, (pp. 41–86). New York: Academic Press.

Goldman, R. (1964). *Religious Thinking from Childhood to Adolescence*. London: Routledge & Kegan Paul.

Goode, W. J. (1951). *Religion Among the Primitives*. Glencoe, IL: The Free Press.

Harris, P. L., Brown, E., Marriot, C., Whittall, S., & Harmer, S. (1991). Monsters, ghosts, and witches: Testing the limits of the fantasy-reality distinction in young children. *British Journal of Developmental Psychology, 9,* 105–123.

Inagaki, K. & Hatano, G. (1996, August). Early recognition of the mind's inability to control bodily processes. Paper presented at the meeting of the International Society for the Study of Behavioral Development. Quebec City, Quebec, Canada.

Johnson, C. N., & Harris, P. L. (1994). Magic: Special but not excluded. *British Journal of Developmental Psychology, 12,* 35–51.

Johnson, C. N., & Wellman, H. M. (1982). Children's developing conceptions of the mind and brain. *Child Development, 53,* 222–34.

Leslie, A. M. & Keeble, S. (1987). Do six-month-old infants perceive causality? *Cognition, 25,* 265–88.

Long, D., Elkind, D., & Spilka, B. (1967). The child's conception of prayer. *Journal for the Scientific Study of Religion, 6,* 101–109.

Oakes, L. M., & Cohen, L. B. (1990). Infant perception of a causal event. *Cognitive Development, 5,* 193–207.

Perner, J. (1991). *Understanding the Representational Mind*. Cambridge, MA: MIT Press.

Phelps, K. E., & Woolley, J. D. (1994). The form and function of young children's magical beliefs. *Developmental Psychology, 30,* 385–394.

Piaget, J. (1929). *The Child's Conception of the World*. London: Routledge & Kegan Paul.

Pillow, B. (1989). Early understanding of perception as a source of knowledge. *Journal of Experimental Child Psychology, 47,* 116–29.

Pratt, C. & Bryant, P. (1990). Young children understand that looking leads to knowing (so long as they are looking into a single barrel). *Child Development, 61,* 973–982.

Rosengren, K. S. & Hickling, A. K. (1994). Seeing is believing: Children's explorations of commonplace, magical, and extraordinary transformations. *Child Development, 65,* 1605–26.

Scarlett, W. G., & Perriello, L. (1991). The development of prayer in adolescence. In: F. K. Oser and W. G. Scarlett (Eds), *Religious Development in Childhood and Adolescence. New Directions in Child Development, Vol. 52,* (pp. 63–76). San Francisco: Jossey Bass.

Spelke, E. S., Phillips, A., & Woodward, A. L. (1995). Infants' knowledge of object motion and human action. In: D. Sperber, D. Premack, and A. J. Premack (Eds.), *Causal Cognition: A Multidisciplinary Debate,* (pp. 44–78). New York: Clarendon Press.

Subbotsky, E. V. (1993). *Foundations of the Mind: Children's Understanding of Reality*. Cambridge, MA: Harvard University Press.

Tversky, A., & Kahneman, D. (1973). Availability: A heuristic for judging frequency and probability. *Cognitive Psychology, 5,* 207–32.

Vikan, A., & Clausen, S E. (1993). Freud, Piaget, or neither? Beliefs in controlling others by wishful thinking and magical behavior in young children. *The Journal of Genetic Psychology, 154* (3), 297–314.

Wellman, H. M. (1990). *The Child's Theory of Mind.* Cambridge, MA: MIT Press.

Wellman, H. M., & Estes, D. (1986). Early understanding of mental entities: A reexamination of childhood realism. *Child Development, 57,* 910–23.

Woolley, J. D., & Phelps, K. E. (1994). Young children's practical reasoning about imagination. *British Journal of Developmental Psychology, 12,* 53–67.

Woolley, J. D., Phelps, K. E., Davis, D. L., & Mandell, D. J. (1999). Where theories of mind meet magic: The development of children's beliefs about wishing. *Child Development, 70,* 571–587.

Woolley, J. D., & Wellman, H. M. (1993). Origin and truth: Young children's understanding of imaginary mental representations. *Child Development, 64,* 1–17.

Zusne, L. & Jones, W. H. (1989). *Anomistic Psychology: A study of Magical Thinking.* Hillsdale, NJ: Erlbaum.

# 5 Intuitive Ontology and Cultural Input in the Acquisition of Religious Concepts

PASCAL BOYER AND SHEILA WALKER

Do children have religious beliefs, and how are they different from adult ones? Clearly, the question is of interest to anthropologists who need to understand how religious representations are acquired and therefore how cultural assumptions are transmitted from generation to generation. The question is also of importance to developmental psychologists, for what children grasp of religious concepts and beliefs may illuminate how they build complex conceptual structures on the basis of limited input. Surprisingly, studies of the development of religious concepts are still few and far between. They are not really satisfactory either, for two reasons. One is that such studies often apply to developmental phenomena views of adult religious concepts that have no sound cognitive basis. Another reason is that such studies generally ignore a wealth of anthropological material concerning the diversity as well as the recurrent features of religious concepts. This is why the first part of this chapter deals with religious representations in adults, introducing a cognitive framework based on anthropological evidence. We then argue that this framework makes it possible to evaluate the relevance of recent developmental evidence to an understanding of religious concepts, and to specify in what ways children's religious concepts differ from the adult versions.

"Religion" in the ordinary sense combines (among other things) at least five different domains of representations, to do with (i) the existence and specific powers of supernatural entities, (ii) a particular set of moral rules, (iii) notions of group identity ("our" religion is not "theirs"), (iv) types of actions (rituals but also daily routines or avoidances), and, sometimes, (v) particular types of experiences and associated emotional states (the main focus of W. James's psychology of religion). Although these different aspects are obviously connected in an individual's religious beliefs, they are not acquired as an integrated conceptual package. This chapter is about the first domain identified above, that of *religious ontologies*: mental representations concerning the existence (and causal powers) of various supernatural entities. What we offer here is a series of directions for research, some of which are supported by evidence and others by considerations of plausibility or theoretical coherence. The domain lags far behind other aspects of cognitive development and our account necessarily includes some speculation as well as demonstrated results.

## "Religion" as a Cognitive Phenomenon: Some Caveats

Lack of serious interest in detailed studies of children's religious concepts is less surprising if we consider that the "psychology of religion" as an academic specialty is not generally concerned with cognitive processes as such. As Watts and Williams (1988) put it, psychologists "have often chosen to study the *externals* of religion," such as explicit claims to belief, "religiosity scales," connections between personality types and religious commitment or between religious beliefs and social relations, and so on. Most of these studies transfer to religion general concerns and methods of social and personality psychology, and therefore leave aside the general cognitive processes involved in religious concepts. Even when this research considers cognitive phenomena as such, it seems to us that the psychology of religion may perpetuate misleading notions of religious concepts. A good illustration is Watts and Williams' (1988) general essay on "religious knowing," which makes a strong case for the fact that religious representations should not be considered as *a priori* different from other conceptual domains, and aims to highlight "essential similarities between religious knowing and other everyday forms of knowing" (p. 38). Watts and Williams (1988), for instance, evaluate the relevance of different cognitive frameworks (prototype theory and metaphor) to an understanding of the (mental) concept of God. They start from the assumption that "religious knowledge is the knowledge of God" and conclude that "religious knowing involves, not so much coming to know a separate religious world, as coming to know the religious dimensions of the everyday world" (Watts & Williams, 1988, p. 151).

Despite suggestive analyses, this type of work illustrates two general problems in the psychology of religion. An important limitation is that the authors consider only Christian religious ideas and practices; more disturbingly, they seem to take for granted, as self-evident, certain aspects of religious thought that are in fact particular to that tradition.[1] One could argue that Western Christian data can be subsequently compared to other cultural contexts. However, this particular focus may conceal some aspects of religious concepts that are crucial to their acquisition. This is a second widespread problem with the psychology of religion. An exclusive focus on Western notions, because of the particular features of the traditions concerned, suggests that there is an autonomous domain of religious cognition, and that its features are generally accessible to consciousness. These two premises are less than altogether plausible, as we will try to show throughout this chapter.

This is why we will start from the assumption that *cross cultural diversity should be a starting point* rather than an afterthought in the systematic study of religious representations. The variety of religious representations to be found in the world is an advantage as well as a challenge for cognitive studies. Consider supernatural agents, for instance. In many societies there are several gods, in others there are no gods at all, or both gods and spirits, or ghosts only, and so on.

Also, we may find that in many places *the domain of religion is not necessarily marked off* from "mundane" or "profane" concerns in quite the same way as in the Christian West. In many societies, representations about souls or ghosts are considered as a description of what there is in the world, in the same way as cultural notions about plants and animals or people, not as a separate domain of speculation. In this sense our common concepts of "faith" and "belief" (in the everyday sense of "believing *in* something") are not quite relevant. They constitute a particular, Western response to seemingly incompatible claims from religion and other scholarly traditions, notably science, but they are not a necessary condition for religious representations. We should also note that having an explicit notion of *a* religion (as opposed to another) is historically specific. True, it may be found in

---

[1] There are many religious traditions in which the very notion of a knowledge of God would seem inconceivable, not to mention the numerous religious traditions in which there is no equivalent whatever to the Christian concept of "god." The same remark applies to other domains of Watts and Williams's work, for example, to their analysis of the act of "prayer" (with no clear equivalent in some cultural environments). The idea of "the religious dimensions of the everyday world" is also culturally specific and would seem odd in other cultural contexts.

diverse circumstances (from China to India or the West and Islam), but it is not universal.

Equally important, *the domain of religious representations is broader than official religion.* The psychology of religion has often focused on "God-concepts." But other representations, such as spells, omens, taboos, magic, divination, or mediumship as well as ghosts, ghouls, fairies, golems, and so on, are part and parcel of religious representations. In Christianity (as well as in other literate traditions, e.g., Islam) such notions and practices are officially considered marginal, unimportant, not part of "religion" proper, or even downright antireligious. There is no reason for cognitive studies to underwrite such social judgments. What is marginal in one culture may be central to another's religion and tap the same cognitive capacities in both contexts.

Finally, we must keep in mind that *adult religious representations are not exhausted by normative accounts.* A developmental description of religious representations must rely on a description of adult religious representations as they are, not on an ideal or official version of those representations. There is little point in comparing children's actual representations to an end point that they do not actually reach.

Most studies in the domain take it for granted that there is a clear-cut domain of religion, that it has to do with God, that it can be described in terms of explicit, officially sanctioned theological statements, and so on. Here, by contrast, we put forward a description of religious concepts and their acquisition that aims to do justice to their cultural diversity and recurrent features, as well as provide a precise understanding of their developmental dynamics. We also show how developmental evidence in other domains may illuminate religious concepts.

## Religious Ontologies: An Anthropological Framework

Let us start with anthropological findings that may shed light on the cognitive underpinnings of religious categories. As we said above, there is undeniable cultural diversity in religious representations, and a proper consideration of this diversity may illuminate questions of acquisition. This cross cultural diversity does not entail that religious concepts are the product of an unconstrained form of imagination. Cultural representations in general are widespread because, all else being equal, they are more easily acquired, stored or transmitted than others (Durham, 1991; Sperber, 1985, 1996), and an account of religious representations requires an explanation of their cognitive salience (Bloch, 1998; Whitehouse, 1997). If we focus on the recurrent patterns underlying the apparent diversity of religious representations, it appears that they are constrained by a small number of principles that are part and parcel of normal, everyday cognition and not specifically religious in nature (Boyer, 1994b; Lawson & McCauley, 1990).

The ontological assumptions found in most religious systems, in otherwise diverse environments, generally constitute direct violations of intuitive expectations that inform everyday cognition (Boyer, 1994a). Consider some widespread forms of religious ontology. Spirits and ghosts are commonly represented as intentional agents whose physical properties go against the ordinary physical qualities of embodied agents. They go through physical obstacles, move instantaneously, and so on. Gods, too, have such counterintuitive physical qualities, as well as nonstandard biological features; for example, they are immortal, and they feed on the smell of sacrificed foods. Also, religious systems the world over include assumptions about particular artifacts, statues for instance, that are counterintuitive in that they are endowed with intentional psychological processes. They can perceive states of affairs, form beliefs, have intentions, and so on.

The notion that such representations are "counterintuitive" simply means that they include some conceptual elements that violate ordinary intuitive expectations of the kind that is routinely described in cognitive (and developmental) accounts of "naive physics" or "naive biology" or "theory of mind."[2] One should not confuse what is intuitively counterintuitive from a cognitive viewpoint with what is perceived as unfamiliar. Some religious assumptions can become part of a cultural "routine"; this is orthogonal to the question of whether they violate tacit, intuitive ontological principles. Most important, when we say that some religious assumptions are counterintuitive, we do not mean to suggest that they are not taken as *real* by most people who hold them. On the contrary, it is precisely insofar as a certain situation

---

[2] Anthropologists are sometimes tempted to say that these religious assumptions are perfectly intuitive to the people who hold them, but this is not based on any experimental evidence, is directly contradicted by everyday life in the cultures concerned, and in any case would make it very mysterious that the people concerned find their religious notions so fascinating.

violates intuitive principles *and* is taken as real that it may become particularly salient. It is the conjunction of these two assumptions that gives such representations their *attention-grabbing* potential.

Religious concepts, then, are constrained by their connection to what could be called an "intuitive ontology": a set of broad categories about the types of things to be found in the world, together with quasi-theoretical assumptions about their causal powers. This provides a first approximation for the range of religious representations that are likely to be "successful" in cultural transmission. Cultural representations need cognitive salience to be acquired at all, and a violation of intuitive principles provides just that. The idea of spirits being in several places at once would *not* be counterintuitive, if there was not a stable expectation that agents are solid objects and that solid objects occupy a unique point in space. In the same way, the notion of statues that listen to one's prayers is attention-grabbing only against a background of expectations about artifacts, including the assumption that they do *not* have mental capacities.

Beyond this, religious representations are further constrained by intuitive ontology. Counterintuitive elements do not exhaust the representation of religious entities and agencies. For instance, ghosts are construed as physically counterintuitive. At the same time, however, people routinely produce a large number of inferences about what the ghosts or spirits *know* or *want*, which are based on a straightforward extension of "theory of mind" expectations to the spirits. Indeed, most inferences that people produce about religious agencies are straightforward consequences of activating those intuitive principles that are *not* violated in the representation of those supernatural entities. These background assumptions are generally tacit and provide the inferential potential without which cultural representations are very unlikely to be transmitted. We rarely observe religious ontologies that do not include this tacit background: Imagine, for example, spirits that are located nowhere, or an omnipotent God who can perceive nothing at all, or the idea that ghosts become inanimate blades of grass or kitchen knives. To take less extreme examples, this requirement of inferential potential also explains the *relative* spread of religious assumptions. The notion of a spirit (an agent with strange physics and standard psychological properties) is symmetrical to that of a zombie (an agent with standard physics and counterintuitive intentional properties). Although both notions are counterintuitive, the former is much more widespread than the latter, probably because ascribing standard psychological properties to a religious agent affords much more inferential potential than construing it as a solid object.[3]

This twofold constraint from intuitive ontology explains why religious ontologies, despite surface variations, are based on a limited number of recurrent assumptions. Intuitive ontologies produce specific expectations that apply to a limited number of broad ontological categories, so that the number of assumptions that directly violate them are limited too. Moreover, not all violations are compatible with maintaining an intuitive background that supports inferences. In this framework, it is not surprising that religious ontologies the world over include such concepts as agents with counterintuitive physical properties (e.g., spirits); agents with counterintuitive biological properties (e.g., immortal gods, or gods who procreate in nonstandard ways, or feed on smells and shadows); agents with counterintuitive psychological properties (e.g. zombies or possessed people); animals with counterintuitive biological properties (e.g., metamorphosed into other animals); and artifacts with intentional properties (e.g., statues that listen, masks that talk.)

However elementary, such a "catalogue" accounts for most of the conceptual assumptions actually found in religious categories.[4] These stem from either *violations* or *transfers* of expectations. In the case of violations, expectations that are activated for a particular ontological category are violated. For instance, gods are represented as intentional agents, activating the standard expectations of such agents as having perception, thoughts, and intentions. But their perceptual processes, for instance, might have counterintuitive properties, such as perceiving future events as well as the present. In the case of transfers, expectations are activated for an ontological category that does not usually activate them. For instance, an artifact is said to have cognitive powers, a mountain to have a physiology, or a tree to have thoughts.

[3] In all cultural environments where one finds notions of "zombies," these nonintentional agents are invariably construed as "remote-controlled" by other agents, which invariably turn out to have all of the usual features of intentional agents as construed by intuitive "theory of mind."

[4] This, obviously, applies to the fundamental principles underlying religious representations, not to the specific set of surface features that accompany them. For instance, the principle of intentional agents with counterintuitive physical properties is widespread the world over; but in each cultural environment it is accompanied with detailed and highly variable explicit notions about the characteristics and behavior of those agents.

The actual distribution of cultural representations seems to confirm the prediction that, all else being equal, representations that combine counterintuitive principles and intuitive background in the way described here are more likely than others to be acquired, stored, and transmitted.

## Implications for the Representation of Religious Concepts

The anthropological argument outlined above leads to particular predictions as concerns the acquisition and representation of religious concepts. These can be tested experimentally. Let us examine those predictions that are directly relevant to the question of acquisition.

*Salience of counterintuitive elements.* The attention-grabbing quality of counterintuitive assumptions should have some direct consequences on recall and recognition, if the attention-grabbing elements are to be transmitted. All else being equal, we should expect such elements to be better recalled or recognized than representations that conform to intuitive expectations. A long time ago, Bartlett studied chains of transmission for mythical stories and argued that subjects tend to "normalize" stories to familiar themes and discard their exotic elements (Bartlett, 1932). A more systematic study of transmission by Barrett (Barrett 1999) shows that subjects transmit counterintuitive elements better than either standard, noncounterintuitive descriptions or descriptions that are strange without being counterintuitive. Using similar material, Boyer studied recall for counterintuitive items that either violate intuitive expectations (e.g. objects that have no shadow or suddenly disappear, people with extraordinary cognitive powers) or transfer expectations to an inappropriate category (e.g., artifacts with psychological processes or biological properties) (Boyer in press). The stimuli were designed to use principles found in recurrent religious representations, although they are not presented as "religious." Results show that such items are better recalled than control, noncounterintuitive items. Also, these simple counterintuitive items are better recalled than combinations of violations and transfers, although the latter are more "strange" and more distant from everyday experiences. In other words, *particular* types of counterintuitive representations, rather than just any odd concepts, seem better recalled. This is not unrelated to the fact that these particular types are more recurrent in otherwise very diverse cultural environments.

*Context and discontinuity of representations.* We said that religious ontologies include counterintuitive elements that violate intuitive expectations. This does not mean that they supplant these expectations, so one should be able to observe the same subjects having divergent representations of the same situation, depending on whether the context makes one anticipate violations. This is illustrated in Walker's study of Yoruba adults' explanations for natural kind transformations in ritual versus nonritual contexts (Walker, 1992). Yoruba adults from southwestern Nigeria refused to accept, for example, that in an everyday context a cat could turn into a dog. Their explanations centered on the immutability of natural kinds. In contrast, when a cat was disguised as a dog and used as such in a ritual context (the efficacy of a particular Yoruba ritual depending on sacrifice of a dog), the same subjects who had just denied that one animal could turn into another now declared unequivocally that the cat had become a dog. Yoruba adults clearly demonstrated their solid knowledge of causal principles with respect to natural kinds, yet in contexts allowing for violations of those principles their explanatory accounts were consistent with an understanding of the special nature of those violations.

*Inferential use of intuitive background.* What drives inferences about supernatural entities is not their attention-grabbing, counterintuitive explicit element but the activation of a background of "default" intuitive expectations, which are not explicitly violated.[5] A dramatic illustration of this phenomenon is a study by Barrett and Keil of concepts of "God" and other nonnatural agents in both believers and nonbelievers (Barrett & Keil, 1996). Barrett and Keil first elicited explicit descriptions of God. These generally centered on counterintuitive claims for extraordinary cognitive powers. God can perceive everything at once, focus his attention on multiple events simultaneously, and so on. The subjects were then tested on their recall of simple stories involving God in various scenarios where these capacities are relevant. In general, the subjects tended to distort or add to the stories in ways that were directly influenced by their tacit, intuitive principles of psychology. For instance, they recalled (wrongly) that in the story

---

[5] In other words, religious representations are not simply bracketed off as "strange" or "awesome," but routinely activated in explanation and prediction. The claim here is that the counterintuitive elements by themselves are insufficient for that purpose because they do not support rich inferences, whereas default assumptions do: Saying that ghosts go through walls does not give one much predictive power; assuming that they have belief-desire psychology produces a rich domain of explanations for their behavior as well as predictions of future behavior.

God attended to some problem *and then* turned his attention to another, or that God *could not perceive* some event because of some obstacle, although such information was not in the original stories. This is particularly impressive in that intuitive principles that specify limitations on cognitive powers (e.g., perceptions are hindered by obstacles between the object and the perceiving subject) are diametrical to the subjects' explicit beliefs about God. The framework summarized above would explain how such contradictions are possible. The two types of representations are distinct and contribute to different aspects of the representation of religious categories: attention-grabbing salience for counterintuitive assumptions and inferential potential for tacit intuitive assumptions. Barrett and Keil use the term "theological correctness" (TC) to denote this tendency for subjects to entertain explicitly a description of supernatural agents that is not actually used in representing or predicting their behavior.[6] Concepts of God seem to comprise an accessible TC part as well as an intuitive component; the two do not seem integrated. Indeed, in this case they deliver opposite expectations.

In summary, there is evidence both anthropological and psychological for a description of religious ontologies as based on a limited, salient, counterintuitive violation or transfer of expectations. This also requires that other assumptions, which are not counterintuitive, are constantly used to produce inferences about supernatural entities. Only the first counterintuitive aspect of religious representations is explicitly transmitted, although full acquisition of these concepts requires both aspects. To acquire religious concepts, people (i) must possess the tacit principles that inform intuitive ontology, (ii) they must be sensitive to violations of these principles, and (iii) they must use nonviolated background assumptions to produce inferences about religious entities; Barrett and Keil's data confirm that the latter aspect is crucial, since background intuitive assumptions drive people's actual inferences and expectations about religious agents. The problem

---

[6] Incidentally, neither TC concepts nor inferences produced by subjects show any difference correlated with the subjects' particular faith, denomination, or even general attitude toward religion. Atheists, Hindus, and Christians of various denominations have similar performances. This may illustrate the fact that religious ontology (the domain that is studied here) is quite independent from the group-identity assumptions that are usually connected with it. So there is cultural variation between these groups, but it does not consist, as is often assumed, in differences in religious categories themselves, but probably in metarepresentations of these concepts.

then is to see to what extent all three conditions obtain in children's concepts and how they develop.

## Direct Studies of Children's Religion

We know that children have religious representations in the minimal sense that they think (and to a certain extent talk) about matters that clearly belong to the religious domain. This may be the special powers of God in Western cultural environments, or the spirits' uncanny behavior in an African village or a shaman's trance in South America. The question is to evaluate the similarities between such representations and those described above as typical of adult conceptions. As we said above, there are surprisingly few systematic studies of religious concepts as a cognitive, particularly developmental phenomenon (see surveys in Gorsuch, 1988; Hunsberger, 1991; Reich, 1993). If we leave aside reports of children's explicit opinions on spiritual matters and theology (e.g. Coles, 1990), which provide intriguing evidence but no account of acquisition, developmental studies often focus on social influences more than cognitive processes (see Ozorak, 1989). However, we will discuss Goldman's Piagetian interpretation of religious representations, the most detailed and pertinent account of the domain yet (Fowler, 1981, provides a very similar account). We will then explain why such "direct" studies of children's concepts (e.g., asking them what God is like or what a prayer consists of) may be misguided and leave out some important aspects of the cognitive processes involved.

In a Piagetian framework, notions of God and other supernatural agents are closely tied to discussions of *animism* (a large domain of causal processes is construed in terms of intentional action) and *artificialism* (many aspects of natural processes are construed as people's intentional creations). Piaget observed that in early and middle childhood subjects tend to see clouds as moving of their own accord, shadows as created by (or emanating from) people, and so on (see Laurendeau & Pinard, 1962, for a general presentation). Also, children tend to see adults and parents in particular as responsible for all sorts of aspects of their daily environment that they then construe as a consequence of natural facts or social constraints. At this stage (before "formal operations") concepts of supernatural agents like God should be based on a straightforward extension of these assumptions. On the basis of Piaget's assumptions, Goldman showed how shifts in children's notions of religious agency could be interpreted in terms of structural developmental stages (Goldman, 1964). The main point of Goldman's studies was that children's religious notions are not just fragmentary or abridged versions of adult representations. Goldman was particularly concerned with the fact that children's concepts diverge systematically from adults', and particularly from the cultural input provided by religious education. Whilst religious teaching in general aims to emphasize the difference between the religious and the profane, and to represent religious matters as incommensurable with everyday ones, children seem to reinterpret religious concepts in terms of familiar situations. Consistent with Piaget's predictions, the child's concept of God is overwhelmingly anthropomorphic up to the "formal operational" stage (after age eleven). God is described as literally having a voice, a face, and so on. Using Biblical stories as his material, Goldman elicited descriptions of God's capacities and agency that highlight this anthropomorphic concept. This extension of everyday assumptions can be observed in other religious domains as well. For seven-year-olds, prayer works because of some physical conduit that allows God literally to hear people just like they hear each other (Goldman, 1964, Ch. 12). It is only at the beginning of adolescence that children take Biblical stories as "symbolic," not as literal accounts of physical events. In the same way, it is at that stage that they grasp complex aspects of Christian morality, for example, the idea that God is good to evil persons as well as good ones. Such studies are not inconsistent with anecdotal evidence, and converge on a view of religious development that charts the gradual emergence of "abstract" religion out of anthropomorphism and the development of a vision of religious messages as symbolic or inspiring rather than literal.

We will not challenge this evidence but argue that it does not necessarily support the developmental schedule hypothesized. To start with, one must notice that Goldman's studies are based on a normative account of religious representations. That is, the experiments highlight children's *actual* representations (how children think) and show how they diverge from adult *ideal* representations (i.e., how adults ought to think, according to theological doctrine). However, there is no evidence that adults really represent religious concepts in the ways prescribed by church doctrine. Indeed, even in cases where Goldman documents age-related differences, we have good reasons to doubt that this is evidence for the developmental shifts hypothesized. Take the case of Biblical stories for instance. For children under thirteen, the story of Moses' crossing of the Red Sea involves a humanlike (though omnipotent) God who physically parts the waves by the power of his voice. Adolescents on the other hand are likely to say that the story is "symbolic" and that miracles do not require God's physical intervention. This is seen as evidence for the construction of an abstract and more "theological" concept of God. However, Barrett and Keil's (1996) results show that such "theologically correct" constructions are only part of people's God concept, and that inferences and expectations are in fact driven by another, intuitive and largely inaccessible component. In view of these results, it seems plausible that Goldman's adolescent subjects have reached a stage at which they are more competent than younger subjects in "theologically correct" representations. That is, they know the culturally correct answers to questions about miracles and God's physical presence, although their actual God concept might well diverge from this official (and meta-represented) version. In particular, the intuitive component is probably just as anthropomorphic as in the younger child's concept, which is contrary to Goldman's interpretation.

These remarks point to some general problems with what we call "direct" studies of religious concepts. Asking children what God is like or how prayer works produces evidence that is difficult to analyze, for two related reasons. First, there is no simple way of telling whether the statements elicited actually correspond to principles that support explanation and inference, or merely belong to a "theologically correct" repertoire that is quoted rather than used. So a study of children's explicit notions gives us only part of the picture, a part that may or may not reveal actual development. Second, children's religious statements cannot be properly explained (nor can development be adequately described) if we ignore the broader ontological background against which they are formulated. For instance, children may state that "God sees everything and remembers everything," but this does not in itself tell us much unless we have a reliable account of children's intuitive notions of perception and memory. The question, "Are children's religious representations different from adults?" may be better tackled by studies focused on their intuitive ontology as well as their construal of counterintuitive, fantastic, and fictional situations.

## Religious Concepts and Children's Intuitive Principles

As we said above, what underpins the transmission of religious concepts is a particular cognitive equilibrium between socially transmitted counterintuitive representations and spontaneous activation of intuitive principles. Children's religious representations are similar to adult concepts insofar as (i) they include counterintuitive assumptions that are salient because of their counterintuitive character, and (ii) they also activate background default principles that support inference. In the course of acquiring a given supernatural concept, children first have to understand the relevant domain-specific principles whose acquisition would then enable them to recognize violations (see Harris, 1994, for a similar line of reasoning about nonreligious, "magical" thinking). What sets many religious concepts apart from "ordinary" ones is this very feature – their violations of causal principles constitute their attention-grabbing potential. This is why surface similarities are not sufficient and we should focus on the general principles that are both violated and activated in the child's concept. Fortunately, we now have a wealth of evidence about the structure and development of ontological categories and intuitive domain-specific principles. This will help us to describe religious development against a conceptual background that is much richer than that assumed by Goldman. One of Goldman's central hypotheses was that the child's principles of causation are largely anthropomorphic and that mechanical causation only gradually emerges from intentional causation. But the evidence for this may be misinterpreted. Children's "intentionalistic" notions about clouds and shadows may have more to do with their lack of empirical knowledge than with an intrinsically different conception of causation (Bullock, 1982). More generally, experimental studies in the last two decades have demonstrated the existence and constraining power of a set of specific causal principles in the preschooler. These principles inform such domains as intuitive physics, belief-desire psychology, and even biology (see Hirschfeld & Gelman, 1994). Also, a number of recent studies have centered on the child's construal of magical or fantastic scenarios (see Woolley, 1997). These findings, together with the anthropological framework described above, give us a much better view of the acquisition of religious representations.

Let us first consider the question of whether children actually have the "intuitive ontology" that religious concepts seem to transgress. As we said above, culturally recurrent religious concepts do not center so much on odd or unfamiliar assumptions as on counterintuitive ones based on the violation or transfer of intuitive domain-specific principles. Now it is striking that the principles violated or transferred are not about peripheral aspects of the ontological categories, but about their central properties. The notion of a god that can perceive everything at once (in parallel fashion) goes against a central assumption of our intuitive "theory of mind" – that attention is a serial process directed at particular objects one after the other. In the same way, mythical accounts of metamorphoses violate a central assumption about biological beings – that membership in a species is a stable, "essential" property and not an accidental one. In the Yoruba religion, for instance, as in countless others, changes in animal identity are allowed, the transformation violating an unassailable intuitive assumption associated with natural kinds. Finally, the notion of a statue that listens to people's prayers violates a core property of the artifact domain–that artifacts are inanimate.

The principles violated or transferred are central to the categories. They are also among the first acquired for each of the domains considered. "Ghost-physics" violates assumptions about solid objects that appear in the first six months (Baillargeon, 1994 Spelke, 1990;). Metamorphoses violate essentialist principles tacitly used by preschoolers (Coley, 1995; Gelman & Markman, 1987) even before they develop a rich understanding of what makes live beings alive (Carey, 1985). Indeed, animals that undergo metamorphoses are construed as changing kind-identity, because metamorphosis is excluded by the child's early understanding of natural growth (Rosengren, Gelman, Kalish, & McCormick, 1991). In the same way, statues with psychological processes go against the preschooler's expectation that artifacts are not agents and cannot in principle move by themselves (Gelman & Kremer, 1991).

Preschoolers, then, seem to have the principles "targeted" by religious representations. But this leaves open the question, Are children sensitive to the counterintuitive quality of these representations? This is a different question, in the sense that children might have the principles yet fail to appreciate in what way they are contradicted by certain cultural representations. But there is evidence that children are in fact sensitive to violations and transfers and notice how they go against intuitive expectations. Indeed, observing the child's reaction to nonstandard predications, counterintuitive concepts, or "impossible" scenarios is the most common research tool in the study of intuitive principles. That is, we can say that the child has the principles mentioned above mainly because we create contexts in which expectations are violated and observe behavioral responses. These range from gaze direction and sucking frequency in infants to laughter or explicit sentence judgment in older children.

Accepting that children have the relevant intuitive principles and are sensitive to counterintuitive representations as such, we can then evaluate whether their reactions to such representations are the same as adults' reactions. Do children construe religious concepts as descriptions of a real yet unobservable domain of reality, or as part of an imaginary world that includes fiction as well as personal fantasies like imaginary companions? Recent evidence concerning the child's "reality-fantasy" distinction is relevant here. First, many studies have established that children do distinguish what is "real" from what is "imaginary" and "magical" in contexts that include salient violations of expectations (Harris, Brown, Marriott, Whitall, & Harmer, 1991; Johnson & Harris, 1994; Woolley & Phelps, 1994). This is linked to the early development of a broader distinction between reality and appearance (see Flavell, Flavell, Green, & Moses, 1990; Gopnik & Meltzoff, 1987). There remain two major questions as regards the proper interpretation of such findings. First, we do not know whether children identify particular situations as "real" or "unreal" on the basis of a general ontological distinction, or, alternatively, by using domain-specific features like animacy for certain objects, tangibility for others, stability over time for superficial properties, and so on. Second, many children have problems applying the term "real" to nonstandard experiences like dreams (Prawat, Anderson, & Hapkeiwicz, 1989). This suggests that the terms "real" or "reality" and the underlying concepts might at this stage be primarily based on a notion of "experienced situation" rather than "actual situation."

It is clear that preschoolers can distinguish between three "worlds": (1) that of experienced reality; (2) the realm of the imagination, where the individual conjures up beings, objects, and events; and (3) the world of fantasy and fiction, found in fairy tales, cartoons, and so on, where agents other than oneself carry out magical, anomalous, or supernatural acts. In the world of fiction, anomalous objects and acts, such as permeable solid objects or inanimate objects becoming animate, are seen as "natural" and acceptable, and such anomalies often delight or amuse young children. On the other hand, such violations of causal principles in real-world contexts often take children completely by surprise, eliciting incredulous utterances or looks of confusion and bewilderment (Chandler & Lalonde, 1994).

Yet, despite being able to make distinctions among what is real, imaginary, or fantastic, children often seem to blur the line between reality and these other worlds. For example, in a study conducted by

Harris et al. (1991), young children expressed fear of an imaginary creature, and in another study, hearing of a fictional child's behavior in a fairy tale, the children's own subsequent behavior implied a belief in supernatural events (Subbotsky, 1994). There seem to be important contextual effects in these reactions, in particular in the extent to which "natural" causal principles or "magical" principles are invoked to guide behavior (Chandler & Lalonde, 1994; Rosengren, Kalish, Hickling, & Gelman, 1994). For example, Harris et al. (1991) found that young children expressed no fear of opening a box in which there was an imaginary rabbit but were fearful of looking into a box supposedly containing a monster. The prospect, however dim, of encountering monsters, those frightful, unfamiliar supernatural creatures, shook the children's certainty of their understanding of the imaginary. Likewise, a number of studies have demonstrated that children often resort to "magical" explanations in contexts where they have difficulty explaining unusual phenomena using natural causal principles (Chandler & Lalonde, 1994; Phelps & Woolley, 1994; Rosengren et al., 1994). For example, in Phelps and Woolley's (1994) study of physical versus magical explanations in young children, two-thirds of the six-year-olds gave magical explanations for the disappearance of a quarter in a mirrored box. Contexts such as this, which present some sort of violation of children's causal assumptions, may evoke "magical" explanations if the children can provide no satisfactory "natural" account. By contrast, in a study investigating young children's judgments and explanations of sensible and anomalous sentences, the children readily recognized the absurdity of the anomalous sentences and easily furnished appropriate causal explanations (Walker, 1999). For example, one four-year-old responded as follows when asked if pigs can have kittens: "Noooo. That's silly; pigs have oink oinks." Here, the anomalous information was not presented in a supernatural context, or one presenting phenomena that went beyond the children's ability to offer an explanation. Consequently, preschoolers had no difficulty identifying sentences as absurd and providing appropriate explanations for why that was so.

So young children do have a grasp of domain-specific causal principles that they can readily access in certain contexts to explain unusual phenomena. However, in explicitly supernatural contexts, or when appropriate "natural" explanations elude them, they frequently resort to "magical" explanations. It is difficult at this stage to disentangle task specificity as such (i.e., whether certain tasks elicit more "magical" speculations) from context or relevance effect (i.e., whether "magical" speculation is more relevant given the context).

As we said above, religious representations derive their attention-grabbing potential from the fact that they are presented as *real* occurrences. This is a crucial factor, and some of the "reality-fantasy" literature may help us to understand how this aspect of religious concepts develops. The oppositions between events that conform to intuitive expectations and those that violate them, on the one hand, and real and unreal ones on the other, are orthogonal. A course of events may be represented as (1) imaginary, yet conform to intuitive expectations, or, conversely, as (2) counterintuitive and real. That these distinctions are orthogonal is clear in children's pretend behavior (the first type of situation) and in their reactions to magician's tricks (the converse case). Johnson and Harris's studies of children's explicit judgments on a variety of "magical" scenarios show that this second type of situation is readily called "magical" by seven year-olds and older children, and that both criteria are equally important; the situations must be represented as both counterintuitive *and* real (Johnson & Harris, 1994), if the latter is understood in the sense of "actually experienced" (see our remarks above on an experience- rather than ontology-based understanding of "real" in young children). This marks off "magical" situations from fictional accounts of various counterintuitive scenarios. It also suggests that this concept of "magic" may extend to phenomena that are not culturally categorized as "magic" by adults, such as light switches or magnets. Without speculating too much, we would suggest that nothing important here hinges on the lexical label itself. Indeed, what seems to distinguish the seven-year-old's reactions from younger children's is not so much the lexical meaning for "magical" as the construction of a particular slot for real *and* counterintuitive occurrences. In this sense, it is plausible that at around age seven the child acquires a conceptual ability that makes his/her religious concepts much more similar to adults', that is, based on counterintuitive assumptions *and* clearly distinguished from fiction.[7]

Additional evidence for this shift comes from Walker's studies,

---

[7] It may be relevant to point out that in many places religious specialists are quite keen to distinguish themselves from magicians. Even in places where religious activity involves trance or possession, it is generally assumed that the less spectacular performances are the more convincing ones. In other words, the delicate balance that allows one to consider these counterintuitive occurences as real is threatened when the violations are so massive that people suspect trickery.

mentioned above (Walker, 1999). As we said, recurrent religious concepts tend to violate or transfer core principles associated with ontological categories. In other words, the domain of possible religious concepts is much narrower than we would suppose if religious concepts are described as only "odd," implausible, or unfamiliar situations. However, most studies of the reality-fantasy distinction use a maximal contrast (between situations in full accordance with intuitive principles and situations that clearly violate them), and it remains possible that young children (before the age of seven) do not readily distinguish such violations from simply unfamiliar, odd, or implausible scenarios. In Walker's experiments, children had to judge the relative "silliness" of statements at three levels of distance from intuitive expectations: statements describing (1) sensible scenarios (e.g., a cow that eats grass), (2) implausible ones (a cow that eats popcorn), and (3) anomalous ones (a cow that has puppies). Even the youngest group (age three) had no problem judging anomalous situations more "silly" than sensible ones. However, "implausible" situations were generally judged "silly" by three- or four-year-olds who did not easily distinguish them from anomalous ones. There is a gradual shift, and by around seven years most children find "implausible" scenarios comparable to sensible ones in that they describe unusual but possible states of affairs.

This may explain the apparently paradoxical finding that children develop more refined religious concepts at the same period when they have a richer representation of causal principles. Several researchers have observed that "magical" thinking decreases with age, as children become more sure of causal principles and hence more skeptical of anything that smacks of "magic" (Chandler & Lalonde, 1994; Harris, 1994; Subbotsky, 1994). Yet, as was observed with the Yoruba adults, explanations that supported violations of causal principles were readily offered in ritual contexts; "magical" thinking was very much in evidence. What seems to happen developmentally is that children acquire a more elaborated supernatural framework that is more intimately tied to supernatural beliefs found in their respective cultures. So, while certain kinds of "magical" explanations (e.g., for how magicians can make objects float in space) may suffer a decline with age, the "magical" thinking that is part and parcel of specific religious belief systems actually increases. For example, it has been noted by several researchers that children do not spontaneously offer supernatural explanations unless the context supports such an explanation or they cannot come up with one based on causal principles (Chandler & Lalonde, 1994; Woolley & Phelps, 1994). Likewise, in a different study that included Yoruba children and adults, Walker (1999) found that Yoruba children did not give supernatural explanations for transformations of animals in nonritual contexts, but a few older children did, as did a number of adults. This finding, combined with those of other studies discussed here, suggests that a well-elaborated, readily accessed supernatural framework takes time to develop, possibly not settling into place until late childhood or early adolescence.

## Conclusions

To return to our central question: Are children's religious representations similar to adult concepts? Strictly speaking, practically nothing in the child's conceptual repertoire is *completely* identical to the adult's, so a negative answer would seem sensible. This, however, hinges on a rather extreme understanding of "similarity" that may not be relevant here. We have provided arguments and evidence that point to a more nuanced, and on the whole positive answer. There are definite continuities between children's and adults' religious concepts. To see them, however, one needs to abandon the narrow view of religious concepts in which they reduce to explicit statements about matters officially labeled "religious." One also needs to take into account the cognitive processes involved in adult religious concepts across cultures.

The main continuity is that religious concepts include (i) socially transmitted, attention grabbing, counterintuitive elements based on violations or transfers of intuitive principles; and (ii) spontaneous inferences from a default background. As far as these two aspects are concerned, there is substantial congruence between the adult's and the six-year-old's way of representing such concepts. However, it is true that there is anecdotal evidence that seems to go against this continuity. Children do say things about religious agencies that adults find strange or funny or just plain wrong, depending on their own concerns. Yet this does not really conflict with our account. Children's explicit statements about gods or spirits differ from the adults' for two main reasons:

1. A six-year-old simply lacks some of the relevant cultural knowledge. Only gradually can one learn that God's being "eternal"

means that he was around before cars were invented, or that God probably does not need to brush his teeth (or that the question is officially considered silly). That the child acquires a richer knowledge base does not entail that the principles under-lying religious concepts have significantly changed over time. Children also say that clouds or rivers move of their own accord. This does not entail that they have a particular conception of causation. It only shows that they do not know enough true facts about clouds or rivers.

2. Many of the alleged discontinuities might be due to our failure to detect the phenomenon of "theological correctness" identified by Barrett and Keil (1996). That is, children's and adult's con-cepts may be continuous, not just because the child already uses most of the tacit principles of adult ontology, but also because the adult's religious concepts are much more governed by early developed principles than adults themselves (or their religious teachers) would like to think.

To highlight the essential continuity of religious principles between early or middle childhood and adult concepts does not mean, how-ever, that we deny important developmental shifts. Two of these are particularly important:

1. Our account is based on the fact that a six-year-old holds most of the intuitive principles contradicted by religious concepts. Now, not all principles emerge or are acquired at the same time. Principles of intuitive physics, for instance, are a very early development, while notions about the stability of species iden-tity are rather shaky even in a six-year-old (Keil, 1989). This leaves open the question, How do children represent supernat-ural agents before they develop the relevant principles? For in-stance, how do they construe a god that perceives everything before they understand the possibility of a false belief? At age three, children have a poor grasp of the complex factors that mediate between a given state of affairs and a representation of that state of affairs in someone's mind. As a result, they ascribe to agents in general the kind of immediate and unerring access to reality that adult believers describe in supernatural agents like God. So one could predict that the child's concept of God at that stage is more "theologically correct" than the adult version. Barrett (in press) has striking evidence that this is indeed the

case. We certainly need more studies of this kind to make any conjectures about early religious concepts before ontological principles are firmly entrenched in the child's expectations.

2. There seems to be a clear shift with the construction of a specific (not necessarily named) conceptual slot for "counterintuitive + real" scenarios. The psychological evidence shows that this is a middle-childhood phenomenon. Anthropological evidence shows that at this point children develop a much stricter distinction between magical, religious representations and fiction. This is crucial, since religious representations owe much of their attention-grabbing potential to the fact that they are presented as descriptions of *real* occurrences and states of affairs.

Here we presented a framework that allows us to explain the development of religious ontologies in a way that is consistent with both psychological and anthropological data. This implies that religious ontological representations are not limited to consciously accessible representations about God, for instance, are not exhausted by conscious reports about the properties of that agency. Tacit assumptions govern people's inferences and expectations about such agents in ways that are not accessible to consciousness. This is why the structure of religious concepts requires experimental studies of intuitive ontology as well as a description of religious meanings as such.

All of this leads to a more general question concerning the extent to which religious concepts can be said to form a specific domain in the sense of the "domains" of domain-specificity. Obviously, religious concepts have some common features, and we tried to describe some common processes underlying their acquisition. However, the notion of a cognitive domain should be understood more strictly if the notion is to be of any theoretical use. The domain of intuitive psychology ("theory of mind") for instance seems to be informed by principles that are both unique (not found in other conceptual domains) and strongly integrated (how one detects gaze direction is linked to how one attributes perception and intentionality to others, which is linked to how one explains their action as goal-directed, and so on). In this chapter, we have suggested that "religion" might not be a conceptual domain in this strong sense, and we must explain why, as this point has practical consequences on how we study the development of religious concepts.

The conclusions and conjectures summed up above are all centered on the domain of religious ontology: claims about the existence and causal powers of various supernatural entities. We tried to show that religious concepts are parasitic on intuitive ontology. They are given in the cultural input, but (i) their salience depends on their counterintuitive nature, relative to prior expectations; and (ii) they are always complemented by default assumptions imported from intuitive ontology. So it would make little sense to describe (or study) the development of religious ontologies while ignoring the development of intuitive ontology. The particular way in which religious ontology develops depends on the wider development of ontological categories.

Now "religion" does not reduce to religious ontologies, as we said at the beginning of this chapter. Other conceptual "repertoires," as it were, are involved in religious representations. As we said at the beginning, religious concepts also activate representations of moral rules, group identity, and private experience. We would contend that: (i) in each of these repertoires we may well find a similar "parasitic" structure, where religious concepts can be explained only against a broader conceptual background; and (ii) there is no overwhelming evidence that the various repertoires are strongly integrated into a unified religious domain. Morality is a domain where specific cultural input seems to activate general principles that have to do, for example, with a distinction between habit and convention and between convention and moral obligation (see, e.g., Turiel, 1983). Religious morality does not develop differently; it only differs from the nonreligious kind in making explicit claims about the connections between morality and supernatural agents, or about the origin of moral imperatives. So we could not really explain the development of religious morality without importing most of our explanation from the development of morality in general. To turn to group identity, concepts of social categories and ethnic differences are informed by specific principles with a specific developmental path (Hirschfeld, 1996). Group identity founded on religious criteria, as opposed to kinship or locality, does not seem to have specific features in that respect. A similar point could be made for the acquisition of cultural routines and rituals, or for the representation of private experiences. In each of these "repertoires," then, it seems that the relevant explanation for conceptual structure and development involves the repertoire as a whole, not just its "religious" subpart.

Further, as we said above, there is no evidence that all of these repertoires are strongly integrated, even though they are often presented, especially in literate traditions, as part of a unified package.

That is to say, a "religion" is presented as a coherent system in which morality for instance is supported by belief in sanction from supernatural agents, as well as connections with group identity, specific practices, and specific experiences. There is good anthropological and historical evidence that these connections between repertoires are *ex post facto* rationalizations rather than the expression of actual inferential links. Historically, ontology may change without disrupting either morality or group indentity, or, conversely, a new morality can be established while preserving ontology, and so on. From a cognitive viewpoint, the connections between repertoires take the form of abductive explanations, providing connections between assumptions that are already there rather than deducing some of them from the others (Boyer, 1994b).

All of this points to the conclusion that there is no domain specialization in "religious thinking." That is to say, we have no good reason to think that there is a distinct domain of "religious cognition" with particular functional characteristics. Obviously, we do not mean to suggest that there is no such thing as "religion." The notion does denote a real social and cultural phenomenon, but this does not entail that religion is cognitively integrated into a domain. To take a distant analogy, "trees" are a distinct kind of reality for all sorts of economic, ecological, or aesthetic purposes; yet "tree" is not a sound biological category.

This question of "domains" and integration is relevant to how we study and explain religious concepts. In our view, studies of cognition in religion so far make both the acquisition and the adult representation of religious concepts rather difficult to understand. If we accept that "religion" makes use of intrinsically diverse cognitive resources, we can better understand its acquisition and behavioral manifestations. Morality and group commitment and construal of private experience are all domains for which there are particular acquisition trajectories, and for which there already exists a rich developmental literature. So a "deflationary" account of religion, even though it may seem to dissolve the originality or specificity of religious concepts, in fact paves the way for a more precise understanding of religious concepts and practices.

### References

Baillargeon, R. (1994). Physical Reasoning in young infants: Seeking explanations for impossible events. *British Journal of Development Psychology, 12* (1), 9–34.

Barrett, J. L., & Keil, F. C. (1996). Conceptualizing a non-natural entity: Anthropomorphism in God concepts. *Cognitive Psychology, 31*, 219–247.

Barrett, J. L. (1999). Transmission advantages for minimally counterintuitive concepts. Invited presentation for the University of Michigan Cognition and Culture Program's mini-conference *The Transmission of Religious Ideas*, March.

Barrett, J. L. (in press). Do children experience God like adults? Retracing the development of god concepts. In: J. Andresen (ed.), *Keeping Religion in Mind: Cognitive Perspectives on Religious Experience*. Cambridge: Cambridge University Press.

Bartlett, F. C. (1932). *Remembering. A study in Experimental and Social Psychology*. Cambridge: Cambridge University Press.

Bloch, M. (1985). From cognition to ideology. In: R. Fardon (Ed.), *Power and Knowledge. Anthropological and Sociological Approaches*. Edinburgh: Scottish Academic Press.

Boyer, P. (1994a). Cognitive constraints on cultural representations: Natural ontologies and religious ideas. In: L. A. Hirschfeld and S. Gelman (Eds.), *Mapping the Mind: Domain-Specificity in Culture and Cognition*, (pp. 391–411). New York: Cambridge University Press.

Boyer, P. (1994b). *The Naturalness of Religious Ideas: A Cognitive Theory of Religion*. Berkeley, CA: University of California Press.

Boyer, P. (in press). Cultural inheritance tracks and Cognitive predispositions: The example of religious concepts. In: H. Whitehouse (Ed.), *Mind, Evolution and Cultural Transmission*. Cambridge: Cambridge University Press.

Bullock, M., Gelman, R. & Baillargeon, R. (1982). The development of causal reasoning. In W. J. Friedman (Ed.), *The Developmental Psychology of Time*. New York: Academic Press.

Carey, S. (1985). *Conceptual Change in Childhood*. Cambridge, MA: MIT Press.

Chandler, M. J., & Lalonde, C. E. (1994). Surprising, magical and miraculous turns of events: Children's reactions to violations of their early theories of mind and matter. *British Journal of Developmental Psychology, 12*, 83–95.

Coles, R. (1990). *The Spiritual Life of Children*. Boston: Houghten Mifflin.

Coley, J. (1995). Emerging differentiation of folk biology and folk psychology: Attributions of biological and psychological properties to living things. *Child Development, 66* 1856–74.

Durham, W. H. (1991). *Coevolution. Genes, Cultures and Human Diversity*. Stanford, CA: Stanford University Press.

Flavell, J. H., Flavell, E. R., Green, F. L., & Moses, L. J. (1990). Young children's understanding of fact beliefs versus value beliefs. *Child Development, 61* 915–928.

Gelman, S. A., & Kremer, K. E. (1991). Understanding natural cause: Children's explanations of how objects and their properties originate. *Child Development, 62*, 396–414.

Gelman, S., & Markman, E. (1987). Young children's inductions from natural kinds: The role of categories and appearances. *Child Development, 58*, 32–41.

Goldman, R. (1964). *Religious Thinking from Childhood to Adolescence*. London: Routledge & Kegan Paul.

Gopnik, A., & Meltzoff, A. (1987). The development of categorization in the second year and its relation to other cognitive and linguistic developments. *Child Development, 58,* 1523–1531.

Gorsuch, R. L. (1988). Psychology of religion. *Annual Review of Psychology, 39,* 201–221.

Harris, P. L. (1994). Unexpected, impossible and magical events: Children's reactions to causal violations. *British Journal of Developmental Psychology, 12,* 1–7.

Harris, P., Brown, E., Marriott, C., Whitall, S., & Harmer, S. (1991). Monsters, ghosts and witches: Testing the limits of the fantasy-reality distinction in young children. *British Journal of Developmental Psychology, 9,* 105–123.

Hirschfeld, L. A. (1996). *Race in the Making: Cognition, Culture and the Child's Construction of Human Kinds*. Cambridge, MA: MIT Press.

Hirschfeld, L. A., & Gelman, S. A. (Eds.). (1994). *Mapping the Mind: Domain-Specificity in Culture and Cognition*. New York: Cambridge University Press.

Hunsberger, B. (1991). Empirical work in the psychology of religion. *Canadian Psychology/Psychologie canadienne, 39,* 497–504.

Johnson, C. N., & Harris, P. (1994). Magic: Special but not excluded. *British Journal of Developmental Psychology, 12,* 35–51.

Keil, F. C. (1989). *Concepts, Kinds and Conceptual Development*. Cambridge, MA: MIT Press.

Laurendeau, M., & Pinard, A. (1962). *Causal Thinking in the Child*. New York: International Universities Press.

Lawson, E. T., & McCauley, R. N. (1990). *Rethinking Religion: Connecting Cognition and Culture*. Cambridge: Cambridge University Press.

Ozorak, E. W. (1989). Social and cognitive influences on the development of religious beliefs and commitment in adolescence. *Journal for the Scientific Study of Religion, 28,* 448–463.

Phelps, K. E., & Woolley, J. D. (1994). The form and function of young children's magical beliefs. *Developmental Psychology, 30,* 385–94.

Prawat, R. S., Anderson, A. L., & Hapkeiwicz, W. (1989). Are dolls real? Developmental changes in the child's definition of reality. *Journal of Genetic Psychology, 150,* 359–74.

Reich, K. H. (1993). Cognitive-developmental approaches to religiousness: Which version for which purpose? *International Journal for the Psychology of Religion, 3,* 145–71.

Rosengren, K., Kalish, C. W., Hickling, A. K., & Gelman, S. A. (1994). Exploring the relation between preschool children's magical beliefs and causal thinking. *British Journal of Developmental Psychology, 12,* 69–82.

Rosengren, K. S., Gelman, S., Kalish, C. W., & McCormick, M. (1991). As time goes by: Children's early understanding of growth in animals. *Child Development, 62,* 1302–20.

Spelke, E. S. (1990). Principles of object perception. *Cognitive Science, 14,* 29–56.

Sperber, D. (1985). Anthropology and psychology. Towards an epidemiology of representations. *Man, 20*, 73–89.

Sperber, D. (1996). *Explaining Culture: A Naturalistic Approach*. Oxford: Blackwell.

Subbotsky, E. (1994). Early rationality and magical thinking in preschoolers: Space and time. *British Journal of Developmental Psychology, 12*, 97–108.

Turiel, E. (1983). *The Development of Social Knowledge. Morality and Convention*. Cambridge: Cambridge University Press.

Walker, S. (1992). Developmental changes in the representation of word-meaning: Cross-cultural findings. *British Journal of Developmental Psychology, 10*, 285–299.

Walker, S. (1999). Culture, domain-specificity, and conceptual change: Natural kind and artifact concepts. *British Journal of Developmental Psychology, 17*, 203–219.

Watts, F., & Williams, M. (1988). *The Psychology of Religious Knowing*. Cambridge: Cambridge University Press.

Whitehouse, H. (1992). Memorable religions: Transmission, codification and change in divergent Melanesian contexts. *Man, 27*, 777–797.

Woolley, J. D., & Phelps, K. E. (1994). Young children's practical reasoning about imagination. *British Journal of Developmental Psychology, 12*, 53–67.

Woolley, J. (1997). Thinking about fantasy: Are children fundamentally different thinkers and believers from adults? *Child Development, 68*, 991–1011.

# 6 On Not Falling Down to Earth

## Children's Metaphysical Questions

PAUL L. HARRIS

In this chapter, I begin with a puzzle – the neglect of religious thinking in psychology, particularly in developmental psychology. Having provided a tentative historical answer to this puzzle, I attempt to sketch what the study of children's metaphysical concepts might involve, had we taken a different route. I argue that it is not too late to retrace our steps, but, in so doing, we need to clear away various assumptions about the nature of cognitive development.

### A Puzzle

Why has the study of children's religious thinking been mostly ignored? There are several possible answers to this question that take a historical and negative approach to the topic itself; they imply that there is something about such thinking that prevents it from being part of a productive research program. For example, it can be argued that children concentrate on the mundane and have no inclination to think about or understand religious matters, so that, at best, the study of religious thinking in childhood is the study of the way in which various adult ideas are thrust on essentially secular thinkers. However, this proposal seems implausible. If children entirely lack any disposition to engage in religious thinking, adult instruction should fall on deaf ears. But few religious educators would accept such a claim. Many religious movements actively seek to instruct children on the grounds that they are particularly receptive to teachings of the right sort–and, so it is alleged–dangerously receptive to teachings of the wrong sort. Indeed, as I shall describe below, children's interest in metaphysical issues is highlighted by the questions that they pose. Hence, this line of argument indicates, at most, that children might not be disposed to adopt any given faith. It scarcely shows that they are immune to the teachings of the faithful.

Another possibility is that religious ideas are so multifarious and undisciplined that no generalizations are possible. Depending on the religion, children must learn that there is only one god or several, that cows may or may not be eaten, that women may or may not be ordained, and that there will or will not be a second coming. How could there be an interesting developmental story to tell in the face of such contradictions? On this argument, children's religious development can amount to little more than a study of the rote learning that children must deploy as they master this or that catechism. This irreverent approach, however, denies the possibility that, notwithstanding appearances, religious thinking centers on a set of core issues and has enunciated a limited set of answers. Yet, as argued elsewhere (Boyer, this volume) – that is a definite and illuminating possibility. An analogy with the study of moral development is not misplaced. Recall that in the 1930s the study of children's moral development all but ran aground because of the apparent heterogeneity of the domain and the inconsistencies displayed by children faced with different sections of it (Hartshorne & May, 1928–1930). Against that backdrop, however, a cognitive-developmental approach to children's moral thinking was slowly constructed, first in the hands of Piaget (1932), then Kohlberg (1969), and more recently through the domain-oriented approach of Turiel and his colleagues (Turiel, 1998). This cognitive-developmental approach holds out the promise of universal applicability, notwithstanding important cultural considerations (Turiel, this volume). It is not inconceivable that the study of religious thinking could follow the same route, albeit more than half a century later.

A third possible answer to the puzzle of why religion has been neglected seizes on an important issue but then proceeds to draw too hasty a conclusion. Arguably, religious thinking could never be the basis for a healthy research program because religious concepts, by their very nature, endlessly gesture at metaphysical possibilities that are, to put it mildly, not about to be either substantiated or displaced. According to this argument, religious thinking is best seen as a quaint but useless excrescence of a cognitive system that was actually designed for other, more useful, epistemic purposes. It is a bit like the ball-balancing ability of the sea lion – a capacity that is certainly demonstrable but not one that tells us much about the creature that exercises it. However, this argument presumes that human thinking is typically directed at observable, mundane reality. It is possible, and even likely, given the long history of human thinking about religion,[1] that this non-empirical mode of thought does tell us something significant about the nature of human cognition. Admittedly, our religious concepts are not testable in any conventional fashion, but this lack of empirical "bite" might reveal an interesting disposition of human mentation.

I conclude that there are tempting but no compelling arguments to show that the study of religious thinking, and its development, is doomed to failure. Such an enterprise could, in principle, be as productive as the study of moral development and could uncover a hitherto neglected cognitive endowment. In the next section, I consider a more contingent and historical explanation for its almost total absence from the relatively wide intellectual horizon of developmental psychology. In particular, I focus on the Piagetian legacy to the study of cognitive development. I argue that it is our selective pursuit of that legacy that has led us to neglect the development of religious thinking rather than any clear-eyed assessment of the feasibility of a productive research program.

## Cognitive Development Simplified

Although there are a variety of debates about how children actually do it, few students of cognitive development would quarrel with the claim that, at least in certain core domains, without any explicit instruction from adults, children move toward a more objective conception of reality – objective in the sense that it includes a more accurate conception of the enduring features of the world, as distinct from the world of appearances. While acquiring a more accurate conception of the world, children shed a variety of mistaken notions. In this orthodox view, cognitive development is mostly aimed at the truth, and it is relatively successful with respect to the nature of physical objects,

---

[1] Inferences from archaeological artifacts are not without their risks given the likely paucity and unrepresentativenes of the sample available. However, it is worth stressing that complex burial patterns, including the adornment of the body, date back 28,000 years (White, 1993). In addition, during the same period of the Upper Paleolithic, there are examples of anthropomorphic art–impossible fusions of human legs with a bison torso. Apparently, the after life and various mythical creatures have been on our mind for some time.

the biology of growth, the foundations of arithmetic, or human psychology.

Much of this vision stems, of course, from Piaget. Indeed, the seeds of that vision were sown very early in his intellectual career, certainly by the early 1920s, when he became convinced that various asocial and nonlogical features of early thinking were gradually supplanted by objectivity and rationality. I think that this progressive vision was bolstered in Piaget's mind by two different considerations. On the one hand, it fit in with his Enlightenment conception of the march of the intellect over historical time, and, more specifically, the historical claim that magical or animistic thinking has slowly given way to scientific thinking. Second, it fit in with Piaget's developmental credo that "autistic" thinking, in which reality is distorted by flights of the imagination, is a characteristically immature mode of thinking, one that is eventually suppressed by the more austere, reality-testing mode (Harris, 1997).

Particularly in his later work, Piaget emphasized a further aspect of cognitive development. Children do not merely contemplate reality: They explore and experiment with it, and by virtue of that activity they get closer to the truth. This emphasis of Piaget does indeed seem especially apt if we consider domains in which it is possible for children to act and observe the outcome of their actions. The infant's developing understanding of how to recover a hidden object offers a plausible example of the way that an initially restricted and. error-prone activity might be corrected by exploration and feedback (Piaget, 1954).[2] Children's understanding of the balance beam (Siegler, 1976) and of number (Nunes & Bryant, 1996) provide two other familiar examples.

Finally, and intimately connected with his emphasis on independent, empirical investigation, Piaget was skeptical of any knowledge that he regarded as merely verbal. Some of his most influential experimental work was guided by the assumption that we shall be misled about what children know if we merely listen to them talk. For example, a child who counts may or may not understand numbers. The acid test is not the ability to count but the appreciation of the invari-

---

[2] Admittedly, an avalanche of data has shown that the infant's conception of a hidden object is more sophisticated than Piaget allowed. At the same time, despite that avalanche, Piaget's claim that the search for a hidden object becomes progressively more extensive and accurate as the infant gets older, still stands.

ance of numbers as indexed by the conservation experiment. By the same token, Piaget was inclined to argue that any knowledge that children acquire merely via language is likely to be at best poorly assimilated, and at worst adopted in a dogmatic and uncritical fashion.

These intellectual preoccupations, with an emphasis on progress toward an objective view of reality, on the role of empirical feedback, and on the obfuscations of mere verbal knowledge, are likely to entail a negative approach to the development of children's metaphysical thinking, in which it is seen as a regressive mode of thought that is eventually outgrown. One aspect of that approach was reflected in Piaget's own early research. He focused on various limitations in the child's initial conceptualization of the world, limitations that are eventually shed with the advance of further observation and increasing objectivity. In this vein, Piaget studied children's dispositions toward animism – the tendency to endow physical objects and events with biological or psychological capacities – and artificialism – the tendency to believe that objects were made by mankind expressly for his own purposes. He argued that both tendencies decline in the course of early childhood. Thus, on one reading, Piaget can be seen as endorsing a historical and developmental opposition: Naive or primitive modes of reasoning, including those that are found in certain types of religious thinking, gradually give way to the objectivity of science.

Admittedly, contemporary investigators have insisted that Piaget overstated the young child's naivete and underestimated the child's rate of progress. Thus, any disposition toward animism or artificialism is alleged to be less widespread than he claimed. Consider, for example, a current, influential view of cognitive development. The child is described as working more or less concurrently, and successfully, in several different "laboratories." He or she is simultaneously constructing independent theories of the physical, biological, and psychological domains (Wellman & Gelman, 1998). In its most radical form, this approach claims that it is not so much that children resemble scientists, but that scientists are fortunate enough to resemble children in having the freedom to pursue the open-minded inquiry that is characteristic of childhood (Gopnik & Meltzoff, 1997). However, these revisions of the Piagetian approach are the dissenting voices of orthodoxy rather than of heresy. The overall conclusion is simply that progress in objective theory construction gets under way more rapidly than Piaget allowed, and is hampered primarily by a lack of access to relevant data. Thus, even if we examine the agenda laid out by the intellectual heirs of Piaget, there is little opportunity to construe the development of religious thinking in progressive terms. Once again, the child as enlightened scientist is assumed to outgrow the child as confused metaphysician.

It is worth pointing out that this contemporary stance does not do full justice to Piaget's epistemological framework. There is a different agenda that could have been derived from his own intellectual struggle with the relation between science and religion, as laid out in a series of publications in the 1930s. He acknowledges that there is a rightful place for metaphysical thinking, one that need not be in opposition to science. At the same time, he does assume that certain modes of religious thinking are undermined – and should be undermined – in the face of scientific advances. Specifically, Piaget contrasts two forms of religious thinking: on the one hand, the traditional stance that postulates an anthropomorphic but transcendent God who is at the same time a *deus ex machina*, an initial cause, and an agent in human history and, on the other hand, the more sophisticated stance that regards the divine as immanent in life, and notably in the normative activity of thought itself, with its alleged propensity toward higher and more encompassing forms of equilibrium. Effectively, Piaget finesses any implication of an irreconcilable divide between religion and science by claiming that science is the divine made manifest.

One possibility with respect to future research is to take Piaget's proposals seriously: to investigate, particularly in adolescence, the extent to which the transcendent stance is displaced by the immanent stance. However, I propose an approach that steps outside various key Piagetian assumptions. I argue that children are not necessarily aiming at a more objective conception of reality, do not rely primarily on empirical feedback, and frequently rely on verbally transmitted collective representations. These interrelated claims yield a different agenda for the study of religious thinking.

## The World of Possibilities

Consider the idea that children are not primarily scientists in the making and that only a small part of cognitive development can be construed as progress toward increasingly stable theories. Consider instead the proposal that an enduring backdrop to cognitive development is the processing of propositional content organized by time and modality. By three or four years, children conceptualize the past, present, and future, and they also distinguish among actual and merely hypothetical or imagined events. Coordinating these temporal and modal frameworks, they can set up a variety of mental spaces, each of which is marked for time and modality. Thus, they can set up mental spaces devoted to the actual present that are kept separate from those devoted to the actual past, or from those devoted to the fictional past, the counterfactual present, or the probable future. In this view, there is room for children to discover in a standard Piagetian fashion truths that apply across various mental spaces, as earlier unsophisticated ideas are replaced by those closer to the truth. At the same time, there is room for expansion and elaboration to take place within these various mental spaces. Thus, children expand their comprehension of the actual past – they contemplate the time before they were born, the time when their parents were children, the age of the Romans or of the dinosaurs. They also expand their notion of the probable future; they begin to contemplate not just the next day, but the arrival of a new sibling, the time when they will grow up, or when their parents will die. Concurrent with this expanding temporal envelope is an expansion of the realm of possibility. Children learn what befell Peter Rabbit or Brer Rabbit. And they may go on to think about other unnerving possibilities: that their parents might not be their real parents; that the universe and all that it contains might never have come into existence; and that there might, or might not, be a God. All of these mental spaces, those that pertain to the probable or the merely possible, and not just those that pertain to the actual, can drive children's emotional systems and engage their curiosity.

The second proposal concerns the role of active, empirically oriented exploration. To the extent that the above claim is correct, children's mental universe rapidly extends well beyond domains in which active experimentation is feasible. With respect to the past and the future, the realm of fiction, and of counterfactual possibilities, children cannot act in a truth-seeking, Piagetian mode. They cannot experiment on the past or check out the afterlife; they cannot discover alternative escape routes from Mr. McGregor's garden or the celestial mechanics of the tooth fairy. Nor can they, except in their imagination, investigate the consequences of having had a different set of parents, of meeting a dragon, or of living in a parallel universe. The implication, therefore, is that once they step outside the vault of the actual, children cannot operate as standard, Piagetian truth-seekers: Direct empirical feedback is not available to correct their thinking.

In some ways, this point is not novel. It has often been remarked that children cannot experiment on the stars, the sun, or the clouds. Hence, it is not surprising that they are more prone to animistic thinking with respect to these entities than those that are more accessible and palpable (Berzonsky, 1971). However, this assertion tacitly presumes that the child's primary domain of operation is the observable universe, albeit one that extends beyond his or her powers of experimentation. My argument, by contrast, is that that observable universe is a lesser fraction of what is on the child's mind and, within that greater fraction, direct empirical observation is out of the question. Nevertheless, mental experimentation is possible. By extrapolation from the known causal mechanisms that apply in the actual world, the child can speculate about possible outcomes in the nonactual world. However, those default assumptions cannot supply all of the answers. In thinking about what happens after death, or how the world began, various gaps and anomalies will be encountered.

The third proposal concerns our species-specific capacity to acquire and exchange new information using language. This important capacity has attracted little systematic attention in the study of cognitive development. It is frequently assumed that major cognitive change – the kind that can be measured in terms of a qualitative shift in the child's mode of explanation – is not brought about via anything as straightforwardly pedagogic as verbal instruction. Even if children are told something in the first instance, it is assumed that they need to digest the message in the context of activity and exploration. The upshot is that we have a limited experimental grip on the extent to which children can take in new information about the actual or nonactual world simply by being told what is the case or what is believed to be the case. Everyday experience, however, suggests that they certainly turn to adults in search of information. Many of these questions arise in the course of pragmatic activities – "Where is my puzzle?" "What's his name?" "Who is outside?" – and receive answers in which a preexisting conceptual slot about the actual world is filled in. However, other questions are concerned with matters beyond the present and actual world. Children want to know how the world began and what happens when people die. In the next section, I describe two expectations concerning such questions.

## Curiosity and Metaphysics

I have made three interrelated claims: that young children, certainly from the age of three or four years, navigate among various mental spaces that are appropriately marked for time and modality. They think about the actual world, but they also think about nonactual, fictional, and metaphysical possibilities located in the past, the present, or the future. Second, if children are to understand the creatures and mechanisms of these nonactual worlds, they cannot rely on active exploration and empirical feedback. That mode of learning can offer help in the case of accessible, manipulable regularities. It starts to break down once children look further afield – at the stars or the clouds. It collapses altogether when they shift out of the actual and present world. Third, children do nevertheless seek to resolve the puzzles that they encounter as they think about these other worlds. In the absence of empirical feedback, they use that alternative, species-specific mode of information gathering, discussion, and conversation to seek enlightenment. In such contexts, they are likely to learn about, and come to rely on, the collective representations of their culture concerning the nature of death, the origin of life, and the power of God. We can reasonably assume that the longevity of such collective representations is not determined primarily by their empirical validity; although claims and predictions may well be made, few of them concern the actual and present worlds.[3] Instead, their collective, cognitive viability will be determined by their ability to survive the winnowing process of repeated transmission from one generation to the next.

These claims lead to two interrelated predictions. First, although children frequently confront gaps and anomalies in their empirical experience of the present and actual worlds, we may anticipate that they will also encounter them in their mental contemplation of other, nonactual worlds. Of necessity, such gaps and anomalies are not thrown up by perceptual experience; they arise only in the context of the child's mental model of the functioning of these other worlds. As the child attempts to visualize or imagine what takes place in such a nonactual mental space, an imagined outcome is recognized as odd or

---

[3] Even when predictions are made about the actual world, their falsification is unlikely to undermine the belief system that gave rise to them (Festinger, Riecken, & Schacter, 1956).

paradoxical, and this puzzlement is translated into a question. The first prediction, therefore, is straightforward: Just as children pose questions about the empirical anomalies that they encounter in their direct exploration of the actual world, so too they will pose questions about the imagined anomalies that they encounter in their mental exploration of the nonactual world. In particular, in line with an acute early analysis of children's why and how questions presented by Isaacs (1930), we may expect children to pose questions when they encounter a tension between what they generally expect to happen and the particular outcome that they are in the process of contemplating, whether with regard to the actual or the nonactual world.

The second prediction flows directly from the first. When the child is engaged in exploration of the actual world, the expectation of regularity can be supplied by the child's own internal schemas, and the oddity can be supplied by observation of a perceived anomaly. For example, the child expects a given object to float, places it in some water, but sees the object sink. At this point, the child can point to the observed anomaly and ask an adult to explain it. In the case of questions about the nonactual world, on the other hand, the situation is more complex. The child must supply both the expectation and the oddity. After all, and to repeat, it is only in the child's imagination that the oddity or paradox is realized. There is no way to investigate the afterlife or the moment of creation to assess whether they conform to expectation. By implication, therefore, certain schemas supply an expectation about what should "ordinarily" happen, whereas other schemas supply a hypothesis or guess about a particular nonactual outcome. Then, in comparing the one with the other, the child will sometimes encounter an anomaly. Thus, the second prediction may be formulated as follows: Children's questions about anomalous outcomes will sometimes be triggered by the tension between an observed outcome and an expectation, but they will also be triggered by the tension between two sets of "expectations" – the local expectations that yield the particular imagined outcome and the more wide-ranging expectation with which that imagined outcome conflicts. In the next section, I take a closer look at some examples of children's how and why questions to evaluate these predictions.

## Examples of Children's Questions

If we look back at surveys of children's questions, we find that investigators have ignored the above distinction between questions that arise in the course of encounters with the actual world and those that occur in the course of reflection about the nonactual world. For example, Piaget (1926) emphasizes that children's questions spring from their "precausal" model of the world, but he makes no distinction between questions that arise in the context of an observed anomaly and those that stem from puzzlement about nonactual worlds. In an acute analysis, Isaacs (1930) takes Piaget to task for his insistence that children's questions arise primarily because they are in the grip of some naive causal epistemology. At the same time, Isaacs, like Piaget, was inclined to think of scientific thinking as the canon against which to judge the child's first questions. And seeing children's "why" questions as the first stirrings of the scientific mode of inquiry, he was not inclined to distinguish between the kinds of questions that an observant "scientific" child might pose in the course of everyday activity and the kinds of questions that the child metaphysician might pose.

However, the disinclination of either investigator to make such a distinction is in some ways reassuring. Because they did not seek out questions of one kind over the other, it suggests that their sampling is unbiased. In Table 6.1, I give examples of questions that appear to be triggered by some observed oddity or anomaly in the child's empirical experience of the actual world. I also give examples of questions triggered in the context of the child's speculation about non-actual worlds.

Inspection of the first group of questions provides support for the claim made by Isaacs (1930): Many of these how or why questions do appear to be triggered by an observed anomaly. Consider, for example, a question put by a child of three years and eleven months: "Why won't it burn?" The question was asked about some wet raffia held in the fire that refused to burn. Presumably, the child asking the question has built up the expectation that when things are held to a flame they usually burn, and this is especially true of items such as sticks or strips of paper. When an item that is similar in shape and texture to these combustible items fails to catch fire, the child is puzzled. Note that the child is not posing a general question about fire ("What makes things burn?") nor a question about what prevents a given class of objects from burning ("Why don't rocks burn?"). Rather, the question is triggered by the gap between the particular outcome that was expected and the particular outcome that was observed. To the extent that the anomaly arises out of an ongoing activity and an empirical observation, it is the kind of encounter that Piaget regarded as an engine of cognitive development. It is interesting to note, nonetheless,

Table 6.1. *Examples of Children's Questions in the Context of "Empirical" and "Metaphysical" Puzzles*

| Empirical Questions | Age | Source |
|---|---|---|
| Why can I put my hand through water and not through soap? | 3; 7 | Sully (1896, p. 457) |
| Why won't it (wet raffia held in fire) burn? | 3; 11 | Isaacs (1930, p. 318) |
| How is it that when we put our hand into the water we don't make a hole in it? (asked when sitting at a table) | 4; 0 | Sully (1896, p. 469) |
| Why does the soap look smaller in the water? | 4; 1 | Isaacs (1930, p. 318) |
| Why do they kill the stags? They don't want their skins, do they? (on being told that seals are killed for their skins) | 4; 3 | Sully (1896, p. 475) |
| Why doesn't the butter stay on top of hot toast? | 4; 4 | Isaacs (1930, p. 318) |
| Why does water spread out flat (in the bath)? Why won't it keep up in the middle? | 4; 5 | Isaacs (1930, p. 318) |
| When I mix red and orange it makes brown, why? | 6; 0 | Piaget (1926, p. 179) |

| Metaphysical Questions | Age | Source |
|---|---|---|
| Where was I before I was born? | 3; 10 | Sully (1896, p. 458) |
| When are all the days going to end? | 3; 11 | Sully (1896, p. 458) |
| Well, the little seed out of the flower drops into the earth and springs up again into a flower. Why can't (dead) people do like that? | 4; 3 | Sully (1896, p. 479) |
| It's only the naughty people who are buried, isn't it, because auntie said all the good people went to heaven. (And, on being told that all people are buried) Oh, then heaven must be under the ground or they couldn't get there. | 4; 7 | Sully (1896, p. 479) |
| How did God put flesh on us and make what is inside us? | 4; 9 | Sully (1896, p. 478) |
| (After being told that clouds are penetrable) Is it another world like this (on the other side)? | 5; 2 | Sully (1896, p. 482) |

168

| | | |
|---|---|---|
| I can't make out how the first man in the world was able to speak. A word, you know, has a sound, and how did he find out what sounds to make? | 5; 8 | Sully (1896, p. 485) |
| I can't make out how it is that God doesn't make us good. I pray to him to make me good. | 5; 8 | Sully (1896, p. 486) |
| Why are angels always kind to people? Is it because angels don't have to learn to read and do nasty things? | 6; 0 | Piaget (1926, . 189) |
| If I was an angel, and had wings and was flying in the fir-tree, would I see the squirrels or would they run away? | 6; 0 | Piaget (1926, p. 189) |
| Why do angels never fall down to earth when there is no floor to heaven? | 6; 6 | Isaacs (1930, p. 319) |

that the child does not engage in solitary reflection or experimentation but instead seeks information from an adult.

A similar analysis can be made of a question posed by a slightly older child, aged four years and four months: "Why doesn't the butter stay on top of hot toast?" Presumably, the child has had innumerable experiences of foods, such as cheese, ham, or even jam, which, like any other solid, remain supported by a flat surface, whether it is a table top, a plate, or a piece of toast. The absorption of the butter into the hot toast provides an anomaly against that regular backdrop. Thus, in both of these examples the analysis provided by Isaacs (1930) works well.

However, turning to another example, an additional important point emerges. Soon after his fourth birthday, Sully's son asked: "How is it that when we put our hand into the water we don't make a hole in it?" In some respects, this question fits the pattern of the two examples just discussed. The child has presumably noticed that when he puts his hand into a variety of palpable substances (mud, sand, paper, flour, and snow) a hole is made. Water is different, however. You can touch it and feel it; you can even poke your finger in it, just as you can with snow; but you don't make a hole. This question, like the previous examples, appears to be triggered by the gap between an expected outcome and the failure of that outcome to materialize. Yet it is worth emphasizing that the question was posed at the table. Moreover, Sully (1896, p. 469) explicitly remarks that the question came out of the blue: "He observed quite suddenly, and in no discoverable connection with what had been happening before..." Thus, even when a how or why question is posed about the actual world, it is not always posed immediately upon observation of the relevant empirical anomaly. Possibly, the child encodes the anomaly, and when mentally rehearsing it later formulates the question; alternatively, the child encodes the anomaly, immediately formulates the question, and then voices it later. In either case, the child finds a way of encoding an anomaly and rehearsing it at a time when it can be discussed.

The analysis of a fourth example reveals a further point: The child aged four years and three months asks about the killing of stags. In fact, this question was preceded by another. Looking at a picture of some seals, he asks: "What are seals killed for?" and is told: "For the sake of their skins and oil." The child's rejoinder, on turning to a picture of a stag, is as quoted in Table 6.1: "Why do they kill the stags? They don't want their skins, do they?" What is interesting about this example is the child's rapid assimilation of a new piece of information supplied solely through conversation: The child has been told that seals are killed for their skins, and appears to infer the general conclusion that, when animals are hunted and killed, it is for the sake of their skins. However, prompted by seeing the picture of the stag, the child generates an anomaly: Stags are presumably not killed for their skins, so why are they killed? Thus, in certain respects, this question fits the standard pattern: The child expects an outcome, notes a case where that outcome fails to materialize, and asks a why question. Yet, it departs from the pattern established so far in two ways. First, the wider expectation, namely, that animals are killed for their skins, is not grounded in empirical experience, but has been formulated on the strength of newly supplied verbal information (concerning seals). Second, the anomalous outcome, that stags are not killed for their skins, is not an anomaly that the child has actually observed whether immediately before asking the question or on some prior occasion. After all, the child has only just learned that animals are killed for their skins. The implication is that the child may sometimes, having been presented with a generalization, engage in a retrospective review, looking for cases that now stand as anomalies in relation to this newly established generalization.

Summarizing, we can say that, although children's why or how questions about the actual world are often triggered by the puzzle of a generalization that is not borne out in a given case, it is not necessarily empirical experience that supplies either the grounds for the generalization or the trigger for detecting the anomaly. In particular, even in discussing the actual world, the child can be puzzled by apparent clashes between what he or she is told and hitherto unproblematic pieces of knowledge. Making the same point differently, it is clear that the portrait of the child as a lone experimenter engaging in hands-on empirical exploration of the actual world and being confronted by puzzling observations – the portrait favored by Piaget and Isaacs alike, notwithstanding their other disagreements – is inadequate. Puzzles also arise in the child's imagination, as he or she tries to reconcile conflicting expectations. As we shall see below, this point is even more evident when we examine children's questions about metaphysical issues.

Sully (1896, p. 478) notes that during his fifth year, his son's interest in religious matters "grew out of the feelings awakened by the thought of death." Many children start to ask questions about death, and have difficulty in grasping its permanence. Sully's son struggled with the relationship between death and heaven. Passing a church-yard, he said to his mother: "It's only naughty people who are buried, isn't it?" And when asked why, he explained: "Because auntie said all the good people went to heaven." The background to the child's question about the fate of naughty people appears to be the following puzzle. When people die, they end up being buried, but in that case, good people are anomalous because (according to auntie) they end up in heaven. So far, the context for this puzzlement parallels what we saw in the case of the stags. The child has established a generalization, probably on the basis of verbally supplied information rather than direct experience, namely, that people get buried in the ground. However, he spots an apparent exception: Good people, he has been told, go to heaven.

Faced with this anomaly, the child does not immediately ask for an explanation but devises a way to resolve the anomaly himself: "It's only naughty people who are buried, isn't it?" Despite the elegance and emotional appeal of this resolution, the child appears not to be totally convinced, and seeks confirmation from his mother. Sadly, the resolution has to be abandoned because his mother replies that all people are buried. The child is left, therefore, with the original puzzle exacerbated: Irrespective of whether they are good or naughty, people get buried in the ground; yet good people end up in heaven. How is that possible? To explain that puzzle, the child switches gears and, instead of questioning the apparently problematic generalization that all people are buried, focuses instead on explaining or minimizing the anomaly surrounding the burial of good people. If good people are indeed buried, but also end up in heaven – "Oh, then heaven must be under the ground, or they couldn't get there."

There are some noteworthy features to this exchange. First, the child apparently accepts without demur that good people go to heaven, and furthermore that they are buried. Second, in trying to form a mental model consistent with both claims, the child appears to be constrained by standard, folk physics: People (including dead peo-ple) cannot levitate from under the ground to heaven. Third, a solu-tion is found by relocating heaven to the nether regions. Effectively, two different bodies of knowledge simultaneously capture the child: one derived from adult "theological" pronouncements and the other from ordinary, physical knowledge. Both are honored in the child's proposed solution. Making the same point differently, the child's mental model of life after death is a hybrid creature if we inspect its origins: It takes input from adult pronouncements and from naive physics and seeks to fit them together.

A question from a child of five years and eight months highlights the same tension between what the child has been told and what the child assumes on the basis of ordinary experience: "I can't make out how the first man in the world was able to speak. A word, you know, has a sound, and how did he find out what sound to make?" Here, once more, the child appears to have accepted an adult pronouncement concerning the creation of man. At the same time, this is juxtaposed with the child's ordinary knowledge of how language is learned, so that the child asks perfectly reasonably how he knew what sound to make. Not surprisingly, the child can supply no answer to this tricky question.

A third question, posed by a child of six years and six months, reveals a similar tension between what the child has been told and ordinary experience: "Why do angels never fall down to earth when there is no floor to heaven." Presumably, the child has learned about the aerial feats of the angels but has not invested them with wings. This somewhat distorted representation does not square with a routine assumption of folk physics, namely, that what goes up must ordinarily come down, unless there is something that keeps it aloft.

Having scrutinized a small selection of children's questions, we can tentatively conclude that the two predictions described earlier are borne out. Children do indeed pose how or why questions when they contemplate a particular outcome that is anomalous with respect to some wider generalization that they have come to accept. However, such anomalous outcomes do not arise only in the context of empirical observations of the actual world. They also arise when the child speculates about the nonactual world and encounters a mismatch between a particular imagined outcome (often constructed on the basis of what the child has been told) and the child's more wide-ranging causal expectations. We may now consider the wider implications of this analysis.

## Coherence in the Nonactual World

An important implication of the above analysis is that when children speculate about nonactual events, whether located in the afterlife or prehistory, they expect them to be constrained by the causal regularities that obtain in the actual world. Is there any further evidence that children are able to transpose their causal knowledge from the actual to the nonactual world in this fashion? Recent research on the imagination of the two-year-old shows that children engage in such causal transpositions from an early age. When they watch a pretend scenario, involving various pretend transformations such as "pouring," "wiping," and "squeezing," two-year-olds expect the causal impact of those pretend transformations to be similar to the impact of their actual world equivalents. For example, if they watch while a cup containing pretend tea (but no real tea) is moved laterally and then turned upside down, children readily grasp that the pretend tea is first displaced in the cup, but then pours out when the cup is inverted and wets the surface below. Thus, they expect pretend liquid just like real liquid to stay inside an upright container, to fall vertically when poured, to moisten a surface with which it comes into contact, and so forth (Harris & Kavanaugh, 1993; Harris, Kavanaugh, & Dowson, 1997). Indeed, children can keep track of embedded, causal sequences, where the imagined outcome of one intervention is the setting for the next (Harris, Kavanaugh, & Meredith, 1994). Obviously, such pretend outcomes cannot be empirically observed. Because there is no real liquid in the cup, nothing gets transported when it is displaced, nothing pours out, and the surface beneath remains objectively dry. Nevertheless, the mental model that the child constructs in their imagination of the pretend situation reflects the causal regularities that would obtain in the actual world.

The above analysis of children's metaphysical questions illustrates a similar transposition. Just as two-year-olds can transpose their causal understanding of the actual world to the pretend world, older children can transpose that causal understanding to various metaphysical worlds as they think about death, the very first man, or the capacities of angels. They assume that a dead person could not ordinarily be hoisted from the graveyard to heaven, that the first man has to learn a language in the same way as the rest of us, and that angels are subject to gravity.

At the same time, on the strength of verbally transmitted collective representations, the child is led to create propositions with missing entries. The child effectively generates a somehow entry and asks how it can be realized. Somehow good people go from the graveyard to heaven – how do they manage that? Somehow the first man was able to speak – how did he find out what sound to make? Somehow angels remain in heaven – how do they avoid falling to earth?

Combining these two points, it is evident that the child must enjoy a system of "double-entry" bookkeeping. On the one hand, the default assumptions about actual causal mechanisms that the child transposes to his or her model of the nonactual world do not overwrite the child's assimilation of information encoded in various collective representations. Conversely, the assimilation of that new information does not undermine the child's transposition of the default causal mechanisms. However, there is a tension or anomaly because the two do not always fit together. As we have seen, the child can be quite inventive in seeking reconciliation. By elaborating on what he or she has been told – maybe good people escape burial or maybe heaven is underground – the child can try to remove the anomaly. However, given the incommensurability of the two frameworks, especially with respect to their causal principles, it is possible that a fault line gradually extends across the child's thinking, dividing mundane causality on the one hand from theological causality on the other.

That fault line, to the extent that it exists, underlines the potential for integration and also for duality that exists in the child's cognitive system. Information is accepted both on the basis of discourse with other people and on the basis of personal observation. When children construct a mental model they take in and integrate information from either source. This dual encoding works fine so long as the two sources of information are consistent with one another. So far as the actual and present worlds are concerned, this is likely to be the case. It may also be largely true of the immediate past; what the child observed and remembered about a given episode may be largely consistent with other people's narratives about it. With respect to the distant past and future, the child is necessarily reliant on discourse rather than observation. As we have seen, however, the child is not particularly daunted by remoteness: He or she simply adopts a default causal framework, that of the actual and present worlds. So far, then, no fault line need emerge. However, given the difference in the causal framework of theological and mundane discourse, complete integration between the two is not sustainable. Yet various zones of influence can be demarcated. To the extent that God operates at the margins of the mundane as the first mover, or as someone looking down on humanity from heaven, conflicts between mundane causality and divine powers are minimized. For that reason, perhaps, the efforts of the young child to fit the two together – to find a passageway from the grave to heaven – strike us as naively constrained by mundane causal regularities. Yet the solutions that are proposed for bridging the gap between the divine and the mundane – that the soul travels unaccompanied to heaven – or that the Holy Spirit comes down among us – must eventually yield to the same constraints. The main advance is that various corporeal impediments are quietly dropped.

## Conclusions

An unnerving implication of this chapter is that there is nothing special about children's religious or metaphysical questions. To make this point more explicit, although children do ask questions that, from our perspective, concern religious or metaphysical issues, in their eyes they are probably asking a question just like any other. As we have seen, such questions are especially likely to arise when the child encounters some anomaly between expectation and outcome. But that context is not especially associated with metaphysics. It also arises in the course of the child's encounters with the everyday world. Admittedly, an important distinctive feature of religious questions is that they do not arise in the context of empirical observation. Yet that does not distinguish them from questions about dinosaurs or dragons. This might be thought to pull the rug out from under the present line of argument: If the grounds for metaphysical and actual world questions are not so different, what is the point of the distinction? In fact, this conclusion is accurate as far as it goes, but it does not go far enough. The more fundamental point to notice is that the child is designed to move equally comfortably in various mental spaces: the actual as well as the nonactual. The child is not designed to stick to the actual, and is not especially curious about its nature. The child is equally curious about the nonactual. For someone like Piaget or Isaacs, that curiosity looked at from an adult perspective seems like the seeds of objectivity or even science. From another perspective, it looks like the seeds of metaphysics or even religion. My guess is that the whole metaphor of a seed, with all of its teleological overtones, is misleading when we apply it to cognitive growth. It has taken a long time to root out that metaphor from our thinking about evolutionary biology. It may take still longer to abandon it when we think of cognitive development. Still, it is worth considering the possibility that cognitive growth is as open-ended – and as directionless – as evolution itself.

### References

Berzonsky, M. D. (1971). The role of familiarity in children's explanations of physical causality. *Child Development, 43*, 715–715.

Festinger, L., Riecken H. W. Jr, & Schacter, S. (1956). *When Prophesy Fails.* Minnesota: University of Minnesota Press.

Gopnik, A., & Meltzoff, A. (1997). *Words, Thoughts and Theories.* Cambridge, MA: MIT Press.

Harris, P. L. (1997). Piaget in Paris: From 'autism' to logic. *Human Development, 40*, 109–23.

Harris, P. L., & Kavanaugh, R. D. (1993). Young children's understanding of pretense. *Society for Research in Child Development Monographs*, Serial No. 231, *58*, 1.

Harris, P. L., Kavanaugh, R. D., & Dowson, L. (1997). The depiction of imaginary transformations: Early comprehension of a symbolic function. *Cognitive Development, 12*, 1–19.

Harris, P. L., Kavanaugh, R. D., & Meredith, M. (1994). Young children's comprehension of pretend episodes: The integration of successive actions. *Child Development, 65*, 16–30.

Hartshorne, H., & May, M. S. (1928–1930). *Studies in the Development of Character* (3 volumes). New York: Macmillan.

Isaacs, N. (1930). Children's "why" questions. In: S. Isaacs, *Intellectual Growth in Young Children*, Appendix A, (pp. 291–349). London: Routledge.

Kohlberg, L. (1969). Stage and sequence: The cognitive-developmental approach to socialization. In: D. A. Goslin (Ed.), *Handbook of Socialization Theory and Research*, (pp. 347–480). Chicago: Rand McNally.

Nunes, T., & Bryant, P. (1996). *Children Doing Mathematics.* Oxford: Blackwell.

Piaget, J. (1932). *The Moral Judgement of the Child.* London: Routledge & Kegan Paul.

Piaget, J. (1954). *The Construction of Reality in the Child.* New York: Basic Books.

Siegler, R. S. (1976). Three aspects of cognitive development. *Cognitive Psychology, 8*, 481–520.

Sully, J. (1896). *Studies of Childhood.* New York: D. Appleton and Co.

Turiel, E. (1998). The development of morality. In: W. Damon (Ed.), *Handbook of Child Psychology*, 5th ed., Vol 3: N. Eisenberg (Ed.), *Social, Emotional and Personality Development*, (pp. 863–932). New York: Wiley.

Wellman, H. M., & Gelman, S. (1998). Knowledge acquisition in foundational domains. In: W. Damon (Ed.), *Handbook of child psychology*, 5th ed., Vol 2: D. Kuhn and R. S. Siegler (Eds.), *Cognition, Perception and Language*, (pp. 523–73). New York: Wiley.

White, R. (1993). Technological and social dimensions of "urignacian-age" body ornaments across Europe. In: H. Knecht, A. Pike-Tay, and R. White (Eds.), *Before Lascau: The Complex Record of the Upper Paleolithic*, (pp. 247–99). Boca Raton, FL: CRC Press.

# 7 Putting Different Things Together

## The Development of Metaphysical Thinking

CARL N. JOHNSON[1]

That the human spirit will never give up metaphysical researches is as little to be expected as that we should prefer
to give up breathing altogether, in order to avoid inhaling
impure air. There will, therefore, always be metaphysics in
the world; nay, everyone, especially every reflective man,
will have it and, for want of a recognized standard, will
shape it for himself after his own pattern.

(Immanuel Kant, 1783/1977, p. 107)

All our attitudes, moral, practical or emotional, as well as
religious, are due to the "objects" of our consciousness, the
things which we believe exist, whether really or ideally,
along with ourselves.

(William James, 1902/1990, p. 55)

In its brief history, cognitive developmental science has offered two
seemingly contradictory pictures of the way children think about the
nature of the world. Early portraits posed children as primitive, magical thinkers, fundamentally confused about the nature of reality. The
current fashion, however, is to present even young children as science-
like theorists, sorting reality into different kinds and causes.

Contemporary researchers have sought to replace the old picture
with the new one, complaining that the earlier depiction fails to do
justice to reality. Piaget's early work is particularly criticized as suffering from poor technique. His questions are said to be too abstract, the

[1] Special thanks go to Kirk Loadman-Copeland for inspiration and guidance laying the
groundwork for this chapter; and to Paul Harris, a longtime friend and faithful critic,
for helpful comments on previous drafts.

subject matter too unfamiliar, and the coding too inadequate to capture the richness of children's early intuitive understanding (see Wellman, 1990).

The problem with this critique, however, is that it fails to do justice to the distinct intent of Piaget's early work. By his own account, Piaget (1929) was looking at something other than children's intuitive understanding. In fact, he acknowledged that young children have a rich, "intuitive" understanding of mental phenomena, being "no less conscious of the content of thought than we are of ours," aware of the "existence of thoughts, of names and of dreams, and a quantity of more or less subtle peculiarities," with a "whole extremely delicate psychology" (pp. 124–25). His intention, in contrast, was to look at "tendencies" in the direction of children's spontaneous reflective thinking when challenged by questions that went beyond their intuitive understanding. He did not confine himself to posing questions that children had already resolved because he was distinctly interested in "children's philosophies" (Piaget, 1933), and enchanted by the prospect that their untutored speculations could provide a fleeting glimpse into the origin of pre-Socratic metaphysical ideas.

From this standpoint, there may still be something to learn from Piaget's early efforts. While contemporary researchers have greatly added to our knowledge of children's intuitive understanding, the origin of metaphysical ideas has been comparatively neglected. The purpose of this chapter is to distinguish these subject matters and to see how they are integrally connected. The guiding idea is that concepts that serve to constrain thinking within science-like domains at a primary, intuitive level equally serve to promote ideas that transcend these categories at a reflective level.

The conceptual roots of this chapter lie in Aristotle's original characterization of metaphysics. Like current theory theorists, Aristotle recognized that individual sciences grow out of the essentialist categories of common sense: "Every demonstrative science investigates with regard to some subject its essential attributes, starting from the common beliefs" (1941, p. 720). But, having distinguished separate sciences of physics, the soul (psychology), and animal life (biology), Aristotle also distinguished a higher order science of metaphysics as the study of Being in general.

For Aristotle, metaphysics was the highest manifestation of the uniquely human capacity to make connections across different experiences: "The animals other than man live by appearances and memories, and have but little of connected experience; but the human race lives also by art and reasonings" (1941, p. 689). Human beings have the capacity to go beyond intuitive experience and practical action to articulate general theories about why things are as they are. Aristotle considered myth as a beginning effort to explain the larger nature of reality. Metaphysics was distinguished from myth by a higher capacity for "theory," constituting a rational science of first principles and causes aimed toward ultimate knowledge, wisdom, and the divine.[2]

This chapter begins with a discussion of the existential ground of metaphysics. The intuitive categories that serve to frame science-like thinking are taken to equally provide the existential ground for metaphysical ideas. We then turn our attention to the conceptual foundation of "ideas" that "transcend" ordinary boundaries of the subjective and objective worlds. Kant's (1781/1965) analysis of such ideas is reviewed, as it anticipates modern cognitive theory and frames Piaget's early thinking about the developmental origins of transcendental, magical, and religious ideas.

With this background, we consider the origins of metaphysical thinking. An emerging reflective capacity in children, characterized by the representation of "intentions," is seen to not only yield an awareness of private, mental states, but equally invisible "intentions" that exist in the world and yet transcend it. A reappraisal of Piaget's early work ensues, wherein magical ideas are seen to be a product of reflective ideation, rather than a primitive ontological confusion. Indeed, an intuitive distinction between thought and things is shown to be a condition for ideas about their magical "participation."

A broad outline of the development of metaphysical thought is then described, distinguishing early magical/mythical ideas from a later capacity for more radical metaphysical theorizing. The chapter then turns to look at the development of supernatural ideas among

---

[2] So lofty was this pursuit that Aristotle questioned whether it may be beyond the human capacity for knowing – that only God could know such things and that people might better stick to more limited kinds of knowledge. But he dismissed this possibility, insisting that metaphysics was the most honorable, although the least necessary of the sciences. Over time, Aristotle's original doubts have become widespread. The one-time "queen of the sciences" no longer even warrants the name of "science." As the empirical sciences have progressed, the limits of a reflective science of metaphysics have become increasingly evident.

adolescents growing up in different religious traditions. In conclusion, emphasis is given to the value of ideas that go beyond the boundaries of domain-specific knowledge.

## Existential Conundrums

Intuitively, it seems obvious that things exist in the world, just as it is obvious that sentient individuals exist who perceive, think about, and act on such things. "Theory theorists" have reasonably argued that such intuitions are embedded in conceptual frameworks (Gopnik & Wellman, 1994). Little considered, however, is how this first-order understanding of existence gives rise to metaphysical puzzles and transcendental explanations.

Drawing on the work of McGinn (1993), Pinker (1997) lists six conundrums that have resisted all efforts toward coherent under-standing: conscious sentience, self, free will, meaning, knowledge, and morality. Efforts to resolve such puzzles are observed to circle around four responses. The first and "favorite solution in most times and places, is mysticism and religion" (Pinker, 1997, pp. 559–60). Other, more typically modern, solutions include ignoring the issue, accepting the existence of these strange objects, or trying to reduce them to something more comprehensible. None of these alternatives, however, has proved to be wholly satisfactory.

With McGinn (1993), Pinker (1997) argues that these existential conundrums reflect something basic about the way human beings think. Evolution has selected for adaptive ways of conceiving the world in terms of different kinds of things and causes but leaves open the problem of how these different kinds of things and causes came into being and are causally connected.

A wealth of recent research demonstrates that young children have at least some rudimentary awareness of these puzzling existential phenomena. Research on children's "theory of mind" documents that even preschoolers have some understanding of the existence of dis-tinctly "mental entities" like intentions, desires, and thoughts (cf. Wellman, 1990). At the same time, young children are also discerning the existence of distinctly moral phenomena (see Turiel & Neff, this volume). The point to be made is that such categories not only serve to constrain thinking at an intuitive level, but equally pose conun-drums that foster mystical and religious ideas.

## Kant's Ideas

The argument that metaphysics arises from intuitive conundrums of thought was originally articulated by Immanuel Kant. Consider the opening statement in his preface to *Critique of Pure Reason*:

> Human reason has this peculiar fate that in one species of its knowledge it is burdened by questions which, as prescribed by the very nature of reason itself, it is not able to ignore, but which, as transcending all its powers, it is also not able to answer. The perplexity into which it falls is not due to any fault of its own. It begins with principles which it has no option save to employ in the course of experience, and which this experience at the same time abundantly justifies it in using.
>
> Rising with their aid (since it is determined to this also by its own nature) to ever higher, ever more remote, conditions, it soon becomes aware that in this way – the questions never ceasing – its work must always remain incomplete; and it therefore finds itself compelled to resort to principles which overstep all possible empirical employment, and which yet seem so unobjectionable that even ordinary consciousness readily accepts them. (Kant, 1781/1965, p. 7)

Kant set the stage for modern thinking about metaphysics, challenging the "queen of the sciences" with a cognitive analysis of the limitations and illusions inherent in reflective thought. In this effort, he depicted a structural framework that is echoed in contemporary theory. Perception was considered to be inherently organized by schema (comparable to modern-day "modules"), the output of which is *intuition*. Inferences based on such intuitive data give rise to *concepts* or *understanding* (currently, "intuitive theories" or "framework theories"). In turn, intuitive concepts become the input for reflective thought or pure reason, resulting in the construction of *ideas*. On this account, Kant concluded that "all human knowledge begins with intuitions, proceeds from thence to concepts, and ends with ideas" (p. 569).

Like contemporary theory theorists, Kant (1781/1965) considered scientific thinking to be grounded in intuitive categories of understanding. But he was equally interested in the source of ideas that "transcend" these intuitive categories. Simply put, he argued that the capacity to reflect on concepts yields ideas that transcend the boundaries of intuition. Ideas are genuinely "transcendental" objects insofar as they represent an ideal order that goes beyond the boundaries of the immanent world. While transcendence is real in this sense, Kant also recognized that the reflective apprehension of this conceptual order is accompanied by inevitable illusions. Just as perceptual experience has natural biases that give rise to illusions, Kant argued that reflective experience has natural biases that yield "transcendental illusions." The capacity to take the output of intuition, namely, concepts, as an input for reflection brings with it certain unavoidable tendencies that "incite us to tear down all those boundary-fences and to seize possession of an entirely new domain which recognizes no limits of demarcation" (p. 299). As Kant elaborates:

> The cause of this is that there are fundamental rules and maxims for the employment of our reason (subjectively regarded as a faculty of human knowledge), and that these have all the appearance of being objective principles. We therefore take the subjective necessity of a connection of our concepts, which is to the advantage of the understanding, for an objective necessity in the determination of things in themselves. This is an *illusion* which can no more be prevented than we can prevent the sea appearing higher at the horizon than at the shore. (Kant, 1781/1965, p. 299)

Transcendental illusions arise from the uncritical assumption that the order that is inherent in concepts exists in reality itself. Examples of transcendental illusions include inferences that because everything has a cause (intuitively), there must necessarily be a first cause; because human agents act freely (intuitively), such action must arise from a source that transcends the boundaries of physical causality; or because the "I" exists as an invariant across variations in state (intuitively), it must refer to some unitary, immaterial substance (i.e., a unitary mind, soul, or transcendental self).

Kant's ideas were powerfully influential in framing the science of cognitive development.[3] In particular, Piaget began his career proposing that children's reflective thinking originally suffers from a kind of transcendental illusion. Ignorant of the constructive processes of the

---

[3] The idea that the human mind is prone to confuse order in the mind with order in the world is well developed in cognitive psychology, although little attention has been paid recently to the "transcendental" implications. Such confusion is at the heart of magical thinking, as Nemeroff and Rozin (this volume) well describe. Particularly notable is Shweder's (1977) revision of magical thinking. In the absence of a higher level of critical, nonintuitive ideas, he argues that magical thinking naturally arises with intuitive thinking as the result of failure to distinguish conceptual relationships in the mind with empirical relationships in the world.

mind, he argued that children initially tend to confuse representations of reality with reality itself. Moreover, Piaget theorized that religious ideas develop from a kind of transcendental illusion, whereby God and ideal order are conceived as arising from a transcendental source, beyond the physical and mental worlds, toward conceiving such order as arising from "immanent" processes of creation (see Chapman, 1988; Vidal, 1994).

## The Ground of Science and Magic

Contemporary researchers have demonstrated that preschool children are coming to infer the existence of imperceptible "theoretical" entities behind the reality of overtly perceptible things. They are variously coming to represent the existence of mental states behind behavior, "essences" underlying things, and reality behind appearances. On this account, children are reported to function like scientists, thinking about the world in terms of an underlying reality of different ontological kinds and causes (Wellman & Gelman, 1988).

Although currently overlooked, Piaget (1926) made a very similar observation about the capacity of young children to distinguish the underlying reality of imperceptible essences and causal forces. What he saw in this achievement, however, was not only the beginning of science-like causal explanations, but equally the ground for magical thinking.

Interested in the development of children's explanatory reasoning, Piaget (1926) marked the emergence of "why" questions at the age of three with a broadly emerging capacity to think about the existence of an imperceptible reality behind the apparent perceptible world.[4] He cited three related achievements: (1) the emerging use of mental verbs

---

[4] Like Piaget (1929), Harris (this volume) notes the importance of children's ability to think about "nonactual" kinds of things, beyond the here and now. This advance opens the door to a wide variety of new kinds of things: future things, fictional things, once-upon-a-time things, heavenly things, supernatural things, and so forth. While Piaget neglected to consider the rich variety of such things, his distinctive contribution was to show that, in the case of metaphysical thinking, children tend to spontaneously construct a kind of transcendental intentionality. Unfortunately, Piaget never developed his proposal with a broader analysis of "intentionality" in the philosophical and phenomenological senses of the term (see Johnson, 1988). He also failed to fully appreciate the genuinely confounding philosophical problems that children are trying to resolve (Matthews, 1994). In part, this seems to be due to his strong personal and professional reaction to the "illusions" of philosophy (see Piaget, 1971).

"to think" and "to believe" that mark a divergence between what is real and what is imagined; (2) the earliest lies; and (3) the use of cases, tenses, and subordinate prepositions that provide the "whole necessary apparatus for the beginnings of formulated reasoning" as it functions to "construct, over and above the immediate world of sensation, a reality supposedly deeper than the merely given world" (Piaget, 1926 p. 234). He concluded that

> all these transformations have this fundamental trait in common, that they indicate an act of conscious realization. From now onwards the child distinguishes between the real as it appears immediately to the senses, and something which precedes events and underlies all phenomena. Let us describe this something by the very comprehensive term – *intention*. (Piaget, 1926, p. 232)

Piaget (1926) used the term "intention" in a distinctly comprehensive way, emphasizing that this notion is not limited to strictly personal, subjective states. As he explains:

> The real, henceforth, becomes crowded with intentions ascribed first to other people, then to things, whether these things are thought of as autonomous or dependent upon persons. Thus the whole world becomes peopled in various degrees – not, it is true, with personified spirits, because at this age the child is still unconscious of its own personal unity, and does not think of ascribing intentions to define "I's" – but of intentions that are impersonal, so to speak, or at any rate improperly localized and multiform. Hence the earliest "whys," "why" being the specific question for seeking the intention hidden behind an action or an event. (p. 233)

Although Piaget did not elaborate on the notion of "intentionality" in a broader philosophical sense of the term (see Johnson, 1988; Searle, 1983), he can be fairly interpreted as proposing that children are initially biased toward construing the world in terms of "aboutness." While Piaget notes that intentions are "ascribed first to other people," the point is that intentionality can be widely extended: Symbolically, meaningfully, any given thing can have an "intentional" relationship with other things. Intentional construals take on different forms in different cases: Agents have subjective intentional states in the form of "seeing," "desiring," or "thinking." Words have "intentions" in the form of meanings. Inanimate things and events have "intentions" in the form of reasons or purposes for being.

Piaget (1926) well recognized that children's earliest "whys" were primarily directed toward inquiring about the psychological causes of human action ("intentions" in the ordinary sense of the term). He appreciated that children are beginning to distinguish between types of explanations. What drew his attention, however, was a clear bias in children's why questions. Not only were most of children's questions about psychological causes, rather than material ones, but this bias appeared to extend to occasional reflective questions about why things are as they are. For example, he cites a child asking, "Why do trees have leaves" (p. 235). In such cases, he observed that children appeared to be biased toward understanding the purposes, or teleology, of things. (For recent supporting evidence of an early teleological bias see Evans, this volume; Guthrie 1993; Keleman, 1999).

At the same time that children are becoming conscious of subjective intentional states of people, they are becoming conscious of impersonal "intentions" in the world. The way in which impersonal "intentions" come into existence can be better appreciated in terms of Searle's (1983) depiction of the structure of intentionality. Intentionality is defined by modes of relationship between a subject and an object with respect to directions of causality and fit. For example, a desire may have a causal role in directing an action that aims toward accommodating the world to fit the desire of the subject. In contrast, a perceptual state, like seeing, is defined by a state of the subject that fits and is caused by something in the world. Searle argues that this structure of intentionality not only frames the existence of subjective, mental states, but equally the existence of impersonal meanings and "representations." These latter phenomena arise with speech acts that give linguistic utterances an intentionality of their own. For example, assertive acts ("judgments" in Kant's terms) have a *word*-to-world direction of fit, just like the mental states of "seeing" or "believing" have a *mind*-to-world direction of fit. In each case, the intentionality is defined by conditions of satisfaction whereby the "representation" fits the world. In one case the "intention" is attributed to a subjective mind, in the other to a word. Words, assertions, or propositions thus come to have an objective kind of "intentionality," or meaning, independent of the subjective states of individual minds.[5]

---

[5] Searle (1983) makes the broader case to show that the structure of intentionality that functions to distinguish mental states also functions to distinguish speech acts. In contrast with assertives, directive and commissive speech acts are like states of desire in that the intent is to fit the world to the representation (to the word in the case of

On this account, a capacity to represent "intentions" marks a remarkable advance, not only in the ability to think about the subjective intentions of persons, but equally about "objective" intentions in terms of representations, meanings, reasons, purposes, and values that appear to exist in the world itself. While contemporary research has emphasized that children can distinguish the existence of private representations from publicly perceptible things (cf. Wellman, 1990), little attention has been paid to children's thinking about representations that appear to have an objective reality of their own. As the philosopher Popper (1972) pointed out, reality not only includes the existence of physical and mental things, but also a "third world" of representational things. Language, word meanings, moral truths, and knowledge all exist in this third world. The metaphysical puzzle is how such things exist and come into being. How is it that words have meanings, that right and wrong exists in the world, and that reality appears to be naturally categorized and purposefully ordered? As will be seen, Piaget's early work makes a reasonable case that these metaphysical puzzles tend to lead children toward magical and theological ideas.

## The Direction of Ideation: Mind and Magic

During the preschool years, children are becoming aware that there are hidden "intentions" behind everything that exists in the world. Where does this intentional bias lead children in the course of development? Certainly it leads them to ask questions that can be satisfied with explanations in terms of the meaning systems and "reflective beliefs" of their culture (cf. Sperber, 1996). But, apart from cultural tuition, this bias leads children's metaphysical thinking in a certain spontaneous direction. This direction was the focus of Piaget's (1929) investigation of children's conceptions of the world.

Explicitly contrasting his investigation from the study of children's intuitive knowledge and instructed beliefs, Piaget set out to explore "how their ideas are formed in response to certain questions and

the speech act; to the mind in the case of desire). Expressives, whereby subjective states are simply reported, distinctly lack a direction of fit. Declarations, such as oaths or pronouncements, are especially remarkable in that they seem to combine both directions of fit. In other words, the speech act itself creates a realty. It seems likely that religious rituals and practices may function in this sort of way, whereby participation genuinely creates a new kind of reality (cf. Boyer, 1994, for an account along this line).

principally in what direction their spontaneous attitude of mind tends to lead them" (Piaget, 1929, p. 123). He pushed children to explain why things are as they are, and was struck by how children often came up with magic-like ideas echoing the metaphysical beliefs of the pre-Socratics.

Piaget (1929) stressed that the magical ideas he elicited from children were weak in comparison to the beliefs of adults: "For our part we fully realize that in all adult society, magic is an eminently social reality and that belief in magical efficacy, therefore, possesses an intensity and a continuity that make it incomparable with the weak and extremely discontinuous beliefs of children" (pp. 391–392). Moreover, he emphasized that "the child does not actually work out any philosophy, properly speaking, since he never seeks to codify his reflections in anything like a system. And yet, however unconnected and incoherent the spontaneous remarks of children concerning the phenomena of nature, of the mind and of the origin of things, may be, we are able to discern in them some constant tendencies, reappearing with each new effort of reflection. These are the tendencies which we shall call "children's philosophies" (Piaget, 1933, p. 534).

Overlooking the distinct object of Piaget's early work, researchers have taken evidence of children's intuitive knowledge to directly refute his findings. Wellman (1990) marshals a particularly strong attack along this line, arguing that Piaget mistakenly confused ontological with epistemological realism.[6] As Wellman (1990) explains:

> Suppose, for example, that at first young children are ignorant as to how thoughts originate from and correspond to things. They simply appreciate that thoughts can originate from encounters with things (you see it; you know it's there) or from mental effort (you think it up, imagine it), but they have no specific understanding of how it works. If children simply assume an unspecified direct connection between thoughts and things, then part of Piaget's original description would be apt: children might well be epistemological realists, albeit not ontological ones. (p. 59)

What Wellman (1990) characterizes as "epistemological realism" is precisely what Piaget (1929) regarded to be the ground of magical

---

[6] In personal conversations, Wellman has been very open to this alternative interpretation and has even entertained similar ideas in his more recent writing (see Wellman & Gelman, 1998, p. 555–56). In any case, there is no question about the importance and validity of his research documenting children's intuitive knowledge.

ideas. This magic, as he put it, consists of "participation" existing "between two beings or two phenomena which it regards either as partially identical or as having a direct influence on one another, although there is no spatial contact or intelligible causal connection between them" (Piaget, 1929, p. 132).[7] It is clear from this description that "participation" presumes a capacity to differentiate "two beings." Participatory magic does not arise from a failure to distinguish between the phenomenal existence of a thought from a thing, but from the idea that there must be some deeper, imperceptible connection between these different things, despite that absence of any "intelligible" causal mechanism.

Wellman (1990) focuses on the capacity of young children to distinguish thoughts from perceptible things. In contrast, Piaget (1929) focused on children's thinking about a deeper, mystical unity. He provided a particularly rich description of this sort of unity of differences in the case of nominal realism. In this case, he noted that children well recognize that utterances (or marks) are different than their referents but nonetheless infer that these different things are more deeply connected. As he explained:

> although children may suppose they need only to look at a thing to know its name, it does not in the least follow that they regard the name as in some way written on the thing. It means rather that for these children the name is an essential part of the thing; the name Saleve implies a sloping mountain, the name sun implies a yellow ball that shines and has rays, etc. But it must also be added that for these children the essence of the thing is not a concept but the thing itself. Complete confusion exists between thought and the things thought of. The name is therefore in the object, not as a label, attached to it but as an invisible quality of the object. (Piaget, 1929, p. 70)

Lacking any natural, "intelligible" causal explanation for the apparent connection between a name and a thing, children assume that there must be some invisible quality, some underlying essence that unites them together. This essence, mysteriously, is in the thing and yet transcends its material existence. Effectively, the idea of an essence arises from an assumption that there must necessarily exist some

---

[7] It is worth noting that the idea of "participation" appears in Plato's theorizing as an explanation of how abstract ideas can be connected with real-world things. Aristotle (1941, p. 701) comments on this matter.

quality of the thing that satisfies the condition of its being what it is labeled to be. The word "sun" is *about* the sun, and is therefore assumed to somehow essentially "fit" the sun. In the absence of any obvious, overt connection between the word and the thing, the tendency is to assume that there must be some deeper, hidden connection.

Ideas of magical participation appear to be constituted by the same essentialist thinking that forms the foundation of children's natural categories. Contemporary theorists laud children's capacity to infer the existence of underlying "essences" as a mark of an ability to infer the existence of imperceptible "theoretical" entities (Wellman & Gelman, 1988). Young children infer that things that are labeled as being the same living kind share some underlying essence, despite overt differences in appearance (Gelman, 1988). But recent work suggests that "essentialism" is not limited to a particular natural domain (see Gelman & Hirschfeld, 1999). Rather, a general capacity to infer the existence of essences opens the door not only for thinking that natural kinds of things essentially differ, but equally for magical ideas about how different kinds of things are connected. On this account, essentialist thinking appears to underlie beliefs that living things share some underlying vital essence, as well as beliefs in contamination, fetishes, and blessings (see also Nemeroff & Rozin, this volume).

Gelman and Hirschfeld (1999) argue that essentialist thinking is recruited precisely in cases where more ordinary explanations fail – in cases of radical transformation and causal anomaly. For example, essentialism appears to be recruited to give an explanation of race, precisely because this category is not otherwise coherent. In the same way, essentialism may be recruited to explain how things as different as words and things are connected. Lacking a better theory of how representations are connected to things, there appears to be a tendency to infer that some hidden "essential" connection exists in the world.

Leaving aside these metaphysical issues, Wellman (1990) argued that Piaget and his followers misinterpreted their data. He recoded Laurendeau and Pinard's data to demonstrate that young children are not literally confused about the difference between dreams and things. To examine this difference in interpretation, consider Laurendeau and Pinard's (1962) description of the responses of a five-year-old that were classified as stage 1, integral realism – the very earliest level of comprehension:

You know what a dream is? – *Yes.* – Do you dream sometimes at night? – *Yes.* – Now, tell me, where does a dream come from? – *In heaven, perhaps. I don't know.* – Do they come from inside of you, or from outside of you? – *From outside of me.* – Who makes the dreams come? – *Jesus . . . I don't know.* – Is it you or is it somebody else? – *Somebody else.* – Who? – *Jesus, perhaps.* – While you are dreaming, where is your dream, where does it go, in what place is it? – *In front of me.* – Is it inside of you or in your room? *In my room.* – Is it in your room for real, or is it only as if it were there? Or does it only seem to be there? – *It is as if it were in my room, but it is not there for real.* – While you are dreaming, are your eyes closed or open? – *Closed.* – Then, where is your dream? – *In my room when I am dreaming.* – When you dream that you are playing in the street, where is your dream, is it in the street or in your room? – *In the street. I cannot dream in the street because I never play there.* – Is there something in front of you, when you are dreaming? – *Yes, but they are not real people* – ( . . . ) – Why do you say that I could not see your dream? – *Because you are not asleep.* – If I were asleep? – *You would see it.* – ( . . . ) – What is a dream made of? – *With nothing. It can be seen the same as I see you there.* (p. 111)

In recoding this interview, Wellman (1990) focuses on the singular fact that this child recognizes the unreal status of dream – *"It is as if it were in my room, but it is not there for real."* In this, he overlooks the fact that Laurendeau and Pinard (1962) acknowledge such understanding but deny that this alone is grounds for concluding that children think that dreams are strictly subjective. As Laurendeau and Pinard (1962) explained:

> To repeat a comparison already suggested by Piaget, the dream is as-similated to that privileged universe of the child which contains, among other things, fairies and ghosts. *The child knows that the dream is illusive; he does not confuse it with real objects and persons. But he nevertheless remains essentially realistic, since he does not yet recognize any subjective element.* In short, to account for the various phenomena of everyday reality, the child creates a second universe for himself, just as objective to him as the first, but reserved for beings who are more alien, or less accessible to him. (pp. 111–12, emphasis added)

What does it mean to say that children do not recognize a "subjective element"? The problem can be seen in the above example as the child struggles to make sense out of the puzzling phenomenal status of dreams. Even though dreams are clearly not "real" perceptible kinds of happenings, they nonetheless appear to arise from outside the self. This puzzling status is well expressed by a six-year-old in Laurendeau and Pinard's (1962) study, categorized as stage 2, mitigated realism. This subject starts out claiming that dreams exist "in the eyes," "in front of ourselves," and "in my room." But he then notes that dreams happen when one's eyes are closed and that they are not observable by others. Pressed further, this child becomes completely perplexed, unable to conceive how these different facts can go together:

> Then, tell me, what do we dream with? – *With the eyes.* – If we could open your eyes while you are dreaming, could we see your dream? – *No.* – Why do you say that we could not see your dream? – *It's in front. It's also inside of me. I'm all mixed up.* – Then, where is our dream? – *I don't know.* (Laurendeau & Pinard, 1962, p. 117)

Like other representational phenomena, dreams appear to exist both inside and outside the self. Dreams are private, immaterial episodes that occur during sleep, in the absence of normal sensory-motor action. Nonetheless, dreams appear to exist as happenings coming from outside of the self. Dreams are not things that are personally "made up" any more than morals or word meanings are personally "made up." These representations appear to have a strange kind of immaterial existence outside of the self.

In efforts to explain the puzzling status of dreams, children in Laurendeau and Pinard's (1962) study frequently offered supernatural explanations, with references to dreams coming from heaven or being made by Jesus. Notably, such references occurred along with a recognition that dreams occur inside the head. Consider the following examples of two different nine-year-olds:

> Then, tell me, where does a dream come from? – *We think . . . It comes into our head.* – Where are the dreams made, where do dreams come from? – *From ourselves, on the forehead . . . no, in the forehead. We think.* – Do they come from inside of you, or from outside of you? – *From within me.* – Who makes dreams come? – *God . . . He says: let them come! . . .* If we could open your head while you are dreaming, if we could look into your head, could we see your dream? – *No.* – Why do you say that we could not see it? – *Because . . . we see it . . . because it's invisible . . . because it's God. If He wants us to see it, we can see it.*(p. 118)

> Then, tell me, where does a dream come from? – *From the dreadful things we have seen or read.* – Where are dreams made, where do they come from? – *From our thinking.* – Do they come from inside of you or from

outside of you? – *From inside of me.* – Who makes the dreams come? – *God.* – Is it you or somebody else? – *Somebody else.* – Who? – *God.* (p. 124)

Laurendeau and Pinard (1962) explain that: "Far from being characteristic of the most primitive beliefs, the recourse to divine or supernatural beings may be observed at all levels. Indeed, even among children who hold the strongest convictions about the subjectiveness and individuality of dreams, a reference to the action of a divine power may often occur" (p. 106). Yet, developmental changes were noted in such accounts. Whereas young children viewed dreams as being literally fabricated and sent by humanlike agents, for older children "divine action is dehumanized and recourse to the omnipotence of God becomes necessary only as a last resort, that is, when naturalistic explanations are no longer satisfactory to the child and he is led to look for a more distant cause." (pp. 106–7)

Supernatural explanations were not limited to the case of dreams. Consider the following responses to inquiries about the nature of mind and the origins of names in Piaget's (1929) original study:

> Tann (8) thinks with his "mind." What is the mind? – *It is someone who isn't like we are, who hasn't skin and hasn't bones, and who is like air which we can't see. After we're dead it goes away from our body.*– Goes away?–*It goes away but it stays, when it goes away it still stays.* – What stays? – *It stays, but all the same it's in Heaven."* Tann has not yet accepted as irresistible the dualism between internal and external . . . (p. 53)

> Pat (10): And who gave the sun its name? – *God.* – And how did we know its name? – *God put it into men's heads.* – If God had not given it that name could they have given it another? – *Yes, they could.* – They knew it was called the sun? – *No.* – And the names of the fishes? – *God put the names into men's heads.* (p. 71)

As these examples illustrate, children may well judge that representations exist as temporary, private states in the head yet still believe that they arise from some transcendental source outside the body. This amorphous status of being something that is inside and outside, subjective and objective, imperceptible and real was widely documented in Piaget's (1929) work. In this vein, Piaget was struck by instances where children spontaneously came up with the idea that thoughts exist in the form of breath or air. Consider the following examples:

Ris (8;6, a girl) . . . stated, without having been previously questioned about thought, that the dream is – *In words*. – And what are the words in? – *The voice*. – Where does the voice come from? – *The air*. (p. 47)

Falq (7;3): You know what it means to think? – *You think of things you want to do*. – What do you think with? – *With something*. – What with? – *A little voice*. – Where is it? – *There* (he points to the forehead). – Where does the little voice come from? – *The head*. – How does it happen. – *By itself*. (p. 49) . . . A few moments later Falq speaks of memory. Where is it? – *Inside there* (showing his forehead) – What is there? – *A little ball*. – What is inside it? – *Thoughts*. – What would one see inside if one looked? – *Smoke*. – Where does it come from? – *From the head*. – Where does the smoke come from? – *From the thoughts* – Is thought smoke? – *Yes*. – Why is thought inside the ball? – *It is a little air and smoke that has come*. – Where from? – *From outside*. . . . What is the smoke? – *Breath* – And the air? – *The same*. (p. 50)

To Piaget (1929), such instances offered a remarkable glimpse into the origins of a pre-Socratic cosmology where air/breath were conceived as the unifying element of the universe, as this entity offered a mediating link between things that are inner and outer, material and immaterial, living and nonliving. In contrast, Wellman (1990) dismisses the significance of these sorts of speculations, insisting that these are mere analogies, as children do not really confuse thought with air. The point here, however, is that a capacity to discriminate these phenomena at an intuitive level does not preclude their integration at a higher theoretical level.

Robin Horton (1993) describes exactly this sort of move with regard to the cosmologies of traditional cultures. Things that are distinguished, but causally connected, at a primary level become identified with one another at a secondary theoretical level. Thus, observations of causal connections between thinking and speaking, speaking and breath, breath and air, breath and life, all point to air as a unifying element. As Horton (1993) explains,

it is significant that ideas about breath and/or wind are so widely associated with pre-scientific explanatory systems, both in contemporary Africa and in earlier Europe. Breath and wind, being visually unobservable, yet able to penetrate the interstices of and thus pervade many bodies, form particularly apt prototypes for theoretical entities, which are inaccessible to the same acts of observation we use to verify statements about events at the material-object level,

and are at the same time coextensive with such events. Ideas concerning these phenomena may well have formed the original bridge
between ideas about hidden goings-on and theoretical ideas *sensu stricto*.
(p. 298)

Recent research further shows why air is such a natural candidate
for this kind of theory. Carey (1991) reports that children initially
conceive of air to be substantially "nothing" and yet to have real
causal powers. This sort of immaterial power seems to precisely characterize initial ideas about the nature of mind.

## Intuitive States Versus Mental Substances

Contemporary theory theorists have argued that young children can
distinguish between physical and mental "entities." The implication
is that young children are already dualists in the sense of dividing up
the world into physical and mental substances. But it is important to
recognize that children can have intuitions about the existence of
mental states without any ideas about the existence of more substantially enduring minds.

There is good evidence to show that young children distinguish the
existence of temporary, ephemeral mental *episodes* well before they
construct more substantial ideas about the mind. Children's first representations of mental phenomena appear to be an extension of their
representations of intentional behavior (see Johnson, 1988; Searle,
1983). Just as children initially divide up the stream of outer behavior
into discrete episodes of perceptual states and motor acts, so too they
divide up the stream of thought into discrete episodes of representational states and acts. Such episodes include thoughts that are intended to "fit" or accommodate something existing in the world (beliefs), as well as thoughts that are not intended to fit anything at all
(imagination or fantasy).

Young children become aware that objects exist independent
of their temporary representation in the same way that they are aware
that objects exist independent of temporary perception. Nor is there
any deep mystery to the fact that representational experiences and
actions occur apart from perceptual experiences and motor actions.
For example, children can readily observe that visual images occur
when the eyes are closed. They can directly "test" whether a thought
is "real" by simply trying to visually explore or physically manipu-

late it. And, they can demonstrate an ability to generate thoughts at will.[8]

What is not accessible to intuition, however, is the idea that there are more enduring mental "entities" that exist independent of these temporary states and acts of mind. This limitation is particularly well demonstrated in research on children's conceptions of the brain. Clearly children do not have "intuitive" information about actual brain functions.[9] But, absent science education, young children appear to assimilate ordinary talk about the brain into an intuitive framework. In the same way that children conceive external body parts as necessary for perception and motor action, so too they conceive the inner "brain" as necessary for inner "mental" states and acts. Just as the eyes are needed to see, and the legs to walk, the brain is judged to be needed to dream, remember, and think (Johnson & Wellman, 1982).

In this initial conception, the brain has no particularly central or important function in human behavior as a whole. The brain is judged to be needed only for inner states and acts, not outer behaviors like seeing or acting. Moreover, inner mental states and acts, like their outer counterparts, exist only as occasional intentional episodes. On this account, children judge that people can mostly get along without a brain (Johnson & Wellman, 1982), just as they judge that people mostly get along without thinking (Flavell, Green, & Flavell, 1995).[10]

---

[8] As James Gibson (1979) emphasized, children have no trouble differentiating between real things and representational things, insofar as they have perceptual information that specifies this difference. A picture of a rock, or a thought of a rock, for example, simply do not have the perceptible qualities of an actual rock. Problems arise, however, when the reality of a representation cannot be directly tested. As Gibson notes, "In storytelling, adults do not always distinguish between true stories and fairy stories. The child herself does not always separate the giving of an account from the telling of a story" (p. 261).

[9] As Piaget (1929) well noted, knowledge of the brain is not something that children spontaneously figure out on their own. In his investigation, this idea showed up at about eight years of age. However, he emphasized that conventional references to the brain as the source of thought were not initially accompanied with the idea that thoughts are essentially internal, private sorts of things. On the contrary, knowledge of the brain was combined with persistent assumptions about the transcendental quality of thought.

[10] Why is it that young children are ignorant of the ongoing flow of thought? Why is it that such information is not intuitively accessible? The answer, as Piaget well recognized, has to do with how things can be "grasped" in consciousness. To move from simple awareness to conscious "representation," children must break up the flow of experience into momentary, episodic states, namely, "intentional states," that are defined by the mode and direction of fit (see Johnson, 1988). Later, through

While the brain is conceived as an inner receptor and enabler of occasional mental states and acts, the critical point is that no enduring mental "entities" are contained within it – no processes, concepts, contents, ideas, or traits. In other words, mental episodes have no more enduring existence than behavioral episodes. Nothing "mental" exists apart from the capacity for and occurrence of occasional representational acts and states. This limitation is particularly strikingly demonstrated in studies of children's inferences about the consequences of a brain transplant (Johnson, 1990; Gottfried, Gelman, & Schultz, 1999). For example, when asked to imagine that a child's brain was successfully transplanted into a pig, children up to the age of eight or nine years judged that the pig would now have the intellectual *capacities* of a child (being intellectually skilled in human ways) but nonetheless would retain the memories, identity, and personality of a pig (Johnson, 1990). Even more startling, Gottfried, Gelman, and Schultz (1999) found that young children judged that personal memories and thoughts would remain unaffected even with a transplant of the entire insides of the individual's body. In other words, children seem to have no idea that subjective mental contents are essentially contained within an individual brain or body.

These findings point precisely to a divide between an intuitive and a reflective theory of mind. Intuition certainly presents the phenomenal existence of occasional representational actions and states. What is not presented, however, is the existence of a more substantially enduring mind. Children regard the human body as an instrument of the self, as a locus of action, experience, and thought but not as a container of enduring subjective minds. In other words, intuition does not provide the characteristically Western idea of a person that Geertz (1975) characterizes "as a bounded, unique, more or less integrated motivational and cognitive universe, a dynamic center of awareness, emotion, judgment and action organized into a distinctive whole..." (p. 48). This idea only begins to take shape toward the end of childhood. At this point, the brain is conceived as containing mental things and operating as a kind of inner self that centrally informs and directs

disciplined acts of meditation, the flow of experience can be rediscovered, as can the illusion of a substantive self or mind. Such was the reflective insight of William James that put him in the company with the metaphysics of early eastern thinkers and modern phenomenologists. In this regard, James, like Piaget, also showed a special allegiance to Bergson (see Taylor & Wozniak, 1996).

all human action and experience (Wellman & Hickling, 1994). This new idea, however, not only functions to explain certain puzzling phenomena, but poses new problems and transcendental illusions.

## Outline of Development

In focusing on children's domain-specific knowledge, contemporary researchers have little considered the development of thinking that stretches beyond domains. As Aristotle saw it, the ability to make connections across categories appears to be a uniquely higher order human achievement (see Mithin, 1996, and Donald, 1991, for contemporary versions of this Aristotelian position). A rough outline of this development is sketched here.

To begin with, an intuitive understanding of what exists is a prerequisite for metaphysical reflections about such existence. In this vein, Piaget (1929) marked an increase in metaphysical questions at the age of six or seven years, with the peak of "mythological artificialism" occurring between the ages of seven and nine years. He argued that beliefs in a supernatural power developed only as a reluctant consequence of the lack of a better explanation. Theological ideas, he insisted, are "foreign to the child's natural thought ... children only bring in God against their will as it were, and not until they can find nothing else to bring forward" (Piaget, 1929, p. 353).

A tendency to appeal to the existence of transcendental powers and forces only occurs when children can discern existential puzzles that defy ordinary explanation. Even in this case, however, the puzzles need not prompt serious explanatory efforts. As Piaget (1929) well documented, only some children became engaged in metaphysical speculation with any conviction; others refused to take the problem seriously, answered at random, or "romanced," inventing answers merely for the fun of it.

Metaphysical thinking requires a capacity to frame existential problems, an appreciation of limits of ordinary causal powers, and a willingness to engage in a serious effort to generate an explanation. Moreover, this explanatory effort requires a leap in imagination, beyond the ordinary boundaries of intuition. Such a leap is well characterized by Holyoak and Thagard (1995) as system mapping. Conceptual systems that originally served to frame the existence of immanent, natural causes and kinds are accessed and recruited to frame ideas about supernatural causes and kinds. Thus, as Boyer and Walker (this volume) well argue, magical and religious ideas are built by the extension of intuitive frames of understanding.

Middle childhood appears to be especially characterized by this sort of growth of imagination. During this period, children commonly entertain ideas about all sorts of fantastical beings, powers, and events, variously considered to be "real," "fictional," or merely "made up," including supermen, sorcerers, aliens, ghosts, tooth fairies, elves, dinosaurs, dragons, and God. Knowledge of the limits of natural powers of mind and body brings attention to the possibility of supernatural powers.

As children's imaginative capacities expand, they certainly do not blithely accept any old fantastical idea as real. Children are generally quite conventional in their beliefs, and they can readily distinguish between the actual world that they know and fantastical possibilities that they can imagine. The problem is not in distinguishing between the actual and the possible, but in discerning the boundaries of the possible. For example, what is the difference between the real existence of once-upon-a-time dinosaurs, the fictional existence of once-upon-a-time dragons, and the dreamed existence of monsters? Absent any means of empirically testing these possibilities, children must rely on their own sense of plausibility and the authority of others (see Gibson, 1979; Sperber, 1996). A major achievement of childhood, surely, is to sort out different genres of possible things – historical things, fairy story things, religious things (see Harris, this volume; Miller, Hengst, Alexander, & Sperry, this volume).

While children remain practically grounded in the everyday world of ordinary objects, people, and events, fantastical possibilities have a place, whether in fictional entertainment or more serious theological ideas. Thinking in middle childhood is thus marked by imaginative extensions of the actual into the possible. Intuitive categories that originally served to frame events in the actual world are accessed to construct new possibilities. These extensions serve to enrich an intuitive frame of understanding, yet do not fundamentally revise it. Cosmological myths offer an explanation of why things are as they are without seriously questioning the intuitive ground of reality itself.

The end of childhood is marked by another potential leap in imagination. More than explaining reality as it intuitively appears, metaphysical thinking may now turn to consider alternatives to the intuitive ground of reality itself. The naive assumptions of ordinary understanding may be opened to epistemological doubt (Chandler,

1987). The actual order of things may be subordinated to the possible (Piaget & Inhelder, 1969). And thinking may be freed to entertain the most far-reaching connections and extraordinary ideas.

The fantasies of children seem conventional in comparison to the radical possibilities that are entertained at higher levels of metaphysical thought (see Johnson, 1997). Consider, for example, the Cartesian idea that everything that exists depends on the existence of thoughts and distinctly mental "substances;" the Socratic idea that the highest knowledge can be derived from reflection; or the mystical idea that a higher, transcendental reality can be discovered in dreams and "visions." At the other extreme, consider the materialist idea that everything that exists is reducible to material entities and causes.[11]

At this level of thinking, there is again the prospect of playful entertainment as well as serious metaphysical belief. Individuals surely differ in the degree to which they seriously entertain metaphysical possibilities as well as ideas they come to espouse. Short of a singular, ultimate expert theory, development can be marked by the acquisition of a kind of pragmatic wisdom, respecting the value and limitations of different ways of framing reality (cf. Piaget, 1971; Labouvie-Vief, 1994).

## Later-Developing Supernatural Ideas

What happens to supernatural thinking at the end of childhood? Piaget (1929) described a widespread decline in magical thinking with the acquisition of competing ideas. Effectively, children acquire explanations and beliefs common in modern Western culture, undercutting a tendency toward magical ideas (see Subbotsky, this volume). But this is not to say that supernatural ideas disappear altogether. As Piaget well noted, magical beliefs not only persist among adults everywhere, but in fact become stronger and more crystallized within culturally shared metaphysical systems of belief (see Piaget, 1929, p. 390). Moreover, as domain-specific knowledge develops – knowledge of

---

[11] In an important sense children grow up in a world of transcendental, socially constructed objects. As Richard Shweder (1990) puts it, children grow up in an "intentional world" of things that are "real, factual and forceful," but nonetheless exist "only as long as there exists a community of persons whose beliefs, desires, emotions, purposes and other mental representations are directed to it, and are thereby influenced by it" (p. 2). This world is "transcendental," however, insofar as it exists with a kind of intentionality of its own.

physical and mental kinds of things – the metaphysical problems do not disappear, but rather shift and expand to present ever more radical questions and possibilities about the ultimate nature of things.

Development can be viewed in terms of changes in local knowledge as well as more general articulation of boundaries between natural and supernatural explanations. Thus, certain mysteries, like where dreams ordinarily come from, may be explained with developing ideas about the unconscious processes of the human mind. Yet, new mysteries may arise. While most dreams may be readily explained to be the result of personal thoughts and memories, certain extraordinary visions may appear to reflect a truly transpersonal order. The developing capacity to conceive the existence of inner selves or minds brings with it the possibility of transcendent souls (Boyatzis, 1997). The developing capacity to role-take, taking a position outside of oneself, brings with it the possibility of out-of-body experiences (see Hunt, 1995) and a reification of a personal "I" (see Zusne & Jones, 1989).

Development also presumably includes more general ideas and preferences regarding what kinds of explanations are suitable for what kinds of problems. In a new line of research, Pepitone and Saffiotti (1997) have specified prototypical conditions under which supernatural categories of explanation are commonly elicited from adults (see also, Pepitone, 1997). These conditions, as seen in Table 7.1, stand out as being both highly significant and uninterpretable in ordinary, natural ways. For example, an amazing recovery of a person from a seemingly incurable illness is commonly explained as a miracle, implying the intervention of some higher power. Or, instances of surprisingly good or bad happenstance are attributed to "luck." In turn, notions of "laws of justice" are invoked when extraordinarily good things happen to good people or bad things happen to bad people. These supernatural categories of explanation are posed in contrast with natural categories of explanations consisting of material or psychological causes as well as the existence of chance.

Eliciting open-ended interpretations of the prototypical events, Pepitone and Saffiotti (1997) have found that the same categories of nonmaterial explanations are employed by adults across cultures as different as the United States and India. At the same time, they also found striking individual and cultural differences. Some highly educated, scientifically minded individuals did in fact eschew supernatural explanations in favor of reference to natural causes and chance.

Table 7.1. *Events and Corresponding Immaterial Beliefs**

| Events | Immaterial beliefs |
| --- | --- |
| 1. *"Meant to Be" Events:*<br>Events that produce outcomes having a marked impact on the life of the victim, and contingent on the particular victim's being in a particular place at a particular time. | Fate |
| 2. *"Miracle" Events:*<br>Events that produce longed-for positive outcomes of high value to the victim but against all odds of happening. | God |
| 3. *"Good/Bad Breaks" Events:*<br>Events with positive or negative outcomes of moderate impact on the victim and relatively low likelihood of happening, and which often give the sense that something about the victim pulled for the desirable or undesirable outcome. | Luck |
| 4. *"Just Desserts" Events:*<br>Events with utterly unexpected outcomes that seem to "even out the score" by creating either an undesirable situation for victims who previously had created a negative situation for someone else (Just Desserts—Deserved") or a desirable situation for victims who had created positive outcomes for others ("Just Desserts—Reward"). | Laws of Justice |

*Definitions quoted from Saffiotti (1990).

And, Indian adults showed a comparative preference for explanations in terms of fate, even while still acknowledging the role of chance.

These findings suggest that widespread tendencies toward supernatural explanations may be crystallized in adult belief systems that serve select explanatory purposes. While basic categories of natural and supernatural explanations may be universal across cultures, certain explanations may be privileged over others. And in some cases, supernatural categories of explanations may be dismissed altogether.

To examine this sort of selective process, I recently adapted the methods of Pepitone and Saffiotti (1997) to study the supernatural explanations and beliefs of young adolescents growing up in two very different religious traditions. This age group was selected because it marks a likely turning point in the development of metaphysical ideas. Roman Catholic and Unitarian Universalist religious traditions were chosen, as these foster very different stances toward the existence of the supernatural. The Roman Catholic tradition supports immaterial intuitions with the idea that there is a divine presence everywhere working in the world. In contrast, the Unitarian Universalist tradition offers no doctrinal support for the existence of a supernatural God, instead fostering a naturalistic, humanistic world view.

In an exploratory study, interviews were conducted with two samples of girls, ages thirteen and fourteen, who regularly attended religious education within their respective churches. The participants were questioned about the prototypical events outlined in Table 7.1, which were adapted for this age group from items originally developed by Saffiotti (1990). The participants were also directly questioned about their beliefs in miracles, fate, immanent justice, and luck, as well as the existence of supernatural things, including God, ghosts, and spirits.

Reflecting their religious backgrounds, the participants interpreted the prototypical events in very different ways. The Roman Catholic girls typically affirmed the existence of miracles, fate, luck, and laws of justice. Moreover, these categories were supported, integrated, and explained with a monotheistic theory with a singular divine force operating behind everything. For example, one girl explained that "God is a higher force that moderates everything; fate means your destination in life that you have no control over and that you cannot change; good luck means fate is on your good side, and if people do bad things, then the greater force – God – has control over their lives." It was not that these girls were unable to conceive of the existence of chance or ordinary causes. Rather, these ordinary explanations were conceived to be subordinate to a higher, nonmaterial reality. In fact, the possibility that the immaterial events were the result of chance was entertained, but dismissed as an illusion, masking a deeper reality of design. As one girl put it, "When things happen by chance it kind of happens for a reason. We don't know why and think it happens coincidentally but God knows why."

The Unitarian participants adopted quite the opposite metaphysical stance. They typically dismissed the idea of supernatural design as an illusion, masking the deeper roles of chance, material, and psychological causes. For example, when asked to explain the seemingly miraculous recovery of a child from a terminal illness, these participants commonly argued that it could be due to an unknown natural occurrence or the power of positive attitude and will.

Although the Unitarian participants dismissed the role of divine intervention and the immaterial categories of explanation, it would be a mistake to conclude that they were materialists. On the contrary, they often emphasized the limits of knowledge and appealed to the existence of "something more" in the form of some kind of spiritual force, although more limited than a traditional God. As one subject explained, "Honestly, I don't believe in someone up in the sky or something like that, but to say that I'm an atheist makes me very uncomfortable. It makes me feel like I'm less spiritual, like I'm just flesh and bones and stuff, and I don't like that idea." For her, God was the "inner light," the "inner pure self."

The Unitarian participants also theorized about the existence of nonmaterial or semimaterial existence of ghosts, spirits, and souls. One girl explained that ghosts consist of a combination of the soul, plus spirits, plus elements of matter; spirits consist of "feelings and thoughts," whereas the soul consists of "just good or just bad thoughts." Another Unitarian participant regarded spirits as split-off, fragmented mental states, and claimed that some people do not have souls. She described such people as being like inanimate objects – "like mannequins or a car" – because they "don't think about things," don't really have their "own thoughts and feelings," and don't "make an impact on anyone's life." She also explained that "I believe that God can co-exist with science because I believe that thoughts can exist outside the body. And I believe in spirits, because they are the thoughts of a person's soul and God is that initial thought."

While the Unitarian participants little believed in a higher supernatural power, they tended to attribute extraordinary powers to the human will and spirit. For example, in response to questions about fate, one subject explained that, "I think you choose your own fate"; another concluded that, "mostly you're in control of your own life." In response to the story about the seeming miracle, the subjects emphasized the potential power of mind over the body. One subject explained: "I believe that some things can happen out of pure will power and pure imagination. You know, like some things I have made happen just by thinking." Having indicated a belief in the extraordinary healing powers of a positive attitude, another subject was asked if such powers are supernatural. She responded, "Well, I think it's something that's beyond our knowledge. Like how body and mind are connected. Like, we can't even determine something as basic as how our visual sense works." Asked if we'll eventually understand such things she concluded that, "There's a certain mystery to everything in life, you know. I don't think we'll ever really know."

We know remarkably little about how youth grapple with such mysteries. It is clear, however, that these middle-class, American adolescent girls are contemplating higher order metaphysical ideas. All of the participants took the matter of mind seriously, puzzling over the immaterial qualities of the human will, self, and consciousness, and speculating about transcendental possibilities of spirits, ghosts, and souls. The difference was that the Unitarian girls limited their speculations about immaterial powers to the existence of human intentionality (however extraordinary it may be). The Catholic girls, in contrast, articulated the idea that a higher intentional power exists that ultimately explains everything that happens.

## Something More

For the most part, children's thinking, like most ordinary thinking, is quite practical, common sensical, and down to earth. From the outset human cognitive systems are adaptively designed to detect relevant information in the world and organize this information in ways that serve to successfully guide ordinary human affairs. Yet, the unique power of the human cognitive system lies in its capacity for thinking that goes beyond local knowledge, making higher order connections between different kinds of things.

The recent emphasis on the development of domain-specific knowledge has tended to downplay the value of thinking that stretches beyond domains, reducing it to a kind of "fantastical" error (Woolley, 1997). Yet the value of this broader thinking is nowhere more evident than in the development of Piaget's own ideas. In his early adolescence, Piaget's intellectual pursuits were focused in the domain of biology. Concerned about this narrow specialization, his godfather took him for a summer holiday with the expressed purpose of broadening his thinking, introducing him to philosophy, especially Bergson's ideas about "creative evolution." This experience, as Piaget relays it, was a tremendous shock. He had not before heard philosophy discussed by anyone but a theologian. And he was profoundly affected, intellectually and emotionally. Intellectually, he remembers being "seized by the demon of reflection and focusing it almost immediately on the problem of knowledge." Emotionally, he was struck by the "profound revelation" that God is life itself, thus integrating the study of biology with "the explanation of all things and of the mind itself." (cited in Vidal, 1994. p. 52)

Returning to school, Piaget decided to devote his life to philosophy, the central aim of which, as he saw it, was to reconcile scientific knowledge with religious values. Yet, this effort subsequently led to a deeper crisis, portrayed in Piaget's autobiographical novel, *Recherché*, in the character of Sebastian. This crisis was characterized as a profound "disequilibrium" combined with a thirst for a higher, metaphysical unity. As Vidal (1994) summarizes, "Sebastian sometimes wonders why faith should not limit itself to the realm of values and leave to science the knowledge of reality. His 'thirst for absolute truth,' however, makes him trust metaphysics as a means of uniting being and value, science and faith" (p. 187).

Piaget was driven by a passionate desire for a higher unity. He was torn between science that offered objectivity, at the sacrifice of value, and religion that offered value at the sacrifice of objectivity. This metaphysical conflict led Piaget to reframe the very way in which "reality" was conceived. He proposed a new science that could explain the immanent development of higher levels of organization and value. Inspired by Bergson, Piaget sought to reintroduce Aristotle's notion of genera into modern science. Effectively, Piaget formulated the metatheoretical ground for an empirical science of cognitive development. The attracting vision was a unifying account explaining how higher levels of organization and value can arise out of creative processes immanent in nature. In the place of a transcendental force, God was conceived as being immanent in the creative processes of nature.

Piaget's metaphysical ideas notably coincide with the development of process theology (see Schrader, this volume) and anticipate current, renewed efforts to integrate science and religion (see Berry, 1988; Barlow, 1997). However, having achieved his own personal equilibrium, Piaget embarked on a scientific career, leaving his metaphysical ideas relatively unarticulated.

What Piaget's metaphysics adds to the study of cognitive development is the role of value. More than distinguishing what exists, metaphysics is the natural outgrowth of a human tendency toward conceiving how different things go together in higher order ways. This integration has been described by the philosopher Robert Nozick (1989) in terms of "intrinsic value," defined as "organic unity" or "unity in diversity." Nozick points out that things of greater unity or organization are intrinsically of higher value. Thus, the "great chain of being" appears to be ordered in terms of increasing higher order organization, beginning with inanimate substances at the bottom and proceeding up through plants, lowly animals, higher animals, people, and finally God at the top. In more contemporary terms, he describes a similar chain: "Rocks exhibit intermolecular forces, plants exhibit these along with organic processes; animals show most of these (although not photosynthesis) and add locomotion; higher animals have their activities integrated over time by intelligence and consciousness, and in the case of human beings, this integration occurs in even tighter ways through self-consciousness." (Nozick, 1989, p. 163)

In Nozick's (1989) account, the things that pose the deepest existential conundrums are of the greatest value. For example, it is by virtue of being bodies with minds, being reflexively self-conscious, capable of thinking, knowing, valuing, and exercising free will that human beings stand out as having a high level of value. But intrinsic value can also be discerned in other organizational schemes. The web of life is intrinsically valuable because of the tight interrelation of different parts. Similarly, theories are valuable insofar as they offer an integration of diversity.

In any case, the mystery of existence does not lie in the mere fact that different things exist, nor that different things are connected together. Reflecting on this mystery, there is a tendency to appeal to the existence of "something more" – to some hidden "intention" that explains why things are as they are. It was this intuition of "something more" that William James (1902/1990) reported to be the one common characteristic across varieties of religious experiences.[12]

In their persistent "why" questions, young children are already oriented to the existence of "something more" beyond the given world. From this standpoint, they seek not only to understand human intentions and local causal mechanisms, but also the intrinsic value and meaning of existence in the world. To this end, children's theorizing is not limited to domain-specific knowledge, but extends to thinking about the larger whole. Like Piaget's Sebastian, children's "thirst for absolute truth" leads them to metaphysics. Their sometimes magical interpretations of the world are part of an integrative search for higher value.[13]

---

[12] This idea was simply expressed by a participant in Robinson's (1983) study who reported that religious experience "is any experience that causes me to feel that there is a 'something-more-than' situation. Stripped of its mystique, the transcendent is no more than the sense of this 'something more'. Meaning, after all, is to be found not in the meaningful object or situation itself but always beyond it." (pp. 146–47)

[13] Of course, individuals are variously attracted by the prospect of "something more" against an adaptive countertendency toward the parsimony of something less. As

## References

Aristotle (1941). Metaphysica (Metaphysics). In: R. McKeon (Ed.), *The Basic Works of Aristotle*. New York: Random House.

Barlow, C. (1997). *Green Space, Green Time*. New York: Springer-Verlag.

Berry, T. (1988). *The Dream of the Earth*. San Francisco: Sierra Club.

Boyatzis, C. J. (1997). Body and soul: Children's understanding of a physical-spiritual distinction. Poster presented at the biennial meeting of the Society for Research in Child Development. Washington, DC.

Boyer, P. (1994). *The Naturalness of Religious Ideas*. Berkeley: University of California Press.

Carey, S. (1991). Knowledge acquisition: Enrichment or conceptual change? In: S. Carey and R. Gelman (Eds.), *Epigenesis of Mind: Studies in Biology and Cognition*. Hillsdale, NJ: Erlbaum.

Chandler, M. (1987). The Othello effect. Essay on the emergence and eclipse of skeptical doubt. *Human Development, 30*, 137–59.

Chapman, M. (1988). *Constructive Evolution*. New York: Cambridge University Press.

Donald, M. (1991). *Origins of the Modern Mind*. Cambridge, MA: Harvard University Press.

Flavell, J. H., Green, F. L., & Flavell, E. R. (1995) Young children's knowledge about thinking. *Monographs of the Society for Research in Child Development.* 60 (1, Serial No. 243).

Geertz, C. (1975). On the nature of anthropological understanding. *American Scientist, 63*, 47–53.

Gelman, S. A. (1988). The development of induction within natural kind and artifact categories. *Cognitive Psychology, 20*, 280–85.

Gelman, S. A., & Hirschfeld, L. A. (1999). How biological is essentialism. In D. Medin and S. Atran (Eds.), *Folk Biology*. Cambridge, MA: MIT Press.

Gibson, J. J. (1979). *The Ecological Approach to Visual Perception*. Boston: Houghton Mifflin.

Gopnick, A., & Wellman, H. M. (1994). The theory theory. In: L. A. Hirschfeld and S. A. Gelman (Eds.), *Mapping the Mind*. New York: Cambridge University Press.

William James well noted, where people stand with respect to metaphysics is an important reflection of their personality. In this regard, it is important to emphasize that even young children have been found to differ in their skepticism or credibility (Johnson & Harris, 1994). Individuals also differ in their susceptibility to sympathetic magic (Nemeroff & Rozin, this volume) and in how seriously they entertain metaphysical questions (Piaget, 1929). In a particularly intriguing study of individual differences along this line, Jones, Russell, and Nickel (1977; cited in Zusne & Jones, 1989, p. 240) reported that individuals who most seriously entertained metaphysical possibilities in terms of magical ideation seemed to be most deeply grappling with metaphysical conundrums, "trying to solve the age-old problem of reconciling the subjective and the objective, understanding the world and oneself from both viewpoints."

210   Carl N. Johnson

Gottfried, G. M., Gelman, S. A., & Schultz, J. (1999). Children's understanding of the brain: From early essentialism to biological theory. *Cognitive Development*, 14, 147–74.

Guthrie, S. (1993). *Faces in the Clouds. A New Theory of Religion*. New York: Oxford University Press.

Holyoak, K. J., & Thagard, P. (1995). *Mental Leaps: Analogy in Creative Thought*. Cambridge, MA: MIT Press.

Horton, R. (1993). *Patterns of Thought in Africa and the West: Essays on Magic, Religion and Science*. New York: Cambridge University Press.

Hunt, H. T. (1995). *On the Nature of Consciousness*. New Haven, CT: Yale University Press.

James, W. (1902/1990). *The Varieties of Religious Experience*. New York: Random House.

Johnson, C. N. (1988). Theory of mind and the structure of conscious experience. In: J. Astington, P. Harris, and D. Olson (Eds.), *Developing Theories of Mind*. New York: Cambridge University Press.

Johnson, C. N. (1990). If you had my brain, where would I be? Children's understanding of the brain and identity. *Child Development*, 53, 222–34.

Johnson, C. N. (1997). Crazy children, fantastical theories and the many uses of metaphysics. *Child Development, 68*, 1024–26.

Johnson, C. N., & Harris, P. (1994) Magic: Special but not excluded. *British Journal of Developmental Psychology*, 12, 35–51

Johnson, C. N., & Wellman, H. M. (1982). Children's developing conceptions of the mind and brain. *Child Development*, 53, 222–34.

Kant, I. (1781/1965). *Critique of Pure Reason*. Translated by Norman Kemp Smith. New York: St. Martins Press.

Kant, I. (1783/1977). *Prolegomena to Any Future Metaphysics*. The Paul Carus translation, revised by James W. Ellington. Indianapolis, IN: Hackett.

Keleman, D. (1999). Beliefs about purpose: On the origins of teleological thought. In: M. Corballis and S. Lea (Eds.), *The Descent of Mind. Psychological Perspectives on Hominid Evolution*. Oxford: Oxford University Press.

Labouvie-Vief, G. (1994). *Psyche & Eros*. New York: Cambridge University Press.

Laurendeau, M., & Pinard, A. (1962). *Causal Thinking in the Child*. New York: International Universities Press.

Matthews, G. B. (1994). *The Philosophy of Childhood*. Cambridge, MA: Harvard University Press.

McGinn, C. (1993). *Problems in Philosophy: The Limits of Inquiry*. Cambridge, MA: Blackwell.

Mithen, S. (1996). *The Prehistory of the Mind*. New York: Thames & Hudson.

Nozick, R. (1989). *The Examined Life*. New York: Simon & Schuster.

Pepitone, A. (1997). Nonmaterial beliefs: Theory and research in cultural social psychology. In: C. McGarty and S. A. Haslam (Eds.), *The Message of Social Psychology: Perspectives on Mind in Society*, (pp. 252–67). Oxford: Blackwell.

Pepitone, A., & Saffiotti, L. (1997). The selectivity of nonmaterial beliefs in interpreting life events. *European Journal of Social Psychology*, 27 (1), 23–35.

Piaget, J. (1926). *The Language and Thought of the Child*. New York: Harcourt, Brace & Co.

Piaget, J. (1929). *The Child's Conception of the World*. New York: Harcourt, Brace & Co.

Piaget, J. (1933). Children's philosophies. In: C. Murchinson (Ed.), *A Handbook of Child Psychology*. Worcester, MA: Clark University Press.

Piaget, J. (1971). *Insights and Illusions of Philosophy*. New York: World Publishing Company.

Piaget, J. & Inhelder, B. (1969) *The Psychology of the Child*. New York: Basic Books.

Pinker, S. (1997). *How the Mind Works*. New York: W. W. Norton.

Popper, K. (1972). *Objective Knowledge*. New York: Oxford University Press.

Robinson, E. (1983) *The Original Vision. A Study of the Religious Experience of Childhood*. New York: Seabury Press.

Saffiotti, L. M. (1990). The selective use of beliefs to interpret major life events. Unpublished doctoral dissertation. University of Pennsylvania.

Searle, J. (1983). *Intentionality*. New York: Cambridge University Press.

Shweder, R. A. (1977). Likeness and likelihood in everyday thought: Magical thinking in judgments about personality. *Current Anthropology, 18* (4), 637–48.

Shweder, R. A. (1990). Cultural psychology–what is it? In: J. W. Stigler, R. A. Shweder, and G. Herdt (Eds.), *Cultural Psychology*. New York: Cambridge University Press.

Sperber, D. (1996). *Explaining Culture: A Naturalistic Approach*. New York: Cambridge University Press.

Taylor, E., & Wozniak, R. (1996). *Pure Experience*. Bristol, England: Thoemmes Press.

Vidal, F. (1994). *Piaget before Piaget*. Cambridge, MA: Harvard University Press.

Wellman, H. M. (1990). *The Child's Theory of Mind*. Cambridge, MA: MIT Press.

Wellman, H. M., & Gelman, S. A. (1988). Children's understanding of the nonobvious. In: R. Sternberg (Ed.), *Advances in the Psychology of Intelligence* (vol. 4). Hillsdale, NJ: Erlbaum.

Wellman, H. M., & Gelman, S. A. (1998). Knowledge acquisition in foundational domains. In: W. Damon (Ed.), *Handbook of Child Psychology* (5th ed.), Vol. 2, (D. Kuhn & R. Siegler, eds.), *Cognition, Perception and Language*. New York: Wiley.

Wellman, H. M., & Hickling, A. K. (1994). The mind's "I": Children's conception of the mind as an active agent. *Child Development, 65* (6), 1564–80.

Woolley, J. (1997). Thinking about fantasy: Are children fundamentally different thinkers and believers from adults? *Child Development, 68*, 991–1011.

Zusne, L., & Jones, W. H. (1989). *Anomalistic Psychology. A Study of Magical Thinking*. Hillsdale, NJ.: Lawrence Erlbaum.

# 8 Versions of Personal Storytelling/Versions of Experience

## Genres as Tools for Creating Alternate Realities

PEGGY J. MILLER, JULIE HENGST, KRISTIN ALEXANDER,
AND LINDA L. SPERRY

After all, the boundaries between fiction and nonfiction,
between literature and nonliterature and so forth are not
laid up in heaven.

Mikhail Bakhtin

This chapter begins with the premise that we owe our ability to envision multiple realities to the tool kit of our culture and that speech genres constitute an important part of the semiotic equipment that every culture provides. Speech genres are prefabricated ways of organizing speech, which simultaneously offer a set of resources for creating individualized performances. Speech genres may be oral or written, and common examples include jokes, lectures, wills, greetings, arguments, psychotherapeutic discourses, political speeches, sermons, scientific reports, and cross-examinations. Even if we limit ourselves to narrative genres, the variety is immense: fairy tales, myths, parables, histories, autobiographies, memoirs, novels, conversational narratives, sportscasting, news reports, confessions, and soap operas, to name but a few.

In this chapter we focus primarily on a single narrative genre, namely, personal storytelling – the verbal activity of recreating past experiences from one's own life in conversation with other people. Our purpose is to use recent developments in genre theory to deepen our understanding of personal storytelling, particularly as it is used by young children in the contexts of everyday family life. In recent years developmentalists have discovered that children are able to participate in this genre of talk from a surprisingly early age. However, as we learn more about personal storytelling within and across communities and cultures, it is becoming clear that here too there is variety – variety in the ways in which personal storytelling is defined and practiced such that alternate versions of personal experience get created.

We anchor this chapter in examples of this diversity, paying particular attention to the different generic constraints that children must learn to become fluent practitioners of personal storytelling in their respective communities. We also emphasize the fact that personal storytelling never occurs alone in any community. When young children are observed as they actually use and reuse stories in the course of their everyday lives, it becomes apparent that their experience of personal storytelling is rooted, from the beginning, in intertextuality; gradually they come to see where the boundaries are between genres and how to combine genres in creative ways. Thus, full participation in speech genres involves more than learning to abide by generic constraints; it also, paradoxically, involves the systematic transgression or blurring of boundaries. In the second half of the chapter we take a close look at one young child's intermingling of personal stories and orally received written stories. In so doing, we expose a distinctive set of cultural practices that are characteristic of some middle-class, European-American families. Guided by Bakhtin's (1986) holistic view of genres as saturated with value, we examine the ways in which this child renarrativized his personal stories and personalized his favorite written story, a story to which he was strongly emotionally attached.

But first we lay the necessary conceptual groundwork surrounding the notion of speech genre itself. Two key insights frame this initial discussion: that speech genres are situated in human activity and that they afford particular ways of envisioning reality.

## What Are Speech Genres?

The term "genre" traditionally has been used in reference to conventional types of literary, rhetorical, or folkloric texts, such as comedy and tragedy or legend, riddle, and proverb. The goal was taxonomic or classificatory, with texts being distinguished on the basis of a static set of mutually exclusive criteria (Bauman, 1992a; Kamberelis, 1995; Swales, 1990). These criteria, often consisting of formal attributes, were used to define ideal types.

Recently there has been a resurgence of interest in the notion of genre, coupled with a reformulation that seeks to encompass formal criteria within a broader understanding of the ways in which genres are tied to social life (see Kamberelis, 1995, for a review). Chief among the scholars taking this situated perspective on genre is Bakhtin, the Russian literary scholar, philosopher of language, and discourse theorist, who is best known for his analyses of novelistic discourse. In a classic paper Bakhtin (1986) argued against a view of genres as static classifications of types of talk based solely on formal linguistic and stylistic criteria. Instead, he defined speech genres along multiple textual and contextual dimensions, including content, linguistic style, relationships among the participants, the overall compositional structures that make up the "whole" of the interaction or sense of generic completeness, and the affective or evaluative stances that participants take up as they use genres. For Bakhtin, speech genres are not rigid templates that are applied to situations, but rather reflect and extend relatively stable histories of use that offer potential meanings to each and every instance of interaction (see Morson and Emerson, 1990). In defining genres along these multiple dimensions, Bakhtin repeatedly emphasized the pervasive heterogeneity of speech genres. These multiple dimensions also point to grounds for pervasive linkages among genres. Speech genres, then, are constantly intermingling in human activity, offering bridges to various typical speech situations.

In addition to Bakhtinian theory, other influential theoretical perspectives have come from linguistic anthropologists and cultural psychologists who seek to understand language use within and across cultures. For example, Bauman (1992a) and Wertsch (1991) describe genres as historically and culturally specific conventions, expectations, or orienting frameworks whose hallmark is flexibility and open-endedness. In his recent book, *Language and Communicative Practices*, Hanks (1996) argues that speech genres – as the site at which formal, ideological, and practice dimensions intersect – provide the basic unit of analysis for describing communicative practice. Like Bakhtin, Hanks emphasizes that speech genres are emergent processes that cannot be reduced to formal categories; they are elements of social practice that both grow out of and create social relationships (see Ortner, 1984). At the same time, Hanks elaborates more than Bakhtin did on the ideological dimension of genres. He acknowledges that genres may be defined, in part, on the basis of native metalinguistic ideologies of language so long as they are not reduced to such ideologies. In other words, the fact that members of a community recognize several different kinds of narratives, which they label "fairy tales," "myths," and "parables," provides researchers with essential clues to local understandings of narratives. However, as Hanks argues, the way participants orient to generic activity does not fully coincide with these explicit labels. Therefore, in taking a situated view of genres, it is necessary for researchers to go beyond what is named by participants to more fully explore generic activity in use.

What we have been calling "personal storytelling" provides a good example of this point. Although telling stories about one's past experiences is common in many mainstream cultural contexts – at dinner tables among family members, in high school corridors among friends, in airplanes among strangers seated next to one another, and on talk show sets in front of seen and unseen audiences – this type of verbal activity is not necessarily named and often goes unnoticed. At the same time, a variety of terms exist in American English to describe subtle variations in personal storytelling, such as "anecdote," "story," "reminiscence," "testimonial," or even simply "talk." These terms imply that adults have folk theories about the existence and definition of personal stories and hold expectations for what such stories should sound like in different situational contexts.

In addition to this ideological dimension, personal storytelling also illustrates the formal dimension of genres recognized by modern theorists. Bauman (1986), Labov and Waletzky (1967), and Polanyi (1985) have described several formal features of stories of personal experience. For example, the narrator and the self-protagonist are one and the same, and this is signaled by the narrator's use of the first-person pronoun. Often, the narrator orients the listener as to time, place, and person before launching into a description of the past event. Typically, the past event is narrated in temporal order: A happened and then B happened and then C happened. Past tense is used, sometimes in combination with the historical present tense. The narrator uses quoted speech or other devices to convey the point or significance of the story. Typically, the listener indicates his or her involvement in the story by way of back-channel feedback ("uh huh") or expressions of interest ("wow!").

Although this configuration of formal features plays an important role in defining personal storytelling, it exists in tension with the open-endedness of personal storytelling as actually practiced. For example, the evaluation of the narrative cannot be established unilaterally by the narrator but must be negotiated with the listener. The narrator may not need to provide any orienting information because the time, place, and persons involved have already been established in the preceding conversation. The narrator may not get beyond the first in a projected series of temporally ordered past acts because the listener challenges the veracity of the narrator's initial claim. In other words, each experiencing of a personal narrative is always constructed moment-by-moment by particular individuals at particular points in space and time, who stand in particular social and affective relationships to one other. At the same time, this particular experiencing resounds for these individuals with the echoed history of previous enactments. We do not develop a meaning from scratch for each personal story that we experience. We make sense of this story by recognizing (tacitly and/or strategically) its connection to other personal stories and to other genres while simultaneously coordinating our evolving perspectives with those of the other participants. Speech genres are thus highly fluid and diverse, always shifting in use.

In sum, the conception of speech genres adopted here is one that acknowledges the relevance of formal and ideological criteria for defining genres yet seeks to encompass these criteria within a larger understanding of genres as fully situated in activity. This conception implies that there will always be a tension between the durable, ready-made, or stable aspects of genres-in-practice and the variable, creative, or emergent aspects (Bauman, 1992b; Hanks, 1996; Wertsch, 1991). The methodological implications of such a view are profound – genres must be studied in ways that respect this tension. That is, our unit of analysis cannot be the disembodied text and formal features alone, for such an approach excludes many of the emergent processes inherent in generic activity. Rather, genres must be studied as they are actually enacted in social life, including the multiple ways in which they come into contact with other genres.

The reader may wonder why we have belabored so long the point that genres are embedded in activity. Our reason is that this reconceptualization is so deeply at odds with the conceptions of genre (and language in general) that are privileged in the social sciences. A sustained presentation of this basic idea is thus necessary at the outset if it is to be "heard" against the dominant discourses of language as a transparent medium and genres as bounded, insular categories. In other words, applying a Bakhtinian understanding to *this* text, we become keenly aware that our view of genres can only be glimpsed in struggle with other more familiar views, and that it is always in danger of being eclipsed.

## Genres as Ways of Seeing

With this background in place, we now move on to another critical characteristic of speech genres, one that is particularly relevant to the topic of this volume. According to contemporary theories, genres are ways of conceptualizing reality. The name that is often associated with this insight is Medvedev. (There is a debate, which need not concern us here, as to whether Medvedev is a pseudonym used by Bakhtin or the name of one of Bakhtin's associates – see Clark & Holquist, 1984, and Morson & Emerson, 1990). According to Bakhtin/Medvedev (1978), speech genres are specific ways of visualizing or imagining aspects of reality.

> Just as a graph is able to deal with aspects of spatial form inaccessible to artistic painting, and vice versa, the lyric, to choose one example, has access to aspects of reality and life which are either inaccessible or accessible in a lesser degree to the novella or drama. (Bakhtin/Medvedev, 1978, p. 133)

Like Bartlett (1932), Bakhtin/Medvedev argued that we do not perceive reality and then find generic forms in which to encode our perceptions. Rather, genres shape what we apprehend; we learn to see reality "with the eyes of the genre" (Bakhtin/Medvedev, 1978, p. 134). As new genres emerge – the novel was a favorite example of a new genre for Bakhtin – our ability to imagine expands. However, it is important to emphasize, as Morson and Emerson (1990) do, that each genre affords both blindnesses and insights. They say that, "Each is adapted to conceptualizing some aspects of reality better than others. That, indeed, is why people and cultures need continually to learn new genres as the compass of their experience expands" (Morson & Emerson, 1990, p. 276).

What, then, are the aspects of reality that personal storytelling enables us to envision? Interestingly, one of the genres that Bakhtin/Medvedev contrasted with the novel is the anecdote, which presumably is similar to what we call stories of personal experience. He says that the anecdote allows us to grasp the unity of a chance situation, whereas the novel allows us to grasp the unity of a whole epoch. For most of us most of the time, the chance situations that we narrate are not very momentous. My printer collapsed as I was printing out the final pages of the final draft of my paper. You were really surprised by the birthday party that your friends hosted. Her toddler fell down and scratched her arm, requiring words of sympathy and a band-aid. These events are significant to a small number of people for a brief period of time. In the case of personal storytelling, then, the "eyes of the genre" are often trained on small matters, on incidents whose importance does not extend very far. Although often limited in scope to the mundane, the thematic content of personal storytelling is oriented to departures from some ordinary baseline or set of expectations: odd, funny, or interesting happenings; gaffes and transgressions; celebrations, holidays, trips, and other happy events; mishaps, accidents, illnesses, fights, or other negative events. The genre of personal storytelling allows us to see within our own mundane experience those outcroppings that are storyworthy.

More generally, we might say that personal storytelling enables each of us to envision reality from a personal perspective. It provides tools for selecting a reportable experience and representing that experience in a way that conveys its meaning to me, from my unrepeatable position in time and space. Although many people may have participated in a particular event – a wedding, the O. J. Simpson trial, a tornado touching down in Urbana, the Vietnam War, the first presidential elections in Taiwan – each will have his or her own stories of personal experience to tell. The insight that personal storytelling affords is insight into the personal. It is the kind of insight that Bakhtin articulated when objecting to totalizing political ideologies: "There is no person in general; there is a definite concrete other . . ." (quoted in Morson & Emerson, 1990, p. 182). Although personal storytelling may be oriented, in the ordinary course of things, to small perturbations, its importance should not be underestimated, for it affords a way of seeing that opposes the tendency to efface the individual in generalizations and abstractions. Even the most public and far-reaching events, the most horrific and the most sublime, can be envisioned from a personal perspective.

The latter part of Bakhtin's statement – "there is a definite concrete other" – points to another important feature of personal storytelling as a way of seeing. As a genre that occurs in a conversational medium, personal storytelling is responsive to one or more concrete others. The story is constructed as a response to what my conversational partner said, and it is shaped moment-by-moment by his or her responses and by my anticipation of later responses. For example, in adult-to-adult conversation, one person's sharing of a story of personal experience often leads to a reciprocal sharing by the other person. This feature of personal storytelling implies that envisioning reality from a personal perspective involves coordinating my perspective with the personal perspectives of concrete others. The fact that personal storytelling is embedded in a conversational medium allows me to see that, just as I have a personal horizon, so do others.

From a fully situated perspective there is still another feature that becomes salient in understanding personal storytelling as a way of seeing. According to Bakhtin, it is impossible to speak without genres just as it is impossible to speak without a language. Genres never occur alone and hence cannot be learned alone. Intertextuality is a basic fact of life. This implies that stories of personal experience constantly come into contact with other genres, and that the boundaries between stories and other genres will be more or less blurred. So, when a mother elicits a personal narrative from her son in the context of accusing him of breaking his sister's toy, they are co-constructing a blending of genres, one in which the son's perspective on the past event (personal narrative) comes into contact with the mother's moral judgment (accusation). Perhaps the son admits to the misdeed; in that case a *confession* has been co-created, a blending of genres that collapses the distance between the child's personal perspective on the past event and his mother's judgment of his behavior. This hybrid genre enables the child to see his own past actions as more or less worthy, according to shared moral standards. On another occasion another child might tell a personal narrative that his mother hears as favorable to the child and to which she responds with approval. In that case the two participants may blend the story into a genre of affirmation. The eyes of this blended genre are oriented toward identifying one's strengths and protecting a positive view of one's self.

As we shall see in the next section, these examples are not hypothetical. When personal storytelling is observed amidst the flow of everyday life, Bakhtin's baseline of intertextuality is evident at every turn. What, then, are the developmental implications of this baseline? We suggest that very young children, who are just beginning to participate in personal storytelling, are likely to experience something of a blooming, buzzing confusion. That is, initially they will participate in personal storytelling without knowing that they are participating in personal storytelling, without any awareness that there are boundaries between genres, and without access to the specialized way of seeing that personal storytelling affords. Gradually they will sort out personal storytelling from the overlapping genres that they hear. In other words, being able to abstract out some sense of personal story-telling as *unblended* is a later developmental attainment. Although Scarlett and Wolf (1979) focus on a different narrative genre, namely, fantasy narratives with fictional characters, our view is thus compatible with their claim that understanding the boundary between fantasy narratives and "real life" is a relatively late development.

We believe that young children will be aided in the task of sorting out personal storytelling by a variety of factors. They will experience personal storytelling recurrently in specific contexts. Again and again they will hear and feel a particular configuration of linguistic, nonlinguistic, and paralinguistic features. Miller and Moore (1989) argued that affectively tinged regularities – such as the rhythmic contour of the story, the shifting voice quality of the narrator, the exclamations of the listener, and the accompanying body involvement of the participants – may be especially salient to young children as they sort out the stories from the rest of talk. Somewhat later in development they may begin to notice the metalinguistic framing devices that speakers and hearers use to signal to one another which orienting frameworks are in play (Wertsch, 1991). Also, somewhat later, more experienced narrators will indicate for them where the boundaries are and what does and does not belong in a story of personal experience. We will elaborate on the latter point in the next section.

In sum, if we think of speech genres as specialized ways of imagining, then personal storytelling can be seen as a genre that is adapted to envisioning reality from a personal perspective. But because personal storytelling constantly comes into contact with other genres in the flow of everyday life, each particular enactment will get hybridized to some degree while still retaining a family resemblance to other enactments of personal storytelling in the individual's experience. The very young child's initial experience of personal storytelling is rooted in these blendings of personal storytelling with other genres. These blendings – especially the routinization of particular kinds of blendings – also turn out to be important in understanding cultural variation's in personal storytelling.

## Alternative Ways of Envisioning Personal Experience: Variations in Personal Storytelling Within and Across Cultures

Although narrating past events from one's own life is a probable cultural universal, there is a great deal of variation within and across cultures in the ways in which personal storytelling is defined and practiced (see Miller & Moore, 1989, for a review). What such stories can be about, whether they can be fictionalized, when to tell them, to whom they should be directed, and for what purposes they are told are highly variable. If we think of genres as ways of seeing, then these culturally different versions of personal storytelling imply differences in the ways in which cultural groups conceive of personal experiences. There is a direct parallel here with Taylor and Carlson's (this volume) discussion of the Hindu conception of what Western psychologists call "imaginary companions." When Hindu children talk to invisible others, their parents assume that they are communicating with real spiritual beings or with remembered persons from a past life. Talking to an entity that the parent cannot perceive thus comes to be understood as a real spiritual experience, intelligible within a particular set of spiritual practices, in one cultural case, but as an imaginary experience akin to pretending in another cultural case. Our claim is that children come to appropriate these alternate interpretations of experience as they participate in different genres of talk to invisible others, genres that are routinely hybridized with religious genres in the Hindu case and with genres of play and fantasy in the American case.

In the case of personal storytelling, the literature contains a number of excellent examples of the different conceptions of experience that get privileged across groups. For example, in a working-class, European-American community in the Piedmont Carolinas, narrators stuck close to the literal truth when relating their past experiences and created self-denigrating protagonists; these storytelling norms contrasted sharply with those in a nearby working-class, African-American community where well-formed stories of personal experience involved fictional embellishment and self-aggrandizing protagonists (Heath, 1983). In the former case, personal storytelling is better adapted to conceptualizing one's past experiences as strictly circumscribed by the literal truth and rife with evidence of personal shortcomings; in the latter case it is better adapted to seeing the possibilities for self-invention and enlargement in one's past experiences. These two versions of the genre thus afford complementary insights and blindnesses. Personal storytelling varies not only in parameters of definition, but in participant structure as well. For example, in many oral traditions the narrator tells the story more or less unilaterally, whereas among Athabaskans in Alaska and northern Canada there is so much negotiation that the audience, in effect, tells the story

(Scollon & Scollon, 1981). This contrast implies differences in the extent to which speakers envision their past experiences as subject to their own or to others' authorial control.

Although most of the research on the developmental roots of personal storytelling has focused on children from mainstream backgrounds, evidence is now accumulating that children from a variety of sociocultural groups participate in the narrative practices of family and community as early as the second and third years of life. The cross-cultural evidence further suggests that these early narrative enactments are already culturally differentiated (Eisenberg, 1985; Miller & Sperry, 1988; Sperry & Sperry, 1995). In keeping with the theoretical emphasis on genres as situated activity outlined above, it is important to underscore a methodological feature of this work, namely, that personal stories are not elicited or treated as disembodied texts; rather, they are observed as they are enacted in ongoing interactions with family members.

For example, in a comparative study of everyday discursive practices conducted in Taipei and Chicago, Miller and her colleagues (Miller, Fung, & Mintz, 1996; Miller, Wiley, Fung, & Liang, 1997) found that both middle-class Chinese and middle-class European-American families engaged routinely in personal storytelling with their two-and-a-half-year-old children. Moreover, in both cases the caregivers told stories collaboratively *with* the child, who participated by making substantive verbal contributions to the story, and they told stories *about* the child, whose participation was usually limited to onlooker or co-present other. However, the Chinese caregivers and children were much more likely than their European-American counterparts to tell stories about the child's past transgressions, to repeatedly invoke social and moral rules, to structure their stories so as to establish the child's transgressions as the point of the story, and to construct story endings in which the didactic implications of the story were developed. Discourse analysis revealed that, even in those rare instances in which a European-American child's past transgression was narrated, a qualitatively different interpretation of the child's experience was constructed, one that acknowledged yet downplayed the child's wrongdoing. The Chinese were more likely to use personal storytelling as a didactic resource for evaluating and correcting young children and conveying moral and social standards, whereas the European-American families were more likely to use personal storytelling as a medium of entertainment and self-affirmation. That is, with respect to personal storytelling, the Chinese parents seemed to place more emphasis on their role as guardians of their children's moral development, and the European-Americans seemed to place more emphasis on their role as guardians of their children's psychological well-being. This was entirely a matter of emphasis, however; both groups of parents found many ways to promote their children's moral development and their well-being.

Applying Bakhtin's insight into intertextuality to this cultural comparison, it becomes clear that in the Chinese case personal storytelling recurrently came into contact with genres of moral evaluation – correction, instruction, criticism, accusation, and confession. This is apparent not only in the hybridized content (e.g., the prevalence of stories about the child's past transgressions) and structure (e.g., the didactic endings) of the stories, but also in the real-time juxtaposition of such genres with personal storytelling. Miller, Wiley, Fung, and Liang (1997) found that the Chinese families were much more likely than their European-American counterparts to respond to the child's here-and-now transgressions by telling a story about a similar transgression that the child had committed in the past. In other words, stories of the child's past transgressions routinely followed events in which the parent judged the child's current action to be wrong. (Note that this finding could be obtained only by studying personal storytelling as it is situated in ongoing activity.) The Chinese parents seemed to be putting into practice the notion of *jihui jiaoyu* or "opportunity education" (Fung, 1994). This notion, expressed by several of the parents in the study, encompasses two interlinked ideas: that it is more effective to situate a moral lesson in the child's concrete experience than to preach in the abstract, and that parents should take every opportunity to provide such concrete lessons. The Chinese caregivers treated the child's here-and-now misdeeds as opportunities to remind the child of a previous transgression, thereby reinforcing and personalizing moral lessons through concrete exemplars. Indeed, they seemed to feel that they would be remiss as parents if they did not take advantage of these opportunities for moral education. The genre of personal storytelling, as constructed by the Chinese caregivers and children, thus invites two-year-olds to see themselves as moral actors, to filter their experiences through shared moral standards. This does not mean that the Chinese caregivers ignored their children's positive qualities; they too found ways to portray their children favorably and to express their affection. Our point is that the genre of personal storytelling, as practiced by Chinese families, invites a particular kind of bias toward personal experience.

The European-American families enacted their own kind of bias, one that obscures rather than highlights the transgressions of two-year-olds. This is well illustrated by an American transgression story in which no one could remember what the child had done wrong. An older sibling and the focal child co-narrated a past experience in which a desired toy had been withheld because they had been "bad boys." But neither child could remember why they had been punished. When the mother, who had been out of the room momentarily, returned and tuned in to the conversation, she commented ironically, "My kids being bad?!" She confirmed that the incident had occurred the week before, but she too could not remember the precipitating misdeed. In other transgression stories, the child's misdeed was narrated as peripheral to the main action of the story, the story was keyed nonseriously, or the story was constructed so as to establish the child's "goodness" as the point of the story in spite of his or her misdeed. The European-American parents were not indifferent to their children's misbehavior, but rather preferred to handle misdeeds at the time that they occurred. They reserved personal storytelling for past experiences that cast the child in a favorable light, hybridizing it with genres of praise, affirmation, and self-protection.

So far we have focused on comparisons across communities or cultures. It is just as important, however, to examine variations within sociocultural groups if we are to fully appreciate the variety of ways that personal experiences may be envisioned. Research conducted by Sperry and Sperry with African-American families from a rural community in the Black Belt region of Alabama provides a good example of how genre serves as a tool to demarcate gender-appropriate behavior (Sperry & Sperry, 1995, 1996). Narrative is highly valued in this community, and two-year-olds' conversations with family members were filled with narrative-like speech, accounting for about one-quarter of their naturally occurring talk. Both boys and girls produced stories about past events that happened to them as well as fantasy stories involving imaginary creatures, with the latter being more prevalent than the former. This finding was not surprising given the fact that the caregivers often invoked frightening fantasy creatures to gain compliance from their children, a practice that was used more often with boys than with girls. Fantasy also occurred in nondisciplinary contexts. According to Sperry and Sperry (1996), "Both caregivers and children enjoyed telling stories of escaping from 'Nicoudini,' the 'Boogabear,' 'Werewolf,' or the spectral deer who entered their home one misty evening; conversely, they enjoyed talk of locking up naughty family members in closets or in the refrigerator. Families told such stories easily and frequently, and children gathered around to be thrilled by the imagined terror and to practice creating it themselves" (p. 462).

Striking gender differences appeared in narrative production as early as twenty-four months of age. Although toddler girls initiated as many of their fictional stories as did toddler boys, boys told many more stories – both fantasy and realistic. Boys were also treated differently by their caregivers in terms of receiving more approbation for fantasy talk. This is illustrated in the following episode in which twenty-eight-month-old Stillman related his fantasy excuse for why he could not comply with his mother's request to get his truck out of the closet where it was stored (Sperry & Sperry, 1996). She accepts his fantasy, and together they elaborate it further:

MOTHER: Where your truck at?

STILLMAN: 'at/ in a 'at/ (gazes at furnace door, then at Mother) [rat]/ in a [rat]/

MOTHER: In a what? (leaning toward Stillman)

STILLMAN: in 'aat!/ (loudly, arching point aimed over Mother's shoulder)

MOTHER: In the closet.

STILLMAN: eh/

MOTHER: Oh, the rat in the closet.

STILLMAN: eh/

MOTHER: You scared to get the truck? (nods, eyes widen)

STILLMAN: mah, mah, mah it scare me rat/ (gazes at floor to the right)

MOTHER: Oh, Lonni gonna get the rat for you?

STILLMAN: eh/

MOTHER: Oh, Okay.

STILLMAN: mah, mah, mah, mah, mah rat go?

MOTHER: The rat'll bite your nose off. (gazes at Stillman)

STILLMAN: mm/ (shakes head "no" briefly) where my rat at?/

MOTHER: In the closet where your truck at.

STILLMAN: unh/ (negatively)

MOTHER: Yes, it is. (nods)

> STILLMAN:  mmm my, my rat in the buh/
> MOTHER:  In the bushes?
> STILLMAN:  eh/
> MOTHER:  There's no rat in the bushes.
> STILLMAN:  a man get 'at in buh/

The gender differences discernible among toddlers in this community appear to be precursors to the gendered reality of adults. In interviews women in the community expressed their awareness of a sharply gendered world. One grandmother said that girls have more pressure on them growing up because they have to "live within the moral bounds." Her grown daughter, in agreement, went on to illustrate, "What's that parent goin say? 'Well, he's a boy and you a girl.' Well, he can stay out later than I can. Why is that? See, that's what you call a double standard. . . . If it's a boy, he gets away with murder. The girl don't get away with nothin." The women also acknowledged that the greater constraints on girls and women extend to the narrative domain. Another grandmother said, ". . . the ladies, they talk casual, like, housekeeping and . . . sewing. Things like that. But men really, they-they-they brag . . . They really brag. You hardly ever catch a, a lady, you know, just getting out doin what they call 'tall-bragging.' They, but men will do it" (Sperry & Sperry, 1995, p. 47). Men were also recognized and admired for their ability to fictionalize real-world events. One mother referred proudly to her husband's fame for telling story lies, "Larry's a good story teller . . . somebody [want to] tell you a story, they get Larry. It be soundin' so true but it don't be true" (Sperry & Sperry, 1996, p. 444).

How, then, does this community manage to hold girls to a higher standard of truth in personal storytelling? Or, to put it differently, how are gender-differentiated generic constraints created and enforced? We have already mentioned one way in which this is accomplished: Caregivers are more accepting of boys' forays into fantasy talk. That is, they are more likely to participate with boys in ways that support and elaborate their fantasy talk. At the same time, they are more discouraging of such talk by girls. Caregivers ignored girls' fantasy talk entirely or responded in the most minimal way. For example, when one little girl told an elaborate fantasy about going for a ride on a tractor and seeing the cows, her mother's only response was "mm hm." Another little girl's fantasy met with a strong rebuke, "We don't say things like that!"

The latter provides a good example of a point we made earlier, namely, that one way in which children learn the specific generic constraints that define personal storytelling in their community is by way of exposure to explicit metalinguistic interventions by more experienced narrators, interventions that are occasioned by the child's transgression of the adult norm. In contrast to this African-American community, both males and females were required to stick close to the literal truth in two working-class European-American communities studied by Miller and her colleagues. As in the Roadville community described by Heath (1983), young narrators in South Baltimore and in the Daly Park (a pseudonym) neighborhood of Chicago were censured for violating a norm of literal truth. For example, for a young child in South Baltimore to say that she got splashed by a playmate was one thing, but to say that she got splashed by a monster was quite another matter, and the caregivers responded promptly, "I believe that's a fib" or "That's a lie and you know it" (Miller & Moore, 1989, p 444). Similarly, when a child in Daly Park told a story in which she went downtown and saw a wolf that talked, her grandmother said, "Do wolves go downtown?" When the child persisted in this vein, her grandmother continued to object, "No silly stuff. Nice stuff." and "What kind of story is this?" (Miller et al., 1990) These were not blanket condemnations of make-believe, for pretend play was valued and encouraged in these communities. Rather, with these explicit interventions more experienced narrators drew clear boundaries between what belongs in a story of personal experience and what does not.

From the standpoint of genre theory, however, these interventions do not simply enforce a normative order; they also privilege one vision of experience over another. In these examples the children's personal experiences were peopled with splashing monsters and talking wolves. Although obviously familiar to the caregivers, these creatures did not appear in *their* stories of personal experience (except when specifically framed as imaginary, e.g., as characters in a movie or TV show). What is at stake, then, are competing visions of reality. The caregivers treated the children's stories as though they were blended or bridged too exuberantly, as though they were insufficiently delimited. They recast the child's vision, typifying it as a lie, as silly, as uninteresting, or as a defective story. In so doing, they were not merely pulling the children's stories away from fictional genres but creating a different kind of bridging toward realistic genres. Thus, drawing boundaries between genres inevitably involves reconfiguring the alliances among genres.

In sum, these examples of variations within and across cultures suggest that personal storytelling is best thought of as a family of genres. Although all of these culturally situated genres embodied a personal perspective on experience – distinguishing them from other families of genres – each culture (or gender within a culture) privileged particular slants on experience. Each version of personal storytelling was specialized in its own way via its association with other activities and genres – toward fictionalization and away from the literal truth, for example, or toward moral evaluation and away from self-affirmation – and the early narrative participation of two-year-olds already mirrored these sociocultural patternings. When young children transgressed the local generic norms, as young children inevitably will, more experienced narrators intervened in ways that explicitly demarcated the boundaries of the genre, thereby privileging their vision of experience and providing a crucial source of information about how the genre is defined.

## Affect and the Intermingling of Genres

In his classic essay on speech genres Bakhtin (1986) made a distinction between simple genres, which he called "primary genres," and "secondary genres," which were constructed out of two or more primary genres. Although personal storytelling qualifies as a primary genre in Bakhtinian terms, this type of generic activity never stands alone, self-contained and immaculate. A key claim running through this chapter is that when we observe everyday family life with young children, we see that personal storytelling, like any genre-in-practice, co-exists with other genres; there is a baseline of intertextuality. We thus agree with Hanks' (1996) recommendation that Bakhtin's distinction between primary and secondary genres be treated not as an absolute distinction but as a heuristic, a scale of relative complexity. From this standpoint, personal storytelling, as described so far, tends toward the less complex end of the scale. In this final section of the chapter we examine a phenomenon that departs from this baseline toward greater complexity, namely, young children's creative incorporation of personal stories into orally received written stories. If Bakhtin (1986) is correct about the nature of this process, then, when situated instances of genres come in contact with each other during the course of human activity, hybrid genres emerge. We would expect personal storytelling as a primary genre to continually interanimate with other generic activities,[1] including instances of written stories, resulting in the development of complex, hybrid genres.

The examples that we draw on in this section come from a series of studies in which young children's emotional "attachments" to stories was the focus of inquiry (Alexander, 1996; Alexander & Miller, 1995; Miller et al. 1993). We conducted interviews with mothers and in-depth case studies of children's sustained affective involvement with their favorite stories, documenting how they used and reused them over time in the course of their everyday lives. We wanted to understand something that many teachers, parents, clinicians, and authors of children's literature take for granted, namely, that stories inspire strong feelings and that children often become captivated by particular stories, interacting with them again and again (Butler, 1975; Hearne, 1990; Paley, 1981; Wolf & Heath, 1992). Curiously, however, developmentalists have ignored children's affective involvement with stories: Although early narrative has attracted a great deal of research attention in recent years, most studies have been concerned with what narrative can tell us about memory or other cognitive skills. Other equally important questions have been eclipsed, questions that have to do with how children relate to stories in a more holistic sense.

The conception of speech genres adopted in this chapter is compatible in several ways with a more holistic conception of genres, one that encompasses affective dimensions. It is not simply that genres affect emotions and emotional development, but that affective perceptions and responses are among the multiple, intertwined dimensions that define genres. According to Bakhtin, for example, speech is saturated with value and this is evident in the responsivity of speech genres. For every utterance that we speak, listeners actively respond, making judgments and evaluations of the utterance and the generic form in which it is cast. The speaker is tacitly aware of and adjusts to this responsivity of the various listeners and is himself or herself responsive to those judgments. Responsivity then is characteristic of both speakers and listeners, who are orienting not only to the present

---

[1] In his classic work on speech genres Bakhtin (1986) limits his discussion of the interaction of speech genres to one direction, arguing that secondary genres "... absorb and digest various primary (simple) genres" (p. 62). It is clear, however, from his general theory of language-in-use that these interrelationships are multidimensional.

utterance but to past and future utterances. These evaluative orientations of speakers and listeners are critical in casting utterances in given generic forms. Bakhtin also argues that speakers must take up an evaluative stance, that is, an expressive affect toward each utterance displayed in the tone of the utterance. This is one way that the individual can mark each utterance with his or her own will, reaccentuating generic forms with his or her own individual and immediate emotional-volitional tone or judgment. Thus, genres, and our creative use of them, help us to make sense, fully affect-laden sense, of the world. The "eyes of the genre" are not neutral; they are colored by affective experience.

### The Interanimation of Kurt's Garden Narratives

What does this process of affective sense-making look like in young children? More specifically, how do written stories become personally meaningful to young children? At this point in our limited understanding of children's affective sense-making, we believe that these questions can be most fruitfully addressed by studying children's naturally occurring emotional involvements with stories. Thus, we turn to examples from the aforementioned studies. These studies suggest that young children make affective sense of written stories by intermingling personal stories with written stories. Let us consider first Miller et al.'s (1993) case study of Miller's two-year-old son, who developed an intense interest in "The Tale of Peter Rabbit" by Beatrix Potter (1980). Kurt was first introduced to "The Tale of Peter Rabbit" during a visit with his grandparents. He was twenty-three months old when his paternal grandmother gave him the collection of Beatrix Potter's stories. Listening to stories read aloud was at this point a taken-for-granted part of his everyday life and a reliable source of enjoyment for him and his parents/grandparents. It should also be mentioned, by way of background, that Kurt shared an avid interest in gardens with his grandparents. He had spent many pleasurable hours in his maternal and paternal grandparents' gardens and was especially gentle with the plants for someone so young. His maternal grandmother had recently told him about the mother rabbit who had a nest of babies in her garden, and his paternal grandmother had written him a small book about the woodchuck who ate the flowers in her garden. Thus, it is not surprising that "The Tale of Peter Rabbit" immediately became Kurt's favorite story; from a Bakhtinian perspective, his response to "The Tale of Peter Rabbit" was not just a response to the story itself but a turn in ongoing conversations with his grandmothers about gardens and the small creatures that inhabit them. Kurt's requests for the story were unceasing over the next month, and his parents accommodated his interest as much as possible, reading the story daily, sometimes several times a day. Kurt sat on his parent's lap, listening attentively and looking at the pictures as the story was read again and again.

During this same one-month period, Kurt's preoccupation with Peter Rabbit was also evident in his spontaneous narratives, which, though in the absence of the book itself, contained references to Peter Rabbit and activities in gardens. Miller et al. (1993) argued that these narratives were Kurt's reworkings of the Peter Rabbit tale. Although Kurt had clearly absorbed many elements from the written story, his Peter narratives were not mere copies but his own creative "revisions" of the story. They also provide evidence for the importance of defining genres in terms of social situatedness in that several features of the interactive context supported Kurt's reworking of the story: A sympathetic listener was always present and responded in ways that affirmed or extended Kurt's verbalizations; his concentration was not disturbed; and he was allowed to exercise authorship of the texts. In other words, these narratives existed in a playful space in which Kurt was permitted to reinvent the Peter Rabbit story as he wished. This playful quality very likely was a carryover from the activity of reading "The Tale of Peter Rabbit."

The first Peter narrative occurred one week after Kurt's initial encounter with "The Tale of Peter Rabbit." He was seated in his high chair gazing out at his grandmother's flower-filled garden when he began to talk about Peter Rabbit's activities in this family garden. This Peter narrative, addressed to his mother, and occasionally his grandmother, was structured as a series of parallel episodes in which Kurt named and pointed to each of several plants in the garden, plants that Peter devoured: a little pine tree, broccoli, plants hanging on the sycamore tree. He characterized Peter as "naughty," the same word that is used in the written story, and later he exclaimed, "uh oh!" and "*that* Peter Rabbit!" Yet his manner of delivery conveyed not censure but excitement about Peter's misdeeds, "Peter Rabbit ate the iris!/ ate them *all* up!/" Throughout this Peter narrative Kurt seemed to side subtly with Peter Rabbit, to enter imaginatively into his experiences.

The second Peter narrative occurred a week after the first, again in proximity to a garden. This time Kurt was standing on his maternal grandparents' front porch next to their flower garden. Unlike the first retelling, which Kurt initiated himself, his mother introduced the topic of Peter Rabbit by saying, "I wonder if Peter Rabbit ate any of these marigolds last night?" This overture triggered an outpouring of talk about Peter Rabbit, "ate that one/ (points to a marigold) Peter Rabbit came around the path/ Peter Rabbit came around the walk/ ate this marigold right there/ he came up on the porch/ he came around the bend/ he walked/ . . ." Again Kurt projected Peter Rabbit onto the family garden and described his destructive acts. But this time he was accompanied by Mother Rabbit, who was distinctly displeased with Peter. She warned him repeatedly not to step on little stalks or walk in areas where things were planted, "mother says, 'no, no don't step in that, Grandma planted stuff right there/ Grandma used a trowel/' mother says, 'no, no, don't step in that'."

These partial, greatly simplified descriptions of Kurt's first two Peter narratives convey something of the emotional flavor of his involvement with "The Tale of Peter Rabbit." (See Miller et al., 1993, for further details and for a transcript of the second Peter narrative.) During his month-long fascination with the story, Kurt produced three more Peter narratives, and much of the analysis presented in Miller et al. (1993) is devoted to describing the systematic changes in content, plot, and affective marking that occur across the successive narratives. For the present purposes, however, our task is somewhat different: We examine these Peter narratives to identify the processes through which the orally and visually received written narrative, Kurt's personal narratives of gardens, and other generic activities interanimate one another – in this case, personalizing "The Tale of Peter Rabbit" and renarrativizing Kurt's experiences.

When examined for evidence of these processes of interanimation, the data collected and analyzed by Miller et al. (1993) as ethnographic background clearly point to the pervasive heterogeneity of activities and genres in which Kurt was routinely participating. Miller et al. (1993) report that Kurt spent many hours visiting his grandmothers' gardens, pointing to, touching, planting, caring for, and, talking about the vegetables and flowers that grew there. Kurt displayed the gentleness of touch that resonated with his grandparents' love of gardening. He experienced these gardens in the company of attentive and supportive grandparents and parents, people tending not only to the garden, but to their relationship with him. Kurt talked and heard about seen and unseen animals in the gardens, animals who lived, played, ate, and grew there. One grandmother had a nest of baby rabbits in her garden, and the other grandmother had a family of woodchucks. He participated in talk with his family and even told narratives about being in these family gardens both while in the gardens and while away from them. None of these garden narratives were routinely recorded, but several were captured on tape. Miller et al. (1993) identified two of these as personal narratives; one was "... about a past event in which Kurt helped his grandmother to plant the garden" (p. 96), and the other "... was a hypothetical narrative in which Kurt excitedly imagined what kinds of flowers and plants he might see in his grandmother's garden when he visits her the following day" (p. 96). Another garden narrative was recorded when Kurt, looking at the garden from his grandmother's porch, began "... fantasizing that a crow built a nest in the marigolds" (p. 102). In addition, Kurt experienced these gardens through written texts that were read to him, including letters written to him by his grandparents and the book that one grandmother wrote for him about the family of woodchucks and how they would eat flowers from the garden. Finally, Miller et al. (1993) make it clear that storybook reading was a routine activity in Kurt's world.

It was into this rich background of gardens and book reading that "The Tale of Peter Rabbit" entered Kurt's experiences. Like his experiences of the family gardens, the story of Peter Rabbit and Mr. McGregor's garden entered Kurt's life as a fully embodied, emotional experience, sitting on grandma's lap and hearing and talking about the book, touching the book and looking at its pictures. Although Miller et al. (1993) reported that no data on the actual readings of Peter Rabbit were collected, they did report that this was a favorite book, one that was read frequently, even multiple times a day. Thus, we know that Kurt frequently revisited Mr. McGregor's garden with his parents or grandparents, those same attentive people who shared the family gardens with him. Kurt heard and talked about the seen and unseen plants and animals, now personified with names (e.g., Peter, Flopsy, Mopsy, and Cottontail) and personalities (e.g., "naughty" and "good little bunnies"). Mr. McGregor's garden was talked about in the presence of the garden (i.e., the pictures in the book) and away from it in other settings.

The interanimation of Kurt's experiences with gardens, his grandparents' and Mr. McGregor's, enriches his narratives of both. Kurt's experiences with family gardens help animate his experiences with the storybook, and his experiences with the storybook help animate the family gardens. Part of what we are seeing in Kurt's narratives, then, is a generic reworking of these various experiences. These processes of interanimation can be seen in three ways.

First, Kurt's narratives mix people and their actions from family gardens and Mr. McGregor's garden. In fact, in three of the five recorded narratives, both Kurt's family members and characters from Peter Rabbit are included. For example, in the second narrative, after quoting Mother Rabbit's prohibitions to Peter ("don't walk in there, don't step in there, mother says/ don't go in there/"), Kurt brings himself and his grandmother into the narrative: "Grandma planted some flowers in there/ Grandma planted some flowers in there/ Kurt did help/." Note that the last three utterances comprise a brief story of personal experience, an account of what Kurt and his grandmother did a few days before this Peter narrative. However, when read within the broader sequence within which it is embedded, this mini-narrative takes on a different meaning than it otherwise could have, for Kurt and Grandma's actions of planting flowers in the flower box are now offered as an explanation for Mother Rabbit's prohibition. Peter should not step on the flower box because Grandma and Kurt planted flowers in there. In contrast with the first Peter narrative, where Kurt seemed to delight in Peter's mischievousness, here Kurt's invocation of his personal experience is affectively different, aligning him simultaneously with the perspectives of his grandmother protecting the garden and the rule-enforcing Mother Rabbit.

A second way this interanimation is apparent is in the full intermingling of agencies. For example, in the second Peter narrative, Kurt says "went in the car to see the boats/ Peter Rabbit went in the grocery store cart to get groceries/ Peter Rabbit and mother went to grocery store to get oranges and cat food/."The evening before this narrative occurred, Kurt had participated in both of these excursions. Here again, fragments of a story of personal experience were embedded within this retelling, but this time there was no formal marking that distinguished them as such; their source in Kurt's own experience was discernible only because his ongoing activities were documented as part of this case study. As Kurt's experiences merge into Peter Rabbit's actions, the affective tone of Peter Rabbit reinflects Kurt's experiences of the family gardens. For example, in the first narrative, he conveyed paralinguistically, his excitement about Peter's misdeeds,

"Peter Rabbit ate the IRIS!/ ate them *all* up!/" Similarly, in the third narrative, he said "and the wheelbarrow SCARED Peter/" and "and the and the and the and the blue jay scared Peter/". At the conclusion to the first narrative, Kurt's excitement about Peter Rabbit seemed to literally propel him into the garden; he demanded to get out of his high chair to walk in the garden. This kind of whole-body enactment is also evident in Butler's (1975) classic case study of her handicapped granddaughter's involvement with books, "At night both her father and I read the story (*The Three Billy Goats Gruff*) to C. ; b3 [3;3 years] again, at her request, and she seemed greatly excited by the troll, clasping her hands in front of her body and kicking her legs with the thrill of it" (p. 65).

Third, processes of interanimation also appeared in the way that immediate physical objects and experiences were incorporated into the ongoing narrative. Three of the Peter narratives occurred in proximity to a garden, and in each of these cases Kurt used the physical resources of his surroundings, what was available in his current visual field, in his developing narrative. Linguistically, this was accomplished through the use of deixis. For example, in the first narrative he pointed to the various plants that Peter Rabbit ate. In the second narrative he said, "ate that one/" and pointed to a marigold. In the fifth narrative he said, "Peter not stepped in this stuff right here/". Here we see that the physical surroundings of the family garden afforded the opportunity to blend Peter Rabbit and Kurt's personal experiences; this is analogous to the earlier example, where such blendings were afforded by more verbal resources (e.g., Peter Rabbit riding in the shopping cart).

It is critical to our analysis of these processes of interanimation to remember that genres are coproduced by "listeners" as well as "speakers" in human encounters. Kurt's five narratives around Peter Rabbit and gardens are available for us to reflect on now because his mother recognized and identified them at the time as retellings of "The Tale of Peter Rabbit." Kurt did not encounter this story alone; his parents and grandparents were reading this story and talking about it as well. Therefore, it was not just Kurt's familiarity with the story that mattered, but also his extended family's familiarity. The family brought to interactions with Kurt their own rich genre resources, cultural understandings of storytelling, familiarity with a variety of children's stories, and their own personal histories with "The Tale of Peter Rabbit." In this extended family at the time of these narratives, the name "Peter" alone seemed to be a powerful link to storytelling genres, casting Kurt's narratives as retellings of this well-known childhood fantasy. In other words, Kurt did not develop these narratives on his own; his and his family's communicative resources and practices combined to cast these situated narratives as creative or personalized retellings of "The Tale of Peter Rabbit."

These embodied and interanimated characteristics of genres-in-use complicate conventional and categorical boundaries. For example, good feelings about family gardens, book reading time, and "The Tale of Peter Rabbit" may link these experiences in ways that our labels of "story narrative" and "personal experience narrative" do not capture or parallel. For other families, it may not be the joy and awe of gardening that offers such links, but the drudgery of gardening, or, as for Peter, the hidden dangers and secret pleasures of sneaking into Mr. McGregor's garden. From a Bakhtinian perspective, these experiential and affective links blur, shift, and multiply not only the boundaries of genres, but also the privileged adult boundary between truth and fiction. It is through these heterogeneous and interanimated activities and genres that the child develops specifically cultural visions of realities.

It is interesting to note that the fifth (and last) recorded Peter narrative displayed less of the visible interanimations outlined above. What we see in this sequence of five Peter narratives is the way that processes of interanimation shifted over time, culminating with a more distilled and story-like narrative than the personalized presentations of the earlier versions. Specifically, this final narrative contained references to all of the characters in the Peter Rabbit tale but none of Kurt's family members. Kurt also maintained his narrator's distance throughout this one. Miller et al. (1993) argue that Kurt's familiarity with the Peter Rabbit tale had improved, that he had worked through his emotional responses, and that he had resolved the problemetizing sequences introduced in the book and in his narratives. We suspect that as Kurt worked and reworked his garden experiences and narratives with his family, he developed particularly rich resources to produce this kind of distilled and cooled off narrative that marked the end, as far as we know, of his Peter narratives.

In the case of these particular garden narratives, Kurt's references to "Peter" helped bring forth a wealth of positive and scaffolded interactions, bringing "Peter" into family garden narratives was *recognized* (i.e., they were recognized by family members as creative retellings of Peter Rabbit), *affirmed* (i.e., Kurt's mother responded to his storytelling in culturally appropriate ways, not interrupting, etc.), and *supported* (the interanimations of gardens were encouraged by family through their own strategic interanimations using books, questions, and comments). However, these kinds of interanimations are not necessarily recognized, supported, and/or encouraged within all cultural groups, by all members within one cultural group, or even for a given member in all aspects of his/her life. Thus, this case study points not only to the ways that Kurt's multiple experiences and narratives interanimate one another, but to the ways Kurt was appropriating particular cultural practices of interanimation, learning dominant generic forms as well as what kinds of generic linkages could be forged and displayed in talk. Starting from a perspective that did not privilege either the story or the "real" events of Kurt's life, this partial reanalysis of Kurt's garden narratives begins to display the kinds of complexities and interanimations of activities and genres through which Kurt simultaneously personalized "The Tale of Peter Rabbit" and renarrativized his and other family members' experiences of the family gardens.

### Some Cultural Beliefs and Practices that Support the Interanimation of Personal Stories and Written Stories

Although this description of the processes of interanimation was generated from a single, richly detailed case, we have collected several other case histories of children's emotional attachments to stories that bear evidence of similar processes (Alexander 1996; Alexander & Miller 1995). An important question raised by these cases concerns how young children learn to intermingle personal and written genres in these ways. One possibility, suggested earlier, is that the baseline of intertextuality – the flow of genre on genre in ordinary family life – provides ample opportunity in and of itself for children to learn to combine genres. This opportunity would presumably be available in any community that exposes young children to both personal stories and written stories. In other words, from a Bakhtinian standpoint, it would be impossible to fully insulate genres from contact with other genres. Another possibility, illustrated by Kurt's garden narratives, is that communities may elaborate a set of specialized beliefs and practices that actively encourage children to intermingle personal and written stories. In this section we examine further some such beliefs and practices as they apply to college-educated European-American families.

In an in-depth interview study, Alexander and Miller (1995) invited twenty-four mothers of preschoolers (two- to five-year-olds) to reflect on their children's emotional involvement with their favorite or "special" stories. Most relevant to the issue at hand were the mothers' responses to questions that asked them to speculate about why the child was so interested in this particular story. There was a high degree of agreement among the mothers that young children find in their special stories parallels to their own lives. The child sees herself as similar to a story character or notices a connection between the events in the story and events in her own life. This connection, the mothers said, provides a basis on which the child can identify with the characters and use the story for emotional purposes. This belief was invoked to support the practice of purchasing books for their presumed relevance to emotional issues in the child's life. For example, one mother said,

> *Afraid of the Dark* has been a big one for him. It's when Ernie is afraid to go to sleep at night in the dark. And I think a lot of that has to do with overcoming his own fear of the dark and things like that. That's why we really like those books. When we had, when we were expecting the baby we bought the Little Critter book, *The New Baby*, and then after we had the baby and it was growing we bought *Just Me and My Little Sister*, they seem real relevant to what's going on in their lives at the time and they're real simple little stories. (Alexander, 1994, p. 33)

The simplicity is important because it offers the situation in simplified terms. It is interesting to note that two popular guides to children's literature, *Choosing Books for Children* (Hearne, 1990) and *The New York Times Parent's Guide to the Best Books for Children* (Lipson, 1991) are organized topically around such issues as the birth of a new sibling, toilet training, moving, and starting school, thereby enabling parents to make informed choices about which books are likely to match their child's current concerns.

Like Kurt, all of the children in the Alexander and Miller study owned many books and were granted a great deal of latitude as to which books they chose to interact with and how often. Even when a child's preference for a particular story lasted for months, mothers were generally accepting. Thus, young children's personalizations of written stories rested on the practice of allowing them to choose the stories that were most interesting to them and tolerating repeated engagements with their favorite stories. These families also furnished toys, clothes, and other props that promoted their children's identification with story characters. A little girl wanted to wear her pink Cinderella dress every day and another tried to look like the Little Mermaid, "The mermaid has long hair, and she won't let me cut her hair. And she likes to wear her hair down, which the mermaid wears her down" (Alexander, 1994, p. 37). Implicit in these several practices was an affirmation of the child's perspective, especially her interests and preferences. Recall that a very similar theme was evident in the biased content of personal storytelling as practiced by middle-class European-American families in Miller, Fung, and Mintz (1996) and Miller, Wiley, Fung, and Liang (1997). Thus, these several studies suggest that the high value placed on literacy and oral book reading by college-educated parents combines with their privileging of the young child's psychological experience to sustain a set of practices that promote the intermingling of personal and written stories.

Apart from these beliefs and practices that recognize and affirm children's interanimations of personal and written stories, did the mothers studied by Alexander and Miller model and scaffold interanimations in the way that Kurt's family did? For example, did they invite the children to make connections between their own past experiences and events in fictional stories (e.g. "I wonder if Peter Rabbit ate any of these marigolds [here in Grandma's garden] last night?")? Some research on emergent literacy suggests that middle-class caregivers encourage their young children to make such connections both during book-reading events in which they model and direct their youngsters to notice relationships between events in the book and events in the world, and at various times during the day when the book is not present but some event occurs that occasions a reference to the book (e.g., Ninio & Bruner, 1978; Snow & Goldfield, 1983; Snow & Ninio, 1986). In what other domains are these types of cross-genre connections encouraged by parents – do they relate real events seen on TV (e.g., the images of Mars from Pathfinder) to books (e.g., Leedy's, 1993, *Postcards from Pluto: A Tour of the Solar System)* or to other real events (e.g., Apollo landing on the moon) or to objects (e.g., a model of our solar system)? We did not ask the mothers to report on their practices at this level of specificity, but these are questions that could be pursued by observing the ways in which parents interact with young children when reading their favorite stories to them.

Although the "mainstream" beliefs and practices described in this and the previous section may seem to confer certain advantages, such as encouraging personally meaningful interactions with books from an early age and validating the child's preferences and emotional experiences, it is important to emphasize that these beliefs and practices – like any culture's beliefs and practices – entail inevitable trade-offs. From the perspective of the Chinese families described earlier, the European-American inclination to affirm the child's perspective carries with it the risk that the children will become too willful, self-indulgent, and insufficiently attentive to voices of authority. From the perspective of the African-American families described earlier, the emphasis on book reading with very young children may seem premature, and the practice of encouraging children to intermingle personal experiences and fictional stories may seem to undermine the moral order, especially for girls. Thus, we want to be clear that mainstream beliefs and practices will not necessarily serve the interests or goals of other cultural groups, and that it is crucial to recognize the political and social overtones of advocating one set of practices over another (Willis, 1995).

In sum, Bakhtin's emphasis on the holistic nature of genres and on the multiple ways in which genres come into contact with other genres points to two areas of relative neglect in developmental research on stories, namely, young children's affective engagement with stories and the interrelationships among narrative genres in young children's speech. A detailed case study of a single child and college-educated European-American mothers' beliefs and practices about their children's favorite stories suggest that young children's sustained emotional engagement with their special stories is a fruitful arena in which to learn about the ways in which young children personalize written stories and renarrativize personal stories within the context of specific cultural practices. At the same time, the exposure of these particular beliefs and practices underscores the need to learn a great deal more about the beliefs and practices of other communities and cultures as they pertain to the relationships among narrative genres in young children's experiences.

## Conclusion

We began this chapter with the premise that human beings owe their ability to envision multiple realities to semiotic resources and that speech genres constitute an important semiotic resource that every culture provides. We illustrated this premise by applying recent developments in genre theory to personal storytelling, a type of narrative activity that qualifies as a ''basic'' narrative genre. Personal storytelling is not only a probable cultural universal, but it is one of the first narrative genres in which young children participate. In addition, it is primary in the Bakhtinian sense of combining readily to form more complex genres. One of the insights afforded by genre theory is that personal storytelling embodies a particular way of envisioning reality, one that privileges the individual's perspective from his or her unrepeatable position in space and time. Compared to a national, political, or scientific narrative, personal stories are limited by their adaptation to the personal and away from the general. But by the same token, these other narratives are limited by adaptation to the general. Can we fully grasp the human meaning of a political movement or a war, for example, without seeing it in terms of the experience of particular persons?

However, the situated conception of speech genres advocated in this chapter implies that my personal perspective may not be readily intelligible to you or yours to me unless we share the same culture-based version of personal storytelling. It also implies that there is no single, fixed personal perspective for either of us. As the studies discussed in this chapter illustrate, this conception commits us to study speech genres as they are embedded in other genres and activities, thereby exposing the variability of generic activity. A particular child in a particular culture participates in many enactments of personal storytelling – each somewhat different from every other and some with clearer boundaries than others – but each bearing a family resemblance to the others. This variability can be a problem for the researcher who wants to reliably identify stories, but for the child it is a resource for envisioning reality from multiple, shifting personal perspectives. When viewed in relation to other cultures, the family of personal stories available to this child represents but a limited subset of the larger family of genres that is detectable across cultures. Thus, we need to speak of *families* and *versions* of personal storytelling both at the individual and the cultural levels. The cultural version of personal storytelling that we experience limits the horizons of our personal perspective while at the same time allowing us to see certain realities with special clarity.

One way in which our personal horizons get widened is by way of interanimation with other genres, other ways of seeing. We have emphasized that when young children bring themselves into Peter Rabbit's story or dress like their beloved Cinderella, they are personalizing these written stories. Each child revises the story from his or her own perspective, creating a personally meaningful version of the story. But at the same time that the child is making the fictional story his own, he is also entering into a new world of forbidden gardens and narrow escapes, of fairy godmothers and magical transformations. We must remember, though, that children do not bring the dominant adult generic expectations of truth and fantasy to their narrative activities. Fairy godmothers and talking animals are just examples of the many characters that children encounter through narrative discourse. Only later will they come to distinguish these characters from those that adults define as real (e.g., presidents, astronauts, great-grandma, a parent's work colleagues, etc.). Thus, through this continual interanimation of genres, not only do children make stories meaningful by personalizing them, but also new hybrid ways of envisioning reality are created – ones that stretch the child's personal perspective to encompass the parameters of multiple social worlds, real and imagined.

We believe that this expansion of the child's vision afforded by the interanimation of genres represents a later step in development that should not be confused with the blooming, buzzing confusion that is characteristic of the child's earliest participation in personal storytelling. Earlier we speculated briefly about the developmental implications of the fact that children do not encounter genres as neatly packaged, self-contained entities, but rather as enactments or events that constantly come into contact with one another in the flow of everyday life. We suggested that initially young children participate in personal storytelling (or any other speech genre) without knowing what they are participating in, without any awareness that there are boundaries between genres, and without access to the specialized way of seeing that personal storytelling affords. Initially, then, whatever distinctions the adults in the community make between fantasy and the literal truth or between written fictions and stories of personal experience simply do not apply to the child's experience.

Beyond this initial developmental moment, we believe that children's development proceeds along at least three dimensions simultaneously: toward more fluent participation in personal storytelling, toward greater awareness of how personal storytelling is constituted and where its boundaries are, and toward more flexible control of how and when to strategically combine genres. Although Kurt had not proceeded very far along these trajectories, he was able to participate with considerable fluency both in personal storytelling and in "The Tale of Peter Rabbit"; he showed some awareness of what he was up to by referring to his retellings of Peter Rabbit as "talk about Peter Rabbit and the mother," and he was able to stay more or less within the boundaries of the two genres on many occasions while also interanimating them on other occasions.

We would like to conclude by underscoring a major point of this chapter, namely, that communities and cultures create their own distinctive pathways within which these developments proceed. Each pathway is constituted out of the kinds of practices described earlier. Most fundamentally, caregivers allow or prohibit, encourage or discourage children from participating in personal storytelling, which is defined in culture-specific ways, privileging the caregivers' own versions of fantasy or the literal truth, moral evaluation or self-affirmation, or any number of other dimensions of experience. Personal storytelling coexists in each community with other speech genres, which are also defined in culture-specific ways, and which come into patterned contact with personal storytelling. In some communities, personal storytelling comes into repeated contact with instruction and criticism, in others with control through the invocation of threatening imaginary creatures, and in still others with written fictions. Each of these patterned juxtapositions helps to form characteristic developmental pathways. But many other practices are involved as well. Caregivers and children together structure children's participation in personal storytelling, creating participant roles of co-narrator, solo performer, overhearer, or eavesdropper, roles that may shift over developmental time. As children become more fluent participants in personal storytelling, they may begin to mark their stories with metalinguistic framing devices, as more experienced narrators do, and caregivers may explicitly correct their transgressions of generic boundaries. At the same time, caregivers may engage in a host of practices that model and encourage the intermingling of personal storytelling with certain privileged genres. In other communities, more attention may be paid to keeping personal storytelling apart from certain privileged genres. In short, developmental pathways, like the boundaries between fiction and nonfiction, between literature and nonliterature, and so forth, are not laid up in heaven; they are made and remade as more and less experienced narrators work together with ready-made generic tools, refashioning them in practice.

## References

Alexander, K. (1994). *Young children's emotional attachments to stories.* Unpublished masters's thesis. University of Illinois at Urbana-Champaign.

Alexander, K. J. (1996). *What stories mean to young children: Low-income preschoolers' emotional attachments to stories.* Unpublished doctoral dissertation, University of Illinois at Urbana-Champaign.

Alexander, K. J., & Miller, P. J. (1995). Young children's emotional involvement with stories. Paper presented at the biennial meeting of the Society for Research in Child Development, Indianapolis, IN, March.

Bakhtin, M. M. (1986). *Speech Genres and Other Later Essays.* Austin, TX: University of Texas Press.

Bakhtin, M. M./Medvedev, P. N. (1978). *The Formal Method in Literary Scholarship: A Critical Introduction to Sociological Poetics*, (A. J. Wehrle, Trans.). Baltimore, MD: The Johns Hopkins University Press.

Bartlett, F. C. (1932). *Remembering.* Cambridge: Cambridge University Press.

Bauman, R. (1986). *Story, Performance, and Event.* Cambridge: Cambridge University Press.

Bauman, R. (1992a). Genres. In: R. Bauman (Ed.), *Folklore, Cultural Performance, and Popular Entertainments: A Communications-Centered Handbook*, (pp. 53–59) New York: Oxford University Press.

Bauman, R. (1992b). Contextualization, tradition, and the dialogue of genres: Icelandic legends of the *kraftaskald.* In: A. Duranti and C. Goodwin (Eds.), *Rethinking Context.* Cambridge: Cambridge University Press.

Butler, D. (1975). *Cushla and Her Books.* Boston: The Horn Book.

Clark, K., & Holquist, M. (1984). *Mikhail Bakhtin.* Cambridge, MA: Harvard University Press.

Eisenberg, A. R. (1985). Learning to describe past experiences in conversation. *Discourse Processes, 8,* 177–204.

Fung, H. (1994). *The socialization of shame in young Chinese children.* Unpublished doctoral dissertation, University of Chicago.

Hanks, W. F. (1996). *Language and Communicative Practices.* Boulder, CO: Westview Press.

Hearne, B. (1990). *Choosing Books for Children* (2nd ed.). New York: Delacourte Press.

Heath, S. B. (1983). *Ways with Words: Language, Life, and Work in Communities and Classrooms.* New York: Cambridge University Press.

Kamberelis, G. (1995). Genre as institutionally informed social practice. *Journal of Contemporary Legal Issues, 6,* 115–171.

Labov, W., & Waletzky, J. (1967). Narrative analysis: Oral versions of personal experience. In: J. Helm (Ed.), *Essays in the Verbal and Visual Arts*, (pp. 12–44). Seattle: Washington University Press.

Leedy, L. (1993). *Postcards from Pluto: A Tour of the Solar System.* New York: Scholastic.

Lipson, E. R. (1991). *The New York Times Parent's Guide to the Best Books for Children* (rev. ed.). New York: Random House.

Miller, P. J., Fung, H., & Mintz, J. (1996). Self-construction through narrative practices: A Chinese and American comparison of early socialization. *Ethos, 24*, 1–44.

Miller, P. J., Hoogstra, L., Mintz, J., Fung, H., & Williams, K. (1993). Troubles in the garden and how they get resolved: A young child's transformation of his favorite story. In: C. Nelson (Ed.), *Memory and Affect in Development. Minnesota Symposia on Child Psychology*, Vol. 26, (pp. 87–114). Hillsdale, NJ: Erlbaum.

Miller, P. J., & Moore B. B. (1989). Narrative conjunctions of caregiver and child: A comparative perspective on socialization through stories. *Ethos, 17*, 428–49.

Miller, P. J., Potts, R., Fung, H., Hoogstra, L., & Mintz, J. (1990). Narrative practices and the social construction of self in childhood. *American Ethnologist, 17*, 292–311.

Miller, P. J., & Sperry, L. L. (1988). Early talk about the past: The origins of conversational stories of personal experience. *Journal of Child Language, 15*, 293–315.

Miller, P. J., Wiley, A., Fung, H., & Liang, C-H. (1997). Personal storytelling as a medium of socialization in Chinese and American families. *Child Development, 69*, 833–47.

Morson, G. S., & Emerson, C. (1990). *Mikhail Bakhtin: Creation of a Prosaics.* Stanford, CA: Stanford University Press.

Ninio, A., & Bruner, J. (1978). The achievement and antecedents of labeling. *Journal of Child Language, 5*, 1–15.

Ortner, S. B. (1984). Theory in anthropology since the sixties. *Comparative Studies in Society and History, 26* (1), 126–166.

Paley, V. G. (1981). *Wally's Stories: Conversations in the Kindergarten.* Cambridge, MA: Harvard University Press.

Polanyi, L. (1985). *Telling the American Story.* Norwood, NJ: Ablex.

Potter, B. (1980). *Peter Rabbit Giant Treasury.* New York: Derrydale Books.

Scarlett, W. G., & Wolf, D. (1979). When it's only make-believe: The construction of a boundary between fantasy and reality in storytelling. In: E. Winner and H. Gardner (Eds.), *Fact, Fiction, and Fantasy in Childhood. New Directions for Child Development. No. 6*, (pp. 29–40). San Francisco: Jossey Bass.

Scollon, R., & Scollon, S. B. K. (1981). *Narrative, Literacy, and Face in Interethnic Communication.* Norwood, NJ:Ablex.

Snow, C., & Goldfield, B. (1983). Turn the page please: Situation-specific language acquisition. *Journal of Child Language, 10*, 551–69.

Snow, C., & Ninio, A. (1986). The contracts of literacy: What children learn from learning to read books. In: W. Teale and E. Sulzby (Eds.), *Emergent Literacy*, (pp. 116–38). Norwood, NJ: Ablex.

Sperry, L. L., & Sperry, D. E. (1995). Young children's presentations of self in conversational narration. In: L. L. Sperry and P. A. Smiley (Eds.), *Exploring Young Children's Concepts of Self and Other through Conversation. New*

*Directions for Child Development. No. 69*, (pp. 47–60). San Francisco: Jossey-Bass.

Sperry, L. L., & Sperry, D. E. (1996). The early development of narrative skills. *Cognitive Development, 11*, 443–65.

Swales, J. M. (1990). *Genre Analysis: English in Academic and Research Settings.* Cambridge: Cambridge University Press.

Wertsch, J. V. (1991). *Voices of the Mind: A Sociocultural Approach to Mediated Action.* Cambridge, MA: Harvard University Press.

Willis, A. I. (1995). Reading the world of school literacy: Contextualizing the experience of a young African American male. *Harvard Educational Review, 65*, 30–49.

Wolf, S. A., & Heath, S. B. (1992). *The Braid of Literature: Children's Worlds of Reading.* Cambridge, MA: Harvard University Press.

# 9 The Influence of Religious Beliefs on Parental Attitudes About Children's Fantasy Behavior

MARJORIE TAYLOR AND STEPHANIE M. CARLSON

Around our house we try to keep our kids from having imaginary companions. I think they are associated with the devil and it would be very bad if they had imaginary companions. I try to emphasize that imaginary companions are bad so he doesn't have an imaginary companion.

This quote is from a mother who participated in our research investigating the role of imaginary companions in children's lives. In this work, an imaginary companion was defined as a vivid imaginary character (person, animal) with whom a child interacts during his/her play and daily activities. The extremely negative remarks of a few parents, who, like the mother quoted above, identified themselves as fundamentalist Christians, stand in marked contrast to the positive view of imaginary companions expressed by most middle-class American parents (Manosevitz, Fling, & Prentice, 1977; Mauro, 1991) and developmental psychologists. Although in the past some researchers have voiced concerns about children who regularly play with imaginary companions (Ames & Learned, 1946), recent research evidence associates having an imaginary companion with a variety of positive attributes, such as the ability to take the perspective of another person (Taylor & Carlson, 1997) and get along well with others (Singer & Singer, 1990), participation in family activities (Manosevitz, Prentice, & Wilson, 1973), and literary creativity (Schaefer, 1969; for a review see Taylor, 1999). More generally, children's capacity to pretend has been linked to a wide range of social and cognitive skills, including language development (Ervin-Tripp, 1991), social competence (Singer & Singer, 1990), memory development (Newman, 1990), exploration and mastery of emotional themes (Bretherton, 1989), and logical reasoning (Dias & Harris, 1990).

We were struck by the comments of the fundamentalist Christian parents in our study, not just because they were more negative than the remarks of the other parents, but because they seemed to reflect a qualitatively different view of the child's activity. Usually when parents express concerns or worries about imaginary companions, they do so within the context of interpreting the imaginary companion as a fantasy creation. For example, a minority of parents complain that children's insistence on including pretend friends in family activities can be inconvenient, that it is age-inappropriate for children beyond the preschool years to play with imaginary companions, or that the existence of an imaginary companion might indicate that the child has some difficulty distinguishing fantasy from reality (Brookes & Knowles, 1982; Newson & Newson, 1976; Rosengren & Hickling, 1994). These parents are interpreting their children's interactions with imaginary companions as nonserious playful activities, and the parents are assuming that the invisible entities are imaginary. This is not the case for parents who associate imaginary companions with the devil. We would argue that these parents' reactions to their children's behavior reflect a divergent perception on the part of the adults of what is real and what is fantasy.

The example of imaginary companions indicates that religious beliefs can be an important source of variability in parental reactions to child behavior. In general, there is very little research investigating the role of religion in child development (Vandenberg, 1992, but see Coles, 1990). This is surprising, because many religions espouse distinctive sets of beliefs about the inherent nature of children. For example, beliefs about when children are capable of faith, and therefore ready for baptism, have been central to bitter theological debates across the centuries, resulting in major divisions within Christianity (Schwartz, 1973). In addition, preferred methods of child rearing believed to properly socialize religious principles are of obvious concern to parents who want their children to become full-fledged participants in their spiritual community.

Religion is interesting to consider in any discussion related to fantasy because there are very large ideological splits between what is considered real and what is considered fantasy across different religious groups. According to Heise (1988), "Truth varies across acceptable social groups and essentially the same belief can be judged as a delusion or a nondelusion depending on the social conditions of the believer . . . Different epistemologies yield different facts, different truths, different realities" (pp. 259–260). Perhaps nowhere are these kinds of conceptual differences in world views more apparent than in the domain of religion. Religions offer a variety of perspectives on the nature and existence of God, angels, the devil, and spiritual beings of various sorts, as well as on the kinds of communications or interactions with the spiritual realm that are possible for children and adults. What is considered essential and very real from one perspective might be dismissed as fantasy from another (Caughey, 1988).

We were particularly interested in religion-based attitudes about children's imaginary companions because the creation of an imaginary companion (either an invisible entity or a special toy) who becomes a regular part of the child's social world is one index of a particularly intense interest and engagement in pretend play (Taylor & Carlson, 1997). In addition, this activity can be construed in a variety of ways. Although the behaviors associated with having an imaginary companion (e.g., a child talking to someone who the parent cannot see) are straightforward to describe, the phenomenon of a child talking to an invisible being could be particularly sensitive to cultural and religious differences in adult interpretation. In this chapter, we discuss three different interpretations of imaginary companions associated with the views of Hinduism, fundamentalist Christianity, and the Mennonite faith. Clearly, this is far from an exhaustive list of the religions that might offer interesting and contrasting views of imaginary companions. We included these three groups primarily because, in each case, there is at least some research for us to draw on and because each provides a unique perspective.

## Hinduism

According to Roopnarine, Hossain, Gill, and Brophy (1994), socialization of the metaphysical aspects of Hindu belief systems occur very early in children's lives. The exact nature of these beliefs vary from region to region and across different sociocultural groups, but one central concept involves Karma and the cycle of birth and death. There is very little research documenting how Indian children play, but one fascinating study by Antonia Mills suggests that the cycle of birth and death is integral to parental interpretations of children's behavior, and to the way children are socialized to process their own experiences (Mills, 1992).

Mills focused her attention on the relation between what is referred to in North America as a child having an imaginary companion and in India as a child remembering a previous life. She began her research in India by conducting an informal survey in which she asked psychologists as well as other adults if they knew of any children who had imaginary companions. The answer was universally "no." At first, she attributed this result to the conditions under which children in India are raised. American children who have imaginary companions tend to have periods of time in which they are alone due to the circumstances of their place in the family (e.g., being an only child or being the youngest child who plays alone when the older children are at school) or where they live (e.g., no playmates readily available in the area). In contrast, Indian children are rarely alone. They sleep, eat, and play with other members of their extended family. Given these conditions, it is possible that Indian children do not create pretend friends because they do not experience a need for extra companionship, or because the extended family setting in which they are raised is not conducive to the creation of imaginary companions. Indeed, this sort of explanation for the lack of pretend friends was offered by the Indians who were questioned by Mills.

Although family environment contributes to the probability that a child will create an imaginary companion (Manosevitz et al., 1973), there was an intriguing alternative explanation for the cultural difference between Indian and North American children in the incidence of imaginary companions. Mills discovered that when Indian children talk to entities that adults cannot perceive, the assumption is that the child is communicating with a very real being who exists on a spiritual realm or is part of the child's past life. Thus, Mills' use of the word "imaginary" in her initial questioning of Indian adults probably had a large effect on their responses. When she started asking about children who had "invisible" rather than "imaginary" companions, she identified forty-nine cases of Indian parents who claimed that their children had memories for past identities. She found that the time frame that is typical for imaginary companions in North America was similar for the phenomenon of memory of past lives, and that most of the children who talked about past lives were the youngest or next to youngest in the family. Overall, memories for past lives was not as common in India as imaginary companions are in the United States (about 0.2% of children in northern India compared with at least 28% of North American children having imaginary companions). Despite these differences, Mills' research suggests that the two phenomena are related.

In addition to the cultural difference in the interpretation of child behavior as belonging to the domain of fantasy or reality, there was a related difference in adult perceptions of their children's activity as serious or playful. The case studies that Mills presents indicate that Indian adults take children's communications with identities from past lives as a very serious business. In many ways, they were emotionally caught up in what the child was doing and encouraged the child in this activity, providing cues about the past identity to improve the accuracy of the child's recall. Reinforcement for past life memory gave way to active discouragement when children reached about the age of seven. Parents then taught their children not to remember the past life, because they were concerned that the children would take on this past identity rather than pursuing their present identity. These observations suggest that parental interpretations of child behavior provide lessons to children about what constitutes fantasy and what constitutes reality within their culture.

## Fundamentalist Christianity

Although mainstream Christianity tends to support children's involvement in fantasy – even toddlers are actively encouraged to participate in rituals involving fantasy characters such as Santa Claus and the Easter Bunny – more fundamentalist sects tend to be less positive about fantasy and to espouse a child-rearing environment that is less conducive to its development. This is not to say that all fundamentalists hold exactly the same views about children's fantasy, or any other issue for that matter. There are many variations of belief systems that might be referred to as fundamentalist, including that of Mennonites, which we discuss in a separate section. In what follows, we mention two types of objections to imaginary companions that seem to be derived from the beliefs of fundamentalist Christians who are part of mainstream American society (i.e., they have not chosen to live in separate communities like the Amish or Mennonites).

The first objection has to do with a general tendency to equate fantasy with deceit. First we should mention that this tendency is not limited to fundamentalist populations. In Newson and Newson's (1976) comprehensive study of seven-year-old children, they found that some parents suspected that fantasy behavior could lead to habitual lying and believed that fantasy should be monitored very carefully. In addition, Brookes and Knowles (1982) found that when lower middle-class mothers (religious affiliations are not mentioned in this study) were asked to describe their reactions to different kinds of child behaviors, their ratings for incidents involving imaginary companions correlated with their ratings for incidents involving children telling lies. The authors interpreted this finding as suggesting that, for these mothers, "fantasy and deceit were part of the same global category of children's behavior" (Brooks & Knowles, 1982, p. 31).

One source of information about the relation between concern for truthfulness and negative attitudes about fantasy comes from research on parental attitudes about children's storytelling. As discussed by Miller, Hengst, Alexander, and Sperry (this volume), very young children are taught culturally defined ways of telling stories that are acceptable to their community. Miller et al. describe how some parents support and scaffold children's personalization of their favorite fantasy stories. For example, Miller repeatedly read her son's favorite story, "Peter Rabbit," to him and supported his own retellings of the tale that incorporated people, places, and events from his own life. In contrast, Heath (1983) describes how the parents in a white fundamentalist community strongly discouraged their children from telling any sort of story that did not conform closely to actual events. Stories with made-up or fanciful characters and imagined happenings were not enjoyed as evidence of the child's growing imagination. Instead, they were considered to be "lies, without a piece of truth" (Heath, 1983, p. 158). If children described any event in which they interacted with a fantasy character, they were severely admonished. "To do so would shock the adults and cause them to accuse her of 'telling a story,' i.e., changing a real incident to make it a lie. In general, only children and the worst scoundrels are ever accused of lying. 'Thou shalt not lie' is an adage on the tip of everyone's tongue, and the community is on the lookout for offenders. 'Don't you tell me a story' means 'Don't tell me a lie.' " (Heath, 1983, p. 160).

Clark also found evidence of parental concern about fantasy as deceitful in an ethnographic study on culturally shared forms of fantasy. There are several cultural myths associated with Christianity. For example, children raised in a Christian tradition are told an elaborate story about a man who wears a red suit, lives at the North Pole, and gives presents to children at Christmas. Parents often go to great lengths to provide concrete evidence that Santa is real (e.g., cookies and milk left out on Christmas Eve) (Clark, 1995). In fact, the entire community is involved in the conspiracy to convince children about Santa (e.g., personal interviews with him on TV and radio), and there can be outrage if someone tells children that Santa Claus does not exist. Rosengren, Kalish, Hickling, and Gelman (1994) have shown that children's belief in fantasy characters such as Santa Claus is correlated with this sort of parental encouragement.

Clark found that parents who identified with fundamentalist Christianity were uncomfortable with cultural myths such as the one about Santa Claus because they were concerned that, once their children found out the truth, they would start to question the existence of God. After all, if parents lied about Santa, how was the child to know the parents were not also lying about Jesus? In fact, many young children do seem to think about Santa and God as connected in some way. According to Allport (1950), young children equate Santa Claus with God. Children in Clark's research suggested that God and Santa must live next door to each other and be friends, that God made Santa, that Santa knows whether children have been good or bad because God tells him, and that God is the one who asks Santa to give presents to children.

Clark found no evidence that when children learn that there is no Santa, they routinely lose their faith in God. However, parents are sometimes directly questioned on this issue. "One father told of his son asking him if he was really Santa Claus. The father had admitted that he was, after which the boy thought for a while, and then asked if his father was also the Tooth Fairy. Again the father admitted that he was. The son then asked if the father was also the Easter Bunny, and when the father said yes, the son asked, 'Are you God, too?' " (Scheibe cited in Clark, 1995, p. 54). Clark points out that Jehovah's Witnesses explicitly discourage parents from teaching children about Santa Claus because they believe that the Santa Claus myth will ultimately have a negative impact on children's belief in God. She provides the following quote from *The Watch Tower*: "One little fellow, sadly disillusioned about Santa Claus, said to a playmate: "Yes, and I'm going to look into this 'Jesus Christ' business too" (Clark, 1995, p. 56).

Most of the parents in Clark's study were very positive about their children's beliefs in Santa and other fantasy characters, but one mother who was a fundamentalist Christian reported that she believed that it was better to tell children the truth about Santa and that it was wrong to give Santa credit for gifts and blessings that should be credited to God. Her son's behavior had raised concerns at school because he told many of the other children that Santa was fake and he refused to join the other children in drawing Santa Claus on decorations for Christmas. When interviewed for this study, he pointed out to the interviewer that Santa was Satan with the letters changed.

The mention of Satan brings up the second type of concern that members of some fundamentalist groups have about fantasy in general and imaginary companions in particular. This concern is espoused by fundamentalists who have a particular interest in or preoccupation with "spiritual warfare." Parents with this belief system are very concerned about protecting their children from evil forces in the spiritual world. For example, one of the major objections that many fundamentalist parents have to public elementary schools is that the curriculum makes these schools "a breeding ground for the occult," exposing their children to dangerous ideas about witchcraft and occult practices (Howse, 1993, p. 161). There is also concern about Halloween because of its perceived connection with the occult, paganism, and Satanism.

Imaginary companions are sometimes explicitly discussed in this context. For example, in their book on spiritual protection for children, Anderson, Vanderhook, and Vanderhook (1996) have the following advice for Fundamentalist Christian parents: "Many children have imaginary 'friends' they play with. It can be harmless unless the imaginary friend is talking back. Then it is no longer imaginary ... A child's dependence on spirit 'friends' will eventually result in spiritual bondage. This must be identified as soon as possible. Satan disguises himself as an angel of light, so young children probably won't see the danger" (pp. 195–96). These authors go on to provide a prayer that parents should teach their children in which they confess to God that they have had an imaginary companion and they renounce this type of activity.

How common is it for parents to worry that an imaginary companion could result in spiritual harm via the devil? Singer and Singer (1990), who have conducted research on children's fantasy for many years, report receiving letters from adults who believe that imaginary companions are evidence of children's contact with the spiritual world, but there are no studies that accurately document the prevalence of this point of view. One difficulty is that fundamentalist parents are likely to be dubious about participation in psychological research. Even when asking questions in Christian bookstores, we have encountered some suspicion about our motives and some understandable concern about being misrepresented or misunderstood.

In our research with 152 parents, only two parents explicitly mentioned concerns about the devil (Taylor & Carlson, 1997; Taylor Carlson, Gerow, & Charlie, 1999). In addition to the mother quoted at the beginning of the chapter, another mother told us that imaginary companions were anti-Christ and that she was very concerned about her six-year-old daughter's fantasies involving unicorns. She reported that sometimes the little girl pretended to be a unicorn, shaking invisible wings and making fluttering sounds, and sometimes she seemed to be playing with an imaginary unicorn. According to her mother, this child played with a unicorn because "she wants to be free. She also wants to be a bird for the same reason." The mother told us that she sometimes played along with her daughter because she loved her, but she tried to hide her daughter's vivid imagination from other people and she prayed every day for the devil to leave her child.

In another study to be described more fully in the next section, five teachers in fundamentalist Christian elementary schools were interviewed about their attitudes concerning pretend play (Carlson, Taylor, & Levine, 1998). Two of the five teachers were suspicious of imaginary companions and voiced concerns about psychopathology or demonic possession. One teacher stated that she would "watch out for an imaginary friend. Children should have real friends." (p. 553). She added that a broken home life can lead to the "wrong kind" of imagination. The other teacher reported that imaginary companions could lead a child into "demon occultist activity." This teacher believed that manipulating make-believe entities in the mind is like witchcraft and thus contrary to a true God.

## Mennonites

> A child unrestrained becomes headstrong as
> an untamed horse.
> Give him no liberty in his youth
> and wink not at his follies.
>       – Menno Simons (1557/1956, p. 951)

The Mennonite faith is a form of fundamentalist Christianity that contrasts sharply with the groups described above. Mennonites (and their Amish subgroups) are much less preoccupied with issues related to spiritual warfare. Instead, they are concerned with leading a simple, truthful life of devotion to God. To accomplish this goal, they live separately from mainstream American culture without the conveniences of modern technology (e.g., phones, electricity, cars) and avoid the outside influences of television, movies, and public education. They espouse agricultural living because it promotes the Puritan values of hard work, thrift, and mutual aid as opposed to the "restlessness, rootlessness, and anxiety" associated with urban mobility (Hostetler & Huntington, 1971, p. 9).

The primary source of information about children in Amish/Mennonite communities is Hostetler's writings based on years of study in the 1960s and 1970s, field visits, and recollections of his own childhood (Hostetler & Huntington, 1971; Hostetler, 1993). Hostetler and Huntington described Mennonite stages of childhood and the socialization patterns characteristic of each stage. "Little children," comprised of children ages one to five years old, are encouraged to participate in the physical world of adults and to be useful on the farm and in the house, but they are kept as far away from the outside world as possible. Whereas initiative in the physical realm is strongly encouraged in little children, intellectual initiative (e.g., asking questions) is severely restricted. Parents caution against new ideas; they feel that it is better for a child to observe and imitate adults on a behavioral level rather than to ask "how?" or "why?"

"Scholars" comprise children in school (ages six to fifteen). The major goal of Mennonite education is to reinforce religious and community values. Schooling ends with the eighth grade. Too much book knowledge is considered to be a detriment to children's enjoyment of physical labor, and therefore it is associated with individual role confusion as well as conflict and instability in the culture as a whole (Peters, 1987). By having their own private schools, Mennonite children and their friends share the same life style and there is no multimedia exposure to alternative ways of living.

Our reading of the Mennonite literature suggests that this community has quite negative attitudes about children's fantasy, but the nature of their objections differs from those of fundamentalist Christians who are concerned about communications with the devil. Instead, in Mennonite society pretend play is seen, at best, as a waste of time. Mennonites believe that free time or "idleness" is detrimental to children's development; thus young children are less likely to have the unstructured time that is believed to promote pretend play (Singer & Singer, 1990). At worst, pretend play is considered a potential threat to the cohesion of the group because of its association with individual freedom of expression. A general rule in Mennonite communities is that personal development must not intrude on the concerns of the group (Redekop, 1989). Thus, adults discourage individual incentive for nonphysical activities because they are viewed as harmful to the group and might lead to personal pride and pompousness (Peters, 1987). In addition, although most Mennonite communities retain high levels of young people in the faith, individual dissension is a constant concern (Hostetler, 1993). This attitude reflects a concern for any activity that makes one stand out from the crowd, including imaginative play. For example, acceptable reading material for children would be stories that represent an American rural way of life and teach a moral lesson (such as the value of hard work). Stories that have a play or fantasy orientation are considered unacceptable. Mennonite parents "do not want their children to read fairy tales or myths; many object to any stories that are not true such as those in which animals talk and act like people or stories that involve magic, such as 'The Pied Piper of Hamlin'" (Hostetler & Huntington, 1971, p. 46).

Very little research has been conducted on the pretend play of Mennonite children, with the exception of our small ethnographic study designed to learn how attitudes about play vary as a function of religion (Carlson, Taylor, & Levin, 1998). Given the traditional Mennonite views of children and the restrictions in the types of activities and reading materials that are acceptable for young children in this society, Carlson et al. (1998) predicted that orthodox Mennonites would have serious concerns about fantasy play, and that this pervasive cultural attitude would be reflected in the play of young Mennonite school children.

Mennonite parents were not accessible to us, so Carlson interviewed eighteen teachers from Mennonite and non-Mennonite private Christian elementary schools in rural Pennsylvania about their attitudes toward fantasy play, practices relating to children's imagination, the importance and usefulness of participating in pretend games, whether dreams and daydreams should be shared with students, whether it was appropriate to read stories about make-believe events in class, and the quantity of fiction versus nonfiction books in the classroom. In addition, the teachers were questioned about the aspects of the classroom environment they thought had the greatest influence on children's development of imagination and how often they thought their students played together outside of school. We were particularly interested in imaginary companions because restrictions on children's activities or in their lives sometimes stimulate this kind of private fantasy activity (Singer & Streiner, 1966; Taylor, 1999). In addition, we found one published case of a Mennonite child who created an imaginary companion. In her account of growing up in a Mennonite community, Weaver (1983) recalled that she and many of her friends had imaginary companions who were "fancy" and thus allowed to wear clothes and play with toys that were off limits to the children themselves.

To gain access for research purposes, Carlson visited one school for six months and assisted the teachers by reading to the children, leading recitation exercises, and correcting workbooks. During these visits, she took great care in her dress, wearing clothing that was very plain and traditional: long black skirt, high-collared blouse or sweater, black stockings, and flat shoes. She kept her hair in a bun and did not wear any make-up, nail polish, perfume, or jewelry. Although the teachers and children were very positive about her visits, the parents in this Old Order community did not approve of her presence. The teacher was reprimanded by the elders of the community at a church meeting, and it was decided that one of their own young people would act as a helper to the teacher. Ultimately, however, Carlson was able to initiate contact with several other schools in the region.

As expected, the results indicated that the Mennonite teachers were significantly less encouraging of pretend play than their non-Mennonite counterparts. For example, the Mennonite teachers tended to disagree with statements like, "I talk to my class about Santa Claus and the Easter Bunny" and "I do not try to control my students' free time, such as recess." In addition, their ideas about which aspects of the school environment influence children's development of imagination revealed cultural differences in attitudes about children's fantasies. Mennonites showed relatively high agreement that stories read aloud, art, and workbook lessons in the school curriculum stimulate children's imaginations. Several of these teachers said that the children themselves prefer realistic stories (such as "Daniel Boone" and "Laura Ingles"). Several non-Mennonite Christian teachers also thought that creative writing exercises stimulate children's imagination. An equal number of these teachers said that "exposure to lots of different things" is an important factor. This idea stands in marked contrast with the Mennonite inclination to shelter children from diverse ideas and life styles. Non-Mennonite Christian teachers also emphasized "freedom to explore," "following a child's pace and interests," and encouraging students to "say their thoughts out loud" as positive influences on the development of imagination. Furthermore, this group was the only one that mentioned fantasy books, television, and computer games in relation to imagination. In fact, one first-grade class was watching a children's music video about "Toby the Talking Computer" while the teacher was being interviewed. It should be noted, however, that despite our efforts to equate these groups on demographic variables aside from religion, the non-Mennonite Christian teachers tended to be older, more educated, and to teach a younger age range than the Mennonite teachers.

Although, overall, the Mennonite teachers were not as positive about social pretense as the non-Mennonite teachers, the reports concerning *private* fantasy activities painted a different picture. Specifically, the Mennonite teachers were more likely than the other teachers to say that they share their dreams and/or daydreams with their class and that they themselves have an active imagination. They also were more positive about imaginary companions. Unlike their non-Mennonite counterparts, at least some of the Mennonite teachers did not believe that imaginary companions were best grown out of as soon as possible. These teachers were also the only ones who reported that their students, or even they themselves, had imaginary companions. They tended to view having an imaginary companion as making up for a lack of social contact with real friends or siblings. Thus, some of these teachers agreed that they would talk to an imaginary companion for a child's benefit and believed that children would end this type of play on their own as they acquired real friends.

The most detailed account of an imaginary companion was a young teacher's description of her own make-believe friend that she "kept" until age fifteen. The friend's name was "Rachel" and she was the same age and size as "Laura," the teacher. Rachel had blond hair, dark brown eyes, and pretty clothes (but not too fancy). She and Laura had the same abilities and did all the same things; they were inseparable best friends. Laura's favorite activities to do with Rachel were riding horses and working together as clerks in a store that she imagined their families owned (in reality her parents were farmers). Laura had four sisters and four brothers living at home while she was growing up, which suggests that, in this case, the imaginary companion was not an antidote to loneliness.

The research with Mennonites points to the importance of examining religious and cultural influences on both social and nonsocial forms of pretense and fantasy. Although Mennonites do not overtly encourage social pretend play, their views concerning imaginary companions suggest that they might have relatively high levels of private, nonsocial fantasies. We suspect that this form of fantasy presents a lesser threat to the cohesion of Mennonite societies than outward displays of imaginative thought.

### How Do Parental Attitudes Affect Child Fantasy Behavior?

Although the focus of our discussion has been the role of religious beliefs in adult attitudes about children's fantasy, it is also important to consider how parental attitudes influence the actual play behavior observed in young children, as well as children's own interpretations of their imaginative experiences. On the one hand, there is no question that parental support and encouragement promote children's engagement in fantasy. After decades of studying the development of imagination, Singer and Singer (1990) place the support of fantasy behavior by a key person in the child's life at the top of their list of common threads in early childhood that are linked to the development of the capacity for fantasy. They base this conclusion on the results of their own empirical studies as well as their extensive review of childhood memories reported in biographies of creative adults. These sources provide evidence that adults can promote imagination in their children by treating children's inventions with delight and respect and by providing children with time, a place, and simple props to stimulate their pretend play.

However, here we are concerned with the impact of negative attitudes on children's fantasy behaviors. Do children continue to pretend even when their parents actively discourage it? Do they create imaginary companions when their parents have negative attitudes about them? There are at least some documented cases of imaginary companions created in very unsupportive environments. For example, Chukovsky (1925/1968) reports the case of one noted Soviet authority on children's education who espoused a negative view of fantasy because he believed that it was detrimental to children's understanding of the real world. This man's son, despite the lack of fantasy stories in his upbringing, created a host of imaginary animals, including a red elephant who lived in his room, a bear named Cora, and a tiny baby tiger that sat in his hand and ate from a small plate beside his own at the dinner table. Chukovsky used this example to support his view that children will create their own fantasy tales to supplement any deficit in the stories provided by adults.

The children of the fundamentalist parents we have quoted in this chapter provide two more examples. Both parents believed that imaginary companions were bad because they opened up channels of communication with the devil. The little girl who pretended about unicorns was clearly very engaged with pretense, despite her mother's strong objections. Perhaps her awareness of her mother's attitude contributed to her decision not to tell the researcher about the fantasy behavior reported by her mother. In fact, her comments at the time of the study were quite negative about fantasy. When the researcher admired the Pocahontas sneakers she was wearing, she replied that she only had them because they had been on sale; she knew that Pocahontas was bad because she did not love Jesus. Thus, not only did this child fail to share her private fantasies with the researcher, she also was apologetic about having the image of a fantasy character from a Disney movie on her sneakers. In contrast, the little boy whose mother was quoted was happy to describe his fantasies to us. While his mother was telling the interviewer that imaginary companions are associated with the devil, the boy was telling a research assistant in the next room about his pretend moose friend. In this case, the mother was totally unaware of her son's private fantasy.

Similarly, Clark (1995) found that, with only one exception, all of the children of fundamentalist Christian parents in her study believed that Santa Claus was real, despite the influence of their churches and parents. Heath (1983) also provides some examples of children pretending even though their parents tend to equate pretending with lying. She describes how one small boy told a lie in which he tried to claim that his toy truck, which he had taken from another child, had been made by another truck: "He got a big truck, it makes lotsa li'l trucks,'n I got this one." When he was scolded for his lie, he replied, "Digger Dan talks." (Heath, 1983, p. 160). He had recently seen a story book at nursery school in which a mechanical crane named Digger Dan was personified. It had a face, a personality, and acted like a hero to little boys and other trucks. The boy seemed to be saying to his mother that his story was no more exaggerated than stories like the one about Digger Dan. According to Heath, even though children in this fundamentalist Christian community were discouraged from "telling stories" in their homes, they were exposed to a wide variety of fantasy materials when they went to nursery school. Only in this setting, and when play time was clearly marked, was it acceptable for children to suspend reality and pretend, such as the little boy above who created trucks that flew, talked, and produced other trucks.

These examples indicate that parents' attempts at curbing their children's fantasy behavior are not entirely successful; the children engaged in elaborate pretending anyway. However, we know less about how these children or others living in a restrictive environment interpret and feel about their own imaginative propensity. It is possible that they view it as having an evil origin and thus, perhaps ironically, they incorporate figures like Satan or the Devil into their fantasy worlds. In fact, Singer and Singer (1990) interpret the evidence from the novels of Samuel Clemens (a.k.a. Mark Twain) as suggesting that, as a child, he had a devil imaginary companion inspired by his mother's fundamentalist beliefs and habitual references to Satan in the home. Satan tends to be mentioned frequently in fundamentalist households. Helen Thomas Flexner, whose parents were members of the orthodox branch of the Society of Friends, writes that Satan was regularly addressed in her household and was believed to be present behind her back ("Get thee behind me, Satan") (Flexner, 1940). She thought of him as being as real as anyone else. Flexner also recalled that she was not allowed to take part in a play made up by the neighborhood children. "Play acting was morally wrong. I was not allowed even to be present as a spectator, and so I found myself excluded from that gay little group of boys and girls" (Flexner, 1940, p. 163).

In the case of Hindu children who converse with invisible entities, their parents' interpretation of their behavior as a sign of spiritual contact with past lives would tend to encourage this type of activity.

Judging from Mills' (1992) estimate of the small number of such cases, however, it appears that Hindu parents do not routinely encourage children to make contact with past lives, but they do perceive it as an important event when it occurs. Mills notes that the children may take this all very seriously because their experience of the imaginary conversations is shaped by their parents' overt reactions and underlying beliefs. That is, they too are likely to interpret their conversations with an invisible entity in a spiritual context.

What about the Mennonite children? Does their behavior in any way reflect the attitudes documented by Carlson et al.? On the one hand, Carlson observed that these children did not seem to have the conceptual understanding of pretense that would be expected in most mainstream American six-year-olds. For example, the children appeared to have difficulty with the language used to describe pretense. Carlson reports an anecdote in which one child brought a doll to school. All of the children gathered around to inspect the doll, but one girl said repeatedly, "It's not a right baby." When questioned by Carlson, it became apparent that the child meant to communicate that the doll was not real. This was only one of several incidences suggesting that the children did not have the vocabulary for talking about fantasy.[1] In fact, one child asked "What's pretend?" when he came across this word in a book, and he was puzzled by the researcher's attempts to explain its meaning. Carlson also found that on the playground Mennonite children's play themes adhered more closely to everyday family roles and activities than did children's play in the non-Mennonite Christian group. This finding is consistent with Hostetler's (1993) claim that Mennonite children are discouraged from engaging in any role-playing that is not directly related to their future place in the community as mothers, fathers, and farmers.

On the other hand, the Mennonite children in this study did engage in pretend play during recess, and with no less frequency than the non-Mennonite Christian children. Although on the whole their play themes tended to revolve around realistic events (e.g., pretending to be a mommy or drive a horse and buggy), a few Mennonite children

---

[1] Although we have interpreted these observations in the light of Mennonite attitudes about pretense, it is important to note that most Mennonites speak German at home. Although these children were fluent in English and did not speak with an accent, their difficulty in understanding the language of pretense might have been at least partly due to their acquisition of English as a second language.

also displayed more decontextualized pretending, such as imperson-ating a rabbit or the bailman at a jail (which was really an outhouse). In addition, some of the Old Order Mennonite teachers suspected that a few of the children in their classes had imaginary companions. For example, one teacher reported that she saw a third-grade boy talking to an invisible friend and another boy talking to an imaginary dog. It is possible that the children in orthodox Mennonite communities rec-ognize what is acceptable – or at least tolerable – behavior in the realms of social and nonsocial fantasy play.

## Conclusion

The ethnographic studies, case histories, and anecdotes that we have discussed in this chapter suggest that religious ideology contributes to substantial variations in adult reactions to and interpretations of child-hood fantasy activities. When a child interacts with an invisible com-panion, the perspective provided by religion may be an important determinant of whether the activity is interpreted as involving pre-tense or as involving a real-world interaction with a spiritual being. In the latter case, the parent might consider the child's communication with spirits to be positive, as suggested by our discussion of Hindu-ism, or as potentially harmful, as in the cases in which the parent's fundamentalist beliefs involve a preoccupation with spiritual warfare and the protection of children from the devil. On the other hand, when the child's activity is perceived as pretense, one religious per-spective raises concerns about the relation between deceit and fantasy, whereas another suggests that there are much better ways for children to spend their time.

Perhaps most of all, our discussion of these issues points to the need for more systematic investigation identifying the range of per-spectives that religions provide and the consequences of parental be-liefs for the activities that children pursue and their interpretations of their own experiences. One limitation of this brief review is that there is too much emphasis on negative interpretations of fantasy behavior based on religious beliefs. We suspect that some beliefs based on religion might contribute to more positive views of pretense. For ex-ample, some of the mothers in Clark's research suggested that chil-dren's participation in rituals involving cultural myths and their be-liefs in fantasy characters contributes to the children's ability to have faith in the absence of concrete evidence, that is, to believe in something that they cannot see for themselves. This experience was believed to be related to the capacity for religious faith. Examples such as this point to the need to document more fully the range of parental perspectives. In addition, we currently know very little about the prevalence of these views, either within the identified religious orientation or in the population at large.

How do parental attitudes about pretend play influence the behavior of children? Our review raises some interesting possibilities. Overall, it seems that children engage in pretend activities even when parental attitudes are negative, but the form their pretense takes and the extent that they are private about their activities is influenced by the cultural perspective of their community. For example, in their play during recess, Mennonite children displayed differences, rather than deficits, in pretend play when compared with their non-Mennonite counterparts. Our research with Mennonite teachers and children also suggested that social and nonsocial types of pretense should be more carefully distinguished in future studies. In some groups, such as the Mennonites, attitudes about social and nonsocial forms of pretense are not necessarily the same. In addition, perhaps nonsocial fantasy, such as having imaginary companions, is less likely to be suppressed by parental disapproval than more social forms of pretense. This possibility is consistent with research showing that older children tend to hide their pretend play from parents who believe that it is age-inappropriate (Newson & Newson, 1976). Similarly, children whose parents disapprove of fantasy for religious reasons might continue to pretend in private ways.

There also is much to learn about children's understanding of the relation between religion and fantasy. Woolley's discussion (this volume) of children's understanding of wishing and praying is an interesting step in this direction. In our own work, we have found that occasionally children mention Jesus when asked if they have an imaginary friend. This response might be due to confusion about the question. Sometimes children do not understand what we mean by "pretend friend," so they answer by describing someone in the ball park of what might be acceptable, usually a friend who is real rather than imaginary. Children might consider Jesus an acceptable response because he is invisible, but they are taught and most likely believe that he is anything but imaginary. Still, it is possible that this type of response reflects some degree of overlap in children's conceptions of religion and pretense.

In summary, there is currently quite limited information about how religion affects parental interpretations of children's fantasy behaviors. However, the preliminary work on this topic provides a variety of interesting observations and insights that have implications for our understanding of the fantasy/reality distinction in adults, children's use of adult cues in their interpretations of their own experiences, and children's developing understanding of religion.

## Acknowledgments

We thank Gerald Levin, Richelle O'Malley, Carolyn Charlie, Tara Fisher, Gretchen Lussier, Sally Anderson, and Lynn Gerow for their assistance with the research described in this chapter.

## References

Allport, G. W. (1950). *The Individual and His Religion*. New York: The Macmillan Co.

Ames, L. B., & Learned, J. (1946). Imaginary companions and related phenomena. *Journal of Genetic Psychology, 69*, 147–67.

Anderson, N. T., Vanderhook P., & Vanderhook S. (1996). *Spiritual Protection for Your Children*. Ventura, CA: Regal.

Bretherton, I. (1989). Pretense: The form and function of make-believe play. *Developmental Review, 9*, 383–401.

Brooks, M., & Knowles, D. (1982). Parents' views of children's imaginary companions. *Child Welfare, 61*, 25–33.

Carlson, S. M., Taylor, M., & Levin, G. R. (1998). The influence of culture on pretend play: The case of Mennonite children. *Merrill Palmer Quarterly, 44*, 539–63

Caughey, J. L. (1988). Fantasy worlds and self-maintenance in contemporary American life. *Zygon, 23*, 127–38.

Chukovsky, K. (1925/1968). *From Two to Five*. Berkeley: University of California Press.

Clark C. D. (1995). *Flights of Fancy, Leaps of Faith: Children's Myths in Contemporary America*. Chicago: University of Chicago Press.

Coles, R. (1990). *The Spiritual Life of Children*. Boston: Houghton Mifflin Co.

Dias, M. G., & Harris, P. L. (1990). The influence of the imagination on reasoning by young children. *British Journal of Developmental Psychology, 8*, 305–18.

Ervin-Tripp, S. (1991). Play in language development. In: B. Scales, M. Almy, A. Nicolopoulou, and S. Ervin-Tripp (Eds.), *Play and the Social Context of Development in Early Care and Education*, pp. 84–97. New York: Teachers College Press.

Flexner, H. T. (1940). *A Quaker Childhood*. New Haven, CT: Yale University Press.

Heath, S. B. (1983). *Ways with Words: Language, Life, and Work in Communities and Classrooms.* Cambridge: Cambridge University Press.

Heise, D. R. (1988). Delusions and the construction of reality. In: T. F. Oltmanns and B. A. Maher (Eds.), *Delusional Beliefs,* (pp. 259–72). New York: John Wiley & Sons.

Hostetler, J. A., & Huntington, G. E. (1971). *Children in Amish Society: Socialization and Community Education.* New York: Holt, Rinehart, & Winston, Inc.

Hostetler, J. A (1993). *Amish Society* (4th ed.). Baltimore, MD: Johns Hopkins University Press.

Howse, B. (1993). *Cradle to College.* Green Forest, AR: New Leaf Press.

Manosevitz, M., Prentice, N. M., & Wilson, F. (1973). Individual and family correlates of imaginary companions in preschool children. *Developmental Psychology, 8,* 72–79.

Manosevitz, M., Fling, S., & Prentice, N. M. (1977). Imaginary companions in young children: Relationships with intelligence, creativity and waiting ability. *Journal of Child Psychology and Psychiatry, 18,* 73–78.

Mauro, J. (1991). *The friend that only I can see: A longitudinal investigation of children's imaginary companions.* Unpublished doctoral dissertation, University of Oregon.

Mills, A. (1992). Are children with imaginary playmates and children said to remember previous lives cross-culturally comparable categories? Paper presented at the American Anthropological Association, San Francisco.

Newman, L. S. (1990). Intentional and unintentional memory in young children: Remembering vs. playing. *Journal of Experimental Child Psychology, 50,* 243–58.

Newson, J., & Newson, E. (1976). *Seven Years Old in an Urban Environment.* London: George Allen & Unwin Ltd.

Peters, J. F. (1987). Socialization among the Old Order Mennonites. *International Journal of Comparative Sociology, 28* (3–4), 211–23.

Redekop, C. (1989). *Mennonite Society.* Baltimore, MD: Johns Hopkins University Press.

Roopnarine, J. L., Hossain, Z., Gill, P., & Brophy, H. (1994). Play in the East Indian context. In: J. L. Roopnarine, J. E., Johnson, and F. H. Hooper, (Eds.), *Children's Play in Diverse Cultures,* (pp. 9–30). Albany: State University of New York Press.

Rosengren, K. S., & Hickling, A. K. (1994). Seeing is believing: Children's explanations of commonplace, magical, and extraordinary transformations. *Child Development, 65,* 1605–26.

Rosengren, K. S., Kalish, C. W., Hickling, A. K., & Gelman, S. A. (1994). Exploring the relation between preschool children's magical beliefs and causal thinking. *British Journal of Developmental Psychology, 12,* 69–82.

Schaefer, C. E. (1969). Imaginary companions and creative adolescents. *Developmental Psychology, 1,* 747–49.

Schwartz, H. (1973). Early Anabaptist ideas about the nature of children. *The Mennonite Quarterly Review, XLVII,* 102–14.

Simons, M. (1557/1956). The nurture of children. In: J. C. Wenger (Ed.), *The Complete Writings of Menno Simons*. Scottsdale, PA: Herald Press.

Singer, D. G., & Singer, J. L. (1990). *The House of Make-Believe: Children's Play and Developing Imagination*. Cambridge, MA: Harvard University Press.

Singer, J. L., & Steiner, B. F. (1996). Imaginative content in the dreams and fantasy play of blind and sighted children. *Perceptual and Motor Skills, 22,* 475–82.

Taylor, M. (1999). *Imaginary Companions and the Children Who Create Them*. New York: Oxford University Press.

Taylor, M., & Carlson, S. M. (1997). The relation between individual differences in fantasy and theory of mind. *Child Development, 68,* 436–55.

Taylor, M., Carlson, S., Gerow, L., & Charlie, C. (1999). A longitudinal follow-up of children with imaginary companions. Unpublished data. University of Oregon

Vandenberg, B. (1992). Sacred text, secular history and human development. *Family Perspective, 26,* 405–21.

Weaver, L. H. (1983). Forbidden fancies: A child's vision of Mennonite plainness. *Journal of Ethnic Studies, 11,* 51–59.

# 10 Religion, Culture, and Beliefs About Reality in Moral Reasoning

ELLIOT TURIEL AND KRISTIN NEFF

In early October 1997, hundreds of thousands of men gathered on the National Mall in Washington DC. Calling themselves the Promise-Keepers, they rallied for a renewed commitment to Christian principles of family responsibility, desirous of turning the tide against "moral deterioration in modern America." These men cried and prayed together, asking for forgiveness for their sins (in one man's case this meant "years of drug and alcohol abuse, spent with hippies, bikers and Buddhists" [*New York Times*, Oct. 5, 1997], and beseeching other men to turn to the Bible for moral guidance. The Bible, not incidentally, was also the reason why there were no women at the rally. The Promise-Keepers promulgated the doctrine that the Bible establishes the rightful place of husbands as leaders of households, and of women as obedient helpmates and caretakers of children. Similarly, in June of 1988, the Southern Baptist Convention declared, through an amendment to its statement of beliefs, that: "A husband is to love his wife as Christ loved the church. He has the God-given responsibility to provide for, to protect and to lead his family. A wife is to submit graciously to the servant leadership of her husband even as the church willingly submits to the leadership of Christ" (*New York Times*, June 10, 1998). While espousing the equality of a wife to her husband before God, she "has the God-given responsibility to respect her husband and to serve as his 'helper' in managing the household and nurturing the next generation."

These statements include several connections between religion and people's behaviors. One is the connection of religious beliefs to morality. For many social scientists, moral values are also seen to stem from religious doctrine or, more generally, from cultural traditions, although religion and culture are often closely intertwined. Are moral judgments reflective of religious beliefs and cultural identities, or is it perhaps the other way around – do people use moral reasoning to critically reflect on religious and cultural traditions? Or are both of these alternatives true, and do other features of knowledge and judgment also play a role? Moreover, because social life involves moral conflicts and tensions, is it the case that religion and culture include social arrangements and practices that make for both moral acceptance and moral opposition? In this chapter we examine approaches to understanding the relationship between morality, culture, and religion, presenting a view of moral development in which multiple sources of knowledge – including those stemming from culture, religion, and everyday social experiences – interact to create a complex moral landscape.

First, we provide the background to our approach and consider the role of beliefs about reality on moral decisions. Then we examine research indicating that there are limits to religious authority in moral judgments – that there is a recognition of the validity of certain moral obligations even if not required by divine law. Next, we try to unpack the concept of culture, challenging current definitions of culture as consisting of shared moral meanings embodied in overarching value orientations such as "individualism" or "collectivism." Special focus is placed on Eastern cultures such as in India, where religion and culture strongly overlap. We argue that there is diversity in Eastern cultural and religious traditions, that individuals' moral judgments often conflict with and contradict such traditions, and that gender and social hierarchy play a central role in generating social conflicts. Finally, we propose that two themes receiving much attention currently, autonomy and connectedness, are human concerns embodied within different religious and cultural traditions.

## Psychological Concepts and Social Construals

Attempts to explain the development or acquisition of morality extend beyond the propositions of developmental psychologists. Social scientists who have theorized about morality and society (e.g., Bellah, Madsen, Sullivan, Swidler, & Tipton, 1985; Durkheim, 1906/1974, 1925/1961) and about morality and culture (e.g., Benedict, 1934; Herskovitz, 1947) have at least implicitly put forth propositions regarding acquisition. In these analyses, as well as in cultural-psychological analyses (e.g., Markus & Kitayama, 1991; Shweder, Mahapatra, &

Miller, 1987), the morality of individuals is regarded to be a function of the acquisition of a code or orientation through their participation in a group (religious, societal, or cultural). In a few instances the moral code acquired is seen as universal. This is the case insofar as it reflects standards that are common across societies or religions (Bennett, 1992; Sommers, 1984). More often, the moral codes and orientations are seen to vary by group. Usually it is culture, and associated religious systems, in which people participate that provide a framework for morality enacted in social practices. In earlier analyses it was usually presumed that a set of standards endorsed by the group was internalized by its members (e.g., Benedict, 1934). More recently, we have seen elaborated conceptions of the morality of groups informed by philosophical analyses (Miller & Bersoff, 1995; Shweder et al., 1987; Shweder, Much, Mahapatra, & Park, 1997). One common formulation is the contrast between individualistic and collectivistic orientations to self and morality. The contrast drawn is between a morality based on rights, emphasizing personal agency, and one based on duties, emphasizing interdependence in the social order.

In our view, individuals' judgments and cultural practices are heterogeneous and entail differentiations of various types. For individuals, there is a heterogeneity of domains of social judgments, as well as distinctions between their judgments and informational knowledge (Turiel & Wainryb, 1994). Cultures, too, are multifaceted, with varying perspectives connected to the different positions that people hold in the social hierarchy (Turiel, 1998b). Our view is based on the propositions that moral and social judgments develop through children's reciprocal social interactions and are connected to a variety of social experiences.

One source of heterogeneity within cultures, therefore, is the different types or domains of judgments that individuals develop. An extensive program of research discussed and summarized elsewhere (Turiel, 1983; Turiel, 1998a; Turiel, Killen, & Helwig, 1987) demonstrates that from an early age children distinguish among moral concepts, which focus on issues of welfare, justice, and rights; social-conventional concepts, which deal with uniformities of behavior within social systems; and personal concepts, which center on actions considered to be under individual jurisdiction. Moral prescriptions are based on principles of fairness, rights, and welfare and are generalizable to other cultural settings. Conventional prescriptions, which are contingent on rules, authority, and existing social practices, are particular to groups and cultural systems. Personal issues are considered to be neither wrong nor right from a moral or conventional standpoint, but matters of personal preference.

The research findings indicate that developmental transformations occur within each of the domains, with the sources of their formation in children's early social experiences (Nucci & Turiel, 1978; Turiel, 1983). In the case of moral events, children form judgments (at least in part) by observing the consequences of harmful acts. For example, if a young girl is hit by another child, she becomes very aware of the fact that physical pain is an unpleasant experience. She can also observe the emotional displays of other children when they experience physical harm, and therefore has a basis for forming the idea that one should not cause harm to others. Such judgments are applied to all people, regardless of whether or not a prohibitory rule is present. A social convention, however, is not wrong because of features intrinsic to the act, but is wrong because it violates a norm designed to regulate and organize social interactions. Conventions, therefore, are considered changeable and relative to the group. Because personal issues are seen to primarily affect the actor and not society at large, they are considered to be contingent on personal preference (Nucci, 1996).

In this view, development does not entail differentiations of moral judgments from conventional or personal considerations – as has been proposed by others (Kohlberg, 1971; Piaget, 1932;). An example of the differentiation model of development can be seen in Piaget's (1932) early work, in which he proposed that children's moral judgments progress form a heteronomous to an autonomous orientation. According to Piaget, by the ages of four or five years, children form a heteronomous morality by which they do not differentiate morality, as entailing justice, equality, and cooperation, from adherence to rules (which children judge as sacred and unalterable), from obedience to authority (a unilateral respect that can override considerations of harm and fairness), and even from the physical and psychological (hence physical rules can be confused with social rules). Whereas at the more advanced level of autonomous morality children participate in the "elaboration of norms," at the heteronomous level children receive them "ready-made" (Piaget, 1960/1995, p. 315).

Piaget proposed that young children enter the realm of morality by feelings of obligation based on unilateral respect for adults and an associated acceptance of their rules as fixed, sacred, and constituting an unalterable reality. Piaget's view was later critiqued by Kohlberg (1963) on the grounds that young children's moral judgments are not based on an acceptance of norms ready-made, or a sense of sacredness of rules, or unilateral respect for authority. Nevertheless, Kohlberg (1971) proposed a model in which children's moral evaluations are undifferentiated from material value and personal goals (referred to as the first stage of punishment and obedience orientation). However, a large number of studies on moral, conventional, and personal judgments have shown that children begin to form distinctive judgments at a fairly early age. Children do not judge moral issues by rules, authority, or material value and sanctions (Turiel, 1997b). The domains of judgment are each associated with different types of social experiences and entail different strands of development (Turiel, 1978; Turiel & Davidson, 1986). Developmental shifts have been identified in judgments about personal jurisdiction (Nucci, 1977), social conventions (Turiel, 1978, 1983), and morality (Damon, 1977; Davidson, Turiel, & Black, 1983).

It is not our aim here to explicate on the developmental changes in thinking within these domains. Rather, our aim is to show that individuals develop a heterogeneous set of social judgments that are not solely determined by a religious or cultural orientation. Other evidence from research with young children supports the proposition of heterogeneity of judgments and actions corresponding to the moral and personal domains. A number of studies have shown that young children manifest positive emotions like sympathy and empathy (Hoffman, 1991), affiliate with others (Dunn, 1987; Kochanska, 1991), and act in prosocial or altruistic ways (Radke-Yarrow, Zahn-Waxler, & Chapman, 1983; Eisenberg & Strayer, 1987). Although this type of evidence is sometimes interpreted to mean that children are mainly oriented to sociability and to acting in positive ways (e.g., Wilson, 1993), there is evidence that, at the same time, children display opposition to others (e.g., mothers), often are involved in social conflicts, and engage in socially prohibited actions (Dunn, Brown, & Maguire, 1995; Dunn & Munn, 1987).

The heterogeneity of domains of social judgments appears in a variety of cultures – including concepts of welfare, justice, and rights (see Turiel, 1998a, for a review). However, the application of moral, social, and personal judgments is associated with the parameters of social situations encountered, in that different types of events can evoke different kinds of judgments. Moreover, individuals draw inferences about persons and interactions and form prescriptive judgments. As a means of illustrating this interactive process, we consider some seemingly straightforward experiments on social influence and conformity. We are referring to the classic social psychological "conformity" experiments of Solomon Asch (1956), which in textbook treatments are often regarded as studies of the effects of the group on individuals (see also Ross & Nisbett, 1991; Turiel & Wainryb, 1994). The experiments were, themselves, simple. The "subject" was put in a group of perhaps eight persons, whose task was to judge the comparative length of lines presented to them. The central component of the experiment, of course, was that all but one of the members of the group were confederates of the experimenter who sometimes gave incorrect responses. That subjects frequently gave the same responses as the rest of the group often has been taken as strong evidence for the idea that the judgments and behaviors of individuals are readily assimilated to groups, even in situations that involve simple judgments about unambiguous physical events.

Were the events experienced by participants in these experiments unambiguous, and were they primarily conforming to group judgments? The results of these experiments, though showing shifts in individuals' behaviors, actually were explained by Asch, himself, to reflect people's interpretations of the total situation, including its physical, social, and psychological attributes. According to Asch, the situation was not unambiguous because of the behavior of the members of the group. Although the judgments about the lengths of the lines may have been straightforward, the behaviors of the others, in that context, were not. Rather than merely accommodating to the group, the participants were attempting to make sense of perplexing judgments on the parts of others, given their own perceptions of the relative lengths of the lines (the physical stimuli). Central to Asch's interpretation is that the participants made social judgments and psychological attributions regarding the situation. In many instances, the participants were led to conclude that their own perceptions of the physical stimuli were flawed since there was no apparent reason for the judgments of the others with regard to the lengths of the lines. The assumption that other people normally give truthful answers meant that perhaps their own judgments were somehow incorrect (see Asch, 1952, pp. 468–72). By contrast, if it were understood why people gave the responses they did, then it would be expected that they would conform less. This expectation was confirmed in a study (similar in design to the Asch experiments) that provided participants with a basis for explaining the incorrect judgments of others in the group (Ross, Bierbrauer, & Hoffman, 1976). Insofar as the others' behaviors could be attributed to particular motives or goals (e.g., to attain a material reward) there was less conformity than when no explanation was readily available.

An important component of Asch's interpretation, contrasting with the conformity explanations, is in the proposition that individuals' behaviors are associated with their judgments about the motives of others and social interactions among them. In this view, social situations are interpreted in ways that the relationships among people and other features are taken into account. Insofar as salient features of situations vary, it would have to be said that the context for the judgments also varies. Asch used the term "objects of judgment" to draw this type of distinction.

A direct demonstration of how the "object of judgment" can vary by variations in the situational context can be seen in research, also conducted by Asch (1952), in which participants were provided with statements containing sociopolitical content and systematic variations in the authorships attributed to the statements. It was found that evaluations of the statements differed in accord with the differences in authors. The studies demonstrated that the different evaluations of a statement were not simply influenced by the prestige or perceived value of the author. Knowledge about the supposed author of the statement contributed to people's interpretations of the meaning of the statement (e.g., a statement thought to be made by Jefferson was interpreted differently from when it was attributed to Lenin). With the use of ingenious experimental manipulations, Asch demonstrated that cognitive context can change by situational contexts. This type of analysis, it should be stressed, does not represent "situationalism" since it is persons' interpretations and construals about features of events that result in contextual variations.

Several different types of features can alter the object of judgment. It can be changes in the behaviors of persons (as in the "conformity" experiments), and it can be background knowledge about the persons involved in a situation (as in the research on attributions of authorship). Another source, directly relevant to moral decisions, is what may be referred to as informational assumptions (Turiel, Hildebrand, & Wainryb, 1991; Turiel, Killen, & Helwig, 1987; Turiel & Wainryb, 1994; Wainryb, 1991). Informational assumptions pertain to knowledge about the nature of reality that may be used in the application of moral judgments. This type of knowledge can be about cause and effect relations, psychological presuppositions, and metaphysical and existential beliefs. Again, an informative example comes from Asch – in this case from his analysis of cultural variations in moral decisions. The example is the practice, in some cultures, of leaving one's elderly parents to die while still in a state of good health. Asch, and others (e.g. Duncker, 1939; Hatch, 1983; Wertheimer, 1935), proposed that this practice is based not on a cultural difference in moral values or reasoning, but on a difference in factual or metaphysical assumptions about an afterlife. Cultures with the practice and those without each hold the moral value that people should further the welfare of the elderly or one's parents. There may be a difference, however, in the assumption that it is beneficial to enter the afterlife in a good state of health. Whether one maintains the assumption that there is an afterlife and assumptions about the most beneficial ways to enter it would have a significant bearing on how moral judgments are applied (also see Hatch, 1983).

It is not only metaphysical beliefs that make for differences in the application of moral judgments. Many controversial social issues hinge on differences in informational assumptions about biology or psychology (Turiel, Hildebrandt, & Wainryb, 1991). For instance, people who differ in their views on abortion do not differ in their judgments about the value of life. Rather, they make different assumptions about when life begins. Another example of the relations between moral judgments, informational assumptions, and moral decisions pertains to the effects of physical punishment on children's learning. Debates about corporal punishment usually do not revolve around whether it is morally right or wrong to inflict physical pain on children. Most agree that it would be wrong to do so. The debates, insofar as they exist, are over the efficacy of physical punishment in teaching children to behave morally. Research has shown that, whereas people agree in the moral condemnation of a father who spanks his child out of frustration unrelated to the child's behavior, evaluations of spanking to correct the child's repeated misbehavior were related to assumptions about the efficacy of physical punishment (Wainryb, 1991).

It should be stressed that moral judgments cannot simply be subsumed under informational assumptions, and that differences in people's informational assumptions do not account for all differences in moral decisions. We are drawing a distinction between moral judgments or moral reasoning (i.e., concepts of welfare, justice, and rights) and the outcome or decisions derived in the application of those moral judgments. It is in the application of moral judgments that factors like informational assumptions and construal of situations are taken into account. Accordingly, people who might maintain similar moral judgments (e.g., that one should not bring harm to others, including parents) might come to similar conclusions in some situations (e.g., you should help your middle-aged parents recover from illness) and different conclusions in other situations (e.g., you should protect your elderly parents from illness and death; you should leave your elderly parent to die at the appropriate time so they will enter the afterlife in a good state of health).

### Religious Beliefs and Moral Judgments

In our view, informational assumptions, metaphysical and existential beliefs, and presumptions about psychological processes must all be taken into account to understand how moral decisions reflect peoples' moral reasoning. A failure to account for the ways that informational assumptions bear on moral decisions can result in misconceptions about differences or similarities among individuals and between groups in moral judgments and their development. The practice just mentioned regarding how elderly parents are treated is an example. It can be concluded, we believe mistakenly, that people who maintain the practice develop fundamentally different moral judgments from those who do not have such a practice.

Another set of examples comes from research on the comparative moral and social judgments of Indians and Americans (Shweder, Mahapatra, & Miller, 1987). Shweder et al. maintained that the morality of Indians differs in kind from that of Americans and, in part, supported this claim with evidence that Indians, unlike Americans, judge actions pertaining to matters like dress and eating practices as morally wrong. By contrast, these are judged as matters of convention or personal preference among Americans. As examples, Indians accepted as morally binding prohibitions against widows eating fish or wearing jewelry and bright clothing, as well as prohibitions against a son getting a haircut or eating chicken immediately after his father's death. These prohibitions can be seen as practices that exist as part of the moral code of one culture but not another. Accordingly, the actions are treated differently in the two cultures. The prohibitions can also be seen as part of a moral code that is based on ideas revolving around duties and the maintenance of social order (see Shweder et al., 1987), as well as a morality of divinity with revealed truths (see Shweder et al., 1997). It is said that some cultures are collectivistic, with a duty-based moral code, and others are individualistic, with a rights-based moral code (Markus & Kitayama, 1991; Shweder et al., 1987; Triandis, 1990). Activities like those pertaining to the eating and dress practices of widows would not be treated as moral obligations in cultures with a moral code based on the freedoms of individuals and their rights to enter into social contracts and have a say in the construction of the social order.

An alternative interpretation of the judgments about particular practices regarding widows and sons would stem from the proposition that objects of judgment can differ in accord with informational assumptions associated with metaphysical beliefs. With regard to these practices, at least, before conclusions can be drawn about differences in moral codes (including duty, divinity, or collectivism), it is necessary to consider possible differences in assumptions about "reality." It does appear that several interrelated beliefs have a bearing on whether the practices are judged in moral terms. These are beliefs in an afterlife, in the existence and transmigration of souls, and that actions on earth can result in consequences for the souls of those who have died (see Turiel et al., 1987, for analyses of these and other examples based on ethnographic material derived from Shweder and Miller, 1985, and Shweder et al., 1987). As an example, beliefs that a widow's or a son's actions on earth can be harmful to a husband's or father's soul result in a perspective on such actions that one would not have in the absence of such beliefs.

Both religion and culture are sources of informational assumptions that influence the application of moral judgments in concrete decisions. If Indians and Americans make the moral judgment that it is wrong to inflict harm on others (and there is evidence that they do), then it would be expected that such a moral judgment would be applied differently in the context of different assumptions as to who can experience harm where. By proposing that religions can be associated with different informational assumptions, we do not mean to say either that religious differences are determined entirely by informational differences or that morality is entirely separate from religious doctrine. We do mean to say, however, that moral judgments are not determined by religious doctrines or revealed truths (nor by cultural moral codes – more on this below). These propositions imply that morality is defined by something other than an orientation given in societal, cultural, or religious systems and that its development stems from children's reciprocal social interactions. As already noted, moral judgments are primarily about welfare, justice, and rights, which are distinguishable from judgments about conventional uniformities in systems of social organization, authority, and personal jurisdiction (Turiel, 1983, 1998a). Indeed, research in several cultures consistently shows commonalities in judgments about welfare and justice (Miller & Bersoff, 1995; Shweder et al., 1987; for a review see Turiel, 1998a).

Our view therefore is that, whereas religious systems usually embody a moral point of view, they neither simply provide members with a unified moral code or moral orientation to assimilate, nor do the members simply acquire morality by accommodating to the system. Distinctions are drawn among various sorts of religious rules and prescriptions, which are analogous to secular distinctions between convention and morality. Moreover, moral judgments are seen as both part of and independent of religious doctrine. To illustrate these points we first consider Martin Luther King Jr.'s blending of religion and justice, as represented in his well-known letter from a Birmingham (Alabama) city jail to eight clergymen who had urged him to cease the demonstrations he had led against racial discrimination – demonstrations the clergymen referred to as unwise and untimely.

Martin Luther King Jr., a minister and religious leader, as well as the foremost civil rights leader of his time, was jailed in April of 1963 while leading a nonviolent demonstration in Birmingham against racial injustice. The occasion for and the content of his letter illustrate that religious precepts do not necessarily provide a straightforward, shared path of moral guidance. First, King's letter was written to respond to public criticisms that had come from fellow men of the clergy. Moreover, King (1963) criticized the "white church" and its leadership from the perspective of one who was also a representative of the church: "I have been disappointed with the church. I do not say that as one of the negative critics who can always find something wrong with the church. I say it as a minister of the gospel, who loves the church" (p. 14). King's most pointed criticism was that church leaders stood on the sidelines "in the midst of blatant injustices inflicted upon the Negro" (p. 14).

Viewing the church as a force for the transformation of society,

King faulted church leaders for their "social neglect and fear of being nonconformists" (in contrast with, as examples, Paul, Jesus, Martin Luther, and John Bunyan). In the face of neglect and fear of nonconformity, King (1963) often asked himself: "What kind of people worship here? Who is their God? Where were their voices when the lips of Governor Barnett dripped with words of interposition and nullification? Where were they when Governor Wallace gave the clarion call for defiance and hatred? Where were their voices of support when tired, bruised and weary Negro men and women decided to rise from the dark dungeons of complacency to the bright hills of creative protest?" (p. 15)

King's criticisms of the behavior of members of the church were derived from conceptions of justice, love, and the dignity of persons – conceptions he regarded as integral to the church. In his view, morality is not based solely on adherence to law, the written word, or the authority of church leaders. That he regarded morality to be, at once, part of religion and not solely given in religion is illustrated by his comments on just and unjust laws: "I would agree with Saint Augustine that 'an unjust law is no law at all.' . . . A just law is a man-made code that squares with the moral law of God. An unjust law is a code that is out of harmony with the moral law. To put it in terms of Saint Thomas Aquinas, an unjust law is a human law that is not rooted in eternal and natural law. Any law that uplifts human personality is just. Any law that degrades human personality is unjust." (King, 1963, pp. 7–8)

It was with great eloquence and clarity of thought that Martin Luther King Jr. expressed his moral sensitivity. Nevertheless, research shows that the messages are consonant with laypersons' orientations to morality and religious precepts. One set of studies (Nucci & Turiel, 1993) examined the judgments of children and adolescents from the following groups: Amish-Mennonites, Dutch Reform Calvinists, and conservative and orthodox Jews. In each of these groups judgments were studied of what might be considered different types of rules. Some were rules pertaining to matters of harm and justice (moral) and others were rules pertaining to nonmoral issues associated with the structure, authority, and rituals of the religions. The moral rules investigated pertained to stealing, hitting, slander, and property damage. Examples of the nonmoral rules included, for the Amish, day of worship, work on Sabbath, women's head covering, and women preaching; for Jews, they included day of worship, work on Sabbath, circumcision, men's head covering, and keeping kosher.

Judgments about these two classes of rules were different among each of the groups. The nonmoral religious rules were judged to be relative to one's religious group and contingent on God's word (e.g., as written in the Bible). That is, the religious rules were not judged as applicable to other religions and it was not considered wrong to engage in acts if there were nothing in the Bible about them. Judgments about the moral issues, however, were not linked to religions or to God in the same ways. Members outside the religion were considered to be under the same obligations to follow the moral rules as adherents to their own religion. Moreover, evaluations of these acts were not judged as contingent on God's word. For example, acts like hitting others or stealing would be wrong even if there were nothing in the Bible or if God had not said anything about them. Such acts were considered wrong because of harm inflicted or their injustice. The responses of an eleven-year-old boy from a conservative Jewish background well convey this kind of thinking:

> Let's suppose that God had written in the Torah that Jews should steal, would it then be right for Jews to steal? *Answer*. No. *Question*. Why not? *Answer*. Even if God says it, we know he can't mean it, because we know it is a very bad thing to steal. We know he can't mean it. Maybe it's a test, but we just know he can't mean it. *Question*. Why wouldn't God mean it? *Answer*. Because we think of God as very good – absolutely perfect person. *Question*. And because He's perfect, He wouldn't say to steal? Why not? *Answer*. Well – because we people are not perfect, but we still understand. We are not dumb either. We still understand that stealing is a bad thing (Nucci, 1991, p. 32).

Dutch Reform Calvinists, who have a strong belief in the compelling nature of God's commands stemming from God's perfection, were posed with the following question: Would it be right to steal if God had commanded Christians to do so? The large majority of participants in the study thought both that such a command would not make it right to steal and that God would not give such a command as it would be in contradiction with God's perfection. Some responses given by adolescents in the study (as reported in Nucci, 1985, pp. 168–169) illustrate the type of thinking involved. A fifteen-year-old female believed that people might steal because it was written in the Bible, but that "it still wouldn't be right." She also thought that God would not give such a command, "because it's the right thing to do, and he's perfect, and if he's stealing, he can't be perfect." Consistent with the fifteen-year-old's evaluation on the basis of the actions involved, a sixteen-year-old acknowledged the possibility of distinguishing justice from God's word: "No, then he wouldn't be a just God. And there are, I'm sure there are people who would go against him, then, if he were an unjust God, even though he had absolute power."

These data indicate that the relation between religion and morality is multifaceted and entails an interweaving of individuals' moral judgments and their perspectives on what exists and should exist in religious doctrine. The data suggest that the influences of religious precepts are not limited to the acquisition by individuals of a preestablished or revealed moral code. Moral criteria, understood by individuals, of welfare, justice, and rights are at least as much applied to religion as religious precepts or God's word are seen to establish the moral. Another study that included children and adults further illustrates the point (De Long, 1991). In that study, Christian children (nine to ten years of age) and adults were posed with hypothetical situations in which God commands what would otherwise have been considered immoral acts (i.e., to commit murder or practice slavery). The children responded somewhat differently from the adults. Whereas most of the children stated that they would not and should not engage in the acts, the adults were divided on the issue. Only a minority of the adults stated that they would not engage in the acts; however, the rest were about evenly divided between those stating that they would engage in the acts and those that could not accept the possibility that God would give such a command. Those who would engage in the acts based it on the presumption that God would have a moral justification for the command, given his perfection and omnipotence. Nevertheless, they were conflicted over the harmful consequences of the acts and their presumptions about God. These findings suggest that, unlike the children, adults conceive of possibilities for God's commands that are unknown to them. The adults might presume that there may be a legitimate moral principle within God's grasp but unavailable to them, or that God may perceive goals based on different informational assumptions.

## Culture, Conflict, and Moral Judgments

Perhaps the conflicts, critiques, and discrepancies between the judgments of individuals and religious doctrines, insofar as they exist, are due to a lessened force of religion in the lives of people in modern

Western societies (Durkheim, 1925/1961). Perhaps it is culture that we should look to for consistency and as the source of revealed moral truth. Indeed, cultures are frequently viewed as entailing shared meanings, with coherence and harmony (Triandis, 1996). However, the conflicts evident in the events surrounding Martin Luther King's letter from the Birmingham jail went beyond disputes with other religious leaders. Much of King's adult life revolved around conflicts, tensions, and oppositions in society more generally, especially those regarding racial discrimination – conflicts and tensions that existed before the 1960s and that continue into the end of the twentieth century. Unless we simply assume that these are conflicts between cultures with different moral codes, they suggest that it is important to consider, within cultures, the heterogeneity of social judgments, the multiplicity of social orientations and types of knowledge, and continual moral and personal tensions. As we have seen, the tensions and discourse over racial discrimination and civil rights, as reflected in King's letter, were over issues of justice, rights, and human dignity. Furthermore, the tensions were over moral issues bearing on institutionalized hierarchical arrangements in culture – in this case, hierarchy based on race. However, King (1963) also recognized a more general, historically sustained and pervasive set of conflicts over social arrangements when he stated in the same letter, "History is the long and tragic story of the fact that privileged groups seldom give up their privileges voluntarily ... We know through painful experience that freedom is never voluntarily given by the oppressor; it must be demanded by the oppressed" (p. 6).

Many analyses of culture and social development are, as stated, based on the idea that collectivities are made up of people who hold shared meanings around a coherent system of personal and moral values. Absent in such analyses are considerations of conflicts and contested meanings stemming from hierarchies in social systems, with persons and groups of persons in positions of greater or lesser power, influence, and status. There is a fair amount of evidence, however, that there are conflicts and disagreements between people in different positions in the social hierarchy (Abu-Lughod, 1993; Goodwin, 1994; Mines, 1988, Okin, 1989; Turiel, 1998b). These conflicts often involve efforts at getting around the requirements of cultural practices through hidden activities. Sometimes there are overt efforts at transforming cultural practices perceived as entailing inequalities, injustices, and unmet needs due to hierarchical arrangements that serve to benefit those in dominant positions (see Turiel, 1997a; 1998b for more extensive discussions).

One manifestation of these types of conflicts within cultures has been that throughout history people have perceived their society to be in a state of moral crisis and degeneration. As current examples, the Promise-Keepers and participants in the Southern Baptist Convention, who we referred to at the start, proclaim that modern society is in moral crisis because individual self-interest has caused people to abandon their responsibilities to family and community in the pursuit of personal pleasure. Moral crisis is also perceived from secular perspectives as well. Many social commentators and social scientists have argued that individualism has led to a loss of interpersonal connection, that a moral sense has been eroded because of a movement away from traditions, that former beliefs in something greater than the self – be it God, the Bible, or the community – have been replaced with egocentrism (Bellah, et al., 1985; Bennett, 1992; Bloom, 1987; Etzioni, 1993). Some see the 1960s as a major turning point in recent American history, when a generation rebelled against the social establishment in favor of personal freedom and jettisoned a more stable, communal, responsible, and moral way of life that characterized the first half of this century. However, in the 1920s many perceived American society to be in moral crisis too. Social commentators made the same kinds of criticisms of the youth of that time as are made currently. They were convinced that the authority of the family, schools, and church was being replaced with "undisciplined individualism," self-gratification, and unbridled freedoms. It was thought that traditional values and a sense of community were being diminished (Fass, 1977). European social scientists in the latter part of the nineteenth century, as well, made similar claims. Sociologist Ferdinand Tonnies (1887/1957) decried the fact that a "Gemeinschaft" society – a paternalistic, community-based way of life in which collective goals and understandings guide individual actions – was being replaced by "Gesellschafts" – where individuals are isolated and rational self-interest overrides concern with others' welfare. Durkheim (1897/1951), for his part, was alarmed by the "anomie" – disconnection, despair, and normlessness – that he associated with "a weakening of the social fabric" in the then modern way of life. From the point of view that morality stems from one's religious beliefs, or from feelings of sacredness associated with group life, or from cultural traditions, then perceived movement away from the societal and religious precepts can be interpreted as a loss of morality. Thus, Bellah et al. (1985, p. 81) wrote that in an individual-istic system, "reasoning remains rooted in a nonsocial, noncultural conception of reality that provides remarkably little guidance beyond private life and intimate relations."

The ubiquitous charges that societies are undergoing decay are often countered by those who believe that changes have promoted positive ends. This was true in the 1920s, when many argued that the social order was being transformed into a more just system with greater individual rights and a curtailment of arbitrary forms of au-thority (Fass, 1977). For many, the 1960s were a time in which a new generation promoted greater racial justice, equality for women, and restrictions on the authority of governments to engage in unjust wars. The claims and counterclaims regarding the course of societies indi-cate that there are indeed many conflicts and differing perspectives within cultures – contested as well as shared meanings.

The conflicts and contested meanings within cultures do not solely stem from differences between people in different positions of power or between those who want to maintain the status quo and those who want change. Matters are more complicated than that. In the first place, most people identify with aspects of culture that they think should be maintained and aspects that they think should be changed. Second, it is important to recognize that those who regard their cul-ture to be in moral crisis and degeneration are often critical of ways of thinking and practices that have become established in the culture. Even though the solution may be couched in terms of a call for a return to practices of the past, they see fault in existing cultural prac-tices and perceive themselves in conflict with those features of the culture. It is equally important to recognize that in many instances people in lower positions of power, who do not entirely accept their position or certain cultural practices, are nevertheless identified with the culture (Turiel, 1998b). In this perspective, participation in culture does not mean total acceptance of cultural meanings or practices, and often does involve ambivalence.

One salient source of ambivalence and conflict, however, stems from the perspectives of those in lower positions in the social hierar-chy (Wainryb & Turiel, 1994). Such conflicts are sometimes between different moral considerations, such as between equality and other goals of welfare. As an example, in the declaration of the Southern Baptist Convention, the espoused role for women was partially based on the view that it would contribute to a strengthening of families and thereby promote the welfare of children and society (perhaps the declaration was also influenced by assumptions about connections between women's nurturing and children's growth and development). The conflicts also are often between moral considerations of equality and fairness for those in subordinate positions, on the one side, and the maintenance of existing conventional arrangements and the promotion of the personal entitlements of those in dominant positions, on the other side (Turiel, 1997a, 1998b; Wikan, 1991).

Although the disputes in Western societies often include considerations of interdependence; community; and the need to maintain a tradition-bound, interdependent, and communal way of life, it is frequently asserted that cultures are primarily oriented to interdependence or independence. That is to say that cultures are seen as either primarily collectivistic or individualistic. However, the contested views in cultures (Western cultures, at least); the heterogeneity of orientations toward morality and religion; and the evidence that individuals construct moral concepts of welfare, justice, and rights through their social interactions suggest that there are limits to the constructs of collectivism and individualism as ways of characterizing cultural orientations to self and morality.

### Individualism, Collectivism, and Heterogeneity

The constructs of individualism and collectivism are used to describe a broad collection of societal and psychological features that are supposed to covary in regular ways. The constructs link aspects of social structure, public ideology, and individual psychology together, assuming a continuity among them. Collectivism is said to characterize societies having firm group boundaries and strong societal constraints on individual activities, and that are authoritarian and hierarchical. Individualism is said to characterize societies with weak group boundaries and minimum societal constraints on individual activities, and that are more egalitarian in allocating decision-making power. These differences occur at the level of social structure and organization. Collectivistic societies are also characterized as having a public ideology that is focused on duty, tradition, and conformity to social conventions (as espoused in certain Hindu scriptures, for instance), whereas individualistic societies are said to have a public ideology that focuses on individual rights and personal expression (as espoused in documents such as the Bill of Rights in the U.S. Constitution). In addition, the constructs are supposed to characterize general psychological differences between individuals belonging to each type of society. Members of collectivistic societies are said to subordinate personal goals to those of the group, to make duty-based moral judgments, and to have a sociocentric and interdependent view of the self. Members of individualistic societies are said to make personal goals primary, to make rights-based moral judgments, and to have an egocentric and independent view of the self (Markus & Kitayama, 1991; Miller, 1994; Shweder & Bourne, 1982; Triandis, 1990). Another way of summarizing these psychological differences is to say that in collectivistic societies people value social connectedness over individual autonomy (at least with in-groups, Triandis, 1990), whereas the reverse is true in individualistic societies.

However, there are often discontinuities between the judgments of individuals and the public ideology of the society in which they live (Spiro, 1993). Although it may be the case that the social structure of a society like the United States, a supposedly prototypical individualistic society, allows for a more equal distribution of personal autonomy than collectivistic societies like India or China, and although it may also be the case that the culture incorporates ideals of freedom, independence, and individual rights in its laws, histories, and myths more than some other cultures, it is not so clear that the moral reasoning of individual Americans can be characterized as predominately individualistic. As has been documented elsewhere (Turiel, 1994; Turiel & Wainryb, 1994), Americans have multiple ways of thinking about the social world that includes concerns with the personal and the collective, and the application of these principles varies between situational contexts. For example, a large-scale public opinion survey that studied Americans' attitudes toward personal freedoms and rights (McClosky & Brill, 1983) found that the majority of the sample supported abstract ideas of freedom of speech and religion as well as the right to privacy, dissent, and divergent lifestyles. However, it also found that these same people did not endorse such ideas when asked, as examples, if the American Nazi Party should be allowed to use a community hall to hold a meeting, or if a newspaper should be allowed to advocate the violent overthrow of the government. In these contexts, concerns with harm to others and community interests took precedence.

We would argue that concerns with autonomy and interdependence, with individual rights and interpersonal duties, coexist and are intertwined in the reasoning of individuals from both types of socie-ties. From the perspective that moral reasoning does not stem directly from cultural or religious sources, but is instead constructed in inter-actions with others and through reflection on cultural and religious traditions, individuals are seen to develop a multifaceted value system in which both concerns of collectivistic and individualistic kinds play a central role.

This is not to say that there are no cultural differences, however. The way in which concerns with autonomy and interdependence are manifested in particular contexts is likely to differ between cultures. In some societies, for example, concern with connectedness between husband and wife might lead to a high value being placed on the stability of marriages and prohibitions against divorce; in others, con-cern with connectedness between husband and wife might be focused on emotional closeness between the pair, leading to a high value being placed on romantic love and the acceptance of divorce in the case of marital unhappiness. We believe that examining the way that concerns with autonomy and interdependence interact and the situations in which they are manifested within cultures lead to more accurate char-acterizations of the relations between moral reasoning, culture, and religion than categorizations of societies through general orientations. To illustrate this point, we take as our example reasoning about auton-omy and interdependence in an ancient, traditional, highly religious culture – India.

## Hinduism, Hierarchy, and Heterogeneity

India is often characterized by social scientists as a duty-bound culture where interdependence and collectivistic thinking predominate over concerns with rights and personal prerogatives. Indians are portrayed as being oriented toward family, tradition, and interpersonal respon-sibility, and as subordinating personal goals to those of family and community (Markus & Kitayama, 1991; Miller, 1994; Shweder & Bourne, 1982); In conjunction with psychological analyses, many of these characterizations are said to stem from analyses of sacred Hindu doctrines (Dumont, 1970). Religious concepts such as *dharma* (a word used variously to mean "law, justice, virtue, duty, innate nature, mo-rality, social obligations and also the acts which result from all these"; Chennakesavan, 1976, p. 199) are viewed as formative of Hindu Indi-ans' moral reasoning (Miller, 1994; Shweder & Bourne, 1982). Because of their belief in *dharma*, it is said that Indians do not experience social restrictions as oppressive, but instead view them as consonant with their personal inclinations (Shweder et al., 1997).

As with Western religions, however, it is not clear or commonly accepted that Hinduism (or Buddhism) embodies positions oriented in one direction or another. By many interpretations Hinduism includes an interweaving of collectivistic and individualistic considerations. Hinduism is oriented to hierarchy (through an acceptance of a caste system), interdependence, and fulfillment of duties, but also to personal goals. Hinduism posits that the Divine is to be found within the individual, allowing each to choose his or her own path for spiritual development. One writer, commenting on the "freedom, spontaneity, and individuality" promoted by Hinduism in spiritual endeavors, writes that for Hindus "religion is a private and personal, not a public and social matter. . . . Hence, we could say it is the religion of individualism rather than a collective or group belief as most religions tend to be. It is the least organized of all religions. It borders on anarchism. . . ." (Frawley, 1992, p. 28). For Hindus, in fact, spirituality is a primary venue for expressions of autonomy and freedom (*moksha*) (Banerjee, 1974). The Hindu concept of *dharma*, taken in its meaning as social duty, also has a significant individualistic aspect. Although the rules of conduct (*dharmas*) specified for each of the castes were designed for the proper functioning of society, the reasons given for fulfillment of these duties entail individual as well as social ends: The law of karma promises that if duties are performed faithfully and selflessly, good results will come to one's soul in a future incarnation (Leggett, 1978; Nikhilananda, 1970). Some have even voiced the complaint that, through an emphasis on individual attainment and personal salvation, "the ethics of sociality came to be sacrificed at the alter of extreme individualism" (Banerjee, 1974, p. 248).

Buddhism, a religion born in India 2,500 years ago, also has individualistic elements, not only in its emphasis on looking inward for spiritual enlightenment, but also in the tenet that Buddhist scholar Robert Thurman (1988) calls "individualistic transcendentalism." Individualistic transcendentalism is the principle expounded by the second-century Buddhist philosopher Nagarjuna, which proclaims that collective interests should not supersede those of individuals, because society is made up of individuals and their interests. Moreover, the establishment of Buddhism itself represented a radical departure from the status quo of Indian culture at that time. In his rejection of the caste system and acceptance of females as full initiates into his monastic order, the Buddha gave equal access to spiritual teachings that had previously been restricted to male Brahmans only. In this sense, many place the principle of equality at the core of Buddhist *dharma*, the word taken here in its meaning of truth or justice (Foster, 1988; Gross, 1993; Nhat Hanh, 1988; Snyder, 1988).

Hierarchy as an essential aspect of the Hindu caste system, as well as paternalistic hierarchy in family relationships as codified in Hindu scripture (Banerjee, 1974; Chennakesavan, 1976), have resulted in descriptions of Indians as more concerned with fulfilling their duties and social role obligations than with asserting their rights. Indeed, Indian girls often are taught from an early age that a wife's duty is to see her husband as a Lord. She is told that self-sacrifice and patient submission to her husband's wants and desires are the highest virtues a wife can attain, and that in fulfilling these duties she will earn respect as a Goddess of the home (Kumar, 1993; Mitter, 1991). As many female Indian scholars have noted, however, husbands are not given the same emphasis on self-sacrifice and duty toward their wives, retaining their status and right of authority no matter if they neglect their wives or physically abuse them. Married women are obligated to cook, clean, labor, and care for their husbands and children, yet tend to receive significantly less food, clothing, health care, education, and material goods than males (Desai & Krishnataj, 1987; Fatima, 1991; Mencher, 1989). They are also commonly beaten by their husbands for disobedience (Flavia, 1988). We might ask, then, does Indian society emphasize interpersonal duty over individual rights, or does it emphasize interpersonal duty for women and individual rights for men?

A study by one of the authors looked into these questions (Neff, 1997). It was premised on the idea that in hierarchical social systems, as is found in Indian families, individual rights and interpersonal duties are actually intertwined: A subordinate's duty to fulfill her superior's needs and desires is also a superior's right to have his needs and desires take precedence (as found by Wainryb & Turiel, 1994, among the Arab Druze). The study was conducted with lower middle-class Hindu families in Mysore, India. The community conforms largely to traditional patterns, with family playing the dominant social and economic role in most people's lives, especially women's. Marriages in these families are normally arranged, with newly married couples often living with the groom's family. Women are responsible for all household chores, including childcare, cleaning, and cooking (meals are always served to men first) and are expected to defer to the wishes of their husbands and in-laws in all important matters.

Male and female children, adolescents, and adults were interviewed about everyday situations in which one spouse wants to fulfill a personal desire but the other spouse wants his or her own needs to be met instead. They were asked what the actor should do and why; thus, they indicated whether they were judging personal or interpersonal concerns to be dominant (i.e., should the actor fulfill his own needs or his spouse's?). The situations involved personal desires such as relaxing after work, going out visiting with friends, or taking dance or music classes, which were in conflict with spousal requests for help in chores, to be kept company at home, or to maintain the house. To see if the participants would be more concerned with duty on the part of wives, and rights on the part of husbands, the role of the protagonist was systematically varied so that the actor was either a husband or a wife. In addition, the conflicts were designed so that the importance of the personal desire increased between the stories, to see if the participants would take this situational variation into account.

It was found that, overall, people were more likely to emphasize personal prerogative for husbands and interpersonal responsibility for wives, reflecting the hierarchical nature of Indian marriages. In other words, people were more likely to say that it was all right for a husband to do what he wants than that it was all right for a wife to do what she wants. As an example of the perceived independence of males, consider the responses given by a male child to a story in which a husband wants to relax after work when his wife wants him to help with the shopping (for similar views of males as self-reliant and independent in a Middle-Eastern traditional culture see Turiel, 1997a):

> *Question*: Do you think Kumar should shop every evening for his wife or should he relax and read a book? *Answer*: He must relax and read a book. *Question*: Why? *Answer*: Because he is the man and he should do what he wants and not what others like his wife tell him. A man can do whatever he wants. (Neff, 1997, p. 104)

However, Indians also took into account the relative importance of personal concerns and the needs of the other in given situations, making personal autonomy judgments for wives as well when the importance of the personal concern was strong (up to 58%). The following response is illustrative; it was given by an adult female for a story in which a wife wants to take dance classes when her husband wants her to stay home and take care of the house:

> *Question*: Do you think Suma should go to dance classes or should she stay at home all day to keep it clean for her husband? *Answer*: She should go ahead with dancing. *Question*: Why? *Answer*: If she wants to do something she has to do it. She need not spoil her interest in learning something because she has to clean the house and her husband asks her not to go. She will lose her identity and individuality if she does this. (Neff, 1997, p. 105)

It appears that Hindu Indians do not have a global orientation toward duty-based reasoning even when thinking about wives' roles. Instead, individualistic ways of thinking are applied to husbands *and* wives when their desires are deemed important and necessary for personal fulfillment. Also note that judgments that endorsed a wife doing what she wants even against her husband's wishes were made in contradiction to the Indian tradition that it is a wife's duty to obey her husband. People were influenced by gender hierarchy, granting more personal prerogative to husbands than to wives, but they also made judgments that were independent of this norm.

Other assessments were included in the study that were designed to investigate Hindu Indians' conceptualizations of the relationship between the individual and society. One question asked whether or not others in society should be involved in enforcing the performance of interpersonal responsibilities by individuals.[1] Most said that this was not society's role, sounding very individualistic in their justifications by claiming that others had no right to interfere in private matters of this sort. Another question assessed whether judgments of the conflicts were dependent on the existence of particular social traditions (i.e., would the judgment that a husband should shop for his wife when she asks him to still hold in the context of another country where husbands didn't usually shop for their wives?). Most did not base their judgments on the existence of social traditions and, instead, often expressed concern with the need to act in spite of, and often in direct opposition to, societal norms. For instance, in response

---

[1] Other researchers have reported that Hindu Indians, due to their collectivistic orientation toward a duty-based morality, see interpersonal responsibilities as socially enforceable (Miller & Bersoff, 1992, 1995, Miller, Bersoff, & Harwood, 1990).

to the story in which a wife wants to take dance classes when her husband wants her to stay at home to take care of the house, a female adolescent stated:

> Whatever the tradition demands is not right always. Many a time tradition seems very absurd. I will not respect a tradition which comes in the way of one's own self interest. How will an individual grow if the tradition becomes a barrier for dynamism? I will surely want Suma to go to the dance class . . . (Neff, 1997, pp. 128–29)

It is important to note, however, that these types of judgments concerning females' rights within marriage often are not actualized in households. Although it is judged that the personal desires of wives *should* be fulfilled, especially when deemed important to their happiness, Hindu women in India have little opportunity to openly fulfill their own wishes and are continually called on to subordinate their interests to those of their spouses. A common phrase that one hears when talking to Indian women is that wives and daughters must "adjust" to avoid discord in their relationships. The reasons women adjust, however, may have less to do with moral judgments and more to do with pragmatics. In India, women are financially dependent on their husbands and in-laws, so subordinating their personal wants to others' may be a matter of survival. One adolescent male said it clearly:

> Suma should do what her husband says or else he will get angry and kick her out of the house. See, eventually she is a loser, she will have no security nor shelter as she is dependent on him completely. She must see that clearly and take a decision about the class . . . See, women here don't marry just the guy but his whole family too, so she ends up making all the changes according to their whims and fancies. It is understood and accepted that a woman makes her new home in the husband's house and will live according to their wants and their rules. (Neff, 1997, p. 141)

Women may not believe that such an arrangement is fair, but since economic and social independence is not an option, they often must do what is asked of them (see also Turiel, 1998b; Wainryb and Turiel, 1994). Thus, it seems that the goals that Hindu women hold for themselves, and the decisions that they think should rightly fall within their own sphere of personal choice, can be at odds with married life as it is actually lived and experienced (Bumiller, 1990; Desai & Krishnataj, 1987; Fatima, 1991; Mencher, 1989).

These findings demonstrate that in a religious, traditional, and hierarchically organized culture like India, concerns with personal prerogative and autonomy coexist with those of duty and interpersonal connectedness. The social context of hierarchy plays an important role in the precedence given to one concern over the other, with autonomy being emphasized when husbands' desires are at issue and duty being emphasized when wives' desires are at stake. However, judgments of autonomy were also made for wives when their personal desires were strong and important, in spite of traditions that demand that wives defer to their husbands' requests. In this way, Hindu Indians' moral judgments appear to be both *reflective of* and *reflecting on* their own society, revealing not only support for duty, tradition, and patriarchal authority, but also assertions of independence, the need for personal fulfillment, limits to society's role in regulating private matters, and dissent regarding established social practices.

Other research supports the idea that Indians have these multiple orientations to morality and self (Mines, 1988; Misra & Giri, 1995). As an example, Misra and Giri (1995) examined the social construals of adult males and females in Central India using measures derived from the work of Markus and Kitayama (1991). Contrary to their original expectations, Misra and Giri found that on various dimensions individuals showed a combination of interdependence and independence:

> In view of previous analysis of self construal it was expected that the participants will display greater tendency toward inter-dependent self construal than independent self construal. The present results, however, do not indicate predominance of interdependent self construal. Instead there appears to be a different mode of self construal in which both interdependent and independent construals are present. The portrait of Indian self as embedded, familial or interdependent does not receive support from this study. (Misra & Giri, 1995, pp. 26–27)

### Social Dissent in India

The heterogeneity of individuals' social judgments implies that individuals or groups should not be divided into those who are part of the system (religious or cultural) and those who oppose it. Rather, individuals often do both. Whereas those in subordinate positions in the social hierarchy do oppose and even try to change the practices that they judge unfair or unduly restrictive of their rights, they also uphold their religious and cultural systems. Indeed, religious precepts are often considered to embody a basis for according oppressed groups their rights and fair treatment. We have already referred to how Martin Luther King Jr. believed that justice, rooted in religion, justified opposition to long-standing oppression and discrimination based on race. This type of thinking and opposition is not limited to Western cultures. In fact, one of the most famous social activists of this century, Mahatma Gandhi, had a profound influence on Martin Luther King. Not only was Gandhi pivotal in the movement to obtain freedom for India from colonial rule, he was also an advocate for changes in the Indian caste system.

Gandhi was a deeply religious man and a fervent Hindu who also believed that those aspects of religious tradition that were unjust or unloving were not "true" religion and should be altered (Andrews, 1930). One aspect of the Hindu caste system of which Gandhi was especially critical was the classing of groups of people as "Untouchables."[2] He believed that the way Untouchables were treated constituted an odious violation of human rights, writing "I have never been able to reconcile myself to 'untouchability.' I have always regarded it as an excrescence in Hinduism. It is true that it has been handed down to us from generations, but so are many evil practices even to this day" (in Andrews, 1930, p. 40). For Gandhi, principles of equality and human rights were prior to particular religious and cultural traditions. Moreover, he saw these principles as consonant with the "true" spirit of Hinduism ("If I found that Hinduism really countenanced untouchability, I should have no hesitation in renouncing Hinduism itself"; quoted in Kripalani, 1970, p. 384), arguing that India needed to abolish the practice of untouchability so that social practices could be brought into line with these core Hindu principles.

Gandhi was also a strong supporter of the feminist movement in India. The movement to gain equal rights for women in India predates Gandhi, however, going back to the nineteenth century, while gaining strength and force all the time (Ali, 1991; Basu, 1992; Devendra, 1994; Dube, 1998; Jain, 1980; R. Kumar, 1993; Raj, 1991). Indian feminists have rallied for a wide range of changes in the traditional social order,

---

[2] The Hindu caste system has four main castes, arranged in hierarchical order – Brahmans, Shattriayas, Vaishyas, and Shudras. Yet there is another class of people who are below the caste system itself. These people are believed to be polluted, inheriting menial, "impure" occupations such as sewage sweeping, so that all physical contact with them by the higher castes is avoided – hence the term "Untouchables."

organizing for the education of women and an end to practices that are harmful to women, such as giving young girls into marriage, sati (widow immolation), dowry, and prohibitions against widows remarrying (R. Kunmar, 1993). The women involved in these campaigns to better women's conditions embraced principles of equality, justice, and freedom in justifying their cause, often turning to Western feminist movements for inspiration in their own struggle. Like Gandhi, however, many Indian feminists have also been committed Hindus, and have felt a tension between their desire to change India's patriarchal traditions and their desire to retain the religious and cultural heritage that they consider basic to their self-identity.

Some have criticized other Indian feminists for simply adopting Western models of feminism and applying them directly to the Indian context, arguing that this has been ineffective precisely because it has come from outside Hindu culture. Such an adoption is not necessary, it has been argued, because, "although Indian tradition has for the major part encouraged the subservience of women, applauded their self-effacement, and thus promoted their subjection, it contains several elements that can be developed toward establishing equality for women and towards a new assertion of the full dignity of their personhood" (Chitnis, 1988, p. 91). Ideals of female power and autonomy, for instance, are contained in depictions of female warrior Goddesses such as Durga and Kali, and they are also inherent in certain social roles, such as that of a mother-in-law (Wadley, 1988). Chitnis argued that these indigenous expressions of autonomy and independence would serve as more relevant and persuasive justifications for the feminist movement in India. Thus, the point is raised once more that, although concepts of rights and autonomy coexist with those of duty and connectedness within traditional cultures, the expression of these ideas is culturally embedded.

One major figure in the history of Indian social reform, Dr. Ambedkar, did not have faith that Hinduism could be internally modified yet still maintained in an egalitarian society (Limaye, 1991). He argued that the Hindu caste system perpetrated such extreme injustices, especially to the Untouchables (of which he was one), and that it needed to be abolished altogether:"just as Swaraj [self-rule] is necessary for India, so also is a change of religion necessary for the Untouchables. The underlying motive in both movements is the desire for freedom. . . . I tell you, religion is for man, not man for religion. . . . The religion that does not teach its followers to show humanity in dealing with its co-religionists is nothing but a display of force" (quoted in Isaacs, 1965, p. 169). As India's first postindependence Law Minister under Nehru, Dr. Ambedkar was instrumental in making the status of untouchability illegal in the new Indian constitution. This change in legal status did not have much effect on the actual treatment of Untouchables, however, who remained as discriminated against as ever. Disillusioned, Dr. Ambedkar made a very public conversion to Buddhism (a religion that was founded by another Indian Hindu who abandoned the caste system), inspiring approximately 2 million other Untouchables to follow suit. This mass conversion stands out as a stark example of the discontent that many Indians feel towards their place in society and their willingness to make radical changes in the cause of justice. It is also an instance of morality determining religion, rather than the other way around.

The theme common to all of these social movements is that, even in the highly traditional and socially prescribed context of India, people bring a variety of moral perspectives to bear on their own experiences. Individuals make critical reflections on their own religious and cultural heritage, and sometimes strive to reform it. Moreover, it is not only those in higher positions in a hierarchy who evidence concern with freedom and autonomy, but those in lower positions also feel the injustice of their domination. Moreover, those who are not outward participants in social reform, who for various reasons are not capable of or willing to express their dissent openly, may also be engaged in subverting the social system in more subtle ways (see N. Kumar, 1994, for several studies of surreptitious means by which Indian women oppose, challenge, and protest patriarchal authority).

### Conclusions

Religions and culture systems do make for differences in social life. There are differences in informational assumptions or metaphysical beliefs that can result in different moral decisions and practices. There are differences of a customary and conventional nature. There are also differences in the types of social hierarchies in cultural and religious traditions that frame dominance and subordination among the people living in a given society. It appears, however, that hierarchies are widespread in the world's societies (Nussbaum & Glover, 1995; Okin, 1989), and that moral judgments based on harm, welfare, and rights are also widespread. Such moral judgments are applied to the practices associated with hierarchical arrangements, often resulting in tensions, conflicts, and efforts at transforming cultural practices. The multiplicity of social judgments and the presence of social conflicts means that cultures should not be defined solely through shared meanings or harmonious relationships.

We have proposed, therefore, that cultures are not adequately characterized as oriented to individualism or collectivism, and that, instead, there is an interweaving of autonomy, independence, interdependence, and connectedness within social groups. In some cases, the requirements of duties and interdependence for one group carries with them independence and personal entitlements for another group (Neff, 1997; Wainryb & Turiel, 1994), making it difficult to dichotomize orientations. In large measure, this is because the application of moral judgments often entails coordination of the different perspectives of people in social relationships. Concerns with persons (including self-expression, personal fulfillment, or meeting one's needs) may leave the personal realm and become moral issues when they are assessed relative to the needs, wants, and desires of others, whether singly or in groups – when there is some conflict of interests between individuals or groups that must be morally resolved (for analyses of these issues, see Nucci, 1996; Nucci & Lee, 1993). Considerations must be made of the welfare and interests of selves and others because, of course, each party is simultaneously both a self and an other, depending on the point of view taken at any one time. Therefore, focusing on individuals as selves entails concerns with autonomy, in the sense of taking into account their personal needs, desires, rights, and welfare, while focusing on individuals as others entails concerns with connectedness, in the sense of being concerned with others' needs, desires, rights, and welfare. Embedded in moral reasoning, therefore, is the simultaneous balancing of concerns with autonomy and connectedness. Moreover, beliefs about the needs and welfare of the self and other, which stem from social interactions as well as from informational assumptions and metaphysical beliefs given in cultural or religious traditions, affect the weighing and balancing processes involved in morally resolving conflicts of interest. It is the idea of various individual and social considerations interweaving in a dynamic fashion that has framed our discussion of morality, religion, culture, and conceptions of reality. It is necessary to examine the intersection of these features to understand people's development of social thought and cultural practices.

**References**

Abu-Lughod, L. (1993). *Writing Women's Worlds: Bedouin Stories.* Berkeley, CA: University of California Press.

Ali, A. A. (1991). *The Resurgence of Indian Women.* New Delhi: Radiant Publishers.

Andrews, C. F. (1930). *Mahatma Gandhi's Ideas.* New York: The Macmillan Company.

Asch, S. E. (1952). *Social Psychology.* Englewood Cliffs, NJ: Prentice-Hall.

Asch, S. E. (1956). Studies of independence and conformity: A minority of one against a unanimous majority. *Psychological Monographs, 70,* (No. 9).

Bahm, A. J. (1958). *Philosophy of the Buddha.* Berkeley, CA: Asian Humanities Press.

Banerjee, N. V. (1974) *The Spirit of Indian Philosophy.* New Delhi: Arnold-Heinemann Publishers.

Basu, A. (1992). *Two Faces of Protest: Contrasting Modes of Women's Activism in India.* Berkeley, CA: University of California Press.

Bellah, R. N., Madsen, R., Sullivan, W. M., Swidler, A., & Tipton, S. M. (1985). *Habits of the Heart: Individualism and Commitment in American Life.* New York: Harper & Row.

Benedict, R. (1934). *Patterns of Culture.* Boston: Houghton Mifflin.

Bennett, W. J. (1992). *The De-Valuing of America: The Fight for Our Culture and Our Children.* New York: Simon & Schuster.

Bloom, A. (1987). *The Closing of the American Mind.* New York: Simon & Schuster.

Bumiller, E. (1990). *May You Be the Mother of a Hundred Sons: A Journey Among the Women of India.* New York: Fawcett Columbine.

Chennakesavan, S. (1976). *Concepts of Indian Philosophy.* New Delhi: Orient Longman Ltd.

Chitnis, S. (1988). Feminism: Indian ethos and Indian convictions. In: R. Ghadially, (Ed.), *Women in Indian Society.* Newbury Park, CA: Sage Publications Inc.

Damon, W. (1977). *The Social World of the Child.* San Francisco: Jossey-Bass.

Davidson, P., Turiel, E., & Black, A. (1983). The effects of stimulus familiarity on the use of criteria and justifications in children's social reasoning. *British Journal of Developmental Psychology, 1,* 49–65.

De Long, B. J. (1991). *Concepts of morality and religion: The coordination of moral prescription and divine authority.* Unpublished doctoral dissertation. University of California, Berkeley.

Desai, N., & Krishnataj, M. (1987). *Women and Society in India.* Delhi: Ajanta Publications.

Devendra, K. (1994). *Changing Status of Women in India (3rd ed.).* New Delhi: Vikas Publishing House.

Dube, L. (1988). Socialisation of Hindu girls in patrilineal India. In: K. Chanana (Ed.), *Socialisation, Education and Women: Explorations in Gender Identity,* (pp. 166–92). New Delhi: Orient Longman Limited.

Dumont, L. (1970). *Homo Hierarchicus: The Caste System and Its Implications,* (M.

Sainsbury, L. Dumont, & B. Gulati, Trans.). Chicago: University of Chicago Press.

Duncker, K. (1939). Ethical relativity? (An inquiry into the psychology of ethics). *Mind, 48,* 39–53.

Dunn, J. (1987). The beginnings of moral understandings: Development in the second year. In: J. Kagan and S. Lamb (Eds.), *The Emergence of Morality in Young Children,* (pp. 91–112). Chicago: University of Chicago Press.

Dunn, J., Brown, J. R., & Maguire, M. (1995). The development of children's moral sensibility: Individual differences and emotion understanding. *Developmental Psychology, 31,* 649–59.

Dunn, J., & Munn, P. (1987). Development of justification in disputes with mother and sibling. *Developmental Psychology, 23,* 791–98.

Durkheim, E. (1951). *Suicide: A Study in Sociology.* Glencoe, IL: Free Press. (Originally published 1897)

Durkheim, E. (1961). *Moral Education.* Glencoe, IL: The Free Press. (Originally published 1925)

Durkheim, E. (1974). *Sociology and philosophy,* New York: The Free Press. (Originally published 1906)

Eisenberg, N., & Strayer, J. (Eds.). (1987). *Empathy and Its Development.* New York: Cambridge University Press.

Etzioni, A. (1993). *The Spirit of Community: The Reinvention of American Society.* New York: Touchstone.

Fass, P. (1977). *The Damned and the Beautiful: American Youth in the 1920s.* New York: Oxford University Press.

Fatima, N. B. (1991). The plight of rural women. In: S. L. Raj (Ed.), *Quest for Gender Justice,* (pp. 12–26). Madras: Satya Nilayam Publications.

Flavia. (1988). Violence in the family: Wife beating. In: R. Ghadially (Ed.), *Women in Indian Society,* (pp. 151–66). Newbury Park, CA: Sage Publications.

Foster, N. (1988). To enter the marketplace. In: F. Eppsteiner (Ed.), *The Path of Compassion: Writings on Socially Engaged Buddhism,* (pp. 47–64). Berkeley, CA: Parralax Press.

Frawley, D. (1992). *From the River of Heaven: Hindu and Vedic Knowledge for the Modern Age.* Delhi: Motilal Banarsidass Publishers.

Goodwin, J. (1994). *Price of Honor: Muslim Women Lift the Veil of Silence on the Islamic World.* New York: Plume/Penguin.

Gross, R. M. (1993). *Buddhism after Patriarchy: A Feminist History, Analysis, and Reconstruction of Buddhism.* Albany, NY: State University of New York Press.

Hatch, E. (1983). *Culture and Morality: The Relativity of Values in Anthropology.* New York: Columbia University Press.

Herskovitz, M. (1947). *Man and His Works.* New York: Knopf.

Hoffman, M. L. (1991). Empathy, social cognition, and moral action. In: W. M. Kurtines and J. L. Gewirtz (Eds.), *Handbook of Moral Behavior and Development, Vol 1: Theory,* (pp. 275–301). Hillsdale, NJ: Lawrence Erlbaum Associates.

Isaacs, H. R. (1965). *India's Ex-Untouchables.* New York: The John Day Company.

Jain, D. (1980). *Women's Quest for Power: Five Indian Case Studies.* Bombay: Vikas Publishing House.

Kochanska, G. (1991). Socialization and temperament in the development of guilt and conscience. *Child Development, 62,* 1379–92.

Kohlberg, L. (1963). The development of children's orientations toward a moral order: 1. Sequence in the development of moral thought. *Vita Humana, 6,* 11–33.

Kohlberg, L. (1971). From is to ought: How to commit the naturalistic fallacy and get away with it in the study of moral development. In: T. Mischel (Ed.), *Psychology and Genetic Epistemology,* (pp. 151–235). New York; Academic Press.

Kripalani, J. B., (1970). *Gandhi: His life and Thought.* New Delhi: Publications division, Government of India.

Kumar, N. (Ed.) (1994). *Women as Subjects.* Charlottesville, VA: University Press of Virginia.

Kumar, R. (1993). *The History of Doing: An illustrated Account of Movements for Women's Rights and Feminism in India, 1800–1990.* New York: Verso.

Leggett, T. (1978) *The Chapter of the Self.* London: Routledge & Kegan Paul Ltd.

Limaye, M. (1991). *Mahatma Gandhi and Jawaharlal Nehru: A Historic Partnership. Vol. IV (1947–1948).* Delhi: B. R. Publishing Corporation.

Markus, H. R., & Kitayama, S. (1991). Culture and the self: Implications for cognition, emotion, and motivation. *Psychological Review, 98,* 224–53.

McClosky, M., & Brill, A. (1983). *Dimensions of Tolerance: What Americans Believe about Civil Liberties.* New York: Russell Sage.

Mencher, J. P. (1989). Women agricultural labourers and land owners in Kerala and Tamil Nadu: Some questions about gender and autonomy in the household. In: M. Krishnaraj and K. Chanana (Eds.), *Gender and the Household Domain: Social and Cultural Dimensions,* (pp. 117–41). New Delhi: Sage Publications.

Miller, J. (1994). Cultural diversity in the morality of caring: Individually-oriented versus duty-based interpersonal moral codes. *Cross Cultural Research, 28,* 3–39.

Miller, J., & Bersoff, D. (1992). Culture and moral judgment: How are conflicts between justice and interpersonal responsibilities resolved? *Journal of Personality and Social Psychology, 62,* 541–54.

Miller, J., & Bersoff, D. (1995). Development in the context of everyday family relationships: Culture, interpersonal morality and adaptation. In: M. Killen and D. Hart (Eds.), *Morality in Everyday Life: Developmental Perspectives,* (pp. 259–82). Cambridge, England: Cambridge University Press.

Miller, J., Bersoff, D., & Harwood, R. L. (1990). Perceptions of social responsibilities in India and in the United States: Moral imperatives or personal decisions? *Journal of Personality and Social Psychology, 58,* 33–47.

Mines, M. (1988). Conceptualizing the person: Hierarchical society and individual autonomy in India. *American Anthropologist, 90,* 568–79.

Misra, G., & Giri, R. (1995). Is Indian self predominantly inderdependent. *Journal of Indian Psychology, 13*, 16–29.

Mitter, S. S. (1991). *Dharma's Daughters: Contemporary Indian Women and Hindu Culture*. New Brunswick, NJ: Rutgers University Press.

Nhat Hanh, T. (1988). The individual, society, and nature. In: F. Eppsteiner (Ed.), *The Path of Compassion: Writings on Socially Engaged Buddhism*, (pp. 40–46). Berkeley, CA: Parralax Press.

Neff, K. (1997). *Reasoning about rights and duties in the context of Indian family life*. Unpublished doctoral dissertation, University of California, Berkeley.

Nikhilananda, S. (1970). *Self-Knowledge*. New York: Ramakrishna-Vivekananda Center.

Nucci, L. P. (1985). Children's conceptions of morality, societal convention, and religious prescription. In: C. Harding (Ed.), *Moral Dilemnas: Philosophical and Psychological Issues in the Development of Moral Reasoning*, (pp. 137–74). Chicago: Precedent Publishing.

Nucci, L .P. (1991). Doing justice to morality in contemporary values education. In: J. Beninga (Ed.), *Moral, Character, and Civic Education in Elementary Education*, (pp. 21–39). New York: Teachers College Press.

Nucci, L. P. (1996). Morality and the personal sphere of action. In: E. Reed, E. Turiel, and T. Brown (Eds.), *Values and Knowledge*, (pp. 41–60). Hillsdale, NJ: Erlbaum.

Nucci, L. P., & Lee, J. (1993). Morality and personal autonomy. In: G. G. Noam and T. Wren (Eds.), *The Moral Self: Building a Better Paradigm*, (pp. 123–48). Cambridge, MA: MIT Press.

Nucci, L. P., & Nucci, M. S. (1982). Children's responses to moral and social conventional transgressions in free-play settings. *Child Development, 53*, 1337–42.

Nucci, L. P., & Turiel, E. (1978). Social interactions and the development of social concepts in preschool children. *Child Development, 49*, 400–407.

Nucci, L. P., & Turiel, E. (1993). God's word, religious rules and their relation to Christian and Jewish children's concepts of morality. *Child Development, 64*, 1485–91.

Nussbaum, M., & Glover, J. (Eds.), (1995). *Women, Culture, and Development: A Study of human Capabilities*. New York: Oxford University Press.

Okin, S. M. (1989). *Justice, Gender, and the Family*. New York: Basic Books.

Piaget, J. (1932). *The Moral Judgment of the Child*. London: Routledge and Kegan Paul.

Piaget, J. (1995). Problems of the social psychology of childhood. In: J. Piaget, *Sociological Studies*, (pp. 287–318). London: Routledge. (Originally published 1960)

Raj, S. L. (1991). Women's liberation: A philosophical perspective. In: S. L. Raj (Ed.), *Quest for Gender Justice*, (pp. 204–29). Madras: Satya Nilayam Publications.

Ross, L., Bierbrauer, G., & Hoffman, S. (1976). The role of attributional processes in conformity and dissent: Revisiting the Asch situation. *American Psychologist, 31*, 148–57.

Ross, L., & Nisbett, R. M. (1991). *The Person and the Situation: Perspectives on Social Psychology.* Philadelphia: Temple University Press.

Shweder, R. A., & Bourne, E. J. (1982). Does the concept of person vary cross-culturally? In: A. J. Marsella and G. M. White (Eds.), *Cultural Conceptions of Mental Health and Therapy,* (pp. 97–137). Boston: Reidel.

Shweder, R. A., Mahapatra, M., & Miller, J. G. (1987). Culture and moral development. In: J. Kagan and S. Lamb (Eds.), *The Emergence of Morality in Young Children,* (pp. 1–83). Chicago: University of Chicago Press.

Shweder, R. A., & Miller, J. G. (1985). The social construction of the person: How is it possible? In: K. J. Gergen and K. Davis (Eds.), *The Social Construction of the Person,* (pp. 41–69). New York: Springler-Verlag.

Shweder, R. A., Much, N. C., Mahapatrah, M., & Park, L. (1997). The "Big Three" of morality (Autonomy, Community, and Divinity) and the "Big Three" explanations of suffering. In: A. Brandt and P. Rozin (Eds.), *Morality and Health,* (pp. 119–69). Stanford, CA: Stanford University Press.

Snyder, G. (1988). Buddhism and the possibility of a planetary culture. In: F. Eppsteiner (Ed.), *The Path of Compassion: Writings on Socially Engaged Buddhism,* (pp. 82–85). Berkeley, CA: Parralax Press.

Sommers, C. H. (1984). Ethics without virtue: Moral education in America. *American Scholar, 53,* 381–89.

Spiro, M. (1993). Is the Western conception of the self "peculiar" within the context of the world cultures? *Ethos, 21,* 107–53.

Thurman, R. A. (1988). Nagarjuna's guidelines for Buddhist social activism. In: F. Eppsteiner (Ed.), *The Path of Compassion: Writings on Socially Engaged Buddhism,* (pp. 120–44). Berkeley, CA: Parralax Press.

Tönnies, F. (1957). *Community & Society (Gemeinschaft und Gesellschaft)* (C. Loomis, Trans.). East Lansing: The Michigan State University Press. (Originally published 1887)

Triandis, H. C. (1990). Cross-cultural studies of individualism and collectivism. In: J. J. Berman (Ed.), *Cross-Cultural Perspectives. Nebraska Symposium on Motivation: 1989, Vol. 37,* (pp. 41–133). Lincoln: University of Nebraska Press.

Triandis, H. C. (1996). The psychological measurement of cultural syndromes. *American Psychologist, 51,* 407–15.

Turiel, E. (1978). The development of concepts of social structure: Social convention. In: J. Glick and K. A. Clarke-Stewart (Eds.), *The Development of Social Understanding,* (pp. 25–107). New York: Gardner Press.

Turiel, E. (1983). *The Development of Social Knowledge: Morality and Convention.* Cambridge, England: Cambridge University Press.

Turiel, E. (1997a). Cultural practices as "funny things": It depends on where you sit. Paper presented at the Fourth Ringberg Conference, Morality in Context, Ringberg, Germany.

Turiel, E. (1997b). Beyond particular and universal ways: Contexts for morality. In: H. Saltzstein (Ed.), *Moral Development in Culture: Particulars and Universals. New Directions in Child Development,* (pp. 87–105). San Francisco: Jossey-Bass.

Turiel, E. (1998a). The development of morality. In: W. Damon (Ed.), *Handbook of Child Psychology, 5th Ed., Vol. 3:* N. Eisenberg (Ed.), *Social, Emotional, and Personality Development* (pp. 863–932). New York: Wiley.

Turiel, E. (1998b). Notes from the underground: Culture, conflict, and subversion. In: J. Langer and M. Killen (Eds.), *Piaget, Evolution, and Development,* (pp. 271–96). Mahwah, NJ: Erlbaum.

Turiel, E., & Davidson, P. (1986). Heterogeneity, inconsistency, and asynchrony in the development of cognitive structures. In: I. Levin (Ed.), *Stage and Structure: Reopening the Debate,* (pp. 106–43). Norwood, NJ: Ablex.

Turiel, E., Hildebrandt, C., & Wainryb, C. (1991). Judging social issues: Difficulties, inconsistencies, and consistencies. *Monographs of The Society for Research in Child Development, 56* (2).

Turiel, E., Killen, M., & Helwig, C. C. (1987). Morality: Its structure, functions and vagaries. In: J. Kagan and S. Lamb (Eds.), *The Emergence of Moral Concepts in Young Children,* (pp. 155–244). Chicago: University of Chicago Press.

Turiel, E., & Wainryb, C. (1994). Social reasoning and the varieties of social experience in cultural contexts. In: H. W. Reese (Ed.), *Advances in Child Development and Behavior, Vol. 25,* (pp. 289–326). New York: Academic Press.

Wadley, S. (1988). Women in the Hindu tradition. In: R. Ghadially (Ed.), *Women in Indian Society,* (pp. 23–44). Newbury Park, CA: Sage Publications Inc.

Wainryb, C. (1991). Understanding differences in moral judgments: The role of informational assumptions. *Child Development, 62,* 840–51.

Wainryb, C., & Turiel, E. (1994). Dominance, subordination, and concepts of personal entitlements in cultural contexts. *Child Development, 65,* 1701–22.

Wertheimer, M. (1935). Some problems in the theory of ethics. *Social Research, 2,* 353–67.

Wikan, U. (1991). Toward an experience – near anthropology. *Cultural Anthropology, 6,* 285–305.

Wilson, J. Q. (1993). *The Moral Sense.* New York: Free Press.

# 11 Beyond Scopes

## Why Creationism Is Here to Stay

E. MARGARET EVANS[1]

Despite more than a century of scientific support, the theory of evolution has not been fully assimilated and embraced in contemporary society. Creationist beliefs continue to be endorsed by many adults (Numbers, 1992) and adherents of creation science now enjoy considerable success at the school district level in the United States, advocating that "intelligent design" theory and evolutionary theory be given equal time (Scott, 1994).

Why are creationist beliefs so persistent? In this chapter I shall argue that this persistence is not simply the result of fundamentalist politics and socialization. Rather, these social forces themselves depend on certain propensities of the human mind. On this account, the persistence of creationist beliefs in a population attests to their cognitive affinity as well as their public availability (cf. Evans, 1994/1995; Shore, 1996; Sperber, 1996).

This chapter offers a broad look at the nature and genesis of beliefs about the origins of species. Recent evidence on the development of children's thinking on this subject is presented in the larger context of an examination of the nature and distribution of creationist and evolutionary beliefs in contemporary society. The chapter begins with a look at the current ideological debate between proponents of evolution versus creation "science." The case is made that their differences are better understood in terms of dissimilarity in ontological commitment rather than in the capacity to reason scientifically. The next section reviews what is known about the distribution of beliefs about

[1] The studies reported in this chapter were supported by a Spencer Foundation Dissertation Grant, a University of Toledo Research and Fellowship Award, and a Spencer Foundation Small Grant.

origins among ordinary adults in the population at large. The final section reports on a series of empirical studies examining the development of such folk beliefs in children growing up in families from fundamentalist and nonfundamentalist communities in the United States.

## Evolution Versus Creation Science

Modern evolution science is derived from Dobzhansky's 1937 synthesis of Darwinian theories about the origin of species and Mendelian genetics (Mayr, 1997). The contemporary scientific establishment accepts both Darwin's theory of natural selection, that species arise naturally through adaptive change, and his theory of a common descent for all species, including humans. These theories are so central that without them modern biology would make no sense (Berra, 1990; Kitcher, 1982; Mayr, 1991; Scott, 1994).

Creation science stands as a modern challenge to evolution science, with the intent of providing empirical evidence to support the Biblical story of creation, the core tenet of which is the creation of separate species through divine, intentional design. Creation science beliefs are rooted in Biblical creationism and derived from the Book of Genesis in the King James English Bible, which is taken literally to be the word of God (Kehoe, 1995). While most Western religious traditions have accepted the scientific truth of evolution, embracing some form of theistic evolution, a subset of fundamentalist Christians have sought to challenge the theory of evolution on scientific grounds.

Like evolution science, creation science is a twentieth-century product. Notwithstanding their outraged response to Darwinian theory, most Biblical creationists of the Victorian era (1850–1900) accepted the geological theories of that time, including the antiquity of the earth (Gregory, 1986; Numbers, 1992). In contrast, contemporary creation scientists are more radical in defending Biblical teachings even with regard to the age of the earth. Creation science, also known as scientific creationism, really came into its own following the 1961 publication of the Whitcomb and Morris book, *The Genesis Flood* (Numbers, 1992). In this work and subsequent publications (e.g., Whitcomb, 1988), the Biblical dictum of a young earth was preserved and the Noachim Flood was invoked to explain the fossil record. The contemporary interpretation of the geological column was discredited and replaced with flood geology. This literature fostered a reappraisal and reawakening of creationist beliefs across the industrialized world (Numbers, 1992). Importantly, modern "creation science" stands as a peculiar "transmogrification of creationism from religion into science" (Numbers, 1992, p. 244) with the expressed purpose of procuring a place for creationism in the science classroom.[2]

## Science in the Service of Religion

In many ways, creation scientists harken back to a time when science was viewed as a "religion's truest handmaid" (Shapin, 1996, p. 142). Seventeenth-century natural philosophers seeking a scientific understanding of God's creation were deemed "priests of nature;" their experimental studies could even be performed, quite properly, on the Sabbath (Shapin, 1996, p. 153). In revealing God's handiwork, the detailed observations of the natural historian were thought to complement those of the theologian, the interpreter of the Holy Scriptures. Nonetheless, the scientist's enterprise differed quite radically from that of the theologian's. Natural philosophers scrupulously investigated the mechanical or efficient causes underlying nature's complex operation, leaving aside questions about final causes (Deason, 1986; Mayr, 1982; Roger, 1986; Shapin, 1996; Schrader, this volume).

The seventeenth century marked the beginning of revolutionary changes in the scientific view of nature. Challenging the teleological and vitalistic beliefs of earlier thinkers, scientists began to look on nature as a passive kind of machine or mechanism (Deason, 1986; Roger, 1986). This "depersonalization of nature" (Shapin, 1996) initially fostered the argument from design as the central tenet of a natural theology. If nature is not itself purposeful, but rather functions like a blind machine, then it followed that this artifact must be the handiwork of some higher power (Dawkins, 1987; Shapin, 1996).

In the absence of any natural explanation for nature's apparent functional design for living, a supernatural account was accepted. But as the study of natural history progressed in its own way, a powerful, naturalistic account of the origin of species emerged. The handmaid of religion thus ended up challenging the authority of religion itself. Modern science has relentlessly challenged all appeals to final causes

---

[2] Notably, this position has not been embraced by hard-core Biblical creationists, who eschew attempts to ground their religious beliefs in any source other than the Bible.

and supernatural intervention as it seeks to explain reality in natural-istic, purposeless terms (Root-Bernstein 1984; Shapin, 1996).

### Creation Science: An Oxymoron?

Creationism has been commonly dismissed as a religion, dominated by faith rather than scientific evidence. The National Academy of Sciences (1984) draws a sharp line between natural and supernatural kinds of explanations:

> The goal of science is to seek naturalistic explanations for phenomena such as the origins of life, the earth and the universe . . . within the framework of natural laws and principles and the operational rule of testability. . . . Religion provides one way for human beings to be com-fortable with these marvels. . . . Creationism, with its accounts of the origin of life by supernatural means, is not science. It subordinates evidence to statements based on authority and revelation . . . its central hypothesis is not subject to change in the light of new data. No body of beliefs that has its origin in doctrinal material rather than scientific observation should be admissible as science in any science course. (p. 26)

In 1987, the U.S. Supreme Court expressed the same opinion, ruling that creationism is a religion and hence should not be taught in science classes. In effect, this opinion finally reversed the outcome of the famous "Monkey Trial" of 1925, in which John Scopes was tried and convicted of the crime of teaching evolution to high school students in Tennessee. The Supreme Court's 1987 decision, however, only prompted creationists to bolster their credentials as scientists (Scott, 1994). Indeed, creation scientists appeal to classic standards of science. For the most part, they look at nature in depersonalized, mechanistic terms. And, their efforts are directed toward challenging the theory of evolution on empirical grounds, independent from matters of faith.

What distinguishes creation scientists is not a general failure to be "scientific" so much as their commitment to an ontological position that denies the adequacy of a naturalistic explanation of origins. Con-sider four positions along this line. At one extreme, the world is viewed in purely naturalistic terms, eliminating any possible role for supernatural forces and final cause explanation. In this case, science, originally the handmaid of religion, effectively becomes the mistress. At the other extreme, a "magical" world view infuses nature with vital forces, with no clear line separating the natural from the super-natural order. For the most part, Western science and religion have marked out positions between these extremes. Creation scientists hold to the more traditional position of an original creator, God, who fabricated the essential kinds of natural entities in the world. In contrast, most Western religions have moved to a middle ground characterized by some form of theistic evolution. The scientific truth of evolution is accepted while crediting God with initiating or guiding the process as well as creating the spiritual soul, if not the biological body (cf. John Paul II, 1996).

Creation scientists are well aware that they must defend their scientific claims on scientific grounds. To this end, they are quite adept at marshaling criticism against the verifiability of evolution as a scientific theory (see Cavanaugh, 1985; Godfrey & Cole, 1995; Numbers, 1992). Creation scientists gravitate toward the epistemological position that there is something inherently wrong with the theory of evolution, at least when compared to theories in the physical sciences (Cavanaugh, 1985; Godfrey & Cole, 1995). For instance, the following has been recently inserted in Alabama biology textbooks: "No one was present when life first appeared on earth. Therefore any statement about life's origins should be considered as theory, not fact" (Applebome, 1996). This argument harkens back to a kind of Baconian ideal of science based solely on induction from unbiased observation (Woodward & Goodstein, 1996).

Perhaps the most telling criticism of creation science is that it has failed to muster a systematic research program to accompany its rhetorical criticisms of the theoretical and factual bases of evolution (Berra, 1990; Cavanaugh, 1985; Kitcher, 1982; Root-Bernstein, 1984; Wise, 1998). Yet, despite efforts to characterize creationist science as a monolithic, scientifically impoverished endeavor, in a careful investigation Numbers (1992) found considerable dissent, with alternative theoretical proposals and a rudimentary research program. Although most of their output was polemical, the Creation Science Institute has supported some credible research, such as Lammerts' work on mutations in roses and Gentry's on radioactive halos in granite.

Despite these fledgling research efforts, however, it is quite apparent that the goals of creation science cannot be sustained in the face of actual empirical research. There are few doctoral-level geologists or paleontologists in the creation science camp, despite the willingness of the Creation Science Institute to support such training. There were several contenders, but once they became immersed in the new theories and data they either turned to a safer research area that did not challenge their world view or to theistic evolution (Numbers, 1992; Wise, 1998). With theistic evolution, it was possible for creationist geologists to maintain the dual ontologies, that of science and that of religion. However, the Creation Science Institute rebuffed this compromise position, because it failed to maintain a central tenet of creation science, the Biblical dictum of the young earth.

In sum, creation science cannot be simply dismissed as religion, oblivious to the standards of science. More accurately, it stands as an ultimately futile effort to use science to defend a particular ontological position. As Chinn and Brewer (1993, this volume) argue, beliefs that are entrenched in deep ontological assumptions are the most resistant to change based on contrary evidence. Insofar as creation scientists and evolutionary scientists are committed to distinct ontologies, it is not surprising to find them interpreting the same evidence in radically different ways. For example, if, consistent with creation scientists' beliefs, fossils are not signs of ancient life but are, instead, the remains of organisms drowned in the Noachim flood, then their placement in the earth's sediments may be considered to be the result of their specific gravity instead of geologic processes. Furthermore, it might follow that human fossils are rare because, when living, humans tried to survive the rising water by moving to the hilltops, where their remains decayed rapidly, rather than being fossilized in the more forgiving debris at bottom of the waters (Whitcomb, 1988; Wise, 1998).[3]

## The Depersonalized Human Versus the Privileged Human

Efforts to dismiss the scientific standing of creationist beliefs typically fail to consider why such beliefs are so entrenched. The persistence of creationist beliefs cannot be accounted for by a naive acceptance of the literal truth of the Bible, nor with general ignorance of the empirical standards of science. In fact, fundamentalists are generally "scientific," even accepting scientific evidence that runs against heliocentrism as presented in the Bible (Scott, 1987, 1994). Evolutionary beliefs

---

[3] Consistent with their thesis, creation scientists have attempted to prove that all fossils are of the same age (Numbers, 1992).

are peculiarly objectionable because they more deeply threaten to undermine the privileged status of God and the human soul in the universe. Without this special status, the fear is that all higher value will collapse, causing a moral decay that is seen to underlie a host of modern secular evils including fascism, communism, Freudianism, humanism, and witchcraft (Scott, 1987, 1994).

In keeping with their essentialist beliefs, members of the Creation Science Institute insist that "The first human beings did not evolve from an animal ancestry but were specially created in fully human form from the start. Furthermore, the spiritual nature of man (self-image, moral consciousness, abstract reasoning, language, will, religious nature, etc.) is itself a supernaturally created entity distinct from mere biological life" (Applebome, 1996). Evolution is seen to radically challenge this privileged status, threatening to reduce humankind to mere animals, absent their special spiritual and moral status. As one parent explained: "If children are nothing more than apes evolved, then we cannot expect them to act more than that to one another. . . . We must instill the belief of their divine worth" (Evans, 1994/1995, p. 124).

The great success of the scientific revolution, viewing nature as a depersonalized mechanism, very soon began to raise doubts about the status of persons in this new order (Shapin, 1996). Fundamentalists clearly fear that if they abandon their literal reading of the Bible, they must also abandon moral certitude. Science has no easy answer to this uncertainty. Mayr (1997) devoted a whole chapter of his most recent discourse on biology to the evolution of morality and ethics (see also Dennett, 1995), concluding that both an "innate ethical predisposition" and an "exposure to a set of ethical norms" were necessary ingredients for a moral child (p. 262). This leaves open a role for both science and religion but lacks the certitude of a higher religious truth. In a recent letter to the Pontifical Academy of Sciences, the Pope clearly drew a line: "to consider the mind as emerging from the forces of matter. . . . is incompatible with the truth about man" (John Paul II, 1997).

How do these ideological concerns play out in the thinking of ordinary people? The foregoing analysis suggests that creationism appears to be sustained by an effort to seek a final cause explanation, combined with beliefs in the supernatural. The notion of evolution, in contrast, offers a purely naturalistic, purposeless explanation of origins. In the stabilization of creationist and evolutionist beliefs, it has been argued, reliance on such ontologies is likely to be at least as important a factor as the ability to reason scientifically. The nature and genesis of the relevant intuitive ontologies is investigated in the next sections, in the folk beliefs of adults and the intuitions of children.

## The Distribution of Creationist and Evolutionist Beliefs

In contrast to the popular idea that creationist ideas are confined to the less well educated of the rural American South, such beliefs are commonly found wherever Protestants have settled, including much of the former British Empire (Cavanaugh, 1985). Creationist literature has been published in ten languages, from Chinese to Czech (Numbers, 1982). Within the United States, according to Cavanaugh, the movement is most longstanding in the midwestern and western states. Creationists are often highly educated (Cavanaugh, 1985; Evans, 1994/1995; Numbers, 1992), although, in general, adults with only a high school diploma are less likely than those with college degrees to endorse evolutionist origins (Miller, 1987).

Numerous polls indicate that the U.S. adult population is almost evenly split between evolutionist and creationist beliefs, with a few fence-straddlers (Miller, 1987; Almquist & Cronin, 1988; Numbers, 1992). A typical Gallup Poll finding is that 47% of the adults surveyed will agree that "God created man pretty much in his present form at one time within the last 10,000 years" (Numbers, 1992). As most surveys confine themselves to the analysis of single questions, they rarely reveal the complexity of adult thinking or much about the nature of their belief structures.

Studies of students' beliefs about species origins have been more thorough. Given the ideological climate discussed above, considerable research has focused on the relationship between creationist beliefs and scientific competencies and attitudes in general: Do courses in scientific reasoning increase students' acceptance of evolution? Are creationist beliefs associated with other unscientific, supernatural ideas such as beliefs in the paranormal? Are creationists generally anti-intellectual or anti-scientific? In contrast, another line of research focuses more specifically on domain-specific learning, considering the preconceptions and misconceptions of students who are being taught evolutionary theory.

## College Courses in Scientific Reasoning: Do They Help?

Although college students are more likely to subscribe to evolution, and less likely to subscribe to beliefs in the paranormal, than the rest of the population (Miller, 1987), they still exhibit some strikingly resistant beliefs (e.g., Harrold & Eve, 1995a). In an extensive survey of over 21,000 students, Almquist and Cronin found 38% of the students agreeing that "The garden of Eden is the point of origin of human life and the origin itself was an act of creation as performed by God, as recorded by Genesis" (Almquist & Cronin, 1988).

Aside from creationist beliefs, Gray (1995) evaluated the effect of three years of college education on students' beliefs in paranormal phenomena, such as extrasensory perception, astrology, and UFOs. He found surprisingly little change and little effect of either general courses in scientific method or specific courses designed to target the fallacious reasoning presumed to be associated with paranormal beliefs. Consistent with Tversky and Kahneman's (1974) research, he concluded that students were selectively biased toward evidence that confirmed their prior beliefs. A larger body of research along this line points to the importance of evaluating the factors underlying students' endorsement's of particular beliefs, as distinct from their reasoning abilities (see also Harrold & Eve, 1995b; Lawson & Worsnop, 1992).

## Creationism and Cult Beliefs: Anti-Intellectual or Anti-Scientific?

An extensive study of students' beliefs in creationism, cult archeology, and the paranormal indicates that "unscientific" beliefs are not all of a kind (Feder, 1995; Harrold & Eve, 1995b). Overall, creationist students were just as likely as other students to have positive attitudes toward science in general and were no more likely to endorse beliefs in the paranormal, cult archeology, or unconventional ideas about the origins of civilizations (e.g., Von Daniken's ancient astronauts; Atlantis). Examining whether creationists are generally anti-intellectual, Harrold and Eve found that they did indeed read fewer books outside classes and were more likely than other students to choose business majors.[4] Unlike cult beliefs in the paranormal, however, creationist beliefs were allied to a restricted world view involving a strongly held value system centering on political and religious conservatism and eschewing secular humanism. Harrold and Eve termed this ideology "cultural fundamentalism."

## Biology Students' Misconceptions About Species Origins.

Investigations of student learning demonstrate that the Darwinian concept of natural selection poses as many challenges ontogenetically as it did historically (Mayr, 1982). Highly educated biology and medical students, and less advanced students alike, show a persistent tendency to misconstrue biological change as a response to an animal's "wants" or "needs." Moreover, biological change is often viewed as a nonrandom process operating at the individual rather than at the population level (Brumby, 1979, 1984; Clough & Wood-Robinson, 1985; Deadman & Kelly, 1978; Greene, 1990; Settlage Jr., 1994). Overall, students tend to endorse a Lamarckian-type mechanism for biological change, with the inheritance of acquired features, as distinct from the Darwinian idea of natural selection from random variation. For example, students report that rabbits change their color in winter to protect themselves from predators, with their offspring also inheriting this tendency. Courses specifically designed to redress such misconceptions seem to have minimal impact (e.g., Bishop & Anderson, 1990). Students' explanations are remarkably teleological, commonly invoking the purposes and needs of the individual organism (Evans, 1994/1995).[5]

In summary, the spread of evolutionary ideas is only minimally helped by courses in scientific reasoning; in fact, such ideas seem quite difficult to acquire. Creationist beliefs are not associated with other beliefs in the supernatural or the paranormal, nor are creationists

---

[4] Otherwise, Cavanaugh (1985) found that young creationists were encouraged to become engineers, and to avoid the humanities. Whether these career choices are merely pragmatic or reflect a desire to avoid hard challenges to core beliefs is unclear.

[5] Care must be taken when interpreting the teleological or volitional explanations of students as they may simply lack a better means of expression, rather that truly believing in the existence of intentional forces. Many of the biological textbooks and television programs to which these students may be exposed often couch their arguments in similar terms (Jungwirth, 1975; Brumby, 1979; Clough & Wood-Robinson, 1985);. Such language is hard to avoid, even by the experts.

generally anti-scientific. There is some evidence to suggest a kind of anti-intellectualism, however, as this may be associated with an open-minded liberalism. Ironically, the beliefs of creationists are more likely to be challenged in the humanities than in the sciences (with the exception, of course, of evolutionary biology). A deeper understanding of these propensities is offered in the next section, reporting empirical studies designed to look at the emergence of beliefs about origins in different subcultural contexts.

## Cognitive and Cultural Factors in the Emergence of Beliefs About Origins

The origin of species can be viewed in two fundamentally different ways. We can imagine that the intricate design of species must be the intentional handiwork of some superhuman maker. Or, we can suppose that species must have come into being by some nonintentional, natural means. Historically, both of these perspectives are evident. Consistent with their naturalistic outlook, many early Greek thinkers adopted a nonteleological and naturalistic theory of origins, namely, spontaneous generation. This view was subsequently upstaged by a monotheistic creationism,[6] which, in turn, has only lately and partly been challenged by theories of evolution (Deason, 1986; Mayr, 1982).

In a study of public elementary school children from a midwestern university town (Evans, 1991, 1994/1995), the ontogenesis of beliefs about the origins of species was found to be remarkably similar to the historical pattern (see Figure 11.1). Children responded to the question: "How did the very first X get here . . . ?"; where X was a human or an animal. Responses coded as spontaneous generationist included any of a variety of nontransformational origins that appealed to a natural cause, whereas those coded as evolutionist had to clearly reference a natural transformation from one distinct species to another.

---

[6] Creationism, however, did not completely supplant spontaneous generation beliefs. Even as late as the seventeenth century the idea that "living beings could arise from non-living matter" by a variety of means was prevalent (Roger, 1986). Of course, caution must be exercised when using a historical analysis as a blueprint for onto-genetic change, as the conceptual base needed for individuals to generate ideas is likely to be very different from the conceptual base needed for the adoption of those ideas. Even so, this is a promising line of attack that has been used with some success to identify intuitive conceptions (e.g., Kaiser, McCloskey, & Profitt, 1986; Vosniadou & Brewer, 1987; Wiser, 1988; Samarapungavan & Wiers, 1997).

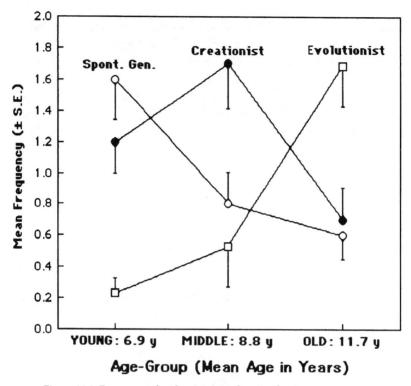

Figure 11.1. Frequency of each origin's explanation by age group.

References to an intentional agent, not necessarily God, were coded as creationist. Mixed spontaneous generationist and creationist responses were generated by the youngest children; consistent creationist beliefs were found in the middle age group, and evolutionist beliefs did not appear until early adolescence, where they predominated (Evans, 2000).

The youngest children were the most variable of all of the age groups, often endorsing both spontaneous generationist and creationist responses. Their spontaneous generationist responses, in particular, offered some clues as to their comprehension of the "origins" questions. From some of their more primitive explanations (e.g. "they were borned here"), it appeared that they failed to appreciate the need to explain why species originally came to be the way they are. The youngest children often seemed limited to proximate-cause arguments for the origins of species, such as growth or birth (e.g., "dinosaur grew on earth from eggs, like a bird), which take the existence and design of the organism to be a given. These children apparently have not yet confronted the "existential" question. Seemingly, they were explaining how an organism becomes manifest, but not how it got to be there in the first place.[7]

I propose that, at least in certain contexts, creationist thinking is a precursor and impetus to the later development of evolutionary theory. By drawing out the analogy between artifacts and species, creationist thinking brings to attention the question of how species came to be existent and have the functional designs that they do. Once the problem of original design is framed, proximal-cause explanations no longer appear adequate. Thinking about the design is naturally linked to thinking about a designer (Dawkins, 1987).

The idea that random, natural processes could explain the intricate design of organisms seems comparatively implausible. In this sense, the theory of evolution is not something that arises intuitively, but rather requires a specific knowledge structure, with attention to special kinds of data. That is, an individual is unlikely to make such an argument without an understanding of the history (fossils) and adaptation of species. It is from this base that a natural, specifically an adaptationist, evolutionary explanation could arise as it forces essentialist assumptions in the stability of species to be overridden (Evans, 2000).

To assess the effect, children in the reported study were questioned about their knowledge of fossils and adaptation. As predicted, such knowledge correlated with whether the children were evolutionist, independently of age. Nevertheless, while allowing for the evolution of species in explaining biological changes, these children were not yet Darwinian. Consistent with the research on college students' misconceptions, these children offered Lamarckian explanations such that animals change with the purpose of adapting themselves to the environment (Evans, 2000). Here again a teleological explanation appears to be readily applied, in the absence of knowledge of other causal mechanisms.

A cognitive account can thus be made for parallels between the historical and ontogenetic development of thinking about origins. However, it is equally important to consider how social factors may

---

[7] Such responses could well have their origin in the apparently spontaneous appearance of new organisms in spring, which preexist in embryonic forms, such as seeds in the ground (Evans, 1994/1995, 2000).

play a role in the story. The developmental sequence reported above was found in a sample of children from a midwestern university town. It seems likely that adults in this highly educated university community would tend to foster evolutionist beliefs. What would the developmental pattern be in a more fundamentalist community that subscribes to creationist views?

## Developing Beliefs About Origins in Fundamentalist and Nonfundamentalist Communities

The impact of social context was examined by comparing the ontogenetic sequence in communities that differed markedly in beliefs about the origins of species. As described earlier, to Christian fundamentalists the mere idea that different species might have come about as a result of natural transformations of animal kinds is quite implausible, even laughable; for them, entities as complex as biological kinds must have been the intended outcome of God's design (Whitcomb, 1972). How would children reared in such communities differ in the development of their beliefs about species origins from those reared in communities that believe that nature, not God, is responsible for the complexity of biological life?

For the purposes of the study, the definition of communities as fundamentalist or nonfundamentalist was determined by school attendance (Evans, 1994/1995, 1999). Fundamentalist families were recruited from two private Christian academies and a Christian Fundamentalist home-schooled group. As far as possible, the nonfundamentalist children were matched by age and the geographical location of their homes to their fundamentalist counterparts, but they attended public schools. All of the children came from rural and suburban areas in the Midwest. In addition to this difference between communities, the study included a survey of parental beliefs, providing a more direct index of adults' beliefs bearing on a child's experience at home. Assessments were also made of a variety of environmental influences, including home, school, and church, to determine the degree to which any child was exposed to a saturated belief system, be it creationist or evolutionist.

The findings for the nonfundamentalist elementary school age children replicated the development pattern found in the first study, reported above (Evans, 2000). In both studies, mixed spontaneous generationist and creationist beliefs predominated in the youngest children (five to seven years), exclusively creationist beliefs were found in the middle aged group of children (eight to ten years), and evolutionist and creationist beliefs were found in the oldest children (10.5–12 years). In the second study adults were also included, and their beliefs resembled those of the older elementary school children (see Figure 11.2).

It should be noted that the nonfundamentalist communities sampled in these two studies differed on several characteristics. In the original study, the children were drawn from a midwestern university town, where it was expected that evolutionist beliefs predominated among the adult population. In the second study, the subjects were drawn from rural and suburban communities, which were more likely to endorse creationism (Almquist & Cronin, 1988), and where adults had fewer years of formal education. These differences were reflected in the proportion of older children from the two communities who endorsed evolutionist rather than creationist beliefs: In the university town population evolutionist beliefs predominated, whereas in the

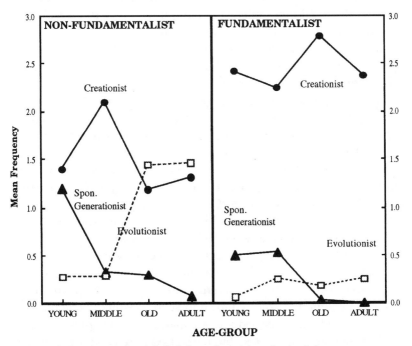

Figure 11.2. Frequency of each belief about the origins of animals by age group in nonfundamentalist and fundamentalist school communities. Age groups: Young (5–7 years); Middle (8–10 years); Old (10.5–12 years).

rural and suburban areas creationist and evolutionist beliefs were both similarly endorsed. On closer examination, this difference appeared to be primarily due to a curious pattern that was peculiar to individuals in the nonuniversity communities. These individuals endorsed evolutionary explanations for nonhuman species, but not for human beings. Humans were thus held out to have a privileged status (Evans, 1994/1995).

The fundamentalist children in this study were drawn from the same geographical areas as the nonfundamentalist children, with parents who had comparable levels of education. An analysis of interests revealed that fundamentalist and nonfundamentalist children were equally likely to enjoy nature studies, dinosaurs, reading, sports, and a number of other activities common to children in this age range. They differed significantly, however, in expressed interest in religious activities and fossils. The fundamentalist children were more interested in the former and nonfundamentalists, in the latter. Likewise, parents from the two communities differed in the degree to which they would encourage these particular activities in their children. Fundamentalist parents were less likely than nonfundamentalist parents to foster their children's interest in natural history and more likely to encourage religious activities (Evans, 1999).

Given this background, the critical question is whether the developmental pattern differs for fundamentalist children as compared to their nonfundamentalist counterparts. The answer is yes. Creationist beliefs predominated in all age groups for fundamentalist children (see Figure 11.2). In the fundamentalist community both naturalistic explanations for the origins of beliefs were suppressed, relative to the nonfundamentalists; evolutionist beliefs did not appear in any age group, and, although there was some expression of spontaneous generationist beliefs in the younger age groups, they were completely eclipsed by creationist beliefs. One interesting correspondence was maintained: Children from the middle age groups of the two communities expressed comparably high levels of creationist beliefs.

The children's creationist beliefs appeared to be linked with a pervasive belief in the essential, unchanging nature of species. Moreover, regardless of their religious leanings, all children, except the oldest group of evolutionists, refused to endorse the possibility that one kind of animal can be transformed into another, even when presented with the explanation (Evans, 1999). Similarly, Rosengren and his colleagues have found that children under the age of seven will not accept metamorphosis as a natural explanation. Adults and offspring of species that undergo metamorphosis are treated as members of different species (K. Rosengren, personal communication, June 13, 1997). From the historical evidence, Mayr (1982) claimed that essentialist beliefs in the stability of species impeded the development of evolutionary explanations, as essentialism was incompatible with idea that species could change through adaptive processes. Essentialism appears to act as a cognitive constraint (see Gelman, Coley, & Gottfried, 1994) that has to be overcome if evolutionist explanations are to be endorsed. Essentialism, however, is perfectly compatible with proximate-cause explanations, such as spontaneous generationism, as well as creationist final-cause arguments.

### Consistency of Belief

Up to this point the two cultural groups, the fundamentalist and nonfundamentalist school communities, have been described as separate entities and treated as if each had uniform cultural meaning systems. Anthropologists often deride such an approach. D'Andrade (1990) argues that beliefs are most likely to be distributed differentially in a cultural group, with some informants exhibiting more coherent or systematic beliefs than others (see also Boster, 1987; Shewder, Goodnow, Hatano, LeVine, Markus, & Miller, 1998; Turiel & Neff, this volume). The following quote from a parent illustrates a kind of complexity that is overlooked in polls and surveys that dichotomize responses: "If we attribute a well written news article, book, or study to a particular author then why are we so quick to assume we are just a chemical accident. Wouldn't such a complex galaxy and beyond lead one to believe in a master blueprint along with a master author and creator. Although our religion doesn't agree with evolution, I feel that, Biblically, people of Christ's era wouldn't have understood . . . but the reference of man coming from dust to me represents some sort of evolution . . . God's planned evolution" (Evans, 1994/1995, p. 124).

Many parents from both school communities acknowledged both evolutionist and creationist beliefs, whereas others were exclusively creationist or exclusively evolutionist. In effect, beliefs about origins were distributed differentially in these populations, and they varied from a consistent creationism, through various combinations of mixed beliefs, to consistent evolutionism.

It was hypothesized that parents who were more consistent and absolute in their views would foster children with similar stances. To the extent that the parents' beliefs were consistent, the child's environment would be relatively more saturated with a particular belief system. At the same time, it was also hypothesized that the capacity of this saturated environment to act as an enabling device would be limited or constrained by the child's intuitive beliefs. Specifically, community-endorsed beliefs would be more or less likely to be transmitted depending on the state of the child's conceptual development. To test these hypotheses, subjects from the two communities were combined into one group and the unit of analysis was the consistency of their belief systems (see Table 11.1).

The results showed highly significant patterns of correlation. Parents who were more consistently creationist tended to have children who were more likely to attend a fundamentalist school and a fundamentalist church. Their children attended church more frequently and were more enthusiastic and interested in religious activities, in general. Children of consistent evolutionists were more likely to attend a nonfundamentalist school or church, or no church, showed less of a preference for religious activities, but had greater natural history knowledge, especially of fossils. Importantly, there was no significant

Table 11.1. *Distribution of Consistent and Mixed Creationist and Evolutionist Beliefs Among Children and Adults from Matched Nonfundamentalist and Fundamentalist School Communities (percent of age group)*

| Age Group | Measure of Belief Consistency* (percent) | | | | |
| --- | --- | --- | --- | --- | --- |
| | (1) | (2) | (3) | (4) | (5) |
| *Nonfundamentalist School Communities* | | | | | |
| Young (5–7 Years) | 0 | 4 | 12 | 44 | 40 |
| Middle (8–10 Years) | 0 | 0 | 4 | 67 | 29 |
| Old (10.5–12 Years) | 12 | 26 | 15 | 26 | 22 |
| Adults | 20 | 17 | 10 | 29 | 24 |
| *Fundamentalist School Communities* | | | | | |
| Young (5–7 Years) | 0 | 3 | 0 | 35 | 62 |
| Middle (8–10 Years) | 0 | 0 | 3 | 31 | 67 |
| Old (10.5–12 Years) | 0 | 0 | 0 | 43 | 57 |
| Adults | 3 | 0 | 3 | 28 | 68 |

*Note:* This measure was derived from scaled, closed-ended questions assessing the degree of agreement (1–4 scale) with creationist and evolutionist explanations for the origins of three animate entities. Spontaneous generationist beliefs were not included in this analysis (Evans, 1994/1995).

* (1) Evolution/No Creation, (2) Evolution > Creation, (3) Evolution = Creation, (4) Creation > Evolution, (5) Creation/No Evolution.

relationship between the consistency of parent beliefs and children's general interests, in sports, reading, and collecting dolls or race cars.

Consistent belief in evolution among the children was significantly correlated with their adaptationist ideas,[8] even when such ideas were not strictly correct. That is, consistent evolutionists tended to endorse the "incorrect" idea that animals acquire new features in response to environmental pressures and that such acquired characteristics can be inherited. The rejection of such beliefs by creationist children appeared to be part of a general reluctance to admit that animals could change in response to environmental influences. For example, when asked, "whether an animal would get a long neck, if it stretched into a tree to get food," one eleven-year-old fundamentalist child explained, "God made it that way, so it can't change" (Evans, 1994/1995, p. 125).

These relationships support the hypothesis that the more consistent the parent's beliefs the more likely the parent was to provide an environment that was relatively more saturated with these beliefs. However, such correlations do not indicate which, if any, of these factors operate independently as predictors of children's beliefs. It is plausible that attendance at a nonfundamentalist or fundamentalist school, for instance, overrides all of the other variables; that is, school attendance might be the major underlying predictor and the others may just be uninteresting correlates of school attendance. All significantly correlated factors were entered into a series of regression analyses, which were carried out separately for each age group.

Saturated environments, as indicated by consistent parent beliefs, did not predict the consistency of child beliefs until the children reached early adolescence. The two significant independent predictors of early adolescents' beliefs were the consistency of parent beliefs and the adaptationist beliefs of the adolescent, together explaining more than half of the variance. The more consistently creationist a parent and the less an adolescent endorsed adaptationist beliefs, the more likely the adolescent was to be a consistent creationist. Conversely, the more consistently evolutionist a parent and the more an adolescent endorsed adaptationist beliefs, the more likely the adolescent was to be a consistent evolutionist. All of the other factors, from the type of

---

[8] This is not an evolutionist belief as there is no claim that a new species results from this process. A sample statement, with which a child could agree or disagree (1–4 scale), was, "If an animal swims a lot it might get webbed feet, and its babies will have webbed feet, too."

school attended to the interests of the child, were subsumed under these major factors.

Only in the early elementary school years (five to seven years) did the type of school attended have an effect on the consistency of the child's beliefs. Attendance at a fundamentalist school increased the consistency of child creationist beliefs, presumably by suppressing or failing to facilitate naturalistic ones, such as spontaneous generationist. The more children in the middle age group (eight to ten years) knew about natural history and the more they endorsed adaptationist beliefs, the more likely they were to be evolutionist, whereas those children who were more interested in religious activities were more likely to be creationist.

These results provide strong support for the thesis that the dissemination of beliefs about origins is a function both of availability and attractiveness. Up through the middle years, children appear generally unreceptive to evolutionary explanations, even in households where parents endorse such beliefs. No matter what their religious leanings, children in middle childhood appeared to be commonly attracted to creationist ideas. Young children also offered naturalistic explanations of spontaneous generation that were never espoused by parents (see also Samarapungavan & Weirs, 1997). Only in early adolescence did access to information about evolution begin to exert a differential effect.

The social environment appears to operate by shaping the expression of intuitive beliefs, by privileging some and suppressing others, and directing attention to particular kinds of activity and data. In fundamentalist communities essentialistic intuitions are deified while evidence of adaptive change is actively reinterpreted and suppressed. The subject of fossils and evolution was not completely ignored in fundamentalist populations, but such information was actively challenged. For example, an eight-year-old stated, "I don't believe that monkey thing . . . they think that monkey's kept changing and then became human . . ." (Evans, 1994/1995, p. 132). And, a twelve-year-old explained, "Sometimes the schoolbooks say . . . this guy named Derwin or something has a theory, but the teachers say the theories that disagree with the bible are not true. His theories are about how some animals changed" (Evans, 1994/1995, p. 132).

While fundamentalist parents appear to successfully support children's involvement in religious activities and creationist beliefs, children of nonfundamentalist parents were more knowledgeable about fossils. Such knowledge appeared to importantly challenge a pervasive creationist and essentialist bias, characteristic of children up to early adolescence.

Consistent with the reported studies of college students' ideas, children's initial adaptationist beliefs were of the Lamarckian variety. Even though erroneous, this understanding appears to be an important step toward a fuller knowledge of evolutionary explanation. The late development of this adaptationist understanding, however, seems to be contradicted by Keil (1994), who demonstrates that even kindergartners grasp the notion of adaptive function, what he calls the design stance. At this point, however, Keil has demonstrated only that young children evince what I would call static adaptation (Evans, 1994/1995, 1999), in which every feature of an organism is seen to be adapted to a specific environment. It is this form of adaptation to which Aristotle subscribed (Atran, 1990) and which is a feature of creationist beliefs. Static adaptation is perfectly compatible with essentialistic beliefs that an animal is destined to fit its surroundings; moreover, it is also, I contend, a feature of early naturalistic beliefs, such as spontaneous generationism. Static adaptation, however, does not take into account the role of the environment as a source of change, which is the crucial feature of the dynamic or Lamarckian adaptationist beliefs of the early adolescent.

**Artificialism Revisited**

From these findings it is clear that parent beliefs underdetermine the beliefs of their children, at least until early adolescence. Most eight-year-olds, for instance, were very likely to embrace creationism, whether or not their parents were avowedly evolutionist. If creationist beliefs are intuitive, how do they arise? The answer, I suggest, is to be found in childhood artificialism (Guthrie, 1993). The creation of artifacts is always done for a purpose, be it functional or aesthetic, and always a human purpose. Childhood artificialism is the application, by children, of these principles to all entities, natural as well as artificial (Piaget, 1929).

A plausible explanation for the derivation of an artificialist explanation is that it arises from an intuitive ontology, specifically a naive theory of mind (see also Boyer & Walker, this volume). By the early elementary school years, children have a well-developed and coherent theory of mind (e.g., Wellman, 1990), and this theory is likely to include some ideas about the intentional origins of artifacts (Bloom, 1996). Children's creationist beliefs about animate origins may simply reflect the "transfer of expectations" (Boyer & Walker, this volume) from the artificialism of an intuitive theory of mind. Rosengren and Hickling (this volume) suggest that it is only when children recognize the impossibility of an event that they are likely to "recruit alternative causal models." What violation of children's expectations might stimulate the emergence of a creationist belief? Piaget (1929) theorized that once the limitations of human capacities become obvious to a child, around the early- to mid-elementary school years, a superhuman might take on the role previously ascribed to the all-knowing, all-powerful parent. The recognition of human frailty might motivate children to transfer their expectations regarding human creative capacities from the realm of an intuitive theory of mind to an alternative model, that of theistic creationism.

If these conjectures have validity, then it should follow that children would initially conflate creationist and artificialist explanations and only later separate out these beliefs. Exactly this sequence was found in the above study, with the conflation being most pronounced for young nonfundamentalist children (see also Evans & Gelman, 1999; Piaget, 1929). In contrast with their fundamentalist counterparts, young nonfundamentalist elementary school children were more likely to conflate creationist and artificialist explanations for the origins of artifacts. By the time they were seven to nine years of age, fundamentalist and nonfundamentalist children alike discriminated between the powers of God and those of the human: God, but not humans, created animals; whereas humans, but not God, created artifacts (Evans, 1999).

Moreover, there is some preliminary evidence for a link between artificialism, creationism, and the existential question. By the time children are seven to eight years of age, they clearly understand first that artifacts are created exclusively by humans and not by God, and second that artifacts did not always, exist. A similarly coherent understanding of animate origins arises a year or so later (see Evans & Gelman, 1999). As outlined earlier, such evidence suggests that an understanding of artifact origins forces children to confront both the existential and the teleological questions. Seemingly, when children have constructed a coherent explanation for artifact origins, they no longer take the existence and design of an entity, artifact or animate, to be a given.

Further findings from this set of studies (Evans & Gelman, 1999), in which preschool and early school age children's creationist and naturalistic beliefs were compared with those of fundamentalist adults, revealed some telling differences. Whereas children are likely to be limited creationists, applying creationist beliefs to familiar animals, only, fundamentalist adults are principled in their beliefs. They apply creationist explanations to all natural entities, animate and inanimate, from unfamiliar prehistoric animals to rocks or ponds. In effect, fundamentalist adults endorsed two principled theories of origins, one is artificialism, in which humans create artifacts, and the second is creationism, in which God creates all natural kinds. The causal model in which adult creationist beliefs are embedded is much more complex and coherent than that of young children's creationism.

## Conclusion

Creationist and evolutionist beliefs about the origins of species became public property in our historic past; now they are part of our collective repertoire of beliefs, transmitted from generation to generation. At one point such beliefs were intuitive (Sperber, 1996), in that they were a product of untutored inferential processes (Atran & Sperber, 1991). Once released and transmitted to other human minds, however, they attained the status of reflective beliefs (Sperber, 1996), largely spread through communication. When a child espouses such beliefs, is it because he or she has acquired them through communication, validated by some authority, be it teacher or religious leader? Or, is it because he or she acquired them through inferential processes similar to those that led to the original development of the belief? Both processes, I have claimed, operate in the emergence and transmission of beliefs about the origins of species (Evans, 1994/1995, 1999).

In an environment in which such beliefs are underdetermined, the child appears to develop both naturalistic and intentional beliefs about origins intuitively, through a process of self-discovery, in the course of normal interactions with the environment. In this case, the ontogenetic sequelae in contemporary elementary school children bear some similarity to those found in early scientists, with shifts from a primitive naturalistic belief, spontaneous generation, along with creationism, to an exclusive creationism, to a more sophisticated naturalistic belief, evolution. However, if children are reared in an environment in which creationist beliefs are overdetermined, as is found in fundamentalist communities, then any naturalistic belief about origins is either suppressed or not facilitated, and creationism predominates in all age groups.

Creationist beliefs are both intuitively attractive and culturally available; evolutionist beliefs are less so. Availability is determined by cultural or societal processes, attractiveness by cognitive processes. At least part of the reason for the easy embrace of creationism seems to be that young elementary school children have a coherent theory of mind, one that is easily extended beyond its natural boundaries. This well-developed intentional system could explain the origins of artifacts, and thus raises the existential question, that of existence versus nonexistence. By analogy this system can also explain the origins of natural entities, in teleological terms, that is, in terms of purpose and design. But a naturalistic explanation at this developmental point has limited explanatory power. It does not explain how species come to have the designs that they do, being limited to proposing proximate causes, such as growth or birth. The shift to evolutionary explanations, albeit of the Lamarckian variety, is only accomplished, it is claimed, when children are exposed to evidence that species have in fact changed. It is knowledge of fossils and adaptation that allows essentialist beliefs in the stability of species to be abandoned; it is in this sense that evolutionist explanations are counterintuitive as they violate such essentialist assumptions.

In summary, by taking a developmental perspective and investigating multiple layers of representation from the individual to the collective, intuitive beliefs can be disambiguated from the cultural meaning systems that support and extend those beliefs. The picture that emerges is one in which preschool and young school age children have a propensity to generate somewhat incoherent, or unprincipled, naturalistic and intentional beliefs about origins. Such competing explanations are typical of developmental systems (Siegler, 1994). These intuitive beliefs are the building blocks for a much more complex system, leading ultimately to evolutionary science and creation science. The environment plays a causal role in selecting and shaping a particular belief system, in part by transmitting information that either facilitates or suppresses these intuitive beliefs. In effect, the environment acts as an enabling device, which is, in turn, limited or constrained by the child's intuitive beliefs. This endorsement by the environment privileges either a naturalistic or an intentional intuitive belief system.

Although these intuitive propensities of the human mind appear to be given more coherent expression by the custom complex (Shewder et al., 1998) in which they are embedded, explanatory coherence is not necessarily a hallmark of adult belief systems. On the face of it, perhaps the most startling findings from these studies is that while some adults were exclusively evolutionist or creationist, many of them endorsed both creationist and evolutionist explanations. Such a result should not, on reflection, be so surprising. Adults, intuitively and reflectively, access both naturalistic and intentional interpretations for biological origins. As proposed earlier, it is the environment that provides the material evidence to extend or suppress such interpretations. Without such support the most reasonable solution is to uphold both explanations, as the one, creationism, offers moral certitude and purpose in life, whereas the other, evolution, offers a compelling natural explanation for biological origins, other than of the human mind. For many of the participants in these studies, as well as for some religious leaders (e.g., John Paul II, 1997), neither explanation is seen to accomplish both objectives. Parents were well aware of the problems that such a solution entails: "One way to avoid two completely contradictory theories is not to think about them," "I don't know what to believe, I just want my kids to go to heaven" (Evans, 1994/1995, p. 105).

## References

Almquist, A. J., & Cronin, J. E. (1988). Fact, fancy and myth on human evolution. *Current Anthropology, 29* (3), 520–22.

Applebome, P. (1996). 70 years after Scopes trial, creation debate still lives. *The New York Times*, March 10, pp. 1, 12.

Atran, S. (1990). *Cognitive Foundations of Natural History: Towards an Anthropology of Science*. Cambridge, England: Cambridge University Press.

Atran, S., & Sperber, D. (1991). Learning without teaching: Its place in culture. In: L. Landsman (Ed.), *Culture, Schooling and Psychological Development*, (pp. 39–55). Norwood, NJ: Ablex.

Berra, T. M. (1990). *Science and the Myth of Creationism*. Stanford, CA: Stanford University Press.

Bishop, B. A., & Anderson, C. W. (1990). Student conceptions of natural selection and its role in evolution. *Journal of Research in Science Teaching, 27*, 415–428.

Bloom, P. (1996). Intention, history, and artifact concepts. *Cognition, 60*, 1–29.

Boster, J. S. (1987). Why study variation? *American Behavioral Scientist, 31*, 150–62.

Brumby, M. (1979). Problems in learning the concept of natural selection. *Journal of Biological Education, 13*, 119–22.

Brumby, M. N. (1984). Misconceptions about the concept of natural selection by medical biology students. *Science Education, 68* (4), 493–503.

Cavanaugh, M. A. (1985). Scientific creationism and rationality. *Nature, 315,* 185–89.

Chinn, C. A., & Brewer, W. F. (1993). The role of anomalous data in knowledge acquisition: A theoretical framework and implications for science instruction. *Review of Educational Research, 63,* 1–50.

Clough, E. E., & Wood-Robinson, C. (1985). How secondary students interpret instances of biological adaptation. *Journal of Biological Education, 19* 125–30.

D'Andrade, R. (1990). Some propositions about the relations between culture and human cognition. In: J. W. Stigler, R. A. Shewder, and G. Herdt (Eds.), *Cultural Psychology.* Cambridge, England: Cambridge University Press.

Dawkins, R. (1987). *The Blind Watchmaker.* New York: Norton.

Deadman, J. A., & Kelly, P. J. (1978). What do secondary school boys understand about evolution and heredity before they are taught about the topics. *Journal of Biological Education, 12,* 7–15.

Deason, G. B. (1986). Reformation theology and the mechanistic conception of nature. In: D. C. Lindberg and R. L. Numbers (Eds.), *God & Nature: Historical Essays on the Encounter Between Christianity and Science,* (pp. 167–91). Berkeley, CA: University of California Press.

Dennett, D. C. (1995). *Darwin's Dangerous Idea: Evolution and the Meanings of Life.* New York: Touchstone.

Evans, E. M. (1991). Understanding fossils, dinosaurs, and the origins of species: Ontogenetic and historic comparisons. *Abstracts of the Society for Research in Child Development, 8,* 246.

Evans, E. M. (1994/1995). God or Darwin? The development of beliefs about the origin of species. Doctoral Dissertation, University of Michigan, 1994. *Dissertation Abstracts International Section A: Humanities & Social Science, Vol. 55(8-A).* Feb 1995, 2335 AAM9500920.

Evans, E. M. (2000). The emergence of beliefs about the origins of species in elementary school children. *Merrill-Palmer Quarterly, 46(2).*

Evans, E. M. (1999). The Emergence of Diverse Belief Systems: Creation versus Evolution. Manuscript submitted for publication.

Evans, E. M., & Gelman, S. A. (1999). Revisiting the argument from design: Artificialism in young children and adults. *Manuscript in preparation.*

Feder, K. L. (1995). Cult archeology and creationism: A coordinated research project. In: F. B. Harrold and R. A. Eve (Eds.), *Cult Archeology and Creationism: Understanding Pseudoscientific Beliefs About the Past,* (pp. 34–48). Iowa City, IA: University of Iowa Press.

Gelman, S. A., Coley, J. D., & Gottfried, G. M. (1994). Essentialist beliefs in children: The acquisition of concepts and theories. In: L. A. Hirschfeld and S. A. Gelman (Eds.), *Mapping the Mind: Domain Specificity in Cognition and Culture,* (pp. 341–65). Cambridge, England: Cambridge University Press.

Godfrey, L. R., & Cole, J. (1995). A century after Darwin: Scientific creationism and academe. In: F. B. Harrold and R. A. Eve (Eds.), *Cult Archeology and Creationism: Understanding Pseudoscientific Beliefs About the Past*, (pp. 99–123). Iowa City, IA: University of Iowa Press.

Gray, T. (1995). Educational experience and belief in paranormal phenomena. In: F. B. Harrold and R. A. Eve (Eds.), *Cult Archeology and Creationism: Understanding Pseudoscientific Beliefs About the Past*, (pp. 21–33). Iowa City, IA: University of Iowa Press.

Greene, E. D. (1990). The logic of university students' misunderstanding of natural selection. *Journal of Research in Science Teaching, 27*, 875–85.

Gregory, F. (1986). The impact of Darwinian evolution on protestant theology in the nineteenth century. In: D. C. Lindberg and R. L. Numbers (Eds.), *God & Nature: Historical Essays on the Encounter Between Christianity and Science*, (pp. 369–90). Berkeley, CA: University of California Press.

Guthrie, S. E. (1993). *Faces in the Clouds: A New Theory of Religion*. New York: Oxford University Press.

Harrold, F. B., & Eve, R. A. (Eds.). (1995a). *Cult Archeology and Creationism: Understanding Pseudoscientific Beliefs About the Past*. Iowa City, IA: University of Iowa Press.

Harrold, F. B., & Eve, R. A. (1995b). Patterns of creationism belief among college students. In: F. B. Harrold and R. A. Eve (Eds.), *Cult Archeology and Creationism: Understanding Pseudoscientific Beliefs About the Past*, (pp. 68–90). Iowa City, IA: University of Iowa Press.

John Paul II. (1997). Truth cannot contradict truth. (From an open letter to the Pontifical Academy of Sciences) *The Scientist* May 12, 8–9.

Jungwirth, E. (1975). Preconceived adaptation and inverted evolution: A case of distorted concept formation in high school biology. *Australian Science Teacher's Journal, 21*, 95–100.

Kaiser, M. K., McCloskey, M., & Profitt, D. R. (1986). Development of intuitive theories of motion: Curvilinear motion in the absence of external forces. *Developmental Psychology, 22*, 67–71.

Kehoe, A. B. (1995). Scientific creationism: Worldview, not science. In: F. B. Harrold and R. A. Eve (Eds.), *Cult Archeology and Creationism: Understanding Pseudoscientific Beliefs About the Past*, (pp. 11–20). Iowa City, IA: University of Iowa Press.

Keil, F. C. (1994). The birth and nurturance of concepts by domains: The origins of concepts of living things. In: L. A. Hirschfeld and S. A. Gelman (Eds.), *Mapping the Mind: Domain Specificity in Cognition and Culture*, (pp. 234–54). Cambridge, England: Cambridge University Press.

Kitcher, P. (1982). *Abusing Science: The Case Against Creationism*. Cambridge, MA: MIT Press.

Lawson, A. E., & Worsnop, W. A. (1992). Learning about evolution and rejecting a belief in special creation: Effects of reflective reasoning skill, prior knowledge, prior belief and religious commitment. *Journal of Research in Science Teaching, 29*, 143–66.

Mayr, E. (1982). *The Growth of Biological Thought: Diversity, Evolution and Inheritance*. Cambridge, MA: Harvard University Press.

Mayr, E. (1991). *One Long Argument: Charles Darwin and the Genesis of Modern Evolutionary Thought*. Cambridge, MA: Harvard University Press.

Mayr, E. (1997). *This Is Biology: The Science of the Living World*. Cambridge, MA: Belknap/Harvard.

Miller, J. D. (1987). The scientifically illiterate. *American Demographics, 9* (6), 26–31.

National Academy of Sciences (1984). *Science and Creationism: A View from the National Academy of Sciences* (Committee on Science and Creationism, National Academy of Sciences). Washington, DC: National Academy Press.

Numbers, R. L. (1992). *The Creationists: The Evolution of Scientific Creationism*. New York: Knopf.

Piaget, J. (1929). *The Child's Conception of the World* (Joan and Andrew Tomlinson, Trans.). Totowa, NJ: Rowman & Allanhead.

Roger, J. (1986). The mechanistic conception of life. In: D. C. Lindberg and R. L. Numbers (Eds.), *God & Nature: Historical Essays on the Encounter Between Christianity and Science*, (pp. 277–95). Berkeley, CA: University of California Press.

Root-Bernstein, R. (1984). On defining a scientific theory: Creationism considered. In: A. Montagu (Ed.), *Science and Creationism*, (pp. 64–93). New York: Oxford University Press.

Samarapungavan, A., & Wiers, R. W. (1997). Children's thoughts on the origin of species: A study of explanatory coherence. *Cognitive Science, 21,* 147–77.

Scott, E. C. (1987). Antievolutionism, scientific creationism, and physical anthropology. *Yearbook of Physical Anthropology, 30,* 21–39

Scott, E. C. (1994). The struggle for the schools. *Natural History,* July p. 10–13.

Settlage Jr., J. (1994). Conceptions of natural selection: A snapshot of the sensemaking process. *Journal of Research in Science Teaching, 31,* 449–57.

Shapin, S. (1996). *The Scientific Revolution*. Chicago: University of Chicago Press.

Shweder, R. A., Goodnow, J., Hatano, G., LeVine, R. A., Markus, H., & Miller, P. (1997). The cultural psychology of development: One mind, many mentalities. In: W. Damon (Series Ed.) & R. M. Lerner (Vol. Ed.), *Handbook of Child Psychology: Vol. 1. Theoretical Models of Human Development, 5th ed.,* (pp. 865–937). New York: Wiley.

Shore, B. (1996). *Culture in Mind: Cognition, Culture, and the Problem of Meaning*. Oxford: Oxford University Press.

Siegler, R. S. (1994). Cognitive variability: A key to understanding cognitive development. *Current Directions in Psychological Science, 3* (1), 1–4.

Sperber, D. (1996). *Explaining Culture: A Naturalistic Approach*. Oxford, England: Blackwell.

Tversky, A., & Kahneman, D. (1974). Judgment under uncertainty: Heuristics and biases. *Science, 185,* 1124–31.

Vosniadou, S., & Brewer, W. F. (1987). Theories of knowledge restructuring in development. *Review of Educational Research, 57,* 51–67.

Wellman, H. M. (1990). *The Child's Theory of Mind*. Cambridge, MA: MIT Press.

Whitcomb, J. C. (1972). *The Early Earth: An Introduction to Biblical Creationism.* Grand Rapids, MI: Baker Book House.

Whitcomb, J. C. (1988). *The World that Perished: An Introduction to Biblical Catastrophism.* Grand Rapids, MI: Baker Book House.

Wise, D. U. (1998). Creationism's geologic time-scale. *American Scientist, 86,* 160–73.

Wiser, M. (1988). The differentiation of heat and temperature: History of science and novice-expert shift. In: S. Strauss (Ed.), *Ontogeny, Phylogeny, and Historical Development,* (pp. 28–48). Norwood, NJ: Ablex.

Woodward, J., & Goodstein, D. (1996). Conduct, misconduct and the structure of science. *American Scientist, 84,* 479–90.

# 12 Knowledge Change in Response to Data in Science, Religion, and Magic

CLARK A. CHINN AND WILLIAM F. BREWER

The purpose of this chapter is to examine the process of knowledge change in the domains of science, religion, and magic. We examine knowledge change in institutions, in expert adults, in nonexpert adults, and in children. Throughout the chapter, we consider (a) similarities and differences in the knowledge change process across the three domains; and (b) similarities and differences in the knowledge change process across institutions, expert adults, nonexpert adults, and children.

Our focus is on how people modify their knowledge in response to anomalous data. Anomalous data are observations of real-world events, or reports of such observations, that contradict current beliefs. For instance, for a child who believes that God always answers prayers, an unanswered prayer would be anomalous data. We have chosen to examine the role of anomalous data in knowledge change because in many instances of fundamental knowledge change, encounters with anomalous data are at the core of the knowledge change process (Kuhn, 1962; Piaget, 1985). We think that anomalous data play a significant role in knowledge change in all three domains and at all levels of expertise.

At the outset, it is important to be clear about how we are defining the domains and the levels of expertise. Scientific knowledge consists of conceptions about the physical and biological world. Religious knowledge includes conceptions of a transcendent reality such as conceptions of God, salvation, heaven and hell, enlightenment, and Buddhahood. The domain of magic includes belief in unusual psychic abilities that go beyond conventional physical and psychological causation. We treat belief in paranormal phenomena as the adult counterpart to children's belief in magic.

Throughout the chapter scientific institutions refer to official organizations such as societies of biologists or chemists. Religious institutions consist of religious organizations such as the Roman Catholic Church, a Buddhist temple, or the Iranian theocracy. In the area of the paranormal, it seems to us that practitioners of ESP, pyramid power, communication with plants, sensing auras, and so on are not members of powerful social institutions as are scientists and religious professionals. In consequence, the domain of the paranormal appears to differ from science and religion in that formal institutions play a much reduced role in the knowledge change of individuals. Therefore, when we discuss institutions, we will restrict our discussion to scientific and religious institutions.

To make fair comparisons among a comparable set of experts in the three domains, we have defined experts as those who publish institutionally sanctioned books and articles. That is, scientific experts are those who publish books and journal articles that pass peer review, as is customary in the institutions of science. Experts in religion are those who publish books and articles that are approved by one or more religious institutions. These experts may include charismatic leaders or mystics as well as university or seminary scholars. In the domain of the paranormal, because of the lack of powerful social institutions, we define experts as individuals who publish widely read books about paranormal phenomena. We do not include professional magicians as expert adults in our discussion of magic and the paranormal because professional magicians do not profess to use paranormal power to perform magic. We exclude parapsychologists because we think that they represent a mixed case of combined scientific and paranormal reasoning rather than the reasoning typical of paranormal believers.

Note that a person who is an expert in one domain is likely to be a nonexpert in the others. A scientist may have expert knowledge in the domain of microbiology and simultaneously be a nonexpert practitioner of Islam or Christianity. An Islamic theologian has expertise in religion but may have only nonexpert, lay knowledge of science. Most adults and children are nonexperts in all three domains.

## The Role of Anomalous Data in Knowledge Change

We think that anomalous data play an important role in knowledge change in science, religion, and magic. In science, detailed historical studies have shown that theory development in such areas as genetics

(Darden, 1991) and plate tectonics (Giere, 1988) is stimulated by the need to explain empirical results that are incompatible with existing theories. Kuhn (1962) observed that revolutionary theory changes in science are frequently preceded by anomalies that resist explanation within the framework of the old theory.

In religion, too, anomalous data can stimulate knowledge change. Many religious conceptions arise as a response to the experiential data of intense, personal religious experiences that cannot be fit into the individual's current conceptual framework. Famous examples include St. Paul's vision in which Jesus spoke to him when he was traveling to Damascus and Siddhartha's experience during meditation of the unity of all life (Batson, Schoenrade, & Ventis, 1993, p. 82). Experiences in which individuals report that they have received divine revelations are an important source of new religious knowledge. Empirical phenomena such as death and human suffering constitute additional data that help shape religious conceptions. In deistic religions, experiences of human suffering may initiate the development of particular beliefs about deities, such as the ancient Greeks' belief that the gods themselves visited tragedies on people or the belief of some Christians that God tolerates suffering as a necessary consequence of granting free will to humans. Some sects of Buddhism have responded to the data of suffering by asserting that suffering is illusory.

Scientific data can also lead to changes in religious ideas. Schrader (this volume) shows how the thought of some twentieth-century theologians has been influenced by theories of modern physics. Although these particular ideas have not spread widely among religious believers, other scientific ideas have had a broader impact. Many Christians have revised their ideas about the origins of species and the extent of God's intervention in natural history because of evolutionary theory and data supporting it (Livingstone, 1987).

Knowledge change in religion certainly occurs for reasons beyond encounters with anomalous data. Much of religious thought is probably not data-driven at all but arises instead to address existential concerns such as understanding the meaning of life, dealing with the prospect of death, and seeking a moral compass (Batson et al., 1993). Religion may exist not primarily to explain but to give meaning. In addition, some sociologists and anthropologists have argued that religious beliefs function mainly to solidify political control; for example, a ruler might exploit belief in a particular god to maintain political control over a group of believers (Dunbar, 1995). However, religious conceptions also represent claims about the real state of the world (e.g., God exists, reincarnation occurs, and so on), so that empirical data about the real state of the world can have an important impact on an individual's beliefs.

In the domains of magical and paranormal beliefs, as in the domain of religion, data are not the sole source of knowledge change. Paranormal beliefs may also arise because of existential concerns; Tobacyk (1983) found that concern about death was associated with greater belief in the paranormal. However, exposure to empirical experiences may help shape magical and paranormal beliefs. For instance, undergraduates' belief in ESP is correlated with reports that an individual has personally had a paranormal experience (Royalty, 1995).

## Two Issues

We examine two core issues regarding how people respond to anomalous data. The first issue concerns the types of responses that people make to anomalous data. We present a taxonomy of possible responses to anomalous data and examine whether there are differences across domains or across levels of expertise in how people respond to anomalous data. Our conclusion, which may be surprising to some, is that experts, adults, and children in all three domains make the exact same range of responses to anomalous data. However, we conclude that there is an important difference across the three domains at the level of the institution. Scientific institutions permit fundamental theory change in response to anomalous data; religious institutions do not.

The second issue addresses the factors that influence how people respond to anomalous data. We briefly discuss a range of factors that can influence responses to anomalous data, and then we focus on two factors that are particularly useful for explaining differences across domains and levels of expertise. These two factors are (a) the epistemological commitments of the individual (or institution) and (b) the degree to which the data that individuals typically encounter in the domain are ambiguous. We conclude that, at an institutional level, science and religion differ both because they employ different epistemological commitments and because religious data are much more ambiguous than scientific data. In general, these two differences at the institutional level reappear at the level of the individual expert. Experts in science, religion, and the paranormal generally apply different epistemological standards, and they also encounter data that differ in their degree of ambiguity. In sharp contrast, we argue that children apply essentially the same epistemological standards across all three domains. However, because physical and biological data encountered by children are less ambiguous than religious data, the application of the exact same epistemological standards yields very different results in the domains of science and religion. Children develop conceptions of the physical world that are remarkably similar across diverse cultures, but they do not develop religious conceptions that are similar across cultures.

In short, one main argument of this chapter is that institutions and experts employ epistemological principles that are highly specific to their domains, whereas children and nonexpert adults employ domain-general epistemological principles that are largely the same across the three domains. A second main argument is that at the levels of institutions, experts, and children, scientific data are less ambiguous than data in the other two domains; however, for nonexpert adults, we argue that data are relatively ambiguous in all three domains. This contrast between nonexpert adults and the other three levels of expertise has important implications for processes of knowledge change.

These two issues have attracted much research in the domain of science, but there is much less relevant research in the domains of religion and magic. Therefore, our discussions of religion and magic are necessarily speculative in many places.

## Responses to Anomalous Data

### Responses of Experts to Anomalous Data

In previous work, we developed a taxonomy of seven possible responses to anomalous data (Chinn & Brewer, 1992, 1993a, 1993b; Brewer & Chinn, 1994). Empirical tests of the original taxonomy led to the inclusion of an eighth category (Chinn & Brewer, 1998a). The eight categories of response are (a) ignoring data, (b) rejecting data, (c) uncertainty about data, (d) excluding the data from the domain of the current theory, (e) holding the data in abeyance, (f) reinterpreting the data, (g) peripheral theory change, and (h) theory change. The eight responses vary along three dimensions: whether the individual believes that the data are valid, whether the individual offers an explanation for the data, and whether the individual alters his or her current theory (see Chinn & Brewer, 1993b, 1998a).

In this section we examine whether this taxonomy applies to the reasoning of experts in science, religion, and the paranormal. In the domains of science and religion, we have chosen evolutionary biologists as examples of scientists and creationists as examples of religious experts. We have focused on creationists because they present an especially interesting case for examining whether there are differences in the knowledge change processes of experts in science and religion. Because many creationists argue that they are applying scientific methods to demonstrate the validity of creationist ideas, we can examine whether their methods really are the same as scientists. Although we agree with Boyer and Walker (this volume) that focusing our attention on one religious group may lead to conclusions that cannot be generalized to other religious believers, we also think that it is valuable to conduct an extensive analysis of the reasoning of one religious group, which can later be compared with the reasoning of other religious groups. In later sections, we will expand the discussion to include religious experts other than creationists.

Table 12.1 presents the eight categories of responses to anomalous data, along with the definition of each category and examples from experts in each of the three domains. The examples in the table indicate that experts in evolutionary biology, creationism, and the paranormal make the full range of responses to anomalous data. In all three domains, experts employ many options for responding to anomalous data besides changing their theories. Six of the responses discount the impact of the anomalous data while keeping current ideas completely intact. The seventh, peripheral theory change, makes only relatively minor changes to the theory. Changing one's theory is just one of eight possible responses to the data.

We think that the full range of responses can be found in the writings of other scientists and other religious experts, as well. Chinn and Brewer (1993b, 1998a; Brewer & Chinn, 1994) have provided many examples of these responses by scientists. Religious experts also appear to make diverse responses to anomalous data. Religious experts occasionally convert from one religion to another (theory change), and they also discount data in various ways. For example, the Jesuit monk Thomas Merton (1967) reinterpreted reports of certain religious experiences of Eastern mystics in terms of a Christian framework. Others might ignore such reports or reject them as invalid.

A question that arises is whether there are domain differences in the frequency of different responses to anomalous data. For instance, are individual scientists more (or less) likely to change theories than

Table 12.1 *Responses to Anomalous Data by Evolutionists, Creationists, and Paranormal Writers*

| Response | Definition | Example from evolutionists | Example from creationists | Example from paranormal writers |
|---|---|---|---|---|
| Ignoring | Individuals who ignore data do not believe the data, nor do they attempt to explain the data. They do not alter their current theory. | Fewer than 30 articles by biologists or geologists per year mention creationism, which suggests that most scientists simply ignore creationist issues (Godfrey & Cole, 1987). | Asserting that archaeopteryx is a true bird rather than a transitional form between reptiles and birds, Gish ignored many skeletal features of archaeopteryx that make them more similar to reptiles than to birds (see Strahler, 1987). | Psychics who profess to be able to help police solve crimes point to their apparently successful predictions but ignore the many predictions that are incorrect (Dennett, 1994). |
| Rejection | The individual does not accept the data as valid but does offer an explanation for how the data were obtained (e.g., a methodological flaw). There is no change in theory. | In response to the creationist claim that fossil human footprints exist alongside fossil dinosaur footprints in the Paluxy River bed in Texas, some evolutionists reject these footprints as a hoax (Miller, 1984). | Creationists have rejected radiometric dating of rocks by claiming that the radioactive decay of substances such as uranium varies (Morris, 1974). | In a test of their dowsing ability, Alaskan dowsers performed no better than chance at locating gold in boxes. The dowsers rejected the data as invalid because something in the green coloration of the boxes made the test invalid (Nickell & Fischer, 1988). |

| | | | | |
|---|---|---|---|---|
| Uncertainty | The individual is unsure about whether to accept the data as valid. There is no attempt to explain the data, and the individual does not change the theory, at least not yet. | Scientists who have studied Precambrian fossils in British Columbia have responded to some incomplete fossils with uncertainty; they are not even sure whether the supposed fossils are of organic origin (Gould, 1989). | After publishing evidence about dinosaur and human footprints side by side in the Paluxy River bed, Whitcomb expressed doubts about whether the tracks were valid data (Numbers, 1992). | On observing spiritual phenomena such as levitating tables, many who were interested in spiritualism were unsure of whether the phenomena could have been produced fraudulently and so repeatedly conducted additional tests (Kurtz, 1985). |
| Exclusion | Individuals declare that the data are irrelevant to the theory. | Evolutionists exclude the Bible or any other sacred book as evidence for any theory of biology. | Creationists have excluded experimental laboratory work dealing with the origins of life because they believe that the ability to create life in the laboratory is irrelevant to the actual emergence of life on earth (Morris, 1974). | Some paranormal believers have asserted that occasional instances in which psychics cheat tell nothing about whether the same psychics use psychic forces on other occasions (Brandon, 1983). |

(continued)

Table 12.1 (continued)

| Response | Definition | Example from evolutionists | Example from creationists | Example from paranormal writers |
|---|---|---|---|---|
| Abeyance | The individual accepts the data but is unsure about how to explain them, often believing that the current theory will one day be able to explain the data. | Acknowledging that there were many missing gaps in the fossil record that presented a difficulty for his theory of gradual evolution, Darwin (1859/1964) argued that later scientists would find the intermediate forms that his theory predicted. | When data about the large size of the universe challenged Setterfield's belief that the universe was created recently, he was at first unable to explain the data (McIver, 1988, p. 247). | William James acknowledged the validity of claims that spiritualists sometimes committed fraud but was unsure of how to interpret these instances of fraudulence (Brandon, 1983). |
| Reinterpretation | The individual accepts the data as valid but explains the data in a way that is completely consistent with the current theory. | McGowan (1984) reinterpreted the Paluxy bed tracks, described above, as footprints of small theropod dinosaurs. | Creationists have reinterpreted the data that more complex forms of life occur in higher geological strata, proposing that during the Biblical flood the more complex land animals were drowned and buried only after they made their way to higher ground (Wise, 1998). | Randall (1982) reinterpreted reports that cockroaches are capable of psychokinesis as instances of the psychokinetic abilities of the experimenters. |

| | | | |
|---|---|---|---|
| Peripheral theory change | The individual accepts the data as valid and explains the data by making a minor change to the current theory. | In Eldredge and Gould's (1972) evolutionary theory of punctuated equilibrium, evolution occurs in rapid change over a few tens of thousands of years. This theory accounts for an anomalous lack of some transitional forms in the fossil data without giving up core beliefs that evolution has occurred. | After reflecting on the troublesome evidence of immense distances between the stars (see above), Setterfield developed the theory that the speed of light had decreased since the time of the creation (McIver, 1988). The speed of light was a peripheral belief that could be changed while protecting a core belief in a young universe. | After a failed prediction that the world would end on December 17, 1996, when angels would arrive to bring 16 years of light without night on earth, one psychic said that ''we were naturally unaware of the fulfillment of his prophecy, since we are now living in a special holographic projection created by the angels'' (Randi, 1997, p. 7). |
| Theory change | The individual accepts the validity of the data and explains the data through adopting a new theory. | Early evolutionists abandoned Lamarckian evolution, in which acquired physical traits could be inherited, in favor of an evolutionary model that does not allow such inheritance. | Creationists have found that when creationist geology students enter Ph.D. programs in geology, the students inevitably give up their belief in a young earth because they become convinced by the geological evidence that the earth could not be young (Numbers, 1992). | The nineteenth-century magician S. J. Davey was initially a believer in occult phenomena but later changed his mind when he caught occult practitioners cheating and then replicated their tricks so well that observers were convinced that he, too, had psychic powers (Hyman, 1985). |

creationists or other religious experts? We are unaware of any research that addresses this question, but it seems to us that any raw differences in response frequencies would be difficult to interpret. If one were to find, for instance, that experts in science change theories more often than experts in religion, one could explain this difference in several very different ways (e.g., scientists are more open-minded, or scientists evaluate theories differently than religious experts, or scientists and religious experts reason in similar ways but scientists have better data on which to base their reasoning). Therefore, to understand whether there are differences in reasoning across science, religion, and magic, it is necessary to consider the factors that influence responses to anomalous data in these three domains. We will address these issues in a later section.

### Responses of Adults and Children to Anomalous Data

*Science.* Chinn and Brewer (1993a, 1993b, 1998a) have presented many examples showing that in the domain of science children and adults make all eight responses to anomalous data. Like scientists, children and adults have at their disposal many ways of discounting anomalous data besides changing their theories.

*Religion.* In religion there is evidence that children and adults also make a broad range of responses to anomalous data. To give several examples among children, creationist children ignore fossil evidence by avoiding contact with it; this is accomplished partly through the guidance of creationist parents (Evans, this volume). Other creationist children respond to anomalous fossil data by interpreting fossils as placed on earth intentionally to confuse humans (Lawson & Worsnop, 1992). This response can be interpreted as peripheral theory change if the children did not believe it prior to encountering the fossil data, or as reinterpretation if the children already held the belief that some data could be disregarded on these grounds. Tamminen (1994) reported that unanswered prayers can be anomalous for children who expect God to answer their prayers. Some children appear to reinterpret this anomalous experience by concluding that God answers prayers in indirect ways. Others respond by reducing their belief in God (Tamminen, 1994), which can be viewed as peripheral theory change, or by becoming atheists (Oser, Reich, & Bucher, 1994), which is an example of full theory change.

Among adults, theory change occurs whenever an adult converts from one religion to another. Two studies (Brock & Balloun, 1967; Schoenrade, 1987, reported in Batson et al., 1993) have found evidence that devout believers prefer to avoid exposing themselves to potentially threatening information, which suggests a predilection for ignoring anomalous data. Burris, Harmon-Jones, and Tarpley (1997) found that many Christian believers reinterpreted evidence suggesting that God had not answered a minister's prayers during a tragic drive-by shooting by affirming that God was acting benevolently but in a mysterious way that humans cannot understand. Batson (1975) reported that some Christian believers responded to anomalous evidence suggesting that Jesus's resurrection was a hoax by strengthening their prior belief, even though they could not explain the new data; this appears to be an instance of abeyance. Finally, Festinger, Riecken, and Schachter (1956) found that members of an apocalyptic cult group who had predicted that the end of the world would arrive on a particular day explained the fact that the world did not end through a peripheral theory change in which they maintained all of their core beliefs and asserted that the world had not ended as a reward for the group's great faith. Such examples suggest that adults as well as children make the full range of responses to anomalous religious data.

*Magic/paranormal.* Developmental research on children's ideas about magic has described the conceptions of children of different ages but has not yet examined how children respond to anomalous data. Some studies do present children with experiential data, such as showing magic tricks to young children (see Rosengren & Hickling, this volume). However, we do not know whether children regard these data as anomalous. If children already have a theory that magical events are possible, then the data would simply confirm prior expectations rather than produce any change in knowledge. Similarly, although a large body of research documents widespread adult belief in the paranormal (see Woolley, 1997), research on how adult believers in the paranormal respond to anomalous data is lacking. Indirect evidence exists that college courses designed to encourage skepticism toward the paranormal have only small effects (Gray, 1987), which implies that many students respond to the anomalous data in the course by discounting the data in various ways rather than by changing theories. We would again hypothesize that in the domain of magic, children and adults make the full range of responses to data that they make in the domains of science and religion, but further research on responses to anomalous data in these areas is needed.

### Responses of Institutions to Anomalous Data

So far we have concluded that experts, adults, and children in all three domains make the exact same range of responses to anomalous data. However, we think that there is an important difference between science and religion at the level of the institution: Scientific institutions permit fundamental changes in beliefs; religious institutions do not. Religious institutions permit, at the most, changes in peripheral conceptions but not changes in core conceptions. Scientific institutions permit theory change, even revolutionary change. The history of science presents many examples of fundamental theory change, such as the shifts from caloric theory of heat to kinetic theory, from phlogiston theory to Lavoisier's oxygen theory, from the fixity of species to Darwinian evolution, and from classical Newtonian physics to quantum mechanics. All of these changes involved changes in core theoretical conceptions, yet the scientists who made these shifts remained respected scientists, fully accepted by their professional institutions.

In many religious institutions, by contrast, fundamental theory change is not tolerated. Religious believers who abandon core conceptions of a religious institution are typically expelled from that institution. After posting his famous theses, Luther was excommunicated from the Roman Catholic Church. Christians who renounce the divinity of Jesus are no longer considered Christians by most Christian churches. Mohammed's teachings met with virulent hostility by contemporary religious institutions. Thus, although a scientist can propose a major theory change and usually remain a respected scientist, a religious expert cannot espouse major changes in religious conceptions without giving up membership in the religious institution. When individuals in a religious institution give up core beliefs, they must break away from that institution and establish or join new ones. Hence, individual conceptual change in religion leads to a proliferation of different religious institutions.

Although religious institutions do not allow members to change core beliefs, they do permit changes in peripheral beliefs. The scope of what is considered a core belief varies from one religious institution to another. Many Christian institutions have permitted individuals to accept much or most of evolutionary theory, but they do not tolerate the abandonment of core conceptions such as a belief in God. Other institutions are much less flexible; creationists who join the Institute for Creation Research are expelled if they deviate from a belief in creationist tenets, which they must affirm in writing as a condition for membership (Godfrey, 1984). By contrast, scientific societies do not require members to affirm creeds before joining.

At the root of the difference between science and religion is that religious institutions are typically organized around a commitment to a particular set of beliefs about the world (e.g., a belief in the Christian Trinity, or the belief that Mohammed was the Seal of the Prophets), whereas most scientific institutions are organized around a commitment to study and explain a particular class of phenomena (biological phenomena, chemical phenomena, etc.) with certain methodological tools. Members of the American Chemical Society are expected to study chemical phenomena, but they are not required to adopt specific theories about these phenomena. Scientists who violate the norms of the institution by choosing to study different phenomena (e.g., the stock market) or by employing nonstandard methodologies (e.g., using a text such as the Bible to establish the age of the earth) are typically not expelled from scientific organizations but, in practice, are socially rejected as working scientists. In religious institutions, social rejection or expulsion can result not only when individuals employ nonstandard methodologies, but also when individuals adopt heretical beliefs about the religious world.

Some observers of science have argued that science is in fact wedded to particular beliefs, such as a commitment to materialism and a rejection of supernaturalism. We think, however, that this view is inconsistent with the history of science, which includes many instances of fundamental changes in ontological beliefs. For instance, in biology there was a shift from a widespread commitment to vitalism (the view that living things contain a special vital force not subject to the laws of physics and chemistry) to the position that no such vital force exists. Acceptance of Newtonian physics involved the acceptance of action at a distance, which had previously been anathema to scientists. And the shift from classical Newtonian physics to quantum mechanics required abandoning foundational beliefs about the nature of causation as well as the nature of matter. All of these beliefs are as fundamental as a belief in materialism. When scientists have found solid evidence that overturns a foundational assumption, they have given up that assumption. We believe that scientists are materialists because they have found no convincing evidence for paranormal phenomena, and if widely replicated evidence for paranormal phenomena existed, scientists would abandon materialism.

## Two Key Factors that Influence Responses to Anomalous Data: Epistemological Commitments and the Ambiguity of Data

Although individuals across the three domains and across different levels of expertise make the same range of responses to anomalous data, this does not mean that all of these individuals reason about anomalous data in the same way. Individuals in different domains, or individuals of different levels of expertise, may differ according to the conditions under which they make a particular response. For instance, experts in science and religion might differ in terms of when they would opt to change theories in response to a particular kind of data or what kind of data they would choose to reject or reinterpret. We turn to this important issue in this section. We examine factors that influence responses to anomalous data, and then we examine how two of these factors may create differences in reasoning across domains and levels of expertise.

Chinn and Brewer (1993a, 1993b, 1998b) proposed that the factors that influence how people respond to new information fall into four clusters: characteristics of the person's prior knowledge, characteristics of the data (if data are presented), characteristics of the new theory (if a theory is presented), and the person's cognitive processing strategies. The factors are displayed and briefly described in Table 12.2. Most of our evidence for the operation of these factors is derived from research in the domain of science (see Chinn & Brewer, 1993a, 1993b).

We think that the factors shown in Table 12.2 can help to explain the differences between science, religion, and magic as well as the differences between institutions, experts, adults, and children. In the remainder of this chapter we will focus on two factors in Table 12.2 that we think are particularly important at illuminating the similarities and differences among domains and levels of expertise. These two factors are epistemological commitments and the ambiguity of data.

Table 12.2. *Factors that Influence Responses to Anomalous Data*

**Characteristics of Prior Knowledge**

*Entrenchment.* Prior knowledge is entrenched to the extent that (a) it is interconnected with other accepted knowledge, (b) it is consistent with a broad range of empirical data, and (c) it helps individuals achieve social goals such as increasing their professional reputations. Entrenched knowledge strongly resists change (Chinn & Brewer, 1993a, 1993b).

*Epistemological commitments.* An individual's epistemological commitments consist of general assumptions about the nature of knowledge and the appropriate grounds for changing or adopting knowledge. Examples include the assumption that conceptions should be consistent with the broadest possible range of data (common in science) and the assumption that conceptions should be aligned with an authoritative holy scripture (common in religion). In science, Chinn and Brewer (1993b) concluded that knowledge change is more likely when individuals are committed to open-mindedness and to a rigorous consistency between theories and data.

*Background knowledge.* Background knowledge refers to knowledge that is not part of the theory currently under consideration. This includes beliefs about methodology as well as beliefs about the world that are not part of the theory under consideration. Background knowledge has obvious effects on how data are evaluated. For instance, different background assumptions about the fossilization process will yield differing interpretations of data involving fossils. Different beliefs about how to set up controls in an experiment will produce different beliefs about whether to reject the results of an experiment.

**Characteristics of New Data**

*Credibility of the data.* New data are more credible to the extent that (a) they come from a credible source, (b) they follow accepted methods of data collection, (c) they are successfully replicated, and (d) they are observed directly. More credible data are less likely to be ignored, rejected, or regarded with uncertainty than less credible data (Chinn & Brewer, 1993b).

*Ambiguity of the data.* Theory change is more likely when the data are unambiguously inconsistent with a theory than when there is a degree of ambiguity. For instance, many children believe that when a solvent and a solute start out at the same temperature, the resulting solution cannot change temperatures. This theory is unambiguously contradicted by a solution reaction in which room temperature reactants become very hot on mixing but is less clearly contradicted by a reaction involving a temperature change of just half a degree.

*Converging lines of data.* Theory change is more likely when there are multiple lines of converging data in support of a theory (Chinn & Brewer, 1993b).

**Characteristics of the New Conceptions**

*Quality of the conceptions.* Alternative theories that exhibit characteristics such as internal consistency, consistency with a broad scope of data, and simplicity are more likely to promote theory change than theories that do not show these characteristics (Chinn & Brewer, 1993b).

*(continued)*

Table 12.2 *(continued)*

---

*Conceptual differences.* When the core components of new conceptions differ in fundamental ways from the core components of old conceptions, theory change is less likely to occur (e.g., Chinn, 1997).

*Explicitness of the conceptions.* Highly explicit explanations of scientific theories promote fundamental theory change (e.g., Chinn 1997), as does telling students about common misconceptions (Guzzetti, Snyder, Glass, & Gamas, 1993).

**Cognitive Processing Strategies**

*Deep processing.* Processing evidence deeply (e.g., thinking carefully about the relationship between different positions and the evidence for them) increases the likelihood of theory change (Eagly & Chaiken, 1993).

*Reasoning strategies.* Epistemological assumptions and specific background beliefs about methodology should translate into reasoning strategies that individuals use when evaluating data or choosing between theories. For instance, background knowledge about the value of conducting controlled experiments should translate into reasoning strategies in which the data from carefully controlled experiments are weighted more strongly than the data from poorly controlled experiments.

---

## Factors that Influence Institutions' Responses to Anomalous Data

At the level of institutions, we argue that here are large differences across the domains of science, religion, and magic in both epistemological commitments and in the ambiguity of data.

*Differences in epistemological commitments.* We think that at the level of the institution, science and religion share some epistemological commitments but differ fundamentally on others. In particular, we think that science is marked by a commitment to exposing theories to data and an insistence on rigorous consistency between theories and data. Religious institutions, by contrast, exhibit epistemological commitments such as deriving knowledge from the interpretation of sacred texts and giving priority to profound spiritual experiences.

*Exposing theories to data.* R. Merton (1942) proposed that one key component of the ethos of science is organized skepticism, according to which scientists are committed to doubting ideas and exposing their theories to data (cf. Popper, 1959). This norm appears to pervade science much more than it does religion. The exposure of theories to data is evident throughout the history of science. Although scientists often fail to expose theories to data as thoroughly as they might (Faust, 1984), they do regularly gather data that have the potential to disconfirm their theories (e.g., Darden, 1991; Giere, 1988).

By contrast, many religions expressly deny that religious ideas can be empirically tested. As John Calvin (1559/1966, p. 166) wrote, "Scripture is indeed self-authenticating; hence, it is not right to subject it to proof and reasoning." Core religious truths are typically viewed as outside the scope of any systematic empirical testing (e.g., Küng, 1978) and sometimes are even viewed as outside the bounds of reason. Zen Buddhism denies that enlightenment can be understood in rational terms (Suzuki, 1959), and Christians such as Tertullian, Luther, and Kierkegaard regarded Christian articles of faith as beliefs that are contrary to reason (see Kaufmann, 1961, p. 114). Sometimes religious institutions deny that it is possible for religious tenets to be contradicted by data. According to Aquinas (1274/1952), "Whatsoever is found in other sciences contrary to any truth of this [theology], must be condemned as false" (p. 6). More recently, Morris (1970), a leader of the creationist movement, wrote, "No geological difficulties, real or imagined, can be allowed to take precedence over the clear statements and necessary inferences of Scripture" (p. 33). Although more liberal religious institutions do not take such a strict stance, it seems to us that even these institutions do not encourage their members to go out and gather data that have the potential to overturn core beliefs.

*Rigorous consistency.* Science and religion both appear to seek broad consistency between data and conceptions, but they appear to do so in very different ways. Science seeks ever more precise theories that encompass an increasingly broad array of data. Religion often seems to accommodate data by developing theories flexible enough to be consistent with almost any data that could occur. Unlike scientific explanations, religious explanations and paranormal explanations posit mechanisms with an essentially unlimited range of effects. For instance, plate tectonics predicts slow, gradual continental shifts but would be unambiguously inconsistent with evidence of rapid continental shifts. Evolutionary theory would be flatly contradicted by evidence that humans were contemporaries of Precambrian life forms. By contrast, deities and psychic forces are almost unlimited in the effects that are consistent with their operation. As a mechanism for raising mountains, the direct action of a deity is equally consistent with mountains rising over millions of years and mountains rising within a week. Similarly, the hypothesis that Providence guides events is consistent with any kind of outcome. A narrow escape from an accident on a highway can be a result of divine intervention, yet so can a crash on the same highway. Both can be interpreted as part of an unknown divine plan. Divine mechanisms that can have any effect whatsoever are indeed broadly consistent with a wide range of data, but they are so imprecisely specified that they are not disconfirmable by data.

*Analyzing sacred texts.* Religious knowledge is often developed and transformed through interpreting and reinterpreting sacred scriptures (cf. Küng, 1978). This epistemological principle is very evident in creationist writings. Clark (1968) wrote, "The Bible must not be judged by men's ideas of science, for scientific theories come and go; on the other hand the Word of God abides forever, and human theories must be brought to the unerring standard of the Word" (p. 19). Morris (1974, p. 15) stated, "It is precisely because Biblical revelation is absolutely authoritative and perspicuous that the scientific facts, rightly interpreted, will give the same testimony as that of Scripture." These creationist sentiments are shared by more traditional theologians. Aquinas (1264/1955) stated that "the sole way to overcome an adversary of divine truth is from the authority of Scripture. . . ."(p. 77). Karl Barth (1936) argued that the Bible is the means through which believers encounter God. Muslims believe that the Koran is authoritative as the Word of God (Guillaume, 1954). Even if believers do not take holy scriptures literally, there are core scriptural ideas that cannot be denied. Even very liberal Christian theologians retain the belief that there is something special about Jesus (e.g., Tillich, 1957; see also Kaufmann, 1961). In contrast to the importance of studying scriptures in religion, most current scientists have probably not even read the original writings of great scientists such as Newton, Lavoisier, and Darwin.

*The primacy of intense spiritual experiences.* In many religious traditions, intense spiritual experiences are given priority as sources of knowledge. These experiences are often interpreted as providing direct information about spiritual reality. Many sacred texts appear to be accepted as authoritative precisely because they are believed to be the direct result of divine encounters. For example, according to the Old Testament, Moses received the ten commandments in a direct encounter with God. Mohammed asserted that the Koran was given to him through divine revelation. Mormons believe that the founder of their religion, Joseph Smith, was directed by a heavenly messenger to a set of thin metal plates from which he translated the *Book of Mormon*. Some religious institutions expect individual members to continue to receive revealed knowledge through such direct spiritual encounters. The Quaker Robert Barclay wrote that God continues to give revelations to people, and these divine revelations cannot be subjected to the test of either scripture of reason: "For this divine revelation and inward illumination, is that which is evident and clear of itself, forcing, by its own evidence and clearness, the well-disposed understanding to assent. . . ." (Barclay, n.d., p. 28). Many practitioners of mysticism in a variety of religions believe that their experiences provide direct insights into a deeper reality (see Kaufmann, 1961; Suzuki, 1959).

The belief that direct revelatory experiences are to be accepted as truth is not shared by members of scientific institutions. Scientists cannot justify their claims on the grounds that they have had the correct theory revealed to them in some way. As a scientist, Newton could not argue that his theory of gravitation was true because God had revealed the theory to him. Rather, he had to show that the theory was supported by the available empirical data. Scientific institutions do not trust feelings of certainty based on personal experiences that others cannot observe. Indeed, scientists are even skeptical of their own sensory observations, often devising methods to gather data mechanically or to double-check sensory observations so as to be sure that individual observations are reliable.

*Differences in the ambiguity of data.* At the level of the institution, we think that a fundamental difference among the three domains is that only in science are data sufficiently unambiguous to permit empirically grounded choices between theories. In religion and the paranormal, data are so ambiguous that choices between theories are largely arbitrary, or they are based on social influences or personal beliefs rather than constraints imposed by the external world. This is not to say that social influences and personal beliefs do not play a role in science, but only that scientific conceptions are more constrained by data than conceptions in the other two domains (see Chinn, 1998).

We believe that three lines of evidence show that science is grounded in unambiguous empirical data in ways that religion and the paranormal are not: (a) the existence of widespread consensus among scientists; (b) the convergence of scientific results using independent methods; and (c) the progress of science.

*Consensus.* The first line of evidence that distinguishes science from the other domains is the existence of widespread consensus among scientists but not among religious experts or paranormal theorists. Scientists throughout the world are in near unanimous agreement about scientific ideas such as the principles of electromagnetism, the basic structure of DNA, and plate tectonics. This widespread consensus transcends national boundaries and cultural identities. Chinese physics is the same as Venezuelan physics. Moreover, the achievement of consensus in science is often astonishingly rapid, as when researchers investigating the structure of DNA rapidly accepted the double-helix structure proposed by Watson and Crick (S. Cole, 1992). In the domain of religion, there is nothing even approaching this uniformity of views or the rapid forging of consensus. Even on such basic issues as whether a deity exists, major religions disagree. Moreover, differences among religions have persisted for millennia and show no signs of moving toward a single consensus. A similar proliferation of theories exists in the domain of the paranormal. Theories of the cause of supernatural effects range from witchcraft and spiritual possession to hyperspace forces and quantum mechanics, with no consensus in sight (e.g., Gardner, 1985).

It seems to us that the best explanation for the greater consensus of science is that scientific knowledge is grounded in data in a way that religious knowledge and paranormal knowledge are not. Chinese physics is the same as Venezuelan physics because both are grounded in a common basis of reliable data. Chinese religions differ from Venezuelan religions because there is no such common core of data that constrains religious beliefs. This does not mean, of course, that the relationship between theory and data in science is one of simple correspondence, but it does mean that scientific knowledge is shaped in part by reliable empirical results.

*Convergence.* A second argument for a more decisive role of data in science than in religion is that in science there is often a dramatic convergence of empirical results using different methodologies and background assumptions. For instance, scientists' confidence in their estimate of the age of the earth is boosted by the fact that several different dating methods relying on different background assumptions all yield similar results (see Miller, 1984). One method is based on a set of assumptions about the decay of uranium into lead. A second method employs a different set of background assumptions about the decay of rubidium to strontium. A third method is based on the amount of meteor dust deposited on the moon over time. All of these methods are quite different and employ very different assumptions, yet they all yield essentially the same result.

Another example is provided by Salmon (1984), who discusses the work of the French chemist Perrin. In a 1914 book, Perrin summarized research aimed at determining Avogadro's number, the number of molecules in a mole of a substance. Fourteen different methods, employing different approaches and background assumptions, all converged on the same value of Avogadro's number. Such convergences are not found in the domain of religion. Different theologians using different methods do not converge on the same characteristics of a deity or the same conclusions about what happens after death. In the same way, writings on the paranormal have not yielded robust findings using a single method, let alone robust findings using multiple methods (Hansel, 1985).

*Progress.* A third line of evidence for the greater role of unambiguous data in science than in religion or the paranormal is that science has progressed in a way that religion and the paranormal have not during the past 500 years. The progress of science has manifested itself in two ways – the increased precision of prediction and the greater capacity for successful technological interventions. Increased prediction is seen in such instances as the precise prediction of the half-life of radioactive elements, the prediction of the exact temperature resulting from a chemical reaction, and the prediction of the effects of a particular hormone on embryonic growth. The greater capacity for intervention is evident in a wide variety of arenas, from placing an unmanned spaceship on Mars to improving crops through gene splicing. It does not seem to us that there has been a comparable increase in prediction or in the power of intervention in religion or the paranormal. This claim is strengthened in the comparison of science with religion by the observation that religious writers sometimes call for a return to the purity of the religious practices of early days, such as the early days of Christianity or the original practices of Gautama. There is no comparable call by scientists to hearken back to the pure science of Aristotle or Galileo. This suggests that many religious believers themselves have a sense that although history may have brought change, it has not necessarily brought progress.

Together, these arguments strongly suggest that data in science are sufficiently clear to disambiguate competing theories whereas data in religion and the paranormal are not.

## The Relationship Between Institutions and Experts

At the level of institutions, we have found major differences both in epistemological commitments and in the degree to which data permit relatively unambiguous choices among conceptions in the domains of science and religion. What do these differences imply for individual experts? In other words, what is the relationship between institutional reasoning and individual reasoning?

One possibility is that the reasoning of individuals mirrors the reasoning of the institution, so that individual scientists reason differently from experts in religion and the paranormal. We think that this is partly correct. Individual scientists do expose their theories to data in their regular practice of conducting experiments in a way that religious experts do not in their everyday practices. Individual experts in religion consult authoritative scriptures; individual scientists consider their classic texts to be targets for revision.

A second possible relationship between individual and institutional reasoning is that the features of reasoning seen at the institutional level are emergent properties that appear only partially at the individual level. For example, the institutions of science may operate so as to require scientists to make theories more consistent with data than they would if there were no institutional pressures (e.g., peer review). Solomon (1992) presented a historical analysis that provides some support for this view. Solomon studied geologists' views of the theory of continental drift during the middle part of this century and found that the geologists paid the most attention to data with which they were personally familiar. For instance, geologists who had not personally seen the close match between geological strata on the coast of South America and the corresponding strata on the coast of Africa were less likely to accept continental drift than scientists who had personally seen these strata. Geologists chose the theory that was consistent with the data that were most salient to them, rather than to all of the data. The institutional pressure to increase the consistency between theory and all known data comes from publications, conferences, and the review process, all of which combine to require scientists to take a fuller range of data into account.

This analysis suggests that some of the features of reasoning that appear at the level of scientific and religious institutions derive from differences in individual experts' reasoning, whereas other features of reasoning arise partly at the level of the institution. Scientists reason differently from experts in religion and the paranormal, but some characteristic features of expert reasoning emerge more strongly at the institutional level.

We think that experts in the domain of the paranormal differ from experts in science and religion on at least two epistemological commitments. Unlike scientists, experts in the paranormal do not appear to systematically expose their conceptions to data. For instance, most psychics are unwilling to have their claims tested by magicians, who are expert at detecting psychic fraud (Brandon, 1983; Randi, 1985). Unlike many religious experts, most experts in the paranormal do not appear to derive knowledge claims from analyses of authoritative texts. Rather, experts in the paranormal appear to focus on attempting to account for unusual empirical phenomena using psychic explanations. We are unsure about whether experts in the paranormal share either of the other two epistemological commitments that we have discussed. Paranormal experts do seem to seek consistency between theories and data, but we are unsure about whether they are as committed to rigorous consistency as scientists are. We are similarly unsure about whether paranormal experts give epistemological priority to intense personal experiences as some religious experts do.

### Factors that Influence Adults' and Children's Responses to Anomalous Data

In this section we discuss how epistemology and ambiguity of the data influence the responses of children and adults to anomalous data.

#### Epistemological commitments.

*Exposing conceptions to data*: In science, it appears to us that children engage only in limited forms of exposing conceptions to data. Young children sometimes engage in exploratory behavior directed at finding out how the world works. Much of this behavior seems directed at establishing generalizations about phenomena, such as the generalizations that dropped objects fall, that magnets stick to metal, or that lights turn on when the switch is turned. Children do not appear to test deeper explanatory conceptions such as the nature of electricity or explanatory theories of color-change reactions. Moreover, their explorations seem limited to only a subset of their conceptions. Although many children believe that sweaters actively produce heat (as opposed to passively retaining body heat), children rarely, if ever, test this belief unless prompted to do so by a teacher. Active testing by adults also appears to be rare.

Except for some exploratory behaviors in children, both children and adults often seem to *apply* their scientific ideas instead of actively *testing* them. That is, if adults believe that turning up the heat on the stove makes water boil at a higher temperature, then when they turn up the stove, they will simply assume, without checking, that the temperature of the water is higher. Sometimes such applications will produce anomalous data. But often, unless systematic measurements are made, the results of the application will not obviously conflict with expectations, and no anomaly will be noted.

In religion, we are not aware of any evidence of exploration analogous to children's exploratory science, but there is some evidence that believers apply some conceptions in a way that can lead to disconfirmation. At least some children and adolescents find unanswered prayers to conflict with their prior beliefs about prayer or about God (Ganzevoort, 1994; Oser et al., 1994). Perhaps some children go so far as to test the efficacy of prayer by asking for something special, which would count as exposing conceptions to data. However, as in science, we suspect that individuals are much more likely to apply religious ideas than to test them in any systematic way.

In the domain of magic, we are unsure about whether children actively test magical beliefs. It is possible that children experiment systematically with wishing for objects to materialize, but we do not know of any research on this issue. Similarly, there appears to be a lack of research on the issue of whether adults ever conduct tests on themselves to see if they have psychic powers.

*Rigorous consistency*: Reif and Larkin (1991) argued that a central difference between everyday reasoning by nonscientist adults and children and reasoning by scientists is that nonscientists are content when they obtain local consistency between conceptions and data, whereas scientists aim for a much more rigorous consistency. Recent studies have shown that children do prefer hypotheses that are more consistent with the presented data (e.g., Ruffman, Perner, Olson, & Doherty, 1993; Samarapungavan, 1992). However, these studies present students with two or three pieces of data and two hypotheses to choose between and do not demonstrate any broader search for consistency. Studies of children who are given the task of conducting experiments in a more complex, multivariate environment indicate that children rarely engage in systematic attempts to make their conclusions consistent with all of the evidence gathered (Penner & Klahr, 1996; Schauble, 1996). When children make valid inferences, their inferences are usually restricted to the experiment just conducted and do not integrate results across experiments. Adults are more systematic in these environments (Schauble, 1996). This suggests that children do not actively strive for rigorous consistency but that adults show an increase in attempting to establish consistency between theories and data. Whether adults' behavior in laboratory studies extends to everyday reasoning is unclear.

A body of research on everyday reasoning provides mixed results on whether children and adults seek rigorous consistency. Studies of children's mental models of the earth's shape (Vosniadou & Brewer, 1992), the day/night cycle (Vosniadou & Brewer, 1994), and speciation (Samarapungavan & Wiers, 1997) show that children develop highly coherent theories that are fully consistent with data known to them. Other studies in the domains of physics (Krist, Fieberg, & Wilkening, 1993; Yates et al., 1988) and chemistry (Chinn, 1997) suggest that there are often inconsistencies in the models of children and adults. This line of research suggests that children and adults sometimes, but not always, manage a moderate degree of consistency between theories and data in science. More research is needed to investigate the extent of consistency in science as well as the other two domains and to determine why the degree of consistency varies from topic to topic.

*Analyzing sacred texts*: Many nonexpert adults share the commitment of religious institutions to making knowledge consistent with sacred texts. For instance, many fundamentalist Christians believe that the Bible is literally true and actively study it. We are not aware of any research on the origins of this epistemological commitment, but it seems probable to us that children learn this epistemological commitment from their parents and from participation in religious institutions.

*Ambiguity of data.* In this section we analyze whether children and adults in the three domains typically encounter ambiguous or unambiguous data.

*Science.* In science, we propose that the developmental trajectory follows these steps: (a) In preschool and early school years, children encounter everyday data that are relatively unambiguous and lead them to develop naive conceptions of natural phenomena. (b) In school, students are presented with data that are often ambiguous and do not decisively favor the scientific theory over their naive conceptions. (c) Students who adopt the scientific theories, or approximations of those theories, do so when they decide that the scientific theory explains the everyday data as well as (not necessarily better than) their naive conceptions. Their knowledge changes are not based on unambiguous data.

There is compelling evidence that supports the position that, prior to instruction, children encounter unambiguous everyday data that powerfully constrain the development of naive theories about some topics. Most striking is the similarity of naive, preinstructional conceptions across children and across cultures. On many topics in the physical and biological sciences, researchers have found that children in different cultures devise nearly identical preinstructional conceptions, which are very different from the conceptions encountered later in school. For example, prior to instruction, children in the United States (Vosniadou & Brewer, 1992), Israel (Nussbaum, 1979), Nepal (Mali & Howe, 1979), and Greece (Vosniadou & Brewer, 1990) develop the theory that the earth is flat. Children in the United States (Chinn, 1997), Scotland (Driver, 1985), and the Netherlands (de Vos & Verdonk, 1987) believe that the smallest bits of a substance become hot as the substance as a whole gets hot. Children in the United States (Rosen & Rozin, 1993), England (Driver, 1985), and Xhosa-speaking sections of South Africa (Slone & Bokhurst, 1992) develop the conception that invisible bits of sugar remain in water as sugar dissolves. Children throughout the world think that heavy objects fall faster than light objects (Driver et al., 1994, p. 166).

The uniformity of these preinstructional conceptions across cultures together with the fact that these conceptions are frequently inconsistent with adult beliefs, strongly suggests that children develop their conceptions on the basis of observational data that are unambiguous with respect to the alternative theories available to children. Because the available observational data are similar across cultures, children in different cultures arrive at very similar conceptions. These conceptions later promote predictable misinterpretations of scientific conceptions encountered during instruction, and these misinterpretations again show remarkable consistency across cultures (see Driver et al., 1994). As one example, children in Sweden (Andersson, 1986), the Netherlands (de Vos & Verdonk, 1987), and the United States (Chinn, 1997) all develop the idea that molecules of a substance have the same properties as the overall substance (e.g., molecules of iron are hard and molecules of water are tiny drops of water). As a second example, children in the United States (Vosniadou & Brewer, 1992), Israel (Nussbaum, 1979), Nepal (Mali & Howe, 1979), and Greece (Vosniadou & Brewer, 1990) develop a similar range of models in response to instruction about the earth's shape. For instance, some children develop the notion that there are two earths, a flat one that people live on and a round one up in the sky, and some develop the notion that the earth is round like a hollowed-out pumpkin, with people living on the flat surface at the base of the inside of the hollow sphere.

There is strong evidence, then, that unambiguous observational data lead children to construct naive conceptions that are very similar across cultures. However, later in school, when students learn about scientific conceptions, we think that schools seldom present evidence that decisively favors the new theory they are learning about. Whereas preinstructional data were unambiguous, instructional data are much more ambiguous.

Four arguments suggest that students do not encounter unambiguous data in school in support of the scientific theories that they are learning (see also Chinn, 1998). First, in many cases, little evidence is presented at all. When evolutionary theory is taught at all in U.S. schools, it is frequently presented as a theoretical structure with very little if any data to support it (e.g., J. Cole, 1983). Second, the data presented to children are often merely suggestive of the new theory. For instance, classroom experiments showing phenomena involving heat exchange can be reconciled with a naive theory that treats heat as a flowing substance; these experiments do not unambiguously support the kinetic theory of heat and temperature. Third, data gathered by students in science laboratories are often highly ambiguous. Because of student error or imprecise laboratory equipment, students in science labs often fail to get the results that they are expected to get (Pickering & Monts, 1982). Far from providing clear evidence to support the scientific theory, the data often actually contradict the theory! Finally, the data that convinced scientists to support a theory are often too technical for students to understand. If a middle-school teacher wants to present evidence for continental drift theory, the teacher cannot present the detailed technical data on the magnetic profiles of seafloor sediments, which were decisive in convincing scientists that the continents have moved, because these data are too complex for middle-school students to understand. Instead, the teacher can only present evidence such as the similarity of coastal fossils in Africa and South America, the similarity in geological strata at the coasts, and the general fit of the outlines of the two continents. But these are just the data that scientists found ambiguous for decades, until the magnetic profile data were reported.

All of these arguments suggest that knowledge change among science students at school often occurs without the benefit of clear, unambiguous data. Science students – both children and adults – appear willing to believe scientific theories on the basis of trusting science authorities, even when they observe no data that decisively favors the scientific theory over their naive theory. Chinn (1998) proposed that science students resist the new ideas until they see how the new ideas are at least compatible with the everyday data that led to their naive theories. Then, once they see that the new theory is at least *as good as* the old theory for everyday data, they are willing to accept the new theory without decisive evidence showing it *superior* to the old theory.

If our proposal is correct, it is ironic that children come to believe conceptions regarded as scientifically incorrect on the basis of observational data but come to believe the accepted scientific conceptions on the basis of trusting authority! Although the scientific conceptions are themselves based on a decisive body of data, students may come to accept these theories without themselves seeing decisive evidence. Further research is needed to explore this interesting paradox.

*Religion.* In the domain of religion, we hypothesize that religious data are ambiguous at all ages and levels of expertise. In contrast with science, there is no evidence that children develop culture-independent religious conceptions. Children in Taoist communities do not develop the same naive religious conceptions as children raised in Muslim communities. This suggests that the empirical pressure toward particular naive conceptions that is found in science does not occur in religion.

One could argue that children and adults do have personal religious experiences that unambiguously point to a transcendent reality (cf. Wall, 1995), even though the experiences might be ambiguous with respect to different religious interpretations of what that transcendent reality is. Indeed, both children and adults report having religious experiences such as feeling the presence of God (Tamminen, 1994). Alternatively, children might spontaneously invent religious conceptions in response to existential issues that they face, such as the death of a loved one or uncertainty about the future. An interesting test of this hypothesis would be to investigate whether children (or even adults) raised without any exposure to religious instruction nonetheless develop naive religious conceptions. We are unaware of any studies on this important issue.

Boyer and Walker (this volume) have convincingly shown that there is a striking cross-cultural commonality among religious conceptions, so that religious conceptions involve violations of elements of naive biology, naive physics, and naive psychology. At first glance, this might suggest that there is a body of unambiguous religious data that leads to these cross-cultural commonalities. However, we think that the commonalities in these conceptions are not based on religious data. Rather, the commonalities are based on cross-cultural similarities that arise in naive biology, naive physics, and naive psychology. The uniquely religious part of the conceptions (e.g., exactly which characteristics of a deity represent violations of naive psychology) are the parts that diverge across cultures. So we think that there are no unambiguous data to guide religious believers in the decision of how to modify naive science and naive psychology to generate characteristics of supernatural beings.

*Magic/paranormal.* In the domain of magic, it is possible that children's conceptions of whether data are ambiguous may undergo a change. Young children may regard magical tricks as unambiguous evidence for paranormal magic. Later, when children realize that some magical events are tricks, they may come to decide that all evidence for magic is fundamentally ambiguous, because any apparent display of magic could be a trick. If this analysis is correct, then there is an interesting difference between children, adults, and experts. A common response by paranormal believers (including adults and experts) when a famous psychic has been caught cheating is to admit that the psychic sometimes cheats but to argue that the psychic demonstrates real powers on occasions when cheating is not detected (Brandon, 1983). If children reasoned in this way, they would conclude that magic tricks are real magic on any occasion when they cannot identify the trick. Instead, it appears that children may reason more like scientists, who tend to conclude that identifying a psychic's trick on several occasions suggests that all similar events produced by the psychic are tricks.

## Summary and Conclusions

In this chapter we have argued that anomalous data play an important role in knowledge change in the domains of science, religion, and magic. Data appear to play a more prominent role in science than in the other two fields. Religion, in particular, exhibits many sources of knowledge change beyond data, including revelation and finding new ways to meet existential concerns. But data do play a significant role in religion as well as the other two domains.

We have investigated differences in how anomalous data influence knowledge change across all three domains and across different levels of expertise. We first examined the range of responses made to anomalous data. We concluded that experts, adults, and children in all three domains make the *exact same* range of responses to anomalous data. At the level of the institution, however, fundamental theory change is permitted in most scientific institutions but not in religious institutions.

Next we analyzed the factors that influence how institutions and individuals respond to anomalous data. We focused on two factors in particular, epistemological commitments and the extent to which data in a domain are ambiguous. Our conclusions are summarized in Table 12.3.

One important overall conclusion is that some epistemological principles of science are unique to scientists and the institution of science. Scientists and their institutions are committed to exposing conceptions to data and to seeking a rigorous consistency between theories and data. These commitments are not shared by religious experts or paranormal experts, nor do they appear to be held by children or adults in any of the three domains.

Two noteworthy epistemological commitments of many religious institutions (giving priority to sacred texts and to immediate revelatory experiences) appear to be shared by adults, although probably not by children. We did not identify any unique epistemological standards in the domain of the paranormal.

Our analysis suggests that children and adults apply many of the same epistemological standards in all three domains. Children, in particular, probably use the same set of general-purpose reasoning strategies across the three different domains. Experts, by contrast, use quite different reasoning across the domains.

There are important differences in the degree of ambiguity of data typically encountered in the different domains. At the level of the institution, data are much less ambiguous in the domain of science than in the other two domains. This leads to conceptions that are much more tightly constrained by empirical data than either of the

Table 12.3. *Differences in Epistemological Commitments and Ambiguity of the Data Across Domain and Level of Expertise*

| | Domains | | |
| --- | --- | --- | --- |
| | Science | Religion | Magic/Paranormal |
| Institutions | Science is marked by distinctive epistemological commitments, including exposing theories to data and seeking rigorous consistency between data and theories that are as precise as possible. Scientific data are often sufficiently unambiguous to permit clear choices between rival theories. | Religion is often characterized by epistemological commitments to granting authority to sacred texts and to accepting the authority of revelatory experiences. Data in the domain of religion are relatively ambiguous, which makes for a lack of consensus in religion. | [Powerful institutions do not exist in this domain.] |
| Experts | Experts in science and religion tend to share the epistemological commitments of their institutions, although some characteristic epistemological features may emerge more strongly at the level of the institution. | | Experts in the paranormal do not appear to share core epistemological principles of either science or religion. |
| Adults and older children | Adults and older children do not share the epistemological standards of scientists, but some may adopt the epistemological standards of religious institutions. Data for adults are relatively ambiguous in all three domains, even in science, because the data known to adults often do not decisively support one theory over another. | | |
| Children | Children do not employ the epistemological standards of either scientists or religious experts. Instead, children apply domain-general reasoning strategies across all three domains. In science, the application of domain-general reasoning strategies yields scientific conceptions that are common across cultural experiences because the data known to children tend to be unambiguous with respect to the available theories. The same domain-general reasoning strategies applied to the other domains do not lead to common conceptions across cultures because of the greater ambiguity of the available data. | | |

other two domains. In science, but not in religion, children encounter data that unambiguously lead them to construct naive theories that are remarkably similar across cultures. In both science and religion, older children and adults choose to adopt new conceptions largely by trusting authorities. In science as well as religion, the data encountered by students during instruction do not appear to unambiguously support new conceptions over old ones.

Taken together, our conclusions are directly opposed to those who argue that experts in different domains, including scientists, share the same epistemological standards. Our analysis points to large differences in the epistemological standards, methodological principles, and types of theories developed. These differences are particularly evident in the contrast between evolutionists and creationists. Evolutionists and creationists do not simply differ in their theoretical positions; they also disagree at the level of epistemological principles for generating and evaluating knowledge claims.

Our conclusions also conflict with the claim that the reasoning of children and the reasoning of scientists are fundamentally the same. Scientific conceptions of the natural world are developed through the application of domain-specific epistemological standards, at least some of which are not shared by children. These standards appear to be learned through specific training within the social institutions of science. Children's conceptions of the natural world are developed through the application of general cross-domain reasoning strategies.

## Acknowledgments

We thank C. Daniel Batson and the editors for helpful comments on an earlier version of this chapter.

## References

Anderson, B. (1986). Pupils' explanations of some aspects of chemical reactions. *Science Education, 70,* 549–563.

Aquinas, T. (1952). *The Summa Theologica Vol. 1 (Great Books of the Western World. Vol. 19).* Chicago: Encyclopaedia Britannica. (Original work published 1274)

Aquinas, T. (1955). *On the Truth of the Catholic Faith: Summa Contra Gentiles. Book One: God* (A. C. Pegic, Trans.). Garden City, NY: Doubleday. (Original work published 1264)

Barclay, R. (n.d.). *An Apology for the True Christian Divinity: Being an Explana-*

tion of the Principles and Doctrines of the People Called Quakers. Philadelphia: Friends' Book Store. (Original work published 1676).

Barth, K. (1936). *The Doctrine of the Word of God. Vol. 1. Part 1. Prolegomenon to Church Dogmatics.* (G. T. Thomson, Trans.). Edinburgh: T. & T. Clark.

Batson, C. D. (1975). Rational processing or rationalization?: The effect of disconfirming information on a stated religious belief. *Journal of Personality and Social Psychology, 32,* 176–84.

Batson, C. D., Schoenrade, P., & Ventis, W. L. (1993). *Religion and the Individual: A Social-Psychological Perspective.* New York: Oxford University Press.

Brandon, R. (1983). *The Spiritualists: The Passion for the Occult in the Nineteenth and Twentieth Centuries.* New York: Alfred A. Knopf.

Brewer, W. F., & Chinn, C. A. (1994). Scientists' responses to anomalous data: Evidence from psychology, history, and philosophy of science. *PSA 1994, 1,* 304–13.

Brock, T. C., & Balloun, J. L. (1967). Behavioral receptivity to dissonant information. *Journal of Personality and Social Psychology, 6,* 413–28.

Burris, C. T., Harmon-Jones, E., & Tarpley, W. R. (1997). "By faith alone": Religious agitation and cognitive dissonance. *Basic and Applied Social Psychology, 19,* 17–31.

Calvin, J. (1966). How do we know God? (extracted from *Institutes of the Christian Religion,* J. T. McNeill, Trans.). In: H. T. Kerr (Ed.), *Reading in Christian Thought,* (pp. 164–66). Nashville, TN: Abingdon. (Original work published 1559).

Chinn, C. A (1997). *A microgenetic study of learning about the molecular theory of matter and chemical reactions.* Unpublished doctoral dissertation. University of Illinois at Urbana-Champaign.

Chinn, C. A. (1998). A critique of social constructivist explanations of knowledge change. In: B. Guzzetti and C. Hynd (Eds.), *Perspectives on Conceptual Change: Multiple Ways to Understand Knowing and Learning in a Complex World,* (pp. 77–115). Mahwah, NJ: Erlbaum.

Chinn, C. A., & Brewer, W. F. (1992). Psychological responses to anomalous data. *Proceedings of the Fourteenth Annual Conference of the Cognitive Science Society,* (pp. 165–70). Hillsdale, NJ: Erlbaum.

Chinn, C. A., & Brewer, W. F. (1993a). Factors that influence how people respond to anomalous data. *Proceedings of the Fifteenth Annual Conference of the Cognitive Science Society,* (pp. 318–23). Hillsdale, NJ: Erlbaum.

Chinn, C. A., & Brewer, W. F. (1993b). The role of anomalous data in knowledge acquisition: A theoretical framework and implications for science instruction. *Review of Educational Research, 63,* 1–49.

Chinn, C. A., & Brewer, W. F. (1998a). An empirical test of a taxonomy of responses to anomalous data in science. *Journal of Research in Science Teaching, 35,* 623–54.

Chinn, C. A., & Brewer, W. F. (1998b). Theories of knowledge acquisition. In: B. J. Fraser and K. G. Tobin (Eds.), *International Handbook of Science Education,* (Part 1, pp. 97–113). Dordrecht: Kluwer Academic Publishers.

Clark, H. W. (1968). *Fossils, Flood and Fire.* Escondido, CA: Outdoor Picture.

Cole, J. R. (1983). Scopes and beyond: Antievolutionism and American culture.

In: L. R. Godfrey (Ed.). *Scientists Confront Creationism*, (pp. 13–32). New York: W. W. Norton.

Cole, S. (1992). *Making Science: Between Nature and Society*. Cambridge, MA: Harvard University Press.

Darden, L. (1991). *Theory Change in Science: Strategies from Mendelian Genetics*. New York: Oxford University Press.

Darwin, C. (1964). *On the Origin of Species* (facsimile of first edition, Ernst Mayr, Ed.). Cambridge: Harvard University Press. (Original work published 1859).

Dennett, M. R. (1994). America's most famous psychic sleuth: Dorothy Allison. In: J. Nickell (Ed.), *Psychic Sleuths: ESP and Sensational Cases*, (pp. 42–59). Buffalo, NY: Prometheus Books.

de Vos, W., & Verdonk, A. H. (1987). A new road to reactions. Part 4. The substance and its molecules. *Journal of Chemical Education, 64*, 692–94.

Driver, R. (1985). Beyond appearances: The conservation of matter under physical and chemical transformations. In: R. Driver, E. Guesne, and A. Tiberghien (Eds.), *Children's Ideas in Science*, (pp. 145–69). Milton Keynes, England: Open University Press.

Driver, R., Squires, A., Rushworth, P., & Wood-Robinson, V. (1994). *Making Sense of Secondary Science: Research into Children's Ideas*. London: Routledge.

Dunbar, R. (1995). *The Trouble with Science*. London: Faber and Faber.

Eagly, A. H., & Chaiken, S. (1993). *The Psychology of Attitudes*. Fort Worth, TX: Harcourt Brace Jovanovich.

Eldredge, N., & Gould, S. J. (1972). Punctuated equilibria: An alternative to phyletic gradualism. In: T. J. M. Schopf (Eds.), *Models of Paleobiology*, (pp. 82–115). San Francisco: Freeman, Cooper.

Faust, D. (1984). *The Limits of Scientific Reasoning*. Minneapolis, MN: University of Minnesota Press.

Festinger, L., Riecken, H. W., & Schachter, S. (1956). *When Prophecy Fails*. Minneapolis, MN: University of Minnesota Press.

Ganzevoort, R. R. (1994). Crisis experiences and the development of belief and unbelief. In: J. Coryeleyn and D. Hutsebaut (Eds.), *Belief and Unbelief: Psychological Perspectives*, (pp. 21–36). Amsterdam: Rodopi.

Gardner, M. (1985). Parapsychology and quantum mechanics. In: P. Kurtz (Ed.), *A Skeptic's Handbook of Parapsychology*, (pp. 585–98). Buffalo, NY: Prometheus Books.

Giere, R. N. (1988). *Explaining Science: A Cognitive Approach*. Chicago: University of Chicago Press.

Godfrey, L. R. (1984). Scientific creationism: The art of distortion. In: A. Montagu (Ed.), *Science and Creationism*, (pp. 167–81). Oxford: Oxford University Press.

Godfrey, L., & Cole, J. (1987). A century after Darwin: Scientific creationism and academe. In: F. B. Harrold and R. A. Eve (Eds.), *Cult Archaeology and Creationism*, (pp. 99–123). Iowa City, IA: University of Iowa Press.

Gould, S. J. (1989). *Wonderful Life: The Burgess Shale and the Nature of History*. New York: W. W. Norton.

Gray, T. (1987). Educational experience and belief in paranormal phenomena. In: F. B. Harrold and R. A. Eve (Eds.), *Cult Archaeology and Creationism*, (pp. 21–33). Iowa City, IA: University of Iowa Press.

Guillaume, A. (1954). *Islam*. Harmondsworth, England: Penguin Books.

Guzzetti, B. J., Snyder, T. E., Glass, G. V., & Gamas, W. S. (1993). Promoting conceptual change in science: A comparative meta-analysis of instructional interventions from reading education and science education. *Reading Research Quarterly, 28*, 116–55.

Hansel, C. E. M. (1985). The search for a demonstration of ESP. In: P. Kurtz (Ed.), *A Skeptic's Handbook of Parapsychology*, (pp. 97–127). Buffalo, NY: Prometheus Books.

Hyman, R. (1985). A critical historical overview of parapsychology. In: P. Kurtz (Ed.), *A Skeptic's Handbook of Parapsychology*, (pp. 3–96). Buffalo, NY: Prometheus Books.

Kaufmann, W. (1961). *Critique of Religion and Philosophy*. Garden City, NY: Doubleday.

Krist, H., Fieberg, E. L., & Wilkening, F. (1993). Intuitive physics in action and judgment: The development of knowledge about projectile motion. *Journal of Experimental Psychology: Learning, Memory, and Cognition, 19*, 952–66.

Kuhn, T. S. (1962). *The Structure of Scientific Revolutions*. Chicago: University of Chicago Press.

Küng, H. (1978). *Does God Exist? An Answer for Today*. New York: Crossroad.

Kurtz, P. (1985). Spiritualists, mediums, and psychics: Some evidence of fraud. In: P. Kurtz (Ed.), *A Skeptic's Handbook of Parapsychology*, (pp. 177–223). Buffalo, NY: Prometheus Books.

Lawson, A. E., & Worsnop, W. A. (1992). Learning about evolution and rejecting a belief in special creation: Effects of reflective reasoning skill, prior knowledge, prior belief and religious commitment. *Journal of Research in Science Teaching, 29*, 143–66.

Livingstone, D. N. (1987). *Darwin's Forgotten Defenders: The Encounter Between Evangelical Theology and Evolutionary Thought*. Grand Rapids, MI: Wm. B. Eerdmans Publishing.

Mali, G. B., & Howe, A. (1979). Development of earth and gravity concepts among Nepali children. *Science Education, 63*, 685–91.

McGowan, C. (1984). *In the Beginning . . . A Scientist Shows Why the Creationists Are Wrong*. Buffalo, NY: Prometheus Books.

McIver, T. (1988). *Anti-Evolution: An Annotated Bibliography*. Jefferson, NC: McFarland & Company.

Merton, R. K. (1942). A note on science and democracy. *Journal of Legal and Political Sociology, 1*, 115–26.

Merton, T. (1967). *Mystics and Zen Masters*. New York: Dell Publishing.

Miller, K. R. (1984). Scientific creationism versus evolution: The mislabeled debate. In: A. Montagu (Ed.), *Science and Creationism*, (pp. 18–63). Oxford: Oxford University Press.

Morris, H. M. (1970). *Biblical Cosmology and Modern Science*. Nutley, NJ: Craig Press.

370    Clark A. Chinn and William F. Brewer

Morris, H. M. (Ed.) (1974). *Scientific Creationism.* San Diego, CA: Creation-Life Publishers.

Nickell, J., & Fischer, J. F. (1988). *Secrets of the Supernatural: Investigating the World's Occult Mysteries.* Buffalo, NY: Prometheus Books.

Numbers, R. L. (1992). *The Creationists.* New York: Alfred A. Knopf.

Nussbaum, J. (1979). Children's conceptions of the earth as a cosmic body: A cross age study. *Science Education, 63,* 83–93.

Oser, F. K., Reich, K. H., & Bucher, A. A. (1994). Development of belief and unbelief in childhood and adolescence. In: J. Corveleyn and D. Hutsebaut (Eds.), *Belief and Unbelief: Psychological Perspectives,* (pp. 39–62). Amsterdam: Rodopi.

Penner, D. E., & Klahr, D. (1996). The interaction of domain-specific knowledge and domain-general discovery strategies: A study with sinking objects. *Child Development, 67,* 2709–27.

Piaget, J. (1985). *The Equilibration of Cognitive Structures: The Central Problem of Intellectual Development* (T. Brown & K. J. Thampy, Trans.). Chicago: University of Chicago Press. (Original work published 1975)

Pickering, M., & Monts, D. L. (1982). How students reconcile discordant data: A study of lab report discussions. *Journal of Chemical Education, 59,* 794–96.

Popper, K. R. (1959). *The Logic of Scientific Discovery.* London: Hutchinson.

Randall, J. L. (1982). *Psychokinesis: A Study of Paranormal Forces Through the Ages.* London: Souvenir Press.

Randi, J. (1985). The role of conjurers in psi research. In: P. Kurtz (Ed.), *A Skeptic's Handbook of Parapsychology,* (pp. 339–49). Buffalo, NY: Prometheus Books.

Randi, J. (1997, July/August). Randi Foundation announces 'Pigasus' Awards. *Skeptical Inquirer, 21,* 6–7.

Reif, F., & Larkin, J. H. (1991). Cognition in scientific and everyday domains: Comparison and learning implications. *Journal of Research in Science Teaching, 28,* 733–60.

Rosen, A. B., & Rozin, P. (1993). Now you see it . . . now you don't: The preschool child's conception of invisible particles in the context of dissolving. *Developmental Psychology, 29,* 300–11.

Royalty, J. (1995). The generalizability of critical thinking: Paranormal beliefs versus statistical reasoning. *Journal of Genetic Psychology, 156,* 477–88.

Ruffman, T., Perner, J., Olson, D. R., & Doherty, M. (1993). Reflecting on scientific thinking: Children's understanding of the hypothesis-evidence relation. *Child Development, 64,* 1617–36.

Salmon, W. C. (1984). *Scientific Explanation and the Causal Structure of the World.* Princeton, NJ: Princeton University Press.

Samarapungavan, A. (1992). Children's judgments in theory choice tasks: Scientific rationality in childhood. *Cognition, 45,* 1–32.

Samarapungavan, A., & Wiers, R. W. (1997). Children's thoughts on the origin of species: A study of explanatory coherence. *Cognitive Science, 21,* 147–77.

Schauble, L. (1996). The development of scientific reasoning in knowledge-rich contexts. *Developmental Psychology, 32*, 102–19.

Slone, M., & Bokhurst, F. D. (1992). Children's understanding of sugar water solutions. *International Journal of Science Education, 14*, 221–35.

Solomon, M. (1992). Scientific rationality and human reasoning. *Philosophy of Science, 59*, 439–55.

Strahler, A. N. (1987). *Science and Earth History: The Evolution/Creation Controversy*. Buffalo, NY: Prometheus Books.

Suzuki, D. T. (1959). *Zen and Japanese Culture*. Princeton, NJ: Princeton University Press.

Tamminen, K. (1994). Religious experiences in childhood and adolescence: A viewpoint of religious development between the ages of 7 and 20. *The International Journal for the Psychology of Religion, 4*, 61–85.

Tillich, P. (1957). *Systematic Theology (Vol. 2)*. Chicago: University of Chicago Press.

Tobacyk, J. (1983). Death threat, death concerns, and paranormal belief. *Death Education, 7*, 115–24.

Vosniadou, S., & Brewer, W. F. (1990). A cross-cultural investigation of children's conceptions about the earth, the sun, and the moon: Greek and American data. In: H. Mandl, E. deCorte, N. Bennett, and H. F. Friedrich (Eds.), *Learning and Instruction: European Research in an International Context, Vol. 2.2: Analysis of Complex Skills and Complex Knowledge Domains*, (pp. 605–29). Oxford: Pergamon Press.

Vosniadou, S., & Brewer, W. F. (1992). Mental models of the earth: A study of conceptual change in childhood. *Cognitive Psychology, 24*, 535–85.

Vosniadou, S., & Brewer, W. F. (1994). Mental models of the day/night cycle. *Cognitive Science, 18*, 123–83.

Wall, G. (1995). *Religious Experience and Religious Belief*. Lanham, MD: University Press of America.

Wise, D. U. (1998). Creationism's geological time scale. *American Scientist, 86*, 160–73.

Woolley, J. D. (1997). Thinking about fantasy: Are children fundamentally different thinkers and believers from adults? *Child Development, 68*, 991–1011.

Yates, J., Bessman, M., Dunne, M., Jertson, D., Sly, K., & Wendelboe, B. (1988). Are conceptions of motion based on a naive theory or on prototypes? *Cognition, 29*, 251–75.

# 13 Theology and Physical Science

## A Story of Developmental Influence at the Boundaries

DAVID E. SCHRADER

Popular intellectual culture has often pictured science and religion as fundamental adversaries, battling for the intellectual allegiances of reflective people. That picture has been buttressed by the well-known story of the conflict between Galileo and the Catholic Church at the turn of the seventeenth century and by the story of the religious conflicts surrounding the work of Charles Darwin since the middle of the nineteenth century (see Evans, this volume). The adversarial picture has been appealing both to religious people of an anti-scientific bent and to scientific people of an anti-religious bent. However, a careful study of the history of the relationship between religion and natural science does not bear out that adversarial picture.

Of course there have been episodes of conflict, such as those surrounding the ideas of Galileo and Darwin, but to view these episodes simply as battles in an ongoing "war between science and religion" would be to misread history. These famous conflicts are clearly situations in which new scientific ideas are in opposition with traditional religious ideas. A careful study of history shows, however, that those traditional religious ideas, at least in the most famous conflicts, had become accepted parts of intellectual tradition in large measure because they had been developed to fit coherently with ideas of the earlier traditional science. These stories of development will comprise the central theme of this chapter.

One of the easiest things to forget about our modern distinctions among various areas of scholarly inquiry is how very modern they are. Prior to the twentieth century, if one wanted to study what we now call "physics" or "chemistry," one would take courses or read in "natural philosophy." Prior to the late nineteenth century, what we now call "economics" was "political economy," and was universally recognized as among the "moral sciences." Psychology likewise, as an independent science, dates back only to the end of the nineteenth century.

At the same time, however, the notion of distinct sciences goes back to Aristotle. The different sciences were distinguished in terms of the genuses that comprised their subject matters and differentiated based on the view that reality is divided into different natural kinds. These sciences were individuated in terms of unchanging essences that accounted for each being the particular kind of thing that it is. Since reality was one reality composed of these various different genuses, the collection of different sciences that gave knowledge of the different genuses necessarily fit together into a unified whole of human knowledge. Accordingly, changes in one branch of knowledge would create a ripple effect of changes across the whole fabric of knowledge.

For a variety of reasons, ranging from the demise of fixed essences to the departmentalization of the twentieth-century universities to studies in the cognitive development of children, we now tend to think of these different areas of human inquiry as constituting distinct and partially separate cognitive domains. This has led us to see the kinds of historical conflicts noted above as battles of domain against domain. Nevertheless, we seem to have retained the earlier insistence that the domains must agree in yielding a unified world picture and hence that if science and religion disagree, one must be right and the other wrong. The view that human knowledge must present us with a fully unified picture of reality, however, would seem to be a victim of the same changes that have led to the rejection of the old fixed essences. Correspondingly, the more disjointed view of reality that replaces a universe of fixed essences may well require a view of knowledge that replaces a fully unified knowledge of reality with a more disjointed view wherein we reject the demand for global consistency in favor of roughly connected domains, each maintaining its own local consistency.

Note the connection here between our view of the makeup of reality and our view of what we should expect in our knowledge of reality. The whole process of changing human understanding occurs within the context of basic frameworks of what might be broadly called metaphysics. These metaphysical frameworks include, most centrally for the purposes of this chapter, understandings of ontology (the basic kinds of things that make up reality), epistemology (how human beings know about reality), and cosmology (how reality came to be).

The central claim of this chapter is that the historical development of Christian theology has been profoundly shaped, both substantively and methodologically, by the historical development of Western physical science. This is not to deny the moments of conflict within that historical relationship. Just as there have been significant conflicts within the course of development of Western physical science and, likewise, within the course of development of Christian theology, there have also been conflicts at the boundary between science and religion. The precise character of those conflicts, however, becomes much clearer when we examine the ways in which theology has been molded to cohere with developments in science.

## A History of the Boundary Influences

The history of Western physical science is commonly divided into three great periods: the period of Aristotelian science, the period of Newtonian science, and the twentieth century. While Aristotle's work predates Christianity, the fact that most of Aristotle's works were lost to the Christian world prior to their introduction through the great Muslim commentators of the middle ages meant that more than half of the history of Christian theology came before there was any physical science with which Christian theology might relate. The intellectual framework of this period was set by the tradition of Platonism. Accordingly, the development of the relationship between Christian understandings of religion and understandings of nature will be divided into four episodes: Christian Platonism, Christian Aristotelianism, Christian Newtonianism, and the Twentieth Century. Table 13.1 serves as a guide to the general metaphysical developments that characterize these four episodes.

## Christian Platonism

For more than the first half of its life Christian theology developed in a context in which there was no science of physical nature. The development of Christian theology from its beginnings until about 1200 took place in an intellectual tradition rooted in the work of Plato (428/7–348/7 B.C.E.). Plato did not think that there could be a science of

Table 13.1. *Metaphysical Frameworks*

| | Christian Platonism | Christian Aristotelianism | | Christian Newtonianism | Twentieth Century |
|---|---|---|---|---|---|
| Ontology | Forms beyond the material world | Forms in matter | | Passive Matter (particles in motion) | End of Unitary Account |
| | | Thomist | Ockhamist | | |
| Epistemology | Rationalism | Abstraction from experience | Experience of particulars | Inductivism | Pragmatism |
| Cosmology | God as formal cause nature | God as efficient, material formal, and final cause of nature | God as efficient and final cause of nature | God as framer of laws giver of impetus | Process? Quantum? ???? |

375

physics. This was a direct implication of both the ontology and the epistemology held by Plato and the subsequent Platonistic tradition.

Plato's ontology is embodied in his well-known "theory of forms." The highest level of reality lies in abstract and immaterial forms. These forms occupy a realm beyond the world of our experience. The material objects of our experience have a reality that is only derivative on the reality of those forms. The epistemology that is consequent on Plato's ontology is a rationalistic epistemology. Since the most genuine reality lies in an abstract, immaterial, and changeless realm, the most genuine knowledge must likewise arise from the human mind's apprehension of that realm. This implies that human knowledge, in its only genuinely secure form, is gained through rational apprehension and reflection on changeless reality. Mathematics, philosophy, and – for the Christian Platonists who arose centuries after Plato's death – theology provided the most secure forms of human knowledge. Accordingly, Plato thought that our views on physics and cosmology could be neither very exact nor very certain. Physics and cosmology, after all, involve the study of material nature, the study of those things that change. It was within the context of this understanding of cosmological and physical speculation that Christian theology developed over its first millennium.

Two fundamental starting points give the root of the Platonistic traditions of cosmology:

P1. "Everything that becomes or is created must of necessity be created by some cause, for without a cause nothing can be created." (Plato, trans. 1961, p. 1161)

P2. What creates becoming must be something in being.

Because physical nature is always in a process of change that is, becoming, that which creates it must be something apart from the physical. This leads to a third fundamental thesis in the Platonistic tradition of cosmological speculation,

P3. That which creates nature must be some form of intelligence.

While the influence of Plato's thought was evident as early as the work of Saint Justin the Martyr (ca. 100–ca. 164), it is commonplace of the history of philosophy that Saint Augustine of Hippo (354–430) was the chief architect of "Christian Platonism." From his own time until the recovery of Aristotle's work in the thirteenth century, the dominant understanding of the theology of creation was an Augustinian-Platonist one.

Augustine's theological account of creation was designed to affirm the central Christian doctrine that God created the whole of creation freely and from nothing. This meant that his cosmology had to depart from Plato's views by affirming that there is absolutely nothing preexistent from which God orders the physical universe. It also differed from the dominant thrust of the larger Platonistic tradition in affirming that God's creative activity is a free act of divine will. The notion that Augustine used to accomplish this twofold task was borrowed from Plotinus (203/4–269/70 C.E.) and eventually traced its philosophical genealogy back to Stoicism. Augustine proposed that the very first creative act of God was God's creation of the *rationes seminales*, or seminal reasons. These seminal reasons are produced from the mind of God. They contain within themselves the potentialities from which the rest of creation develops. In this sense, the *rationes seminales* constitute a kind of intermediary that allows God to create from nothing. They also allow God to maintain an appropriate distance from the world of changing things.

There are clear differences between this account of Augustine's and the various earlier forms of Platonistic accounts. In particular, and in keeping with the scriptural affirmation of the goodness of all creation, God is portrayed as directly responsible for matter. Nevertheless, the Platonistic spirit of the account is unmistakable. The utter transcendence of God is maintained by giving to the causal reasons the concrete job of unfolding the "nuts and bolts" of creation. Likewise, both God's initial creation of spirit and matter, as well as God's impressing the *rationes seminales* on the intellect of the spiritual creation, are maintained as acts of divine free will. Augustine's account is both powerfully and authentically Platonistic and at the same time powerfully and authentically Christian. Its strong appeal is borne out by the influence it exercised among Christian thinkers for well over 1,000 years.

It may, perhaps, go without saying at this point that Christian Platonism did not support any form of argument from a knowledge of physical nature to a knowledge of God. Since genuine knowledge within the Platonistic tradition can only be of the unchangeable, it follows that our knowledge of the changeable physical world cannot be as secure as our knowledge of an unchangeable God, and can therefore provide no support for that knowledge of God. The rational theology (theology based on natural human reason) that developed during the period of dominance of Christian Platonism argued to conclusions about God from premises that make no reference to changeable, physical things. This was the period of St. Anselm of Canterbury's (1033–1109) famous development of the ontological argument for God's existence, arguing that God's existence follows simply from the definition of 'God' as "that than which nothing greater can be conceived." It was also the period in which Augustine, in *De Libero Arbitrio*, argued to God's existence from the existence of other truths that are necessary and changeless. Accordingly, what we see in the period of dominance of Christian Platonism is an intellectual setting in which knowledge of physical nature was of a distinctly inferior sort, and accordingly had little to contribute to a productive approach to theological understanding beyond a general framework for speculation about physical nature.

As indicated in Table 13.1, the ontology of the entire Platonistic tradition is rooted in eternal forms beyond the material world. Its epistemology is rationalistic, involving the rational apprehension of and reflection on those forms. The cosmology of Christian Platonism takes God (ultimately) and the eternal "seminal ideas" in the mind of God (more proximately) as something akin to what Aristotle would characterize as the "formal causes" of material nature.

### Christian Aristotelianism

Aristotle (384/3–322/1 B.C.E.) was the father of Western physical science. His *Physica* was the first self-conscious attempt to set forth a scientific knowledge of physical nature. Similarly, his *Posterior Analytics* was the first systematic treatise on scientific method. Aristotle's discovery of, or should we say invention of, science arose from the innovations of his metaphysics. Aristotle's metaphysics constitutes a clear move away from the absolute transcendence of Plato and the later Christian Platonists. At the level of ontology, Aristotle maintained that every existing thing is a combination of both form and matter. Form is what makes a thing the kind of thing that it is, while matter makes it the particular individual thing that it is. Thus the reality of material nature is not merely a derivative for Aristotle as it was for Plato. Accordingly, Aristotle's epistemology, in taking cognizance of the genuine reality of the material, had to recognize a fundamental role for experience in the acquisition of human knowledge.

The problem of how to explain the role of experience in knowing would generate a fundamental division in the high middle ages between what we might call the "full-blown" Aristotelian followers of Saint Thomas Aquinas and what we might call the "modified" Aristotelian followers of William of Ockham. This division would have monumental consequences in the area of cosmology and was important in the development of science. This division was also important in the most fundamental theological conflict in the history of Christianity, the Protestant Reformation.

The following eight claims embody most of what is central to Aristotle's science of physics:

A1. Motion (which for Aristotle covers any kind of change) involves the transformation of an underlying thing, T, from a condition, $c_1$, to its contrary condition, $c_2$. (Aristotle, trans. 1941c)

A2. There are four kinds of causes: material, formal, efficient, and final. (Aristotle, trans. 1941c)

A3. "It is the business of the physicist to know about them all." (Aristotle, trans. 1941c, p. 248)

A4. Space and time are dependent on the things or changes that occupy them. (Aristotle, trans. 1941c)

A5. "Everything that is in motion must be moved by something." (Aristotle, trans. 1941c, p. 340.)

A6. Motion is eternal. (Aristotle, trans. 1941c)

A7. There is a first unmoved mover. (Aristotle, trans. 1941c)

A8. The most fundamental motion is circular locomotion. (Aristotle, trans. 1941c)

Clearly Aristotle's physics is much richer than the cosmological speculation of the Platonistic tradition. Aristotle's A5 is largely the same claim as Plato's P1. While Aristotle's physics seems to leave open whether we might want to regard Aristotle's first unmoved mover (A7) as a form of creative intelligence (trans. 1941b). Aristotle claimed explicitly that the first mover is a form of intelligence. Thus it is easy to see Aristotle's A7 as making a claim very similar to Plato's P3. Aristotle's A6, by contrast, is quite foreign to the spirit of Platonism. The rest of Aristotle's physics is simply a new, different, and richer analysis than anything found in the Platonist tradition.

At the level of epistemology, the key to Aristotle's understanding of scientific knowledge, "as opposed to knowing . . . in the accidental way in which the sophist knows" (trans. 1941a, p. 111), is the notion of demonstration. Aristotle claimed that scientific knowledge is superior to any other form of knowledge or pseudoknowledge. Scientific knowledge is knowledge that rests on demonstration. A demonstration is a syllogism the premises of which must be "true, primary, immediate, better known than and prior to the conclusion" (trans. 1941a, p. 112). In addition to definitions and principles of logic, the premises of demonstration must include hypotheses that state the necessary attributes of the subject genus of the demonstration. This requirement of necessity produced a difficulty for Aristotle's account. Aristotle accepted the presumably obvious claim that our knowledge of physical nature must start with experience, and yet experience, as he noted (trans. 1941a), cannot give us necessity. Aristotle's resolution to this problem was that an inductive process enables us to elicit a "commensurate universal" from the number of particulars given in experience. These commensurate universals provide the necessity required for scientific demonstration. Unfortunately, Aristotle did not provide an adequate account of how induction can succeed in this eliciting. It was the attempt to resolve this problem in Aristotle's position that signaled the important parting of the ways among philosophers in the high Middle Ages.

As noted above, most of Aristotle's work had been lost to the Christian world until its recovery through contact with the great Muslim commentators in the twelfth century. Christian scholars were quick to recognize the power of the framework set out by Aristotle, and by the midthirteenth century Saint Thomas Aquinas (1224/5–1274) had developed a full-blown systematic understanding of all reality, both natural and supernatural, based on Aristotle. Aquinas resolved the problem of how to generate necessary universals from a particular experience by claiming that human beings have an "agent intellect" capable of transforming the particulars of perception into "intelligible species" (trans. 1945, I, p. 749). Of course Aquinas recognized that some elements in Aristotle's physics had to be qualified to make it compatible with Christian theology. In particular, Aristotle's A6, affirming the externality of motion, had to be abandoned. Similarly, A8 had to be modified to claim only that circular locomotion was the most fundamental form of locomotion, not of all motion in general. Moreover, Aquinas subtly shifted the basic characterization of physics or natural philosophy. For Aristotle, physics was the study of those things that had within themselves a principle of motion (trans. 1941c). For Aquinas, by contrast, physics or natural philosophy was the study of "mobile being" (trans. 1963, p. 4). This modification left physics as a subscience of a broader science of being in general.

This qualified Aristotelian physics provided a framework for the development of Aquinas's theology at several levels. At the level of the theology of creation, Aquinas maintained substantial continuity with the Augustinian-Platonist theology of creation that had dominated theology prior to his own work. Yet the Aristotelian understanding of physics, combined with a "full-blown" Aristotelian epistemology, led to a far richer view of cosmology on which to develop a theology of creation. In particular, Aristotelian epistemology implied that the physicist could know all four of Aristotle's kinds of causes. This led to a cosmology according to which God was the cause of physical nature according to all four kinds of causality. The Augustinian-Platonist notion that creation involved the emanation of the world out of original divine ideas produced from the mind of God was modified to account for God as the formal cause of the created universe. Aquinas maintained that God was the final cause of all creation in the sense that all creation is "for the sake of" God's own goodness (trans. 1945, I, p. 432). God, as the agent that brought about the universe by an act of God's own will, constituted the efficient cause of creation. Aristotle's notion of material causality, however, constituted the most serious problem for Aquinas's theology. God, as a purely spiritual being, could not possess matter. Accordingly, God could not be the material cause of the universe in any straightforward manner. Rather, since God's creation of the universe was a creation out of nothing, there was a sense in which created nature could have no material cause. Nevertheless, Aquinas's theology did recognize God as the creator of the original "prime matter" out of which the universe was formed (trans. 1945, I). Thus Aquinas was able to construct a theology of creation that recognized God in some manner as the cause of the universe in each of Aristotle's four kinds of causality.

Perhaps the most important impact of Aristotelian physics on Aquinas's theology lay in its ability to ground a natural theology, a set of arguments based on the accepted analysis of physical nature and leading to the conclusion that there must be a God. Like the theology of creation, this natural theology followed from the Aristotelian epistemological claim that the physicist could know all four kinds of causes of physical nature. Aristotle's physics, as already noted (A7), affirmed that nature required a first unmoved mover. It would have been surprising if Aquinas had not assimilated Aristotle's first unmoved mover to the God of Christianity, despite the fact that Aristotle's first unmoved mover was the original cause of motion only with respect to final causality. In *Summa Theologica* (trans. 1945), Aquinas developed his hugely famous "five ways" by which God's existence "can be demonstrated from those of His effects which are known to us" (*Summa Theologica*, I, 2, p. 2). The first of Aquinas's "ways" argued to God as the source of motion in the most general sense. Each of the remaining four argues to God as the cause of natural phenomena in one of Aristotle's four kinds of causality.

The third level at which Aristotelian physics shaped Aquinas's theology was in his sacramental theology. On the traditional characterization given in the early twelfth century by Hugh of Saint Victor, a sacrament of the church is "a visible form of invisible grace conveyed in it." Aquinas's explanation of the working of the visible form of the sacrament of the Eucharist was quite naturally given in what he regarded as the appropriate framework for talking about visible forms, Aristotelian physics. The Aristotelian terms for explaining the transformation of an underlying thing, T, from a condition, c1, to its contrary condition, c2, were substance and accident. The underlying thing was the substance, and the changing conditions were the accidents. The sacrament of the Eucharist, however, constituted a unique problem. The underlying thing in the sacrament changes from ordinary bread and wine to the body and blood of Christ. By contrast, the conditions, the texture, the taste, color, and so on, remain constant through the sacrament. The standard Aristotelian categories for physical change had to be turned on their heads. The substance is transformed while the accidents remain the same. It is for this reason that Aquinas's sacramental theology required that the institution of the sacrament involve a miracle, and not just an ordinary form of change. It was this Aristotelian understanding of the sacrament that was to provide one of the central loci of theological debate during the Protestant reformation in the sixteenth century.

The final way in which Aristotelian science shaped Aquinas's theology lay in the area of method. An acceptance of Aristotle's view of science required that if theology were to provide knowledge of the highest order, then theology must be a science according to Aristotle's understanding of science. Thus at the beginning of the *Summa Theolo-*

*gica* Aquinas developed an account of the "science of sacred doctrine" as a demonstrative Aristotelian science. Since the only way in which testimony (e.g., revelation) could provide premises for a proper demonstration was if the subject of the testimony were itself the deliverance of a higher order science, Aquinas had to find a way of holding that the revelation given to the Church was itself a scientific deliverance. Accordingly, Aquinas posited "the science of God and the Blessed" as the divine source of knowledge made known through God's revelation to the Church (*Summa Theologica*, trans. 1945, I, p. 7). The notion that divine knowledge possessed a demonstrative structure introduced a number of additional theological problems, but was necessary if theology were to be regarded as a science in the strict Aristotelian sense.

Aquinas's was not the only resolution to Aristotle's dilemma of how to elicit necessary universals from a particular experience. The tradition that followed the work of William of Ockham (ca. 1285–1349), drawing on important medieval developments in the logic of terms, maintained that natural science deals with mental contents that are embodied in names (hence the appellation, "nominalists") that stand for collections of particular objects. While the nominalists did not develop a substantive physical science alternative to Aristotle's, several of the early nominalists were among those who rejected Aristotle's account of motion (A5) in favor of an impetus theory, according to which motion was initiated and changed by impetus, but required no continuing cause. The important difference between Ockham's and Aquinas's positions lay at the level of epistemology. This also had important implications for cosmology as well. For Ockham, experience played a far more central role in generating scientific knowledge. Because of the fact that what unity science has comes from its being about a collection of particulars rather than an intelligible universal, the need to ground scientific knowledge in demonstrations rooted in premises giving the necessary characteristics of subject genuses fell by the way. This allowed for knowledge to derive from a number of different sources, none of which needed to be subordinated to any other. In particular, testimony stood on all fours with demonstration as a source of the most certain forms of knowledge. In addition, Ockham's emphasis on the particulars of experience led to the rejection of the Aristotelian epistemological claim that the physicist could know formal and material causes. Final and efficient causes were the only concerns of genuine scientific knowledge. At the level of cosmology, this implied that God could only be viewed as the final and efficient cause of physical nature.

In the century and a half following Ockham's death the "via moderna" of Ockham and the "via antiqua" of Aquinas vied for allegiance in the numerous universities across Europe. One of the bastions of the "via moderna" was the University of Erfurt, where Martin Luther (1483–1546) enrolled as a student in 1501. Two of Luther's most significant professors at Erfurt were Jodokus Trutfetter and Bartholomaeus Arnoldi. Both were committed nominalists.

Again and again both of them cited one basic notion as the decisive principle and characteristic of the via moderna: All philosophical speculation about the world must be tested by means of experience and reality-based reason, regardless of what even the most respected authorities might say to the contrary. Arnoldi emphasized that this was to be no different in the case of theology: All theological speculation is to be tested by the authority of the Scripture as interpreted by the Church. Hence experience and Scripture were the only valid norms in the realms of philosophy and theology (Oberman, 1983/1989, pp. 118–19).

The nominalist commitments that Luther acquired in his Erfurt education led to three central methodological principles in his theology and shaped his understanding of the general relationship between theology and natural science. The first methodological principle that Luther adopted from his nominalist teachers is an empiricist epistemology according to which theology originates in human experience, rather than in metaphysical principle. Theology is not concerned with an "objective doctrine of God," but rather with God as discovered in the human being's relationship with God (Althaus, 1963/1966, p. 9). Human experience reveals an inchoate sense of unease in the world, being in opposition to rightness. This is the starting point for theology.

The second methodological principle of Luther's theology is expressed in the traditional phrase, "*sola Scriptura.*" The nominalist affirmation of the epistemological authority of testimony undergirded Luther's affirmation of Scripture as the fundamental source of Christian teaching. The Word of God, revealed both in Scripture and in the event of the life and death of Christ, addresses humanity in its experience of unease. That Word contains two messages. The message of Law lends clear shape to the primal sense of unease by explaining that unease as a condition of opposition to or rebellion against God. The message of Gospel proclaims the resolution to the unease through

God's gift of salvation achieved through the incarnation, death, and resurrection of Christ. The Gospel message announces that the human being can be, through the act of Christ, *"simul iustus et peccator,"* at the same time justified and yet a sinner. This is surely Luther's most fundamental characterization of the experience of the person who has encountered and accepted the Word of God, both law and gospel.

The third methodological principle of Luther's theology is the need to evaluate theological positions on the basis of "reality-based reason." Luther has often been portrayed as an opponent of reason. In fact, however, Luther distinguished between reality-based reason and theory-based reason. The reason of Aristotelian theory, for which Luther reserved some of his most heated invective, was theory-based reason. It claimed that there were certain categories into which reality had to be placed. Luther explained in a letter to a Saxon prince, "When I speak to a carpenter, I must use his terms, namely angle bar and not crooked bar, axe and not hatchet. So one should leave the words of Christ alone and speak of the sacraments in *suis terminis* (his terms) . . ." (cited in Oberman, 1983/1989, p. 170). It was on this basis that Luther rejected the Catholic doctrine of the Eucharist (transubstantiation) as an Aristotelian distortion of God's action in the sacrament. The doctrine of transubstantiation required that Christ's act of giving himself to the believer through bread and wine be understood in the categories that Aristotle developed to construct a science of nature. Such an understanding, Luther maintained, replaced Christ's words (and the content they represent) with those of Aristotle.

Luther regarded reason as a gift and a tool. Reason is a good tool but, like anything human, an imperfect tool. Reason is incapable of ultimately laying bare the truth before us. This implies that science must be somewhat humble in its pretensions to reveal reality, but at the same time it implies that science must be free from the controlling pretensions of theology. Reason and natural science are both "world-bound." This world-bound character of natural science also ruled out any significant prospect for a natural theology. The fact that science is world-bound implies a certain relativity and a certain conjectural character for scientific knowledge. Natural science does not have the capacity to yield ultimately and finally true results about reality. It is the best we have in the way of investigating nature, but it remains fallible. Accordingly, the attempt to constrain scientific research on the basis of theological considerations is misdirected. It rests on the misunderstanding of science as a claimant of ultimate truth. At the same time, such a world-bound science is, for the very same reason, not capable of leading to truth about the divine.

This position of Luther's on the relationship between theology and natural science denies that theology and natural science need to be fully consistent with each other. This is because Luther's epistemology held that human cognitive capacities are incapable of laying out a complete and adequate understanding of reality. Rather, our cognitive capacities lay out partial and provisional understandings. Partiality and provisionality imply that the parts and pieces of our understanding at any given point may fit together only roughly and imperfectly. Human experience comes only in more or less connected bits and pieces. This implies a more fundamental separation of science from theology, and of the several sciences from one another. Any final and perfect understanding of reality is simply not available to the earthly human condition. As noted above, one of the most important particular consequences of this was Luther's rejection of the Catholic doctrine of transubstantiation. The sacrament of the Eucharist was given by Christ and must be understood as Christ instituted it, not as reinterpreted according to Aristotle. How the physical elements of the sacrament can convey the reality of Christ's body and blood is a puzzle that cannot be resolved by translating the operation of the sacrament into the categories of current (Aristotle's or more recent) physics.

In this long and important period of Christian Aristotelianism, we see again, as indicated in Table 13.1, a constant ontology that views reality as form given in matter. Both the epistemology and the cosmology of this period divide around the question of how general knowledge can arise from particular experience. The followers of Aquinas held to an epistemology that claimed an abstractive power for the human intellect and insisted that efficient, material, formal, and final causes could be known by the human investigator. This led to a cosmology according to which God must be viewed as a cause of physical nature according to all four notions of causality. The followers of William of Ockham, by contrast, adopted an epistemology that placed greater emphasis on the particularity of experience and affirmed that the generality of science lies at the level of mental contents only. This limited human investigators to knowledge of efficient and final causes. Accordingly, this led to a cosmology that emphasized God's efficient and final causality of physical nature.

## Christian Newtonianism

The sixteenth and seventeenth centuries witnessed a number of developments that challenged aspects of Aristotelian physical science. Until the publication of Sir Isaac Newton's (1642–1727) *Mathematical Principles of Natural Philosophy* in 1687, however, there was no comprehensive system of physical science to replace Aristotle's. Nearly two centuries earlier Nicholas Copernicus (1473–1543) had challenged the Aristotelian claim that the earth lay at the center of the universe surrounded by the other heavenly bodies. Johannes Kepler (1571–1630) maintained that the planetary orbits were elliptical rather than circular. This constituted an important challenge to A8, the Aristotelian claim that the most fundamental form of motion is circular locomotion. And of course Galileo Galilei (1564–1642) maintained that his explorations with the newly invented telescope confirmed Copernicus's claim that the earth revolved around the sun, and not vice versa. Moreover, Galileo's corpuscular mechanics directly contradicted the Aristotelian basis of the Church's doctrine of the sacrament. This, even more seriously than his astronomy, led to conflict between Galileo and the Church of his day.

With the publication of Newton's *Principia*, however, the challenge to Aristotelian physics ceased to be piecemeal. Newton's physics came very quickly to replace Aristotelian physics, at least within the mainstream scientific community. By the time of Newton's death, Aristotelian physics was largely a relic of history outside of those circles whose primary intellectual commitment was to retain traditional Catholic doctrine.

The heart of Newton's physics lay in his three laws of motion:

N1. "Every body continues in its state of rest or of uniform motion in a right line unless it is compelled to change that state by forces impressed upon it."

N2. "The change of motion is proportional to the motive force impressed and is made in the direction of the right line in which that force is impressed."

N3. "To every action there is always opposed and equal reaction; or, the mutual actions of two bodies upon each other are always equal and directed to contrary parts." (Newton, 1687/1946, p. 13)

Newton's physics provided a rational mathematical explanation of all motion. In particular, it united celestial and terrestrial motion, which had been seen as importantly different within Aristotelian physics. The picture of the physical universe that emerged from Newton's physics was that of a well-coordinated machine, with all movements caused by a set of attractive and repulsive forces that operate according to clearly defined mathematical laws. These mathematical laws reflected an unchanging rational structure to the physical universe.

Newton's physics was both the effect and the cause of continuing change in metaphysical views. In ontology, the work of impetus theorists and mechanists like Rene Descartes (1596–1650) and Thomas Hobbes (1588–1679) contributed to the demise of Aristotle's ontology of form and matter. In its place came a twofold ontology of inertial matter (particles in motion) and active minds both understanding matter and initiating its motions. In epistemology, the Ockhamist move toward greater empiricism was radicalized into Sir Francis Bacon's inductivism. The publication in 1621 of Bacon's *The New Organon* signaled a perceived need to replace the old Organon of Aristotle with a view of scientific epistemology capable of grounding a new science. Bacon's inductivism, despite the fact that it could not possibly have characterized the actual methodological practice of Newton, became the canonical epistemology of the scientific tradition that gave rise to Newton's work and was powerfully strengthened by that work. In cosmology also, Ockhamism prepared the way. Newton himself was deeply committed to the Ockhamist rejection of formal causality. Thus it was quite natural for him to see God's creative activity as that of giving initial impetus to the particles of nature and of setting down the mathematical laws by which those particles would move.

The theological implications of the new physics were profound. The two central themes in the Newtonian theology of creation as just noted were mechanism and voluntarism. The view of the universe as machinelike led to a view of its Creator as a designer-engineer, contrasting with the earlier view of Creator as contemplator. The creation of the universe was not seen as a process of emanation from divine ideas, but as a process of structural design and execution of that design. Similarly, both the development of the design and its execution were manifestations of divine will. This voluntarism was again a theme drawn from the tradition of Ockham. God's creation of the universe was seen as radically free, unconstrained by any antecedent structures of divine rationality.

Perhaps even more importantly, Newton's physics led to a distinctive new form of natural theology that might appropriately be called a "Newtonian natural theology." On the Newtonian understanding of physical nature, the most remarkable feature of nature was the manner in which the diverse parts of nature were coordinated according to strict mathematical laws. The various inputs of impetus that made physical nature operate had to be just right. For 150 years following Newton's *Principia* it was widely argued that there could be only one plausible explanation for the coordination of natural diversity, and that explanation was a rational designer, God. As Newton himself and a host of followers maintained, that coordination could not plausibly be explained either by chance or by natural necessity. The only remaining alternative was the work of a God (Newton, 1687/1946, p. 546).

It was this particular Newtonian form of natural theology that generated the central conflict with the evolutionary biology of Charles Darwin (1809–1882). Darwin's *The Origin of Species* provided an account of how nature might generate order (coordination) out of disorder (diversity) of her own accord. Thus, Darwin's work provided an alternative explanation for the coordination of nature. Since the Newtonian natural theology argued by appeal to God as the only plausible explanation of the coordination of diversity in nature, Darwin's provision of another plausible explanation devastated that natural theology. Religious reaction to Darwin's work in the last half of the nineteenth century was mixed. Many theologians of a generally conservative orientation, such as Benjamin Warfield (1851–1921), found little difficulty reconciling Darwin's biology with their theologies. The only out and out conflict between Darwinian evolution and theology comes for those who maintain that Scripture can only be understood literally. That literalist position has been denied by most major Christian traditions at least since Aquinas's discussions of the language of Scripture (see trans. 1945, I). Darwin's work did, however, undermine the natural theology that arose in response to Newton's physics.[1]

It should be noted here that the Newtonian physical science was wholly without influence in sacramental theology. This is because of

---

[1] Darwin had done substantial study of William Paley's *Natural Theology* during his theological training. His awareness of the fact that his own work provided an explanation alternative to the designing hand of God is clear from the contrast between Paley's comparative anatomical treatment of the eye (Paley, 1828) and Darwin's chapter on "Organs of Extreme Perfection and Complication" in *The Origin of Species*.

the particular sacramental positions held by the three main divisions within Christianity. The Catholic Church maintained steadfastly the Aristotelian understanding of the Eucharist developed by Aquinas. The Lutheran Church denied the need to reconcile its sacramental theology with current views in physics, and the reformed tradition of Protestantism had long claimed that the physical elements in the sacrament of the Eucharist functioned only as symbols of the body and blood of Christ. Therefore the working of the Eucharist involved only a symbolic presence and not any real presence (other than ordinary bread and wine). In short, the only Christian tradition whose sacramental theology required a full reconciliation with physics was also the only Christian tradition that was committed to maintaining the basic framework of Aristotelianism.

The new science that developed over the sixteenth and seventeenth centuries also generated a new view of scientific method. The canonical exposition of that view of method was Sir Francis Bacon's *The New Organon*. As Aristotle's logical and methodological works, generally collected under the heading of The Organon, provided the methodological basis for the old science, Bacon and others thought that the new science required a new Organon. The heart of the new view, which was foreshadowed in the position of the medieval nominalists, was that science was constructed on the basis of induction from experience. A second important methodological stricture of the new view was that science at its best was primarily concerned with uncovering the mechanical laws governing the structure of nature. Ockham had earlier urged the abandonment of concern with formal and material causes. Bacon and his followers also urged that concern with final causes should be abandoned outside the sphere of human behavior. The Newtonian natural theology differed, for example, from the "fifth way" of Aquinas in that the latter argued to God as the final cause of natural motion, while the former appealed to God as the best explanation for the initial impetus and the law structure of the coordination of nature.

The inductivist view of method also led to a substantial debate over miracles during the eighteenth century. While it was generally acknowledged during that century that the observation of nature provides ample evidence that a god of some sort exists, the particulars of the Christian faith are given only through revelation. The peculiar epistemic role of miracles was to establish the reliability of those whose testimony conveyed the Christian tradition. If miracle reports could be shown to be reliable instances of testimony, then those whose words were accompanied by miracles could be taken as reliable recipients of divine revelation. This discussion of miracles continued throughout the period in which Newtonian natural theology was widely held.

Finally, while Roman Catholic theology generally attempted to retain its rootage in Aristotle through this whole period, the inductivist epistemology did have its impact within Catholic circles. The Benedictine "Maurists" of the eighteenth century pursued an extensive program of careful historical research aimed at producing definitive editions of historical chronicles of the Church. Likewise, the group of Belgian Jesuits known as the "Bollandists" engaged in comprehensive research into the historical lives of the saints. Both of these programs were inspired by the inductivist concern to root testimonial authority in unquestioned historical fact. These particular movements, along with the larger "modernist" movement within nineteenth-century Catholicism, show the influence of the inductivist view of method. Nevertheless, the Church's continued commitment to the doctrinal formulations of Aquinas, along with the general inductivist rejection of authority as a legitimate source of knowledge, meant that in the end the Catholic Church would have to reject the new science. It did this officially in 1879 with Pope Leo XIII's encyclical, *"Aeterni Patris,"* affirming that the understandings of Aquinas would continue to be the official teachings of the Church.

A word of summary is in order as we look at the relationship between theology and physical science at the end of the nineteenth century. The Roman Catholic theological tradition had largely accepted Aquinas's version of Aristotelian theology, a theology solidly rooted in Aristotelian physics and, consequently, in the metaphysics that undergirded it, from well before the Protestant Reformation. Throughout its subsequent history, Catholic theological movements were influenced by Ockhamist nominalism and later by the methodological inductivism that accompanied Newtonian physical science. Although Catholic thought could not ignore the monumental success of the Newtonian account of physics, the Church's commitment to a universal faith made it difficult to abandon its Aristotelian roots. At the end of the nineteenth century it had clearly decided against abandoning those roots. The Lutheran theological tradition, by contrast, developed around a firm commitment to epistemological fallibilism, as well as to a commitment that total explanations of reality lay beyond the limitations of the human condition. These commitments led Lutheran theology to develop relatively independently of substantive developments in physical science and to regard developments in scientific method as largely nonthreatening. The impact of Newtonian physical science, then, was most significantly felt within the reformed Protestant tradition and, more generally, within English Protestantism.

In looking at the episode of Christian Newtonianism, we again see the grounding of both scientific and theological changes in the metaphysical changes (see Table 13.1). The ontology of form in matter was replaced by one of passive matter (particles in motion) and active mind. The epistemological role of experience was radicalized into Bacon's inductivism. Cosmology shifted in the direction of explaining the lawlike order witnessed in nature's diversity. Initially it was overwhelmingly believed that only a God-like mind could bring mathematically ordered motion out of passive matter. Near the end of the Newtonian period, however, Darwin provided a powerful kind of explanation of how nature might be able to generate order by its own resources.

**The Twentieth Century**

On November 7, 1919, one of the headlines carried by *The Times* of London read, "Revolution in Science, Newtonian Ideas Overthrown" (Chandrasekhar, 1979, p. 216). The 200-year reign of Newton's physics was over. The demise of Newtonian physical science was very different from the demise of Aristotelian physical science. Aristotelian physics succumbed to a series of piecemeal challenges over a span of roughly two centuries. At its final demise it was replaced by Newtonian physics, which constituted an alternative comprehensive and unified account of nature. By contrast, the demise of Newtonian physics was swift, and it has not to this day been replaced by any alternative comprehensive and unified account of nature. Rather, physics after the demise of Newton became a "marriage between quantum mechanics and special relativity" (Rohrlich, 1987, p. 189). The marriage of quantum mechanics and relativity theory, however, has never succeeded in making the two of them into "one flesh."

The disunity that has become accepted as a part of the "standard model" of twentieth-century physics has brought with it a like disunity in metaphysics. Ontology is strictly up for grabs. Matter and energy are convertible. There may or may not be any fundamental and irreducible particles at the root of nature. Physical forces may or may not be unifiable into a common account. Epistemology has tended to become strongly pragmatic. Success in knowledge acquisition is success in problem solving. Cosmology has become fascinatingly speculative, yet equally tentative, awaiting the latest reports from the Hubble telescope, measurements of radiation from distant space, or any other kinds of data that may tell more about distant space and distant past time. What role God might have played, or how God might have played any role, in the origins of nature is equally open.

The demise of Newtonian physics was brought about on May 29, 1919, when a solar eclipse produced a deflection of light rays passing through the sun's gravitational field of roughly twice what traditional Newtonian physics would predict. The actual angle of deflection was what was predicted by the newly developed relativity theory of Albert Einstein (1879–1955). The heart of Einstein's theory lay in the abandonment of the Newtonian concept of absolute time. Rather, time and space were both held relative to inertial systems.

The other partner in the marriage of twentieth-century physics developed as Newtonian mechanics proved unable to account for the observed pattern of energy radiation from atoms. By 1900, Max Plank (1858–1947) had recognized that emissions of energy from the atom could only come in discrete units. This recognition led Neils Bohr (1885–1962) to a revised understanding of atomic structure wherein atoms could only exist in certain discrete, stable states. Accordingly, following any standard interaction with other atoms, an atom will return to one of these stable conditions. These results led to the replacement of traditional Newtonian mechanics by the statistical mechanics of quantum theory. At the same time, the discovery of the composite character of the atomic nucleus led to a new account of the various fundamental forces operating within physical nature.

While many physicists have been interested in the project of providing a fully unified account of physical nature that would bring relativity theory and quantum mechanics together in a Grand Unified Theory (GUT), the explanatory power of both relativity theory and quantum mechanics within their respective areas has led to a universal acceptance among physicists of the need to carry on their work without such a unification. Partial explanations and localized consistencies have replaced complete explanations and global consistency within twentieth-century physical science.

Both relativity theory and quantum mechanics have had some influence in theological development, but the fact that each of them offers only a partial account of physical nature has limited the ability of either to attain broad theological influence. The key relativistic idea that both space and time are relative to inertial frames of reference, as filtered through the process of metaphysics of Alfred North Whitehead (1861–1947), proved to be the fundamental inspiration to the development of twentieth-century process theology. Process theology, centered as it is on a revised concept of time, primarily provides a theology of creation and an eschatology.

Process theology starts out with its ontology. To be real, whether for the created or the Creator, is to be in process. Since time is relative to an inertial frame of reference, there is neither a creation in time nor an expectation of an end of time. Rather, God and the created world are correlative notions. God's existence requires a world of some sort, and any world's existence requires God. The created universe is an evolving organism, with God providing the impetus for coherence, purpose, and change. God's creative power is God's functioning as a lure directing the process of world evolution. The hope of the believer is that he or she is ongoingly made a part of the divine experience and memory. While process theology has proven to be an interesting and significant development among a number of twentieth-century academic theologians, its influence has not been broadly felt outside the academic theological community. Nevertheless, in a century where many people have felt distress at the loss of the old unified ontology, process- style ontology has not been without influence in the popularity of religious views (e.g. new age) alternative to orthodox Christianity.

Perhaps more influential has been the twentieth-century variety of natural theology that has developed in response to twentieth-century quantum cosmology. As noted above, quantum mechanics has led to the recognition of the composite character of the atom and to the recognition that parts of atoms can be combined in different manners to form different elements. This fact implies the fundamental mutability of matter.

Late twentieth-century scientific technologies have enabled physicists to observe a number of important things about the universe. First, the universe is extremely large and largely empty. Most of the matter of the universe is collected in stars, which are themselves grouped into galaxies. The huge spaces between galaxies are largely devoid of matter. Second, matter is very unevenly distributed with respect to atomic size. Roughly 90% of matter is composed of hydrogen, the smallest and simplest atom. Most of the remaining 10% is composed of helium, the second smallest and simplest atom. Third, spectral lines from increasingly distant galaxies exhibit an increasing shift toward the red end of the light spectrum. This provides evidence that these distant galaxies are moving away from our galaxy faster than are closer galaxies.

The general cosmological picture to which these observations point is that the universe emerged in the very distant past from a "Big Bang," a process wherein an original singularity composed of all matter compressed into a virtual point started a process of expansion. A number of twentieth-century theologians and physicists (e.g., Richard Swinburne, John Polkinghorne, and Paul Davies) have argued that the development of a universe containing intelligent life from a process originating in such a "Big Bang" is intelligible only on the supposition of an intelligent creative agent. There is, of course, a strong kinship between this contemporary form of natural theology and the earlier natural theology of the Newtonian tradition. While this twentieth-century, quantum-based natural theology has its devoted advocates, it is not surprising that it has not attained anything like the influence of its seventeenth-and eighteenth-century ancestor. The force of Darwin's work continues to provide a way of explaining the emergence of order without an intelligent orderer.

Certainly one of the most striking features of twentieth-century physics, by contrast with its various predecessors, is its lack of theoretical unity. This lack of unity has required address at the level of understandings of scientific method. There have been two positions on the methods and aims of science that have had substantial impact in the twentieth century on views of how to conduct theology. Also, while it is always difficult to speak clearly of the present, there appears to be an emerging consensus at the level of method in the sciences. These reflections on twentieth-century physical science will conclude with a brief look at what I take to be this emerging consensus and what its impact on theological method might be expected to be.

Methodological writing in the first half of the twentieth century was dominated by a reluctance to accept disunity as a fundamental feature of science. The logical positivists, working from a commitment to a unified view of science, developed a radically empiricist view of epistemology that dominated methodological discussions for most of that period. The positivists held that genuine knowledge is only possible where there is a determinate way, either through observation or the principles of logic, of deciding the truth of claims. In fact, the meaning of any truth claim is determined by the steps that would be taken to prove it true. As a part of this program, one of the aims of logical positivism was to eliminate the entire discussion of metaphysics, despite the fact, which seems so clear in retrospect, that logical positivism itself assumes its own highly controversial metaphysical foundation. The implications of this position for theology are substantial. Theological claims are not based either on direct observation or the principles of logic. Unless it can be shown that there is some form of religious experience that carries the same objectifying character as ordinary perceptual experience, religious claims can be neither true nor false. They may be expressions of emotion, commitments to live life in a certain manner, or perhaps a perspective on one's own life, but they are simply not the kinds of claims that can bear truth. Clearly this places theology in a very defensive position. There are two possible tasks for the theologian. Either the theologian can attempt to provide an objectifying account of religious experience – a difficult task indeed – or the theologian can present an account of what exactly religious claims are if they are not bearers of truth. Not surprisingly, the largest number of positivists simply thought religious language was a piece of nostalgic nonsense.

A second important position on the method of science that has been significant in shaping twentieth-century views on theological method takes its roots in the work of Wilhelm Dilthey (1833–1911). Dilthey advocated a fundamental methodological division between the natural sciences and what he referred to as "Geisteswissenschaften," or the human sciences. Dilthey's distinction has roots in John Stuart Mill's (1806–1873) earlier distinction between the natural and "moral" sciences, although Dilthey's distinction is clearly not the same as Mill's. According to this second position, while the aim of the natural sciences is explanation, the end of the human sciences is understanding. "Explanation" in this context is generally taken to mean the inclusion of individual phenomena under a general rule, in contrast to understanding, which considers the individual in the context of the whole to which it belongs (Pannenberg, 1973/1976). Central to the methodology of the human sciences is hermeneutics, the study of the understanding of meaning.

The inclusion of theology among the human sciences has led to the development of an important strain of "hermeneutical theology" in the twentieth century. The project of theology, according to hermeneutical theology, is to provide a comprehensive understanding of human experience in terms of the most general possible context of that experience. Certainly one of the most important hermeneutical theologians of the twentieth century, especially in terms of self-conscious attention to theological method, has been Wolfhart Pannenberg (1928–   ). Pannenberg characterizes theology as "the science of God, but a science which can approach its subject-matter only indirectly, through the study of religion" (Pannenberg, 1973/1976, p. 346). Also, "[theological construction] are to be evaluated by their success in giving a coherent interpretation of the data of the religious tradition and the systems of meaning of present experience." (Pannenberg, 1973/1976, p. 345) Needless to say, the underlying methodological presupposition of hermeneutical theology, that the sciences as a whole can be divided into the relatively monolithic natural sciences and the relatively monolithic human sciences, has not gone without challenge in the twentieth century.

A far more comprehensive disunification of science is one of the central features of the pragmatist epistemology of science that has become increasingly dominant in the closing years of the twentieth century. On this view, solving problems is the central concern of science. There is nothing in general that provides unity to scientific problems.

If problems are the focal point of scientific thought, theories are its end results. Theories matter; they are cognitively important insofar as – and only insofar as – they provide adequate solutions to problems. If problems constitute the questions of science, it is theories that constitute the answers. The function of a theory is to resolve ambiguity, to reduce irregularity to uniformity, and to show that what happens is somehow intelligible and predictable; it is this complex of functions to which I refer when I speak of theories as solutions to problems (Laudan, 1984, p. 13).

This last understanding of scientific method has not, thus far, had any substantial influence on the development of understandings of the theological method. It would be somewhat surprising if the pragmatist understanding of method should fail to have such impact in the early part of the twenty-first century. In any case, such a view of method would dictate that the first task in the development and evaluation of theology is to become clear about the problems that theologies aim to solve. This approach suggests a kind of disciplinary autonomy for theology that is perhaps somewhat similar to that advocated by Luther against the comprehensive view of Thomistic Scholasticism. It is, however, a methodological development that lies in the future.

The story of the twentieth century, then, has been one of the demise of a unified metaphysics. The disjointed ontology, pragmatic epistemology, and tentative and changing cosmology that have characterized the past century have been both liberating and disorienting. Popular religious culture has become a battle ground filled with partisans of various unifying metaphysical frameworks, from fundamentalist Christianity to popularized Buddhism to various forms of new age speculation. Each of the proposed unifying frameworks has gained adherents among those who feel the need for a unifying metaphysical vision. At the same time, the fragmentation of the twentieth century may provide for the possibility that humans think through their religious and various scientific understandings in ways that are more true to the many facets of a multifaceted human experience.

## Conclusions

This chapter has presented a story outlining the developmental influence of Western physical science on Christian theology. That one important domain of human reflection and analysis should be influenced by another domain over the course of history should be anything but surprising. While we now recognize physics and theology as clearly different domains of human thought, this has not always been so. Most of Western intellectual history has developed under the influence of unifying visions of metaphysics. A unified ontology told what kinds of things made up reality. A unified epistemology told how humans could know that reality. A unified cosmology told how that reality came to be. Aristotle, for example, taught that different sciences were distinguished in that they had different genuses of things for their subject matters. Those different genuses were distinguished by the abiding essences that constituted them as what they are. As a result, a unified knowledge of reality could be had by putting together the results of the several sciences. Their subject matters were, after all, but different parts of one comprehensive domain, reality.

This way of looking at matters is supported not only by the force of history, but also, as other chapters in this volume argue, by innate tendencies in children's patterns of cognitive development. We have learned from evolutionary biology and from atomic physics that species and genuses are not as fixed as the Aristotelian scheme would suggest. Likewise, if it is true that experience is at least one of our primary vehicles for learning, it is important to recognize that our experience does not come as a unified whole, but as a collection of more or less related parts. We experience reality in different domains, different pieces of reality, carved up in different ways to resolve various different human problems. These domains of thought do not exist in neat, hermetically sealed isolation. In the first instance, there are many boundary issues wherein different domains of thought address common issues. In the second instance, the fact that human experience does not present us with neatly separated and discrete realms leads us to apply methods of investigation of the various domains right up to and across the boundaries of those domains. Boundary questions and boundary conflicts are by no means peculiar to the science-religion boundary.

The contemporary recognition that we think in distinct domains has its roots in the nominalism of William of Ockham. It was perhaps first taken with full seriousness in Luther's critique of scholastic theology. And it was only forced on the general intellectual consciousness by the dissolution of unity in twentieth-century physics. Accordingly, the boundary lines between different domains are both recent and changing. It would be a serious mistake to take cognitive domains as fixed species within an unchanging cognitive psychological reality, each domain fixed by its own unchanging essence.

For a collection of reasons, presumably both psychological and semantic, human beings are uncomfortable with inconsistency. We are rightly reluctant to claim that it is both raining and not raining. This discomfort with inconsistency has undergirded a general belief in Western intellectual history that the totality of our beliefs, those about physics, theology, psychology, and so on, should be mutually consistent. Yet this demand is almost certainly impossible. Each of us maintains a huge number of beliefs in widely divergent areas of reflection. Global consistency would seem to be a suitable characteristic of computers, with their capacity to bring the full contents of their memories together in extremely short order; but not of human beings. Human beliefs come in smaller domains. Even within these smaller domains it is all too easy for inconsistencies to lie hidden. The German philosopher and logician, Gottlob Frege (1848–1925), failed to realize that his foundational system for arithmetic contained an inconsistency until it was pointed out to him by a young Bertrand Russell (1872–1970). Nevertheless, once Russell pointed out the inconsistency, it was universally recognized that Frege's system required major revisions. While global consistency may lie beyond the limits of human capacity, local inconsistency is not easily tolerated.

Concerns for local consistency and global consistency have both been involved in the story of physical science's influence on theology. The ideal of a globally consistent picture of reality provided a clear motivation for the grand system of Thomistic Scholasticism. Likewise, the project of Newtonian physics and theology was guided by the demand for a globally consistent picture. At the same time, the more limited concern for local consistency forces a certain level of mutual influence between physical science and theology. At one level, a position like the traditional Catholic doctrine of Eucharistic transubstantiation, which was developed in application of one form of physical analysis, cannot easily be maintained in conjunction with an account of physics that is inconsistent with it. This recognition, as Redondi (1987) has noted, lay at the heart of the inevitable conflict between Galileo's mechanics and the Church of his time.[2] At a more general level, as long as theologies affirm that God is the creator of all that is, physical and otherwise, theologies must give at least a partial account of God's relation to the physical world. Concerns for local consistency seem to require that those partial accounts be consistent with both the remaining structure of theology and with intellectually respectable scientific accounts of the nature of the physical world. Accordingly, certain large-scale changes in the development of science must inevitably generate accommodating changes in the development of theology.

The popular story of the "warfare between science and religion" is thus a story that is often wrongly told. The famous episodes of conflict between science and religion are not strictly conflicts between science and religion. Rather, they are instances of a more general conflict that arises within the process of changing metaphysical frameworks. Gali-

---

[2] See Redondi (1987) for a detailed analysis of the conflict between Galileo and the Church.

leo's work did not conflict with Christian theology in some general sense (whatever that might mean). What it did was conflict with a theological formulation that was developed to cohere with an earlier scientific vision. Likewise, Darwin's work did not conflict with the religion in any such general sense. Rather, what it did was demolish a particular form of natural theological argumentation that became an accepted part of a theological formulation rooted in Newton's physics, a form of natural theological argumentation that received perhaps its most classic statement in the "General Scholium" to Newton's *Principia*. There are those in the present time who would claim that contemporary work in psychology or neuroscience conflicts with religion by denying the "soul." Yet the "soul" came into Christian theology through Plato and Aristotle. The canonical affirmation of Christianity, given in the "Apostle's Creed," is in the "resurrection of the body." The "soul psychology," like Newtonian natural theology and the Eucharistic doctrine of transubstantiation, is a piece of theology developed in an effort to cohere with an earlier science. There are, then, conflicts between particular scientific formulations and particular theological formulations, but not a general "warfare between science and religion." As science changes theology changes, the boundaries between theology and science change, and the areas for both conflict and conciliation change.

The time of individuating discrete sciences, distinguished in terms of the genus of their subject matter, may well be past. Yet it is surely clear to philosophers and psychologists alike that human beliefs fall into a variety of general domains. As long as the beliefs within those domains come together in single minds, and as long as those domains meet in discourse about some common subject matter, there cannot fail to be important developmental influences at the boundaries.

### References

Althaus, P. (1966). *The Theology of Martin Luther* (Robert C. Schultz, Trans.). Philadelphia: Fortress Press. (Original work published 1963)

Aquinas, T. (1945). *Basic Writings of St. Thomas Aquinas*, 2 Vols., (Anton C. Pegis, Ed.). New York: Random House.

Aquinas, T. (1963). *Commentary on Aristotle's Physics* (Richard J. Blackwell, Richard J. Spath, and W. Edmund Thirlkel, Trans.) New Haven, CT:Yale University Press.

Aristotle. (1941a). *Analytica Posteriora* (G. R. G. Mure, Trans.). In: Richard

McKeon (Ed.), *The Basic Works of Aristotle*, (pp. 110–78). New York: Random House.

Aristotle. (1941b). *Metaphysica* (W. D. Ross, Trans.). In: Richard McKeon (Ed.), *The Basic Works of Aristotle*, (pp. 689–934). New York: Random House.

Aristotle. (1941c). *Physica* (P. Hardie and R. K. Gaye, Trans.). In: Richard McKeon (Ed.), *The Basic Works of Aristotle*, (pp. 218–398). New York: Random House.

Ashbaugh, A. F. (1988). *Plato's Theory of Explanation*. Albany, NY: State University of New York Press.

Augustine. (1982). *The Literal Meaning of Genesis*, 2 Vols. (John Hammond Taylor, S. J., Trans.). New York: Newman Press.

Bacon, F. (1960). *The New Organon* (Fulton H. Anderson, Ed.). Indianapolis, IN: Bobbs-Merrill. (Original work published 1620.)

Barbour, I. G. (1971). *Issues in Science and Religion*. New York: Harper and Row.

Barbour, I. G. (1990). *Religion in an Age of Science*. San Francisco: Harper Collins.

Brecht, M. (1985). *Martin Luther: His Road to Reformation 1483–1521* (James L. Schaaf, Trans.). Minneapolis, MN: Fortress Press. (Original work published 1981).

Chandrasekhar, S. (1979). Einstein and general relativity: Historical perspectives. *American Journal of Physics, 47*, (3), 212–17.

Clayton, P. (1989) *Explanation from Physics to Theology*. New Haven, CT: Yale University Press.

Cobb, J. B., Jr., and Griffin, D. R (1976). *Process Theology: An Introductory Exposition*. Philadelphia, PA: The Westminster Press.

Darwin, C. (1958). *The Origin of Species By Means of Natural Selection or the Preservation of Favoured Races in the Struggle for Life*. New York: New American Library. (Original work published 1859).

Davies, P. C. W. (1977). *Space and Time in the Modern Universe*. Cambridge, England: Cambridge University Press.

Davies, P. C. W. (1983). The Anthropic Principle. *Science Digest, 91*, 24.

Einstein, A., Lorentz, H. A., Minkowski, N., and Weyl, H. (1952). *The Principle of Relativity* (W. Perret and G. B. Jeffery, Trans.). New York: Dover Publications. (Original work published 1922).

Fennema, J., and Paul, I. (Eds.). (1990). *Science and Religion: One World – Changing Perspectives on Reality*. Dordrecht: Kluwer Academic Publishers.

Gale, G. (1986). Some Metaphysical Perplexities in Contemporary Physics. *International Philosophical Quarterly, XXVI* (4), 393–402.

Gamow, G. (1990). Modern cosmology. In: J. Leslie (Ed.), *Physical Cosmology and Philosophy*, (pp. 51–63). New York: Macmillan. (Original work published 1954. *Scientific American, 190* (3), 55–63)

Gray, A. (1963) *Darwinian: Essays and Views Pertaining to Darwinism* (A. Hunter Dupree, Ed.). Cambridge, MA: Harvard University Press.

Hacking, I. (1987). The inverse gambler's fallacy: The argument from design. The anthropic principle applied to wheeler universes. *Mind, 76*, 331–340.

Hefner, P. (1993). *The Human Factor: Evolution, Culture and Religion.* Minneapolis, MN: Fortress.

Kenny, A. (1969). *The Five Ways: St. Thomas Aquinas' Proofs of Gods Existence.* New York: Schocken Books.

Klaaren, E. M. (1977). *Religious Origins of Modern Science.* Grand Rapids, MI: Willam B. Eerdsmans.

Kusukawa, S. (1995). *The Transformation of Natural Philosophy: The Case of Philip Melanchthon.* New York: Cambridge University Press.

Lang, H. S. (1992). *Aristotle's Physics and Its Medieval Varieties.* Albany, NY: State University of New York Press.

Laudan, L. (1984) *Science and Values.* Berkeley, CA: University of California Press.

Leslie, J. (1986). The scientific weight of anthropic and teleological principles. In: N. Rescher, (Ed.), *Current Issues in Teleology,* (pp. 111–19). Lanham, MD: University Press of America.

Leslie, J. (1989). *Universes.* London: Routledge.

Leslie, J., (Ed.) (1990). *Physical Cosmology and Philosophy.* New York: Macmillan.

Lindberg, D. C. (1992). *The Beginnings of Western Science.* Chicago: University of Chicago Press.

Luther, M. (1957). Disputation against scholastic theology (Harold J. Grimm Trans.). In: H. Grimm (Ed.), *Luther's Works, Vol. 31, Career of the Reformer: I,* (pp. 3–16). Philadelphia: Muhlenberg Press. (Original Work published 1517)

Moore, J. R (1979). *The Post Darwinian Controversies: A Study of the Protestant Struggle to Come to Terms with Darwin in Great Britain and America 1870–1900.* Cambridge, England: Cambridge University Press.

Murphy, N. (1990). *Theology in the Age of Scientific Reasoning.* Ithaca, NY: Cornell University Press.

Newton, I. (1946). *Mathematical Principles of Natural Philosophy* (Andrew Matte, Trans.). Berkeley, CA: University of California Press. (Original work published 1687).

Oberman, H. A. (1989). *Luther: Man Between God and the Devil* (Eileen Walliser Schwarzenbart, Trans.). New York: Doubleday. (Original work published 1983).

Oldroyd, D. R. (1980). *Darwinian Impacts: An Introduction to the Darwinian Revolution.* Atlantic Highlands, NJ: Humanities Press.

Paley, W. (1828). *Natural Theology: Or, Evidences of the Existence and Attributes of the Deity, Collected from the Appearance of Nature.* In *The Works of William Paley, D. D.,* Vol. II London: Henry Fisher, Son, and P. Jackson.

Pannenberg, W. (1976). *Theology and the Philosophy of Science* (Francis McDonagh, Trans.). Philadelphia: The Westminster Press. (Original work published 1973)

Pannenberg, W. (1981). Theological questions to scientists. In: A. R. Peacocke (Ed.), *The Sciences and Theology in the Twentieth Century,* (pp. 3–16). Notre Dame, IN: University of Notre Dame Press.

Pannenberg, W. (1988). The doctrine of creation and modern science. *Zygon,* 23 (1), 321.

Pannenberg, W. (1993). *Toward a Theology of Nature: Essays on Science and Faith* (Ted Peters, Trans.). Philadelphia: Westminster/John Knox Press.

Peacocke, A. R. (Ed.). (1981). *The Sciences and Theology in the Twentieth Century.* Notre Dame, IN: University of Notre Dame Press.

Peacocke, A. R. (1990). *Theology for a Scientific Age.* Oxford: Basil Blackwell.

Plato. (1961). *Timaeus* (B. Jowett, Trans.). In: E. Hamilton and H. Cairns (Eds.), *The Collected Dialogues of Plato,* (pp. 1151–1211). Princeton, NJ: Princeton University Press.

Polkinghorne, J. C. (1986). *One World: The Interaction of Science and Theology.* Princeton, NJ: Princeton University Press.

Polkinghorne, J. C. (1990). A revived natural theology. In J. Fennema and I. Paul (Eds.), *Science and Religion: One World – Changing Perspectives on Reality,* (pp. 87–97). Dordrecht: Kluwer Academic Publishers.

Polkinghorne, J. C. (1993). *The Faith of A Physicist: Reflections of a Bottom-Up Thinker.* Princeton, NJ: Princeton University Press.

Redondi, P. (1987). *Galileo Heretic* (R. Rosenthal, Trans.). Princeton, NJ: Princeton University Press. (Original work published 1983)

Richardson, W. M., and Wildman, W. J. (Eds.). (1996). *Religion and Science: History, Method, Dialogue.* New York: Routledge.

Rohrlich, F. (1987). *From Paradox to Reality: Our Basic Concepts of the Physical World.* Cambridge, England: Cambridge University Press.

Russell, C. A., (Ed.). (1973). *Science and Religious Belief: A Selection of Recent Historical Studies.* London: The Open University Press.

Swinburne, R. (1979). *The Existence of God.* Oxford: Oxford University Press.

William of Ockham. (1990). *Philosophical Writings* (Philotheus Boehner, Ed.). Indianapolis, IN: Hackett.

# Author Index

# Subject Index